W9-DBW-846

RESPONDING TO INTERNATIONAL OIL CRISES

RESPONDING TO INTERNATIONAL OIL CRISES

EDITED BY
GEORGE HORWICH AND
DAVID LEO WEIMER
FOREWORD BY SENATOR BILL BRADLEY

American Enterprise Institute for Public Policy Research
Washington, D.C.

This report was prepared with the support of U.S. Department of Energy Grant DE-FG01-85PE77035. Any opinions, findings, conclusions, or recommendations expressed herein, however, are those of the authors and do not necessarily reflect the views of the Department of Energy.

Distributed by arrangement with

UPA, Inc.
4720 Boston Way   3 Henrietta Street
Lanham, Md. 20706   London WC2E 8LU England

Library of Congress Cataloging-in-Publication Data

Responding to international oil crises / George Horwich and David Leo Weimer, editors.
   p. cm.
   Includes index.
   ISBN 0-8447-3639-2 (alk. paper)
   1. Petroleum industry and trade—United States. 2. Petroleum industry and trade. 3. United States—National security.
4. National security. I. Horwich, George. II. Weimer, David Leo.
HD9565.R47 1987   87-25941
338.2'7282'0973—dc19   CIP

1   3   5   7   9   10   8   6   4   2

AEI Studies 464

Printed in the United States of America

Contents

The American Enterprise Institute for Public Policy Research

Founded in 1943, AEI is a nonpartisan, nonprofit, research and educational organization based in Washington, D.C. The Institute sponsors research, conducts seminars and conferences, and publishes books and periodicals.

AEI's research is carried out under three major programs: Economic Policy Studies; Foreign Policy and National Security Studies; and Social and Political Studies. The resident scholars and fellows listed in these pages are part of a network that also includes ninety adjunct scholars at leading universities throughout the United States and in several foreign countries.

The views expressed in AEI publications are those of the authors and do not necessarily reflect the views of the staff, advisory panels, officers, or trustees. AEI itself takes no positions on public policy issues.

Contributors

JOSEPH M. ANDERSON is a vice president of ICF, Inc., where he directs projects on energy markets, long-term economic and demographic change, and the impact of that change on government transfer programs, health care expenditures, housing, and other sectors. He has published articles and book chapters in these areas.

DANIEL B. BADGER, JR., served as a principal administrator in the Oil Industry Division of the International Energy Agency from 1980 to 1985. Before that he was a senior analyst in the Office of Policy, Planning, and Analysis of the U.S. Department of Energy. He is currently with the consulting firm of Putnam, Hayes & Bartlett in Cambridge, Massachusetts.

DOUGLAS R. BOHI is chief economist and director of the Office of Economic Policy of the Federal Energy Regulatory Commission. He was formerly a senior fellow at Resources for the Future, where his research on the International Energy Agency was conducted. He is the coauthor (with Michael Toman) of *Analyzing Nonrenewable Resource Supply* and (with David Montgomery) of *Oil Prices, Energy Security, and Import Policy.*

RICHARD N. COOPER is Maurits C. Boas Professor of International Economics at Harvard University. A former professor of economics and provost of Yale University, he served as under secretary of state for economic affairs from 1977 to 1981. He has written widely on international trade and finance, including *Currency Devaluation in Developing Countries, The Economics of Interdependence, Economic Mobility and National Economic Policy,* and *A Reordered World.* His most recent book is *The International Monetary System: Essays in World Economics.*

GEORGE HORWICH is professor of economics and Burton D. Morgan Professor for the Study of Private Enterprise in the Krannert School of Management, Purdue University. He was a senior economist at the Department of Energy in the Office of Policy, Planning, and Analysis in 1978–1980 and again in 1984, when he was also a special assistant for contingency planning. He is the coauthor (with David Leo Weimer) of *Oil Price Shocks, Market Response, and Contingency Planning*, the editor of *Energy Use in Transportation Contingency Planning*, and the coeditor (with Edward J. Mitchell) of *Policies for Coping with Oil-Supply Disruptions*. He is an AEI adjunct scholar.

HANK JENKINS-SMITH is deputy director of the Institute for Public Policy and assistant professor of political science at the University of New Mexico. In 1982–1983 he was a policy analyst in the Office of Policy, Planning, and Analysis at the Department of Energy. He has published papers on the Alaskan oil export ban and the strategic petroleum reserve and is the editor of the forthcoming issue of the *Natural Resources Journal*, "Natural Gas Policy in the Western United States: Perspectives on Regulation in the Next Decade."

BRADLEY A. MILLER is a Ph.D. candidate in economics at the University of California, Berkeley. In 1983–1984 he was a regulatory impact analyst in the Office of Policy, Planning, and Analysis at the Department of Energy. His current research is the simulation and analysis of dynamic and regional equilibria in natural gas markets.

RODNEY T. SMITH is director of the Lowe Institute of Political Economy and associate professor of economics at Claremont McKenna College. He has published works on the economics of water law and the regulation of petroleum and natural gas.

MICHAEL A. TOMAN is a fellow in the energy materials division of Resources for the Future and a professorial lecturer in international economics at the Johns Hopkins School of Advanced International Studies. He is the coauthor (with Douglas Bohi) of *Analyzing Nonrenewable Resource Supply* and the author of papers on oil stockpiling, international energy security, and natural gas markets and regulation.

DAVID LEO WEIMER is professor and deputy director of the Public Policy Analysis Program at the University of Rochester. He served as a senior economist at the Department of Energy in the Office of Policy, Planning, and Analysis in 1980–1981. He is the editor of the *Journal of Policy Analysis and Management*, the author of *The Strategic Petroleum Reserve*, and the coauthor (with George Horwich) of *Oil Price Shocks, Market Response, and Contingency Planning*.

JOHN P. WEYANT is director of the Energy Modeling Forum and associate professor of engineering-economic systems at Stanford University. He has been a consultant to the Rand Corporation, the California Energy Commission, the Department of Energy, the Office of Technology Assessment, and the Environmental Protection Agency. He also serves on the editorial boards of the *Energy Journal*, *Operations Research*, and *Petroleum Management*.

Foreword

The recent rise in oil imports has brought with it a perceived rise in our vulnerability to an oil supply interruption. The Senate debate on the 1987 Trade Bill included a full discussion of U.S. import dependency and strategic vulnerability. It was argued that we have learned nothing and done nothing to protect ourselves from the chaos that accompanied energy crises of the past decade. On the contrary, we have made significant adjustments. We have learned from our mistakes. First, and most important, we have developed a far more adequate strategic petroleum reserve, which can cushion the economy from the effects of an oil supply disruption. Second, we have abandoned our reliance on domestic price controls and mandatory allocations, which severely hampered our adjustment to higher energy prices in the 1970s.

We have learned just how interdependent the world oil market is. That is why I have urged other consumer nations to create national strategic oil stockpiles and add to those that already exist. These stockpiles will provide a lifeline of crude oil in the event of a world market disruption. I have also encouraged negotiations with friendly oil-producing nations such as Venezuela, Mexico, and Canada, to encourage new exploration that can add to worldwide production capacity. Excess capacity worldwide—not meaningless slogans such as U.S. energy independence—will best ensure the continued energy security of our own economy.

One legacy of the 1970s energy policy is the energy program of the International Energy Agency (IEA), to which the United States is a signatory. While the IEA works to promote worldwide cooperation and coordination, its principal method of coping with an oil supply disruption is mandatory oil sharing. Those of us who believe that the market generally offers the most efficient response to supply losses are skeptical of the prospect of international oil sharing. Not only may sharing result in a less efficient distribution of oil worldwide, its implementation may require domestic mandatory allocations that could lead to full-scale controls. Congress has rejected the notion of government allocation of supplies. It seems an appropriate time, therefore, to reconsider the role of international programs that have the same effect.

The Department of Energy, the American Enterprise Institute, and Professors Horwich and Weimer and their colleagues offer a valuable assessment of the IEA's emergency program. The authors hold diverse views and have come to different conclusions regarding the efficacy and desirability of the IEA's emergency measures. The last two chapters, by Professor Cooper and Professors Horwich and Weimer, assess the various findings and permit readers to form their own conclusions on the costs and benefits of the IEA program.

The threat of international oil shocks promises to stay with us in the foreseeable future. This book will be an important reference in the continuing public debate on the role of the IEA and the appropriate emergency policy response.

BILL BRADLEY
U.S. Senate

Preface

The International Energy Agency was established in 1974 by the free world industrial countries as their response to the Arab oil embargo of 1973–1974. The agency featured as its primary emergency response a system of oil demand restraint and oil sharing known as the International Energy Program. Through a collection of original economic studies, this volume examines the actual record of demand restraint and the likely impact of sharing if it were to be implemented after a new disruption of the world oil supply. The IEA's guidelines for accumulation of oil stocks and proposed coordination of stock drawdown are also analyzed.

The occasion for the volume is the tenth anniversary of U.S. ratification of its membership in the IEA, which occurred on January 1, 1986. From that date the United States could withdraw from the agency by giving one year's notice. A systematic assessment of the International Energy Program, which had not previously been undertaken by an outside independent team, thus seemed especially timely. Not only was a close examination of the emergency measures indicated, but analysis of a number of institutional changes and historical experience also seemed appropriate: possible changes in the structure of the world oil market; changes in various domestic policies of IEA members, including the removal of price controls and mandatory allocations and the development of national oil stockpiles; and whatever evidence might have accumulated on actual IEA performance in past crises.

A grant by the policy office of the U.S. Department of Energy to the American Enterprise Institute, which administered the grant, became the funding source for the proposed assessment. The institute asked us to assemble a group of qualified analysts who together would evaluate the International Energy Program or its essential aspects in individual studies. The analysts represented a broad spectrum of views and included both known advocates and critics of the IEA program, as well as several who had not previously recorded their views. Although members of the team were expected to interact with one

xvii

another and did so through several informal meetings held at AEI, the studies were to be the independent products of their authors. There was no requirement that a consensus be reached or that a single set of recommendations be offered.

To lend cohesion to our efforts, we asked Richard Cooper, a distinguished economist and former under secretary of state for economic affairs, to present his views on the program against the background of the several studies. We offer our own critical summary of the volume and our policy recommendations in the final chapter.

The chapters by Cooper and by Daniel Badger, a former IEA administrator, support the IEA claim that demand restraint and oil sharing together can help to calm disrupted international oil markets and limit both the short-run and the longer-run rise of oil prices. Simulations and empirical results reported by Rodney Smith and ourselves and collaborators find both demand restraint and oil sharing to be either ineffective or a negative force in reducing the costs of disruptions. The critics of the International Energy Program argue that the information required for sharing is unlikely to be available, that allocations under sharing will tend to reduce welfare generated by market forces, and that any import quotas imposed under demand restraint obligations could perversely encourage price increases by oligopolistic producers. An econometric investigation by Joseph Anderson of the world oil market during the major disruptions provides evidence both for and against the premises underlying the program.

In our summary we interpret the balance of findings as supporting U.S. withdrawal from the sharing agreement. We urge continued U.S. participation in the IEA's information-gathering activities and in attempts to achieve coordination of stock drawdown. We do not, however, regard such coordination as essential to the successful use of national stockpiles.

In chapter 1 Daniel Badger sets forth the rationale of the sharing agreement—the attainment of lower oil prices by defusing otherwise panicked and disorderly markets and the removal of the allocation burden from private firms (who do not want that responsibility). Badger's thesis, simply put, is that uncontrolled markets cannot handle severe disruptions and quickly become chaotic. Something like IEA sharing is absolutely essential to improve the efficiency of the market.

Chapter 2, by Rodney Smith, is a broad survey and analysis of the entire IEA experience. Smith provides a detailed account of the IEA structure and institutional evolution and describes the agency's policy goals and specific actions during disruptions. He simulates a disruption in a model of world oil markets and imposes sharing, which, overall, reduces the welfare (social surplus) of IEA members. He examines the political aspects of oil sharing. Smith also analyzes import control and demand restraint measures, focusing on the difficulties of coordination, the tendency of import quotas in a noncompetitive market to raise the world price, and the actual experience of the IEA in 1980 in enforcing demand restraint among members. He concludes with a detailed analysis of oil stockpiling policies, again examining the difficulties of coordination and the actual effects of stock building and drawdown in the 1979–1980 disruptions. Smith's assessments of the effectiveness and desirability of IEA coordination of energy emergencies, based on both theoretical and empirical evidence, are uniformly negative.

In chapter 3 George Horwich, Hank Jenkins-Smith, and David Weimer carry out a detailed simulation of oil sharing using the Department of Energy's elaborate oil trade model. Their simulations involve scenarios of complete and incomplete information about the consumption of members after a disruption and both complete and partial implementation of the sharing agreement. Under partial implementation countries with selling obligations must, as in all cases, stay within their supply ceilings, but countries with buying rights are not required to accept additional oil. The direct effect of partial implementation could be welfare enhancing, but the indirect adjustment costs would almost certainly negate the direct benefits. In all cases of complete implementation, under both complete and incomplete information, oil sharing reduces the net welfare of IEA members.

In chapter 4 George Horwich and Bradley Miller conduct extensive simulations of import quotas imposed in a model of the world oil market. The quotas, imposed by countries with a selling obligation, are shown, under a wide range of assumptions, to create significant price increases in a market containing noncompetitive producers. The results are surprisingly robust, particularly for small-to-moderate mandated reductions of imports and even for very modest magnitudes of noncompetitive oil output. These simulations, pointing to perverse price increases, seriously undermine the case for employing the sharing agreement under any circumstances in the post-1973 world oil market.

In chapter 5 John Weyant shifts the focus from oil sharing to stockpile coordination. He discusses the costs and benefits of unilateral acquisition and drawdown and outlines a coordinated drawdown plan involving the larger IEA countries. It is an automatic plan triggered by an agreed-upon rise in the spot price of oil.

In chapter 6 Douglas Bohi and Michael Toman examine a broader range of emergency responses—stockpile coordination, demand restraint measures, and no action at all. Their analysis, carried out

xix

within a game-theoretic framework, looks at strategies designed to overcome the tendency of individual countries to free-ride on others in the emergency response. In effect, they address the thesis of Rodney Smith that the self-interest of individual countries tends to make any coordinated IEA program unworkable. They urge a mixed strategy, with primary emphasis on stockpile use by the United States and on market-oriented demand restraint by other IEA members.

Chapter 7, by Joseph Anderson, is the first systematic empirical study of the world oil market during the critical period since the late 1960s. Anderson finds that U.S. oil prices, fully adjusted for differences in oil quality and transportation charges, tended to be somewhat higher than in other countries during the 1973–1974 embargo but less so during the 1979–1980 disruptions. His test of the hypothesis that the same structural framework applies to disrupted as to nondisrupted periods is upheld for some variables but not for all.

In chapter 8 Richard Cooper argues that critics of the sharing agreement exaggerate the ability of the world oil market to equilibrate supply and demand quickly and smoothly in disruptions. Contract prices, in particular, are sticky, causing the spot price to rise disproportionately. As the contract price rises to the level of the spot price, the Organization of Petroleum Exporting Countries (OPEC) responds by reducing output, thereby maintaining contract prices at the higher level for prolonged periods. The process is reinforced by stockpiling, which is spurred by the realization that the higher spot price results in higher long-run contract prices. Sharing oil under the agreement can defuse the rise of the spot price, a proposition that Cooper believes is supported by empirical evidence in the study by Anderson. The agreement does not, moreover, require that oil surplus countries restrain demand by imposing import quotas. A variety of other measures are available to reduce demand to what are, in fact, loosely defined goals, not rigid ceilings.

In chapter 9 Horwich and Weimer deny, on theoretical grounds, that the movement of spot prices in disruptions is likely to be significantly influenced by any rigidity in the contract price. They argue that, historically, the U.S. petroleum regulations—in particular, the entitlements system—appear to have played a far greater role in raising spot prices. Their analysis of the dispersion of prices paid by major importers during 1979–1981 suggests that prices in fact adjusted with reasonable rapidity, well in advance of any contribution that sharing could make. They argue that sharing is indeed administratively cumbersome, is likely to entail the use of import quotas, and may promote the widespread imposition of mandatory domestic allocations and price controls. If a cooperative measure is desired, they regard a disruption tariff as superior to sharing. They urge primary reliance, however, on drawdown of government or government-controlled stocks, which need not be coordinated to be effective but should be at least partially triggered by a market-based mechanism. They advocate continued U.S. membership in the IEA but withdrawal from the sharing agreement.

AEI's director of energy studies, Edward Mitchell, provided valuable advice in defining the scope and contents of this study. Edward Kutler, also of AEI, played a crucial role in coordinating and directing our efforts from start to finish. This included the provision of a broad review process that exposed us to the views of academia, industry, and government, including the IEA. The forum for the exchange of ideas was a series of meetings and luncheons at AEI and the annual meetings of the International Association of Energy Economists in Tokyo in 1986 and Calgary in 1987, at which we reported on our progress.

We especially wish to acknowledge discussions with the following persons and their comments, often in writing:

- At the IEA: Helga Steeg, director; David Jones, director of the Office of Long-Term Cooperation; and Keiichi Yokobori, director of the Office of Information and Emergency Systems Operations.
- At the Department of State: Alan Larson, deputy assistant secretary for international energy and resources policy; Daniel Serwer, director, Stuart Allan, deputy director, and the staff of the Office of Energy Consumer Country Affairs; Martin Bailey, economic adviser, and Eric Melby, special assistant to the under secretary for economic affairs.
- In industry: Michael Canes, vice president of the American Petroleum Institute; and Tor Meloe, chief economist of Texaco, Inc.
- At the Department of Energy: John Brodman, director of the Office of International Energy Analysis; John Stanley-Miller, director, and Peter Karpoff, senior economist, of the Office of Oil and Natural Gas Policy; Finn Neilsen, director, and Jill Hill, staff member, of the Office of Energy Emergency Plans and Integration; and our former colleagues in the policy office who, like ourselves, are no longer at the department but with whom we have had the good fortune to remain in continuing dialogue: Jerry Blankenship, Stephen Minihan, Lucian Pugliaresi, Glen Sweetnam, William Taylor, and Thomas Teisberg.
- At the Congress: David M. Gustafson, formerly counsel with the Subcommittee on Fossil and Synthetic Fuels of the House Energy and Commerce Committee.

- In academia: John Carlson, of the Department of Economics at Purdue University; Joseph Kalt, of the Kennedy School of Government at Harvard University; Charles Phelps, of the Public Policy Analysis Program at the University of Rochester; and Glen Toner, of the Department of Political Science at Carleton University in Canada.

We also wish to thank Kazuhiko Togo, director of the Energy Resources Division of the Japanese Ministry of Foreign Affairs, for his many insightful comments.

GEORGE HORWICH
DAVID LEO WEIMER

1
International Cooperation during Oil Supply Disruptions: The Role of the International Energy Agency

Daniel B. Badger, Jr.

The International Energy Agency (IEA) was created thirteen years ago to assist its twenty-one member countries in attaining the following objectives:

- equitable sharing of available oil during supply emergencies
- reduced dependence on imported oil through cooperative efforts toward conservation, research, and accelerated development of alternative forms of energy
- cooperative relations with oil producers and nonmember consuming countries
- a better understanding of the international oil industry

In fulfillment of this mandate, the IEA's work has evolved in several directions, the most important of which are information systems, promotion of long-term policies, and emergency response.

The IEA inherited certain statistical reporting systems on energy activities in member countries from the Organization for Economic Cooperation and Development. The agency has improved and extended its reporting capabilities so that today its information systems on energy markets are without equal. By making available to the public its *Monthly Oil Market Report, Quarterly Oil and Gas Statistics, Quarterly Coal Statistics,* and *Quarterly Price Statistics,* the agency has become the standard international point of reference for data and analysis of trends in world trade of oil, gas, and coal. The agency's *World Energy Outlook,* supplemented by special reports such as "Coal Prospects to 2000," "Natural Gas Prospects to 2000," and others,

1

provides some of the best analysis outside the oil industry itself on the long-term direction of energy markets.

The agency's primary activity in promoting long-term policies has been periodic review of energy policies in member countries to identify obstacles to successful structural adjustment to high-cost energy. Attention most often focuses on policies that impede market forces, as these are (or should be) the driving force behind structural change. In addition, recognizing that market incentives for research and development may be inadequate, the IEA's long-term activities include a substantial program to organize and monitor funding for collaborative research and demonstration projects.

These information systems and public reports provide the starting point for increased "transparency" of energy markets. Additional activities in this area are directed toward the oil industry and toward non-IEA-member countries. The IEA staff performs periodic analyses of the financial condition of the oil industry and regularly invites industry representatives to present their perspectives to member government officials on topics related to oil and other energy markets. Officials of the IEA themselves travel widely to explain the organization's policies and programs in member countries and elsewhere, and IEA staff maintain a broad program of research on energy developments in nonmember countries.

The IEA's emergency response programs, described in detail in this chapter, have evolved considerably since their initial formulation in 1974. This evolution reflects both the structural change in the oil market since that time and lessons learned from actual oil market events and from simulated tests of supply disruptions. With its "coordinated stockdraw" decision of July 1984, the IEA Governing Board strongly supplemented the 1974 "emergency sharing" agreement, though this remains a major component of the overall emergency response plan.

The Political Imperative

If the IEA did not exist, someone would have to invent it. Oil supply disruptions are politically traumatic events. Global supply disruptions—the kind the IEA was created to respond to—have the potential to traumatize international relations. They create sudden, unforeseen hardship and mete it out unevenly among nations and economic interests. A major supply disruption means that certain factories must be idled and workers laid off; certain tractors may not move, and certain crops cannot be harvested; certain heating and cooling systems must be shut down; certain vacations may not be taken, and certain

2

restaurants and hotels must therefore be shut down and staff curtailed. And inevitably, consumers will spend time waiting in line.[1]

With citizens' fundamental interests touched so deeply, governments in most industrialized democracies would find it difficult to stand aside and allow market forces alone—exaggerated as they would be in disrupted or scarcely functioning market conditions—to allocate the pain; and many of the firms who make up "the market" are, under these circumstances, unwilling to assume the responsibility. Political institutions for agreeing on what constitutes equitable burden sharing exist, of course, at the national level. At the international level, however, after security of oil supplies became a global concern in October 1973, governments found it necessary to create an international body with formal programs for responding to supply disruptions. The lack of such an organization would place unacceptable strains on their overall relations, jeopardizing gains from collective action in areas of mutual interest extending far beyond the domain of oil supply.

Another reason for governments to work together to enhance the workings of a severely disrupted oil market was that the market itself, or at least its major participants, did not relish the job. The banking and securities industries long ago recognized that when panic sweeps their markets, they cease to be markets at all in any acceptable sense of the word. These industries accept that at some point there is a need for government action to help restore conditions under which the markets can function properly.

International oil companies were in a difficult position during the oil embargo imposed by the Arab members of the Organization of Petroleum Exporting Countries (OPEC) in the autumn of 1973. The dozen or so oil companies with multinational production and marketing operations, holding large shares of the market in most industrialized countries, found themselves with short supplies and caught between the conflicting claims of their local affiliates and their home and host governments. As it turned out, available oil did reach its various destinations without serious imbalances among regions, but not without decisions that were both difficult (based on insufficient information) and unwelcome (involving political responsibilities).

The international oil companies supported the creation of the IEA because the IEA emergency programs would provide a clear picture of supply flows in a disrupted market and at the same time transfer political responsibilities to other hands. The IEA's disruption simulations have shown that actions taken by the companies on their own initiative are very much consistent with the IEA sharing formula. This is not accidental. The companies' preferred policy in a disrupted market is proportional allocation of supplies among the various markets

3

they serve. This was broadly the case in both the 1973–1974 and the 1978–1979 disruptions. The IEA sharing program was not implemented in either case (it was created in late 1974), though the emergency information system was activated in early 1979. Without that information system, government officials would have no way of knowing until after the event whether the companies were pursuing proportional allocation and no way of demonstrating this pursuit to their concerned constituents. The IEA's emergency program helps both companies and governments out of this difficulty by providing to the IEA Secretariat a detailed view of the supply situations in twenty-one countries and of the activities of forty-five companies in those countries.

In addition to the benefit of transparency afforded by the emergency information system, the emergency sharing formula insulates companies from host government pressure for special treatment. The sharing formula is designed to depoliticize the market. By lifting from the industry the political responsibility for international supply allocation decisions, companies find it easier to get on with their primary business of moving oil to the market.

The Economic Rationale

Beyond the political imperative is an important economic rationale for a collective government response to oil supply disruptions. There are ways in which markets by themselves, when faced with supply disruptions, do not achieve the most efficient outcome for oil-consuming nations. These may be remedied to some degree by government actions. Their efficacy may be diminished if they are undertaken unilaterally but enhanced if the responses are coordinated.

First, market forces alone do not induce consumers to buy enough insurance—in the form of inventories—against supply disruptions. Because oil fuels so much of the economic activity of an industrialized society, the total economic costs of a supply disruption are certain to exceed the sum of losses to individual oil consumers. Therefore, the amount a society should be willing to pay for disruption insurance exceeds the amount of protection that market participants will buy on their own. This is especially true when the portion of consumption "covered" by the insurance constitutes a significant share of the total world market. In this case, drawdown of emergency reserves not only substitutes for lost supplies, but also yields additional benefits by reducing the price of all oil consumed.[2]

A second problem derives from the fact that 40 percent of IEA member countries' oil is imported. In principle, when a resource suddenly becomes scarce, economic efficiency is served best if competing

4

users bid freely and the price rises to market-clearing levels—never mind the redistribution of income that may accompany this process. When some oil is imported, however, the transfers that accompany the market-clearing process divert national income to foreign producers, reducing total economic welfare.[3]

In the medium term, efficiency also requires prices to return to something approaching the long-run marginal cost path following a supply disruption.[4] Sustained deviations from this path send distorted price signals throughout oil-consuming and oil-producing economies, resulting in inefficient resource allocation. The inefficiency of deviations above this path is compounded by the continuing loss of income to producers noted earlier.

The pattern of real oil prices before and after the two supply disruptions of the 1970s suggests that the market did establish a price well above the efficient path, especially after 1979.[5] Only in hindsight, however, is this apparent. The factors that drove the post-1979 price path were not inherent in the structure of the world oil market, and it was by no means foreordained that the market's medium-term course would be inefficient.[6] Thus, while the consequences of the market's going awry potentially are much worse in the medium term than in the short term, the short-run failings are more predictable and provide a more secure basis for government response. If the short-term response produces medium-term benefits as well, so much the better.

The IEA's Emergency Program

The specific objectives of the IEA's emergency program, are

- to forestall upward price pressures in the open market, thereby limiting economic losses arising from the disruption
- to respond to physical shortages affecting individual countries differently by sharing available supplies
- to provide a sufficiently clear picture of supply flows during a disruption to allow both governments and oil companies to function normally without unduly interfering with each other's objectives

The agency's member governments have established an informal arrangement for drawing stocks and taking such other measures as demand restraint in a coordinated manner, as well as a formal scheme for sharing available supplies during a severe disruption. The informal program can be viewed as a first line of defense, which could be brought into play regardless of the size of the disruption. It reduces price pressures and the attendant economic damages in the early

5

stages of any disruption. The formal sharing agreement only comes into play when a disruption reaches major proportions (loss of at least 7 percent of supply). In that case, as the formal system is brought into operation, action taken under the informal agreement would continue to counteract price pressures and help to maintain an orderly market.

The Informal Response Plan. The chaotic market conditions that followed the fall of the shah of Iran in early 1979 demonstrated to IEA member governments that smaller supply shortfalls—in that case about 5 percent—could do as much damage as larger ones, especially in a climate of overall supply uncertainty. They therefore began to search for steps that could operate outside the rigid framework of the Emergency Sharing System. Although these discussions originally focused on oil companies' stock behavior during and after the disruption, attention soon shifted to ways to inject volume on the supply side of an overheated market by drawing on stocks owned or controlled by governments. The discussions resulted in a July 1984 decision by the IEA Governing Board that in the event of a significant disruption—whether or not large enough to trigger emergency sharing—member governments would quickly meet to determine whether a coordinated draw of stocks and other complementary measures would be appropriate.

The stocks that governments could bring into play in such situations fall into two categories: stocks owned by governments, principally in the United States, Germany, and Japan; and stocks held by or on behalf of companies in fulfillment of compulsory stockholding obligations, principally in countries of the European Community.[7] Very substantial quantities of stocks exist in each of these categories. Governments own about 700 million barrels, while about 300 million barrels could be made available by relaxing compulsory requirements. These reserves, taken together, could replace the loss of very significant portions of total supply for many months.

Member governments generally believe that additional advance agreements or commitments, beyond the 1984 decision itself, are unnecessary. Formal agreements for coordinating a stockdraw at the international level do not, therefore, exist. Governments control substantial volumes of oil stocks and have adequate authority to sell or release the oil when they choose. They also can reduce mandatory stockholding requirements. If the July 1984 decision were implemented, it is likely that governments first would decide how much stockdraw would be needed to counteract the economic consequences of the disruption. Then, on the basis of each country's level of stocks

6

and share of IEA oil consumption, it would be decided how much each could contribute. Unlike the more formal sharing agreement, there is no preestablished formula for determining the size of stockdraw or its allocation among countries. Like the sharing agreement, the informal agreement also recognizes that demand restraint may achieve the same ends as stockdraw in responding to supply disruptions.

The importance of the July 1984 decision and the procedures it envisages is political as well as economic: providing that countries will jointly consult on the early use of stocks or on equivalent measures minimizes the possibility of "free riding" by individual countries. The coordinated approach should thus remove one of the possible major domestic objections to using a country's emergency stocks: that the benefit of these stocks would flow to other consuming nations that failed to make an equal effort. The coordinated stockdraw decision therefore makes it easier for member governments to justify use of their own emergency reserves.

The July 1984 agreement marked a shift in thinking, or perhaps in the balance of opinion, from the philosophy of "last resort" toward the philosophy of "first use." The former view holds that stocks should only be drawn when all else has been tried, including demand restraint and emergency sharing. This philosophy reflected the experience of 1973–1974, when emergency reserves—at least those in the hands or under the control of governments—were practically nonexistent, and also of 1979–1981, when emergency reserves were still comparatively small. In both cases, the margin of reserves was, for good reason, regarded as vulnerable to sudden erasure by another disruption. If emergency stocks were used at the outset of a disruption, it was asked, what protection would be left if the supply situation subsequently got worse rather than better?

"First use," by contrast, is the view that stocks should be deployed at the outset of a disruption in the hope of avoiding the need to resort to more drastic interventionist measures. It was no accident that this shift of emphasis from last resort to first use came when government stockholdings had been increased significantly and when the world surplus of production capacity had come to be recognized as an indefinite, if not permanent, feature of the landscape. In this context, supply disruptions are more easily seen as temporary events, after which circumstances are likely to return to normal. Worries about what might happen if the second shoe falls no longer seem so relevant.

Given today's surplus capacity, it should be relatively easy for governments to decide to use stocks at the outset of a disruption. And it is unlikely that, during the disruption, oil companies would

7

invest heavily in inventories that make economic sense only on the assumption of higher prices in the medium term. Both governments and companies could therefore be expected to react more calmly today than they did in 1979 and to act in ways that would diminish rather than exacerbate market pressure. But the hard test for the IEA's coordinated stocks agreement will await the return of the 1978 supply/demand situation, when disruption tipped the balance in a gradually tightening market, pushing it suddenly into a deficit condition from which no short-term relief could be seen. Under these circumstances, the differing views about "first use" and "last resort" could reemerge. One virtue of the 1984 agreement is that it accepts the importance of both stockdraw and demand restraint. A clash of philosophies need not therefore interfere with practical action.

The Formal Response Plan. The IEA's main line of defense in responding to supply disruptions is the formal Emergency Sharing System of the International Energy Program (IEP). Its purposes are to improve market transparency so as to allow governments and oil companies to function with adequate and comprehensive information and to reduce the economic losses and political strains resulting from the short-run effects of competitive forces in a severely disrupted market. The system may also prevent significant economic losses in the medium term, but it is not designed to resist or modify long-term market forces.

Member governments and the forty-five reporting companies have agreed to a large-scale monthly reporting system to support emergency sharing. This reporting system allows each country's and reporting company's supplies to be monitored throughout the disruption. In contrast to the situation in previous supply disruptions, the availability of such information

- gives governments a clear, comprehensive, and quantitative description of the disruption and increases their confidence that it is being properly handled
- provides the same information to oil companies, which may diminish their tendency to overreact
- allows the general public to be reliably informed and thus reduces undue anxiety based on insufficient information

The arithmetic of the sharing formula itself is somewhat daunting when set down on paper, but the underlying principles are fairly straightforward: total supply available to all member countries is to be shared roughly in proportion to each country's consumption in a recent historical base period.[8] Each country's "supply right," calculated

8

in this way, is then compared with the supply actually available to it in the form of indigenous production plus *scheduled* imports. Inventories are not counted as available supply. Countries with available supply in excess of their supply right have an obligation to give up oil, principally by redirecting scheduled imports to those with a deficit relative to their supply right. Conversely, those countries with a smaller available supply than their supply right have the right to obtain the difference from those with an excess supply.

Any shortfall between a country's actual consumption and the supply right must be made up by some combination of stockdraw and demand restraint. Member countries are free to choose the combination that best suits their circumstances.[9] This agreement relieves the pressure on international prices by (a) limiting the allowable level of imports by the group as a whole to the amount of undisrupted oil available to them on the world market, and (b) specifying each member's allowable share of those imports, thereby removing the incentive for competition among members.

The international oil industry is also formally involved in the sharing program. Forty-five of the largest oil companies doing business in the member countries have agreed to act as "reporting companies" when the sharing program is triggered. They will provide detailed information on available supplies and cooperate in the reallocation of supplies in line with the sharing formula. The remainder of the oil industry—mainly smaller independent producers, refiners, and trading companies—are tied indirectly into the IEA program through officials in each member government who participate on behalf of the nonreporting companies in their countries.

IEA tests and actual experience in 1973–1974 and 1978–1979 have shown that, before any IEA involvement, the international oil companies would achieve a certain amount of reallocation on their own. Residual imbalances relative to the IEA sharing formula must then be evened out by means of arm's-length transactions between independent companies. If, through stockdraw and demand restraint, all member countries successfully reduced their demand for imports to precisely the levels allowed by the formula, companies would tend to make these arm's-length transactions without any guidance from the IEA. The only buyers in search of oil would be those operating in "deficit" countries, while those holding excess oil destined for "surplus" countries would have to sell to buyers in deficit countries if they sold at all. To the extent, however, that some countries' available supplies continue to exceed their supply rights and other countries' supplies are less than their rights, the IEA's reallocation program is called into action to balance out surpluses and deficits.

Companies planning to import oil into a surplus country would be requested instead to make oil available for sale to companies wishing to import into deficit countries. The IEA Secretariat, advised by a group of oil company supply experts, would match offers to buy and sell on the basis of quantity, quality, and location. The system is based on the voluntary cooperation of the companies but backed up by the possibility of government-mandated action. Only if voluntary company action failed to achieve the required reallocation would governments have to enter the picture to mandate reallocation.

When voluntary arm's-length commercial transactions occur, the question of price becomes important. The sharing program specifies that prices should be based on "the price conditions prevailing for comparable commercial transactions." Later in this chapter it is argued that the likely result would be prices somewhat higher than predisruption levels. Here it is simply noted that no more than 5 percent of the undisrupted international oil trade would be likely to involve reallocations requiring arm's-length price determinations.[10]

The Market Response to Emergency Sharing

Were the international oil market one in which the IEA member governments were themselves participants and the only participants, the sharing agreement would eliminate international competition for the limited supply available. A country whose actual supply was less than its allowable supply would have no incentive to bid for additional imports because the agreement guarantees that oil scheduled for delivery to other members would be diverted to make up the difference. Similarly, no country would bid to obtain more than its allowable supply, since it would not be entitled to keep the difference. The agreement would limit demand for imports so as exactly to equal the supply available for import. Under these theoretical conditions, there would be no upward price pressure on the international market.

The situation within national borders, however, could be different, depending on national policies. In countries adopting some form of nonprice rationing (allocation and price controls, for example), domestic price pressures would be minimized. In countries choosing to adopt a hands-off policy, market-clearing prices would be higher than predisruption prices since allowable supply would be less than predisruption supply. How high prices would rise would depend on the degree to which stocks were used to fill the gap between demand and the supply right under the IEA formula.

In the real world this simplified theoretical picture is complicated

10

in two important respects. First, IEA members actually account for only 70 percent of all oil imported by the free world's net importing nations. The remainder of the market is not bound by the sharing rules. The agreement states, "It is not an objective of the Program to seek to increase the share of world oil supply that the group had under normal market conditions." Thus in theory the agreement discourages IEA members as a group from bidding against "outsiders" in order to increase their supply, since in practice an individual IEA country that did so would have to share any increase so obtained with other IEA countries and give up most of the benefit. Of course, price pressure could be generated to some degree by IEA members' bidding to keep their collective share from shrinking. To what degree is not clear, but the financial resources available to IEA members to protect their share are considerably greater than those available to other countries to make inroads into it.

The second real-world complication is that (for the most part) companies rather than countries are the buyers and sellers of internationally traded oil. The forty-five most important of these companies have agreed to participate in the sharing arrangements and can generally be expected to support the program. Beyond these forty-five are the many independent refining and trading companies whose activities are taken into account in determining available supply and whose cooperation must be secured by individual member governments.

The practical implications for companies participating in IEA emergency sharing are as follows: refining companies (or refining affiliates of integrated companies) operating in surplus countries under the sharing formula must voluntarily restrain themselves from bidding to increase imports on the world market, though they may bid as necessary to maintain levels of imports. Some of these refiners will then have to be induced to sell some of their offshore supplies to refining companies in deficit countries.

Here the matter of price enters the picture. Pricing of reallocated supplies is sometimes cited as the Achilles heel of the emergency sharing agreement. Critics of the sharing program believe that the difficulties of agreeing on price for reallocation transactions are likely to prove so intractable that the entire edifice of sharing will crumble when put to the test. This is unlikely to be the case. Sellers are unlikely to accept, nor would buyers realistically expect, prices for these transactions substantially below prevailing spot levels. At the same time, in the interest of making the system work, sellers would be unlikely to insist on the highest of the spot quotations mooted in the

11

trade press. As long as spot prices remain above predisruption levels, the result is likely to fall within a band above predisruption prices, but below the highest spot quotations.

Critics may ask what the point of emergency sharing is if buyers have to pay spot prices, since supplies are presumably available at these prices on the spot market. The answer is clear: the system is designed not to provide cheap oil, but to reduce the competitive scramble and thereby dampen upward price pressure. Spot prices rise when no one is willing to sell at the current price. Emergency sharing would reduce spot price pressure by providing companies operating in deficit countries access to willing sellers at prices within the current range.

Trading and refining companies not participating in the system pose special problems, especially for countries in which domestic price levels are allowed to rise substantially above international market levels. Since they are less directly involved in the sharing system, these companies provide channels through which additional supplies could enter countries already supplied in excess of their allowance under the formula. Governments can encourage these companies to dispose of supplies through the IEA reallocation program. But if this remedy is insufficient to stem the flow, governments must then choose between restricting their activities (for example, by imposing import quotas and licensing) and offsetting their activities by persuading participating companies to sell off additional supplies. The first approach involves a potentially complex escalation of the level of government intervention. The second approach subjects participating companies to the possibility of losing their market share to nonparticipating companies. Many countries would resolve this problem by implementing limited internal reallocation ("fair sharing"), thereby compensating companies for selling supplies into the international reallocation program. The IEP in fact anticipates this problem by requiring member countries to have in place such "fair sharing" programs whose objective is to protect companies against loss of market share as a result of cooperating with IEA international sharing.

Conclusion

Many difficulties would unquestionably arise in implementing the IEA emergency programs. It would be unrealistic, however, to expect to cope with a supply emergency without difficulty. What is important is that the broad framework for keeping the market functioning in an orderly fashion and limiting economic damage is in place. Coordinated stockdraw, emergency information, and emergency sharing together would restore order to a severely disrupted market, reduce price pressures, and at the same time make it politically possible for governments to attend to problems at the margin, while allowing the oil companies to get on with their job. The invisible hand is undeniably the best way to allocate resources in orderly markets with large numbers of buyers and sellers. But when the market for an internationally traded commodity with the economic and strategic importance of oil is severely disrupted, invisibility ceases to be a workable principle.

During the middle 1980s, as OPEC's share of the world oil market fell steadily, many analysts and observers moved to the view that security of oil supply had disappeared forever from the agenda of international economic policy making. Today almost no one believes that. Demand has been rising since 1985, and non-OPEC supplies, which rose steadily after 1979, now seem poised to begin a long-term decline. Supplies will now become concentrated increasingly in the volatile Gulf region.

The IEA's mandate therefore remains as important today as it was in 1974 for the international economic and political order. To plan for and insure against the gradual erosion of the ample and diverse oil supply situation of the mid-1980s is a major challenge for policy makers, not least because both memories and horizons are short.

To continue working toward structural reductions in oil requirements has the highest priority, both because this is the surest solution and because the lead time for achieving it is so long. The IEA's long-term program is therefore being pressed vigorously in all fruitful directions. Its success will both diminish the likelihood that the emergency response measures will ever have to be used and reduce the difficulties they would encounter if they should be called into action.

Notes

The views expressed here are those of the author and do not represent the views of the IEA or any of its member governments. The author wishes to acknowledge a debt of gratitude to J. Wallace Hopkins for his substantial and perceptive assistance and to the late Dr. Ulf Lantzke for his useful comments on early drafts.

1. Supply/demand imbalances and gasoline lines would unquestionably occur even were governments to maintain a completely "hands-off" posture. In the United States, for example, the contractual structure between the refinery gate and retail outlets guarantees that supplies will be reduced on a more or less pro rata basis to all retailers, regardless of demand patterns. Most retailers, in turn, with an eye toward preserving customer relations, are unlikely to charge the kinds of prices that will eliminate lines or the need to put customers on allocation.

2. The U.S. market, for example, is sufficiently large that an important part of the benefits of its strategic petroleum reserve program derives from the downward pressure of SPR drawdown on world oil prices. The greater the proportion of the world market that participates in a government stocks program, the larger are these benefits.

3. Income transfers abroad are net losses of economic welfare for which there is no offsetting gain elsewhere in the system. While foreign oil producers may spend or invest this income in the consuming countries, the magnitude of the income loss itself remains the same. In the one case money flows abroad to the producers, and in the other what flow are goods, services, and returns on investment of equal value, which otherwise would have been enjoyed domestically.

4. The long-run marginal cost path is a function of geological and technological imponderables. The most that can be said with any confidence about the efficient oil price path is that it lies above short-run marginal cost of extraction and that in the absence of any dramatic geological or technological breakthroughs or disasters it should rise slowly and steadily over time. These characteristics of the price path reflect the high costs of finding and producing new reserves in relation to the costs of reserves currently being produced. And costs rise as exploration and production move to more remote or less productive areas.

5. The real price of oil rose 400 percent during the winter of 1973–1974 and then remained virtually flat for 4½ years. The price then rose 90 percent during 1979 and 7 percent in 1980. From 1981 through 1985 it declined at an annual rate of around 3 percent before plunging about 30 percent during 1986. It cannot be excluded a priori that such a path might represent an efficient adjustment to developments in long-run marginal extraction costs, but it is difficult to make a good case for this, especially for the post-1979 period. The 30 percent rise in 1973–1974 was in large part a correction for the failure of real prices to rise, as due consideration for long-run extraction costs might have required, during the 1960s and early 1970s. After the Iranian revolution and the onset of the Iran-Iraq war, the indefinite loss of access to much of the vast Iranian and Iraqi reserves on which the market had been relying for the 1980s undeniably justified a discontinuous jump in the long-run path in the 1980–1981 period. But the subsequent decline—at the same time that long-run extraction costs are rising steadily—shows that a 90 percent increase overshot the mark by a wide margin. Although the 1986 drop almost certainly brought the price back down to (or below) the efficient path, the correction took seven years to accomplish. To safeguard efficient levels of oil consumption and production after 1979, the market should have accomplished the adjustment in no more than seven months.

6. A primary cause of the price path's veering off course after 1979 was mistaken notions of price elasticity. The medium-term (one to five years) elasticity of demand was seriously underestimated by the industry, leading companies to continue paying high prices to accumulate inventories in the expectation that demand was only temporarily depressed (this had been the pattern after the 1973–1974 supply disruption and price increase). There is,

14

of course, no necessary reason for the industry to underestimate elasticity, and no guarantee that it will do so during or after the next disruption. The second reason why the medium-term price path remained above the efficient path for so long after 1979 is that the supply side of the world oil market was (and is) heavily influenced by a producers' cartel whose members were willing to reduce output rather than price as the true effects of price elasticity became manifest. By the time of the outbreak of the Iran-Iraq war in September 1980, and only twelve months after the group achieved its record production level, OPEC members had shut in some 6 million barrels per day, or 20 percent of export capacity. Although over half of this shut-in capacity was in Iran, 2.5 million barrels per day were shut in elsewhere in OPEC. Saudi Arabia, the only OPEC member that favored returning to a lower price path during this period, continued to produce at what was regarded as the prudent maximum but lacked the ability to enforce its will with production increases sufficient to offset the others' decreases. The Saudi preference for a lower price path was undoubtedly in that country's best interests in view of its extremely high reserve/production ratio. The Iranian preference for higher prices and lower production, however, may have been equally rational given that country's relatively low ratio. Libya, Venezuela, Nigeria, and Indonesia, all important producers, had interests similar to those of Iran, for the same reason. There is no predicting how these conflicting interests would be resolved after any future disruption, especially since political factors would be at least as important as the economic ones. It is certainly possible, however, that those in favor of a rapid return to the efficient path would prevail.

7. In Germany, the Netherlands, Denmark, and Austria, a large portion of the oil companies' compulsory stockholding obligation is satisfied by separate stockholding organizations, of which the companies are members and to which they pay fees to defray storage costs. While legal regimes differ, member companies generally would have first claim on the oil in the event a supply disruption caused governments to release the compulsory reserves.

8. In fact, the formula is not strictly proportional to consumption but is weighted somewhat to the benefit of countries with indigenous oil production. In a disruption of between 7 and 10 percent, a country's "supply right" is calculated as 93 percent of its consumption in the base period minus the product of the remaining percentage shortfall times the country's share of IEA net imports in the preceding calendar year. Thus, for example, in a 10 percent disruption in 1985, the United Kingdom (a net exporter) would have had a supply right equal to 93 percent of base period consumption, while the corresponding percentages for Japan and the United States would have been 88 percent and 91 percent, respectively.

9. Under the IEP, member governments prepare a program of contingent demand restraint measures enabling them to reduce consumption by either 7 percent or 10 percent, depending on the severity of the disruption (Article 5). Stocks held in excess of those needed to satisfy the ninety-day emergency reserve commitment may be substituted for demand restraint when the system is activated (Article 16).

10. The disruptions simulated in IEA tests typically require that around 10

15

percent of international crude oil trade be reallocated to destinations different from those intended before the disruption. Around half of this has been reallocated by the companies acting on their own initiative. The remaining reallocation takes place under direct IEA coordination.

2
International Energy Cooperation: The Mismatch between IEA Policy Actions and Policy Goals

Rodney T. Smith

The disruption of oil supplies during the Arab-Israeli War of 1973 was a call for action by Western governments. Policies adopted by the Organization of Petroleum Exporting Countries (OPEC) had threatened the strategic and economic interests of the Western world. The central policy question for Western governments became what policies they should pursue in response to the destabilizing political forces in the Middle East.

The Agreement on an International Energy Program was created within this historical context. It has been ratified by twenty-one of the twenty-four members of the Organization for Economic Cooperation and Development (OECD). It has two purposes: to limit OECD losses from future oil supply disruptions and to reduce long-term OECD dependence on oil imports from OPEC. To achieve these goals, the treaty created the International Energy Agency (IEA), which has devised a complex oil-sharing plan and imposed policies of demand restraint, import control, and oil stockpiling.

The IEA generally receives high marks as part of an effective, even an essential, multilateral effort that achieves significant objectives in energy policy and Western diplomacy. Former Secretary of State Henry Kissinger has heralded the program as "one of the great success stories of the last decade and a half."[1] The program has also been viewed as part of a U.S. effort to revitalize U.S.-Atlantic and U.S.-Japanese alliances in the aftermath of the 1973 oil embargo.[2] It has also been criticized, as by Senator Howard M. Metzenbaum, who viewed the whole effort as "merely a mirage."[3]

Despite the program's prominence, no systematic investigation of its actual, as opposed to its promised, economic effects has been

17

undertaken. This chapter examines IEA decision-making procedures and policies. It considers the potential for economic conflict among member countries within IEA decision rules. It also focuses on how IEA policies affect the economic incentives of its members to alter their oil consumption, importing, stockpiling, and pricing policies.

The purpose of the analysis is to discover the link, if any, between IEA policy actions and the stated goals of the program. Understanding the reasons for success or failure of IEA actions identifies which policies achieve real gains from international energy cooperation and which are counterproductive.

The first section is an overview of the structure of the IEA. The second describes the institutional and organizational background, including the policy mechanisms, of the IEA. The third looks at specific policy actions undertaken by the agency, particularly during the Iranian revolution and at the outbreak of the Iran-Iraq war. The economic consequences of oil sharing are examined in the next section, which simulates a world oil supply disruption affecting IEA countries differentially. The fifth section analyzes import controls, focusing on coordination problems and possible OPEC pricing responses, and examines the record of general petroleum consumption restraints in 1980. Oil stockpiling is analyzed both as a general economic phenomenon and as an object of IEA coordination in the sixth section, which also offers an econometric analysis of experience in the 1970s and 1980s. The final section considers less formal assessments of IEA policies, including evaluations by the IEA itself.

Analytical Framework

Figure 2–1 diagrams the IEA's role in the complex array of economic and political forces that govern the international petroleum market. The treaty specifies when IEA policies are binding on signatory countries. Yet the IEA alone does not control the international marketplace. Its effectiveness in achieving its goals depends on how its decision-making structure and policy actions interact with other economic and political forces.

For simplicity, figure 2–1 depicts only OPEC producers and OECD countries. OPEC, of course, is a potential source of future supply disruptions, and its marketing and pricing policies have been the subject of IEA policy discussions. OECD countries are important in two regards: (1) individuals in those countries make resource decisions and their governments adopt national policies that jointly influence the international marketplace; and (2) those countries, through the committee structure of the IEA, formulate IEA policies.

18

FIGURE 2-1
THE IEA IN THE INTERNATIONAL ENERGY MARKETPLACE

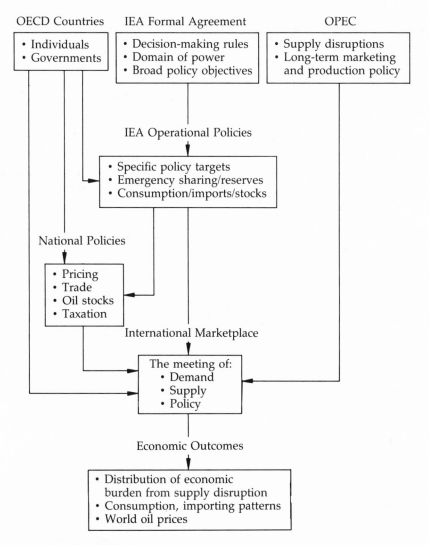

In principle, the IEA's structure and policies have been based on two premises about the energy security of IEA countries:[4]

- The oil supply security of each participating country will be more enhanced by cooperation than by independent action.
- Resistance to OPEC market power can be strengthened by developing countervailing power.

19

International organizations, however, cannot serve as independent sources of restraint on the actions taken by sovereign governments without their consent.[5] A member country will follow IEA policies and meet its obligations only if it is in fact—not just in theory—better off by honoring the agreement.

The bottom box in the figure lists the economic outcomes on which the IEA has focused its attention. The key question is whether IEA policies, which are only one among several influences, will significantly affect the enumerated variables.

The Institutional Structure of the IEA

The International Energy Program was developed after widespread dissatisfaction with the initial responses by Western governments to the 1973 oil embargo. The Organization of Arab Petroleum Exporting Countries (OAPEC) had halted all oil shipments to the United States and the Netherlands because of their support of Israel. The United Kingdom and France were declared exempt. West Germany, Italy, and others were scheduled for a reduction of 5 percent per month in their oil shipments.[6] This differential treatment of OECD countries created tensions in the Western alliance and ultimately influenced the policy approaches included in the program.

Initially the OECD countries disagreed on their response to the OAPEC embargo. Germany and the Netherlands advocated a "coordinated policy" response, while the United Kingdom and France wanted to let the "embargo work."[7] Without a consensus OECD countries engaged, according to some observers, in a "competitive scramble" for oil supplies:

> The European Economic Community (EEC) countries, which had an emergency oil sharing agreement, broke ranks during the embargo as some tried to win favored status with individual oil exporters. Afterward, Japan and the major European nations . . . engaged in a scramble to conclude bilateral agreements with the major exporters, offering economic and political concessions.[8]

With disarray in Europe and the Far East and the United States worried about the "oil weapon" threatening the independence of its foreign policy, the Western alliance met to rethink its response to the OAPEC embargo.

The Process of Agreement. Twelve major oil-consuming nations participated in a conference in Washington, D.C., in February 1974. Policies for coping with future embargoes were discussed. U.S.

20

representatives feared that the United States would be the target and therefore advocated emergency plans for oil sharing as a central feature of the IEA.[9] In response to an original lack of interest in oil sharing on the part of the Europeans and Japanese, the agenda was broadened to facilitate reaching an agreement. In the words of Mason Willrich and Melvin A. Conant:

> The assumptions initially underlying the [program] were narrow. They were largely a reflection of immediate American interests during the Arab oil embargo. In order to obtain sufficiently broad-based industrial country cooperation . . . U.S. diplomacy forged a link between industrial energy security and economic and even military security.[10]

By November 1974 sixteen of the twenty-four OECD countries had signed the International Energy Program agreement, which established the IEA as an autonomous body within the OECD (see table 2–1). IEA membership grew throughout the 1970s. Greece, New Zealand, and Norway joined during 1976–1977. Australia joined in March 1979. Portugal was the last to join, in May 1980. These countries are important actors in the international petroleum market. In 1980 they consumed about 75 percent of the world petroleum produced outside the Soviet Union and China.[11]

Only France, Finland, and Iceland remain as OECD countries outside the IEA. France disliked both the early tone of confrontation between the IEA and OPEC and the apparent U.S. leadership role.[12] Finland and Iceland, unlike other OECD countries, rely mainly on oil imports from the Soviet Union and therefore experience different political considerations in their supply sources.[13]

The IEA administers the policies and programs set forth in the agreement. Although its budget ($9.8 million in 1980) is part of the OECD budget, the IEA maintains control of its own operations. It has four main goals:

1. to prepare participating countries against the risk of a major disruption in oil supplies and to share available oil in the event of an emergency

2. to foster cooperation among participating countries so as to reduce excessive dependence on oil through energy conservation, development of alternative energy sources, and energy research and development

3. to develop an information system on the international oil market and to consult with oil companies

4. to stimulate cooperation with oil-producing and oil-consuming countries with a view to developing a stable international energy trade

21

TABLE 2-1
MEMBERSHIP HISTORY OF THE INTERNATIONAL ENERGY AGENCY, 1974-1987

Group	Countries
Energy coordinating group (drafted International Energy Program agreement in February 1974)	Belgium Canada Denmark Ireland Italy Japan Luxembourg Netherlands Norway United Kingdom United States West Germany
Original signers of International Energy Program agreement, November 1974	Austria[a] Belgium Canada Denmark Ireland Italy Japan Luxembourg Netherlands Spain[a] Sweden[a] Switzerland[a] Turkey[a] United Kingdom United States West Germany
Later joined IEA Before Iranian revolution (1976–1977)	Greece New Zealand Norway
After Iranian revolution (1979–1980)	Australia Portugal

NOTE: OECD countries not members of IEA: Finland, France, Iceland.
a. Not included in energy coordinating group.
SOURCE: Interview of staff at International Energy Agency.

as well as rational management and use of world energy resources in the interests of all countries[14]

The duration of the agreement was to be ten years, and it continues after January 19, 1986, unless the IEA Governing Board, acting by majority vote, decides to terminate it.

Organization and Decision Making. The IEA has four major components: a Governing Board, a Management Committee, various standing groups, and a Secretariat.[15] The Governing Board is the major policy-making entity, the other units serving in an advisory role. Various oil industry advisory committees have also been established, though not mandated by the agreement. These voluntary groups advise the standing groups, as allowed by Articles 54–58.

Table 2–2 summarizes the responsibilities and functions of each unit. Two committees are of critical importance. The Standing Group on Emergency Questions (SEQ) is responsible for informing the Governing Board about developments that concern emergency preparedness. Its most important functions include the emergency sharing and reserve systems. These policies are the cornerstone of the IEA's attempt to "bring order" to international oil markets during supply disruptions.

The remaining committees collect information that enables the Governing Board to oversee the implementation of policy. The Standing Group on Long-Term Cooperation (SLT) conducts annual reviews of member countries' research and development (R&D) efforts and coordinates IEA jointly sponsored R&D projects.

IEA decisions are made at the ministerial level by the Governing Board. The voting system has two components: general voting weights (three per voting member) and an oil consumption voting weight (100 total votes divided among voting members according to their relative amounts of consumption). Table 2–3 shows the distribution of those votes. Norway is a nonvoting member because it has reserved the option not to participate in the oil-sharing scheme and other programs.[16]

The required voting plurality depends on the kind of issue considered. Unanimity is required for obligations not specified in the treaty and for all other decisions not covered by the rules on the use of majority and special majority rule. Majority rule is required for a proposed decision that imposes specific obligations on members already specified by the treaty. A majority is defined as 60 percent of the total combined voting weights and 50 percent of the general voting

TABLE 2-2

IEA COMMITTEE STRUCTURE

Organ	Membership	Function	Decision Making
Governing Board	One or more ministers or their delegates from each country	Adopts decisions and makes recommendations to carry out objectives of International Energy Program Delegates powers to other IEA groups, mainly Secretariat Appoints executive director of Secretariat Reviews international energy developments	Takes actions (binding) Makes recommendations (nonbinding)
Management Committee	One or more senior representatives of government from each country	Functions as assigned by Governing Board Examines and makes proposals to Governing Board on any matter within scope of International Energy Program Can be convened at request of any member country	Makes proposals to Governing Board
Standing Group on Emergency Questions	One or more representatives of government from each country	Functions delegated by Governing Board Functions described in chapters 1–4 of agreement Functions listed in annex of agreement:	Reports to Management Committee Also works with Secretariat

		reserve commitments, demand restraint, allocation, activation, information system May consult with oil companies	
Standing Group on Oil Market	Same as other standing groups	Functions delegated by Governing Board Functions assigned by chapters 5–6: specify information system, review operations, establish framework for consultations with oil companies, prepare reports and evaluate results of consultations	Reports to Management Committee Submits annual reports on consultations
Standing Group on Long-Term Cooperation	Same as other standing groups	Functions delegated by Governing Board Functions assigned by chapter 7	Submits annual reports to Management Committee
Standing Group on Relations with Producer and Other Consumer Countries	Same as other standing groups	Examines and reports on cooperative actions in conservation, development of alternative energy sources, R&D, uranium enrichment Reviews efforts of participating countries to promote cooperative relations with non-IEA countries	Reports to Management Committee
Committee on Energy R&D	Same as standing groups	Performs annual review, published with review by Standing Group on Long-Term Cooperation	
Ad Hoc Group on International Relations		Set up after formal agreement, deals broadly with international energy relations	

(Table continues)

25

TABLE 2-2 (continued)

Organ	Membership	Function	Decision Making
Secretariat	Executive director staff	Day-to-day working group responsible to Governing Board and standing groups	
		Intermediary between member governments and industry advisory groups	
		Functions assigned by all groups and committees above	
Industry Advisory Board	Seven major oil companies, eleven independent and national oil companies	Advises on emergency oil-sharing questions	Advises Standing Committee on Emergency Questions
		Assisted in drafting of IEA Emergency Management Manual	
Industry Supply Advisory Group	Oil industry representatives	Assists operation of emergency oil sharing	
Industry Working Group	Oil industry representatives	Develops and maintains oil market information system	Advises Standing Group on Oil Market and the Secretariat

SOURCE: *Agreement on an International Energy Program (as Amended to 19th May 1981).*

TABLE 2–3
DISTRIBUTION OF VOTING RIGHTS AMONG IEA MEMBERS, 1980

Country	General Voting Weights	Consumption Voting Weights	Combined Voting Weights
Australia	3	1	4
Austria	3	1	4
Belgium	3	2	5
Canada	3	5	8
Denmark	3	1	4
Germany	3	8	11
Greece	3	1	4
Ireland	3	0	3
Italy	3	5	8
Japan	3	15	18
Luxembourg	3	0	3
Netherlands	3	2	5
New Zealand	3	0	3
Portugal	3	0	3
Spain	3	2	5
Sweden	3	2	5
Switzerland	3	1	4
Turkey	3	1	4
United Kingdom	3	6	9
United States	3	47	50
Total	60	100	160

NOTE: Norway is a nonvoting member.
SOURCE: *Agreement on an International Energy Program (as amended to 19th May 1980)*, Art. 62, p. 33.

weights. A majority therefore requires the consent of at least ten countries with at least ninety-six combined voting weights.

Special majority rule further increases the importance of general voting weights. It is required on issues that pertain to preparing, activating, and implementing the crisis management program. The agreement defines two kinds of special majorities: (1) 60 percent of the combined voting weights and forty-five general voting weights (fifteen countries) and (2) 60 percent of the combined voting weights and fifty-one general voting weights (seventeen countries). The first special majority is required of actions associated with the entire participating group; the second is required of actions that pertain to an individual member country (see table 2–4).

TABLE 2–4

IEA ACTIONS REQUIRING SPECIAL MAJORITY RULE

Special majority of 60 percent of combined voting weights plus forty-five general voting weights
- Increase emergency reserve commitment
- Not activate the Emergency Sharing System when the Secretariat finds that the group has suffered a sufficiently large shortfall of oil supply
- Take any action when 50 percent of emergency reserves have been drawn down
- Deactivate emergency measures on basis of Secretariat's assessment of group's oil supply situation
- Deactivate emergency measures wholly or in part when Secretariat has not made a finding supporting the action

Special majority of 60 percent of combined voting weights plus fifty-one general voting weights
- Not activate the Emergency Sharing System when the Secretariat finds that an individual country has experienced a 7 percent shortfall of oil supply
- Maintain emergency measures when the Secretariat finds that an individual country no longer experiences a 7 percent shortfall of oil supply
- Deactivate the emergency measures for an individual country when the Secretariat has made no finding supporting the deactivation

SOURCE: *Agreement on an International Energy Program (as Amended to 19th May 1980).*

Policy Mechanisms Established by the Agreement. The agreement specified procedures, administered by the SEQ, by which the IEA was to prepare its members for oil supply emergencies. Preparation included devising a plan with emergency reserve requirements, demand restraint obligations, and stock drawdown obligations. The plan, called the Emergency Sharing System, includes rules for activation, assignment of buying rights and selling obligations, and pricing policies. Close inspection reveals that "the scheme becomes bewildering in its complexity."[17]

Readiness for emergency situations. The backbone of the effort is the emergency reserve requirement, whereby each member agreed to establish an oil supply reserve. Each country would accumulate sufficient reserves to sustain consumption for a sixty-day (after 1980 for a ninety-day) total disruption in net oil imports. Article 2 specified the pertinent consumption and net oil import levels as the average daily amounts for the previous calendar year. This reserve commitment need not be satisfied entirely by accumulating stocks. Article 3 allows each country to satisfy its commitments by an unspecified combination of fuel stocks, fuel-switching capacity, and standby oil production.

Only reserves that are absolutely available to member governments are to be counted in measuring a country's commitment to the targets. Reserves for military purposes and stocks at sea are expressly excluded. Because absolute availability is difficult to define, Article 1, item 3, of the annex established the rule of thumb that stocks should be measured as actual stocks minus 10 percent.

Each country must also have in place two programs that would reduce its domestic consumption of finished petroleum products by 7 and by 10 percent (see Articles 5, 13, and 14). These percentages are measured from a base period defined as the four most recent calendar quarters, with a one-quarter lag for reporting delay. The agreement did not impose specific obligations about how these programs should operate or what they should include. The SEQ assesses whether each country's programs are sufficient to achieve the required demand restraint. A country may substitute the use of emergency reserves in excess of its emergency reserve commitment for demand restraint obligations.

The Emergency Sharing System is activated by either the Governing Board or the Secretariat; it can be triggered when the IEA as a group sustains or is expected to sustain a 7 percent reduction of the average daily rate of its (base year) consumption, or any participating country sustains or is expected to sustain a 7 percent reduction, or a major region of participating countries sustains or is expected to sustain a 7 percent reduction. Any participating country may request the Secretariat to make a finding on whether the conditions to trigger the system exist (see Article 21).

Once the system is triggered, the agreement calls for accounting computations that define buying rights and selling obligations for member countries. Each country's "right" to oil supply depends on its base period consumption, demand restraint, and obligations to draw down its reserves:

Supply right = base period consumption
− demand restraint − stock drawdown

Nothing in this accounting system requires actual demand restraint or stock drawdowns. The system simply uses the implications of assumed actions.

The magnitude of the supply disruption affects the demand restraint assumed in the calculations. If the group shortfall is less than 12 percent, a 7 percent figure is used for demand restraint. This

29

computation makes permissible consumption 93 percent of that during the base period. If the shortfall equals or exceeds 12 percent, the demand restraint figure used is 10 percent.

The stock drawdown obligation is the balancing transaction in the accounting system. The total IEA shortfall is computed as the difference between permissible consumption (base period consumption less demand restraint) and available oil supplies. If the targeted consumption exceeds the available supply, the agreement assumes that a coordinated drawdown of reserves occurs according to the following formula:

Country stock drawdown obligation $= (PRC/TRC)(PCON - ASUP)$

where PRC is the country's reserve commitment, TRC is the total IEA reserve commitment, $PCON$ is the total IEA permissible consumption, and $ASUP$ is the total IEA supply during the disruption.

The buying right or selling obligation of a country is determined by comparing its "supply right" with its actual supply of oil. The latter is defined as the sum of normal (not actual) domestic production and actual net imports of crude oil and petroleum products. If a country's supply right is less than its actual supply, it has an obligation to sell its excess supply to other IEA countries. If its supply right is more than its actual supply, it has a right to buy the difference between its supply right and its actual supply.

The price at which mandated transactions are to take place is not specified by the agreement. Article 10 states, in its entirety:

1) The objectives of the Program shall include ensuring fair treatment for all participating countries and basing the price for allocated oil on the price conditions prevailing for comparable commercial transactions.
2) Questions relating to the price of oil allocated during an emergency shall be examined by the Standing Group on Emergency Questions.

The guidance offered in section 1 is ambiguous.[18] IEA members have avoided clarifying the pricing policy. Instead they have established a Dispute Settlement Center to arbitrate the inevitable differences of interpretation by buyers and sellers during a supply emergency.[19] If the center proves incapable of arbitrating disputes successfully during a crisis, the Governing Board must exercise its ultimate authority to administer the obligations under the treaty. Decisions would be made under the less stringent special majority rule, not unanimously, because pricing involves the disposition of an issue specified by the treaty.

In summary, the Emergency Sharing System uses an accounting method to allocate oil among IEA members during a supply disruption. If the IEA shortfall exceeds 7 percent of the previous year's consumption, the system is activated unless the Governing Board votes not to implement the program proposed by the Secretariat. Drawdown obligations are used to limit the decline in consumption to the levels specified by the demand restraint obligation.

Implementation during a crisis. The complexity of the Emergency Sharing System is matched by the complexity of its implementation plans. Under current protocols it may be four months after a crisis begins before the oil-sharing plan reaches full operation. Willrich and Conant have summarized the process outlined in Article 19 as follows:

> Within 48 hours (Secretariat finding [of a supply disruption]), the Management Committee meets and reviews the accuracy of the Secretariat's report. Within a further 48 hours (Secretariat finding + 4 days), the Committee reports to the Governing Board. . . . Within a further 48 hours (Secretariat finding + 6 days), the Board meets to review the Secretariat's finding in light of the Management Committee's report. Within a further 48 hours (Secretariat finding + 8 days), the activation is "confirmed" unless the Governing Board by special majority decides otherwise. Implementation begins within 15 days of confirmation (Secretariat finding + 23 days). Any "decisions" of the Management Committee or the IEA Governing Board may be reversed by the Board by a majority vote.[20]

In tandem with its internal decision making, the Secretariat plans to employ a three-phase approach to oil sharing.[21] Phase I would rely on voluntary action by oil companies, with the hope that oil would flow in a way that approximately achieved IEA targets. Phase II would begin when the Secretariat, on the basis of data generated by phase I, issued its initial schedule of national allocation rights and obligations for the current and subsequent two months. The release of this information, it is hoped, would generate voluntary offers of oil shipments to correct any imbalances. If later data showed continuing supply imbalances, phase III would begin, and the Secretariat would approach the governments of members with a sales obligation. According to Edward N. Krapels, "This is a request that a government order a company or companies to ship oil to countries that still have allocation rights, with the hope that the government will accede and the companies will obey."[22]

31

Long-term policies. The second major function of the IEA is to formulate cooperative policies that reduce long-term dependence on oil imports from OPEC (see chapter 7 of the treaty). By their membership participating countries have agreed to undertake national programs and take part in IEA cooperative ventures in conservation, development of alternative energy sources, energy R&D, and uranium enrichment. Under Article 66, each member is obligated to "take the necessary measures, including any necessary legislative measures, to implement this Agreement *and* decisions taken by the Governing Board." The implied attempt to influence domestic energy legislation has been identified as an important long-term goal of the IEA.[23] Yet the agreement does not establish guidelines for any such effort. The sparse protocol to coordinate long-term coordination stands in stark contrast to the complex framework to administer emergency oil sharing. The next section discusses how long-term issues have actually been approached.

IEA Policy Actions

The IEA has implemented a number of programs and actions designed to achieve its goals. While it prepared the protocols for the Emergency Sharing System, it devised formal and informal policies in response to supply disruptions created by the Iranian revolution and the Iran-Iraq war. Table 2–5 lists the important milestones of IEA activity. The following discussion explores these actions and the IEA's effort in R&D.

Setting Up the Machinery. Between November 1974 and November 1978, IEA countries ratified the agreement, established the organizational structure of the IEA, and held ministerial meetings to decide how the mechanisms and goals of the agreement could be implemented. The agreement did not formally enter into force until January 1976, when the conditions stated in Article 67 were satisfied: at least six countries, holding at least 60 percent of the combined voting weights, deposited notification of consent to be bound by the agreement.

The May 1976 meeting of the Industry Advisory Board was the first important IEA milestone. The meeting drafted the Emergency Management Manual, which set out the logistics and operating procedures for administering the Emergency Sharing System during a supply disruption. Although this manual has been revised, an operable system has still eluded the Industry Advisory Group. Recent exercises revealed that the system was unable to operate under the

32

TABLE 2-5
MAJOR POLICY MILESTONES OF THE IEA, 1974–1984

	Action
	Setting up institutional structure and implementing initial program
February 1974	Washington Energy Conference to establish energy coordinating group
November 1974	International Energy Program and IEA established
May 1975	First ministers' meeting
January 1976	International Energy Program agreement enters into force
May 1976	Drafting of Emergency Management Manual
November 1977	Ministers' meeting adopts *Principles for Energy Policy, Program for Long-Term Cooperation,* and group objective
April 1978	Ministers meet to review first *Review of National Energy Policies* and *Review of National Energy R&D*
	Actions and programs after the Iranian revolution
March 1979	IEA ministers negotiate 5 percent voluntary demand restraint
Spring 1979	Sweden requests activation of IEA Emergency Sharing System
May 1979	IEA ministers adopt *Principles for IEA Action on Coal*
December 1979	IEA adopts country-specific import ceilings for 1980 and implements quarterly monitoring
January 1980	Emergency oil reserve requirements changed from sixty days' to ninety days' net oil imports
May 1980	IEA ministers agree on medium-term measures of import yardsticks and ceilings
	Actions and programs after the advent of the Iran-Iraq war
October 1980	Agree to stock drawdowns and measures to limit "abnormal" spot market purchases
December 1980	Ministers reconfirm October actions; agree to "informal" system for sharing oil
December 1980	Ministers adopt *Lines of Action for Energy Conservation and Fuel Switching*
June 1981	Ministers meet to address whether IEA should have formal stock policy
December 1981	Ministers set 1981 stock levels at ninety days of 1980 import levels
July 1984	Ministers decide that stock drawdowns be used as "first line of defense" during disruptions

SOURCE: Compiled by author.

33

comfortable environment of test conditions, let alone during the turbulence of an actual crisis.[24]

The November 1977 ministerial meeting adopted the following twelve principles to promote the long-term goals contained in Articles 41–43:

- to develop programs to reduce or limit oil imports through conservation, increased domestic production, and oil substitution
- to reduce conflicts between environmental concerns and energy requirements
- to allow domestic prices to reach levels that will encourage conservation and fuel switching
- to slow the growth of demand for energy relative to economic growth through conservation and substitution
- to convert oil-fired electricity generation to other fuels
- to promote international trade in coal
- to reserve natural gas for premium users
- to expand nuclear generating capacity
- to emphasize R&D and international collaborative projects
- to establish a favorable investment climate and give priority to exploration
- to plan alternative responses to supply shortfalls in the event that conservation or supply goals are not met
- to cooperate in evaluating the world energy situation, R&D, and technical requirements with developing countries and other international organizations

The ministers proposed to use these principles in regular reviews of national energy policies.

A remarkable feature of these principles is their vagueness as a guide to action. As in the pertinent articles of the agreement, no actions or commitments were specified. The meeting did agree on a group objective of limiting IEA net oil imports to 26 million barrels per year by 1985, but no actions were specified for achieving this goal.

The next ministerial meeting, in April 1978, produced the first review of national energy policies and R&D. The major conclusions were four:

- Cooperation with the IEA and national energy efforts had been showing some progress yet were viewed as insufficient.
- Efforts had been inadequate to achieve the group objective of limiting net oil imports by 1985.
- The development of energy programs varied considerably from country to country.

34

- A world oversupply of oil had contributed to insufficient conservation and fuel switching.

Unfortunately for the outside analyst, the evidence used to reach these conclusions was not made public, but the following IEA statement about its "early years" is revealing:

> Due to substantially higher oil prices and reduced economic activity, oil consumption in OECD countries declined sharply during 1974 and 1975. . . . Energy issues tended to recede from public consciousness over this period and by mid-1978 there was cautious optimism that the basis existed for a renewal of sustained and balanced economic growth. It was recognized that energy adjustments would have to be made and that oil availability over the medium and long term could become a constraint on growth; but it was felt that adequate time existed to make the necessary structural adjustments to the energy systems of the OECD countries.[25]

Had this organization found that the marketplace and national policies continued to march to their own tune and were unaffected by IEA pronouncements of policy principles? Later sections of this chapter investigate this possibility.

The Iranian Revolution. The Iranian revolution prodded the IEA into action, even though the 7 percent shortfall needed to trigger the Emergency Sharing System was not satisfied. A variety of short-term interventions were attempted to coordinate national energy policies.

The first major action came at the March 1979 ministers' meeting. Anticipating a 5 percent reduction in the total oil supply available to IEA countries, the ministers agreed to reduce their countries' demand for oil by 2 million barrels per day. This target was to be met by an unspecified combination of fuel switching, conservation, demand restraint, and, where possible, increased domestic production. Although this was called the "most important meeting of the IEA since the 1973–74 oil embargo period,"[26] no specific policy commitments were made. All the proposed actions were voluntary.

By spring 1979 Sweden experienced a significant shortfall and requested the activation of the Emergency Sharing System. The Secretariat denied the request and urged Sweden to "work it out" with the oil companies.[27] The IEA sought to function within the context of its voluntary demand restraint program.

Uncertainty remained about the duration and severity of the supply disruption. In July the Governing Board adopted a proposal urging IEA countries to achieve their 5 percent reduction in consumption by

35

October instead of at year-end as originally planned. Again no specific actions were taken to ensure achievement of the goal.

Countries began searching for multilateral ways to place specific responsibilities on members (see table 2–6). Participants at the June Tokyo summit—the United States, Japan, Canada, Germany, France, the United Kingdom, and Italy—developed plans for a program of oil import ceilings, which was eventually adopted by the IEA at its December ministerial meeting. The final ceilings were the result of strenuous bargaining, especially within the European Economic Community (EEC), where disputes arose between large and small countries.[28] Quarterly monitoring was planned to ensure that the ceilings were not exceeded.

In December the ministers also discussed private stock accumulation, which they interpreted as "speculative buying" that unnecessarily raised oil prices on the spot market.[29] The Governing Board agreed to consult with governments and oil companies on their stock policies, evaluate the ninety-day emergency reserve requirement, and formulate other proposals for a flexible stock management policy.[30] As before, no formal actions were taken.

Two final meetings solidified the IEA's response to the Iranian revolution. In January 1980, in accordance with Article 2, the ministers increased the emergency reserve requirement from sixty to ninety days of net oil imports. In May 1980 they attempted to formulate a policy to intervene during smaller disruptions than were specified by the treaty, but no agreement was reached. The communiqué from the meeting stated that each minister was to give weight to a point raised in the Secretariat's 1979 review: "'Yardsticks and ceilings' should be

TABLE 2–6

ATTEMPTS AT IEA COORDINATION OF OIL IMPORT POLICIES WITH
OTHER MULTILATERAL EFFORTS, 1979

	Multilateral Action
June 1979	Tokyo summit adopts country-specific import ceilings
December 1979	EEC countries adopt country-specific 1980 import targets
December 1979	IEA adopts country-specific import ceilings for 1980

NOTE: Tokyo summit members: the United States, Japan, Canada, Germany, France, the United Kingdom, Italy. EEC members: Belgium, Denmark, France, Germany, Ireland, Italy, Luxembourg, the Netherlands, the United Kingdom.
SOURCE: Compiled by author.

36

adopted for the purpose of monitoring progress towards medium-term goals." The ministers agreed to meet again if "tight market conditions appear imminent." They viewed ceilings as "represent[ing] a political commitment which stated the degree of self-restraint which individual countries were willing to impose on themselves." This new emphasis on medium-term and more expansive, yet unspecified, policy actions reflected the ministers' finding that the current market situation did not require any adjustments in 1980 import ceilings or creation of ceilings for 1981 imports.

The Iran-Iraq War. Within a few months of this assessment, Iran and Iraq went to war and created another supply disruption. The Governing Board called a special meeting in mid-September to formulate its policy. While IEA country stocks were generally high, uncertainty about the duration and severity of the disruption was seen as placing severe pressure on international spot markets and was therefore of great concern.

In its October 1980 meeting the Governing Board determined that stock drawdowns were to be the principal means of responding to the supply disruption. Governments were urged to restrain spot market purchases by exerting their political influence on oil companies. As before, no specific obligations or means of implementation were specified. This approach was reaffirmed in a December meeting, when a communiqué summarized various strategies to be attempted during the fourth quarter of 1980 and the first quarter of 1981. The aim was to reduce first-quarter net oil imports by 10 percent.[31]

The December meeting also discussed "informal" oil sharing. The Secretariat was instructed to monitor supplies and identify potential imbalances among IEA countries. IEA governments were to support the implementation of "possible solutions" identified by consultations with oil companies.[32]

Two final ministerial meetings completed the development of IEA policy in 1981. In June the ministers addressed a number of questions. Should the IEA have a formal stock policy instead of relying on the efforts of its members? Should the IEA own stocks directly instead of attempting to influence the stock policies of oil companies? Should required stock levels under the emergency reserve commitment be based on different importing levels from those of 1980? In December the ministers reconvened and answered no to all these questions.

The final major pronouncement of policy occurred in July 1984, when the ministers decided to rely on coordinated stock drawdowns as the "first line of defense" during supply disruptions.[33] This approach replaced the earlier reliance on national policies to restrain demand,

37

which have recently received severe criticism.[34] As in other IEA actions, members have avoided any specific commitments.[35]

Research and Development and Long-Term Efforts. In addition to its crisis management, the IEA attempted to coordinate multilateral efforts to reduce long-term dependence on oil imports from OPEC. The Standing Group on Long-Term Cooperation focused its 1976 efforts on two areas that created much dissension among members: establishing a minimum safeguard price of $7.00 per barrel and prohibiting discrimination among IEA members by abolishing export controls.[36] The first idea was widely criticized as an example of international agreements' concentration on the perverse. The second was quickly defeated because it conflicted with domestic political objectives in the United States and Canada.[37]

Table 2–7 lists the major attempts at long-term cooperation after this inauspicious beginning. The *Twelve Principles for Energy Policy* elucidated in October 1977 were to form the cornerstone of all efforts. The problem lay in translating these ideas into concrete policy.

Principles for IEA Action on Coal was issued in May 1979. Three actions were intended to promote substantial expansion of coal use, production, and international trade:

- to ensure that national policies preclude the building or replacement of oil-fired plants and encourage the building of coal-fired plants
- to ensure that fiscal regimes do not adversely affect coal-mining projects
- to encourage national actions to remove constraints on using coal arising from inadequate port and transport facilities

TABLE 2–7

IEA LONG-TERM ACTIONS FOR COORDINATING MEMBERS'
ENERGY CONSERVATION AND R&D EFFORTS, 1977–1980

	Action
October 1977	Ministers adopt group objective and the *Twelve Principles for Energy Policy*
May 1979	Ministers adopt *Principles for IEA Action on Coal*
December 1979	Group objective lowered; national import goals set for 1985
December 1980	Ministers adopt *Lines of Action for Fuel Switching and Energy Conservation*

SOURCE: Compiled by author.

As usual, no specific obligations were created. Implementation was left to the discretion of individual countries.

The next long-term action accompanied the December 1980 ministers' meeting. The meeting's communiqué stated the premise of IEA policy:

> In order to give greater public focus to energy conservation and fuel-switching and to move from statements of general intention to more specific actions to achieve results, they (the ministers) adopted lines of action for energy conservation and fuel-switching which they will implement in their national policies.

To these ends five new proposals were advanced. Governments should

- allow energy prices to reach a level that encourages moves away from oil to other sources of energy
- encourage efficiency by creating an economic climate that fosters investment
- improve the efficiency of automobiles
- create measures for better building insulation, new building codes, and the like
- reduce oil-fired production of electricity

Some analysts have had difficulty finding specific actions rather than the statement of general intentions in IEA policy making. In the words of Willrich and Conant: "In one way or another, the IEP contains suggestions for every possible strategy to deal with the new world energy situation and an impressive commitment to none."[38]

Research, development, and demonstration of new technologies constituted the final area of long-term cooperation. The agreement provided participating countries with the opportunity to carry out any cooperative programs they desired. The objectives of these efforts were "to assure the development and application of those new and improved energy technologies which offer the potential of making a significant contribution to our energy needs, and which can help in reducing long-term dependence on oil."[39] The programs are reviewed annually by the Committee on Energy Research and Development, which also makes recommendations to the Governing Board.

Summary. The IEA's record shows a greater emphasis on intentions to cope with the "energy problem" than on the actual consequences of its policies. Most IEA policies, whether short-term management of supply disruptions or long-term reductions in oil dependence, are general statements of principles. No effort has been made to compare

39

what the agreement aspires to do with what could be achieved in the international marketplace without it. Specific obligations for members, except for oil import ceilings, have been absent. In no case has there been a means of enforcement to punish members who ignore the agreement or the communiqués issued by the Governing Board. Any compliance is assumed to result from the general interest of members in mitigating economic losses created by the "energy crisis." Yet no link has been found between IEA policies and actual economic improvements in adjusting to higher world oil prices. The remaining sections of this chapter investigate the relation between IEA activity and economic outcomes.

The Economic Consequences of Supply Disruptions and Oil Sharing

Disruptions of international oil supplies inevitably inflict economic hardship on oil consumers and oil-importing nations. Without oil sharing, market forces would determine the effects of a disruption on oil prices, consumption patterns, and the distribution of economic losses among countries. Consumers would reduce their demand for petroleum products. Private traders would draw down their inventories to offset, in part, the decline in foreign oil supplies.

The Emergency Sharing System attempts to alter these economic outcomes. The economic effects of oil sharing can be identified by comparing the patterns of consumption cutbacks and income losses that would occur during supply disruptions with and without oil sharing. By understanding the economic effects and political disputes likely to arise under oil sharing, we can determine how effectively the Emergency Sharing System would achieve its stated economic and political goals.

Supply Disruptions. Many analysts have concluded that the political and economic structure of international oil markets threatens the energy security of Western countries. The geographical concentration of petroleum reserves, especially in the Middle East, means that political problems in one or two countries can reduce world oil supply significantly.[40] For example, at the time the IEA was established, 60 percent of Persian Gulf oil exports passed through three ports with eight critical pump sites that controlled the flow of oil.[41] By design or accident, actions taken by or against key supply areas can quickly move international oil supply from a situation of plenty to one of crisis.

The price increases created by disruptions are perceived as substantial and are expected to inflict "huge short-term economic losses" on oil-importing countries.[42] Historical experience suggests that six categories of supply disruptions may occur:[43]

1. political disagreements that lead to deliberate export restrictions in an effort to influence political events, such as the Arab embargoes of 1946, 1957, 1967, and 1973–1974
2. production disruptions due to internal unrest in OPEC countries, such as those created by the Nigerian civil war of 1967–1970 and the Iranian revolution
3. sudden supply reductions for domestic economic reasons, such as occurred in Libya and Kuwait after 1973
4. terrorist acts and sabotage
5. war involving OPEC states, such as the Iran-Iraq war
6. superpower conflicts that jeopardize oil supplies from the Middle East

Disruptions in the first, probably the fourth, and the sixth categories are intended to inflict harm on Western countries. Those in the second, third, and fifth categories would also inflict harm on Western states but only as a byproduct.

For any disruption a benchmark for policy analysis is the market response without oil sharing. That response provides the base case on which oil sharing may either reduce or increase economic losses, limit or extend their duration, and deter or encourage individuals or organizations that aspire to wield the "oil weapon" to further their own political agendas.

Market Response without Oil Sharing. The economic losses a country suffers from a supply disruption depend on the actions taken by all countries. For example, the international oil market defeated the OAPEC embargo in 1973 by redistributing non-Arab oil supplies through commercial transactions.[44] Consider the responses of domestic producers, private storers, and consumers.

How much prices increase in response to a disruption depends on the supply of non-OPEC producers. Non-OPEC producers with idle capacity will rapidly expand their supply to offset, in part, the decline in net imports from OPEC, provided that they receive higher prices for their oil. The 1967 Arab oil embargo, for example, was overcome by expanded production from idle non-Arab sources of supply. In contrast, the lack of excess capacity in non-OPEC sources in 1973 has been held partly responsible for the large price increase that accompanied reductions in OPEC oil shipments.[45]

Private storers will draw down their stocks to replace, in part, the decline in foreign oil because they profit from sales at abnormally high prices during supply disruptions.[46] In fact, past disruptions have been met with immediate, extraordinary drawdowns of stocks, which were rebuilt at the end of the crises.[47] Stock drawdowns limit the magnitude of the price increase, and the more so the greater the initial level of stocks.[48]

Consumers will also respond to higher oil prices by reducing their use of petroleum products. They will substitute away from petroleum and toward other goods and services, even if their real incomes remain the same. But they will cut back their petroleum consumption by additional amounts because higher petroleum prices reduce their real income.[49]

Three disruptions were modeled to simulate the economic effects of supply reductions. The disruptions ranged from the minimum needed to trigger the Emergency Sharing System, 7 percent, to 10 and 15 percent declines in total supply (defined, as the IEA defines it, as the sum of domestic production and net imports of crude oil and refined products).[50] These disruptions would cause an annual loss to IEA member countries of about 800, 1,100, and 1,700 million barrels under the 1983 market conditions assumed to prevail before the disruption. The world spot market price for oil is estimated to increase from $28 per barrel before the disruption to $38, $44, and $56 per barrel during the supply disruptions.

The modeling was based on four assumptions. First, each disruption lasts one year. Second, private storers follow their historical storage rules in drawing down stocks. Third, consumers substitute away from petroleum in accordance with their past responses to changes in spot market prices. Finally, international arbitrage allocates oil among countries to equalize domestic and world spot market prices.

Appendix A describes the underlying equations for consumption, import supply, and stock drawdown for each IEA country. Appendix B gives estimated parameter values.

The amount and distribution of losses of national income from supply disruptions. Table 2–8 reports the losses of consumers, the gains of domestic producers, and the income losses and capital gains of private storers, which combine to determine the net effect on national income, for key groups of OECD countries. In 1983 private storers were building stocks and therefore would suffer income losses from paying higher prices on the original volume of planned storage. These small losses account for the discrepancy between the estimated effects on national income and the difference between the losses sustained by consumers and the gains enjoyed by home producers.[51]

The United States and Japan suffer about the same losses of national income from each supply disruption, which are slightly smaller than the loss suffered by the EEC. The remaining European countries suffer, as a group, the smallest losses of national income. The Japanese suffer the greatest per capita loss, followed by residents of the EEC, the United States, and non-EEC European countries. The other OECD countries (Australia, Canada, New Zealand) would enjoy slight gains in national income.

Variations in the loss of national income partly reflect the presence or absence of significant domestic petroleum resources. For example, over 75 percent of the loss of U.S. consumers is offset by gains by U.S. producers. In contrast, the virtual absence of indigenous petroleum resources in Japan means that the losses experienced by Japanese consumers are not offset by gains for Japanese producers. In general, the per capita loss of national income for a country is proportional to its per capita income, higher for countries that depend more on imports, and lower for countries with higher oil stocks.[52]

Supply and consumption cutbacks. Table 2–9 reports the distribution of supply cutbacks (domestic production plus net imports), consumption cutbacks, and stock drawdowns during the supply disruptions. The United States experiences the greatest supply cutback in absolute terms. The cutbacks are 30 percent smaller for the EEC, and Japan experiences cutbacks about 40 percent less than those suffered by the EEC. The remaining countries suffer small losses in absolute terms. Supply cutbacks per capita are almost proportional to national income but independent of import dependency and stock levels.[53]

For the OECD as a group, stock drawdowns limit consumption cutbacks to 75 percent of supply cutbacks. The significance of stock drawdowns as an alternative source of supply during disruptions holds for all regions and all disruptions, although their relative importance varies among countries.

The Economic Consequences of Oil Sharing. Three assumptions govern the analysis of oil sharing. First, the discussion ignores the numerous operational difficulties encountered during test runs of the system.[54] Second, it assumes that the IEA will correct a fundamental inconsistency in its current accounting system that makes aggregate sales obligations exceed aggregate purchase rights.[55] Finally, it assumes that oil sharing simply reallocates available oil supplies among IEA countries after a postdisruption allocation by market forces.[56] That is, the demand restraint described by the treaty is used solely to compute each member's purchase rights under oil sharing.

TABLE 2-8
Distribution of Economic Burden from Supply Shortfalls among OECD Countries and Domestic Consuming and Producing Interests without IEA Oil Sharing

Country/ Shortfall	Loss of National Income			Loss of Home Country Consumers			Gross Gain of Home Country Producers			Inventory ($ billions)	
	Total ($ billions)	Per capita ($)	%	Total ($ billions)	Per capita ($)	%	Total ($ billions)	Per capita ($)	%	Non-recurring gain	Loss from planned stock purchases
United States											
7%	16.34	69.67	0.50	50.95	217.28	1.56	38.63	164.72	1.19	14.75	4.01
10%	24.13	102.89	0.74	77.40	330.07	2.38	59.45	253.51	1.83	22.70	6.17
15%	38.12	162.56	1.17	128.80	549.24	3.96	101.19	431.50	3.11	38.63	10.51
Japan											
7%	16.53	138.57	1.40	15.08	126.44	1.27	0.04	0.35	0.00	5.04	1.49
10%	25.25	211.76	2.14	23.03	193.09	1.95	0.06	0.54	0.01	7.76	2.29
15%	42.46	356.02	3.59	38.67	324.25	3.27	0.11	0.93	0.01	13.21	3.90

44

EEC											
7%	21.96	83.65	1.04	29.50	112.37	1.39	10.45	39.83	0.49	9.04	2.91
10%	33.40	127.23	1.58	45.00	171.44	2.13	16.09	61.29	0.76	13.91	4.48
15%	55.69	212.15	2.63	75.44	287.40	3.56	27.39	104.33	1.29	23.67	7.63
Other Europe											
7%	8.22	60.04	1.45	10.55	77.06	1.86	3.09	22.56	0.55	3.36	0.76
10%	12.46	91.07	2.20	16.05	117.25	2.84	4.75	34.72	0.84	5.18	1.17
15%	20.69	151.14	3.66	26.78	195.71	4.74	8.09	59.09	1.43	8.81	1.99
Other OECD											
7%	−0.36	−6.98	−0.03	7.17	137.32	0.61	7.91	151.51	0.67	1.69	0.37
10%	−0.66	−12.66	−0.06	10.93	209.42	0.92	12.17	233.18	1.03	2.60	0.58
15%	−1.42	−27.13	−0.12	18.31	350.88	1.55	20.71	396.90	1.75	4.42	0.99
Total											
7%	62.67	46.64	0.52	113.24	79.43	0.88	60.12	39.55	0.44	33.88	9.55
10%	94.58	70.54	0.78	172.40	121.00	1.34	92.52	60.87	0.67	52.14	14.70
15%	155.54	116.46	1.29	288.00	202.34	2.24	157.49	103.61	1.15	88.74	25.02

NOTE: Loss of national income = consumer loss − producer gain + loss from planned stock purchases. Negative numbers denote gain in national income. EEC: Belgium, Denmark, France, Germany, Ireland, Italy, Luxembourg, the Netherlands, the United Kingdom. Other Europe: Austria, Finland, Greece, Iceland, Norway, Portugal, Spain, Sweden, Switzerland, Turkey. Other OECD: Australia, Canada, New Zealand.

SOURCE: Computed by author; see appendix A.

45

TABLE 2-9

DISTRIBUTION OF CONSUMPTION CUTBACKS, STOCK DRAWDOWNS, AND
TOTAL SUPPLY CUTBACKS AMONG OECD COUNTRIES
DURING SUPPLY DISRUPTIONS WITHOUT OIL SHARING

	Consumption Cutbacks			Stock Drawdowns			Total Supply Cutbacks		
Country/ Shortfall	Total (mil.bbl)	Per capita (bbl)	%	Total (mil.bbl)	Per capita (bbl)	%	Total (mil.bbl)	Per capita (bbl)	%
United States									
7%	274.59	1.17	5.75	52.58	0.22	3.91	327.16	1.40	6.36
10%	387.46	1.65	8.11	74.19	0.32	5.52	461.65	1.97	8.98
15%	569.20	2.43	11.91	108.98	0.46	8.11	678.18	2.89	13.19
Japan									
7%	77.36	0.65	5.54	52.57	0.44	11.44	129.93	1.09	8.47
10%	112.35	0.94	8.04	76.35	0.64	16.61	188.70	1.58	12.31
15%	173.64	1.46	12.43	118.00	0.99	25.68	291.64	2.45	19.02
EEC									
7%	159.97	0.61	5.84	69.62	0.27	8.46	229.60	0.87	7.64
10%	230.77	0.88	8.42	100.16	0.38	12.17	330.93	1.26	11.01
15%	352.72	1.34	12.87	152.35	0.58	18.50	505.07	1.92	16.80
Other Europe									
7%	68.22	0.50	6.92	18.74	0.14	6.12	86.96	0.64	8.25
10%	98.03	0.72	9.95	26.75	0.20	8.73	124.78	0.91	11.83
15%	148.96	1.09	15.12	40.22	0.29	13.13	189.18	1.38	17.94
Other OECD									
7%	23.37	0.54	3.51	4.38	0.10	2.85	27.75	0.64	3.96
10%	32.58	0.75	4.89	6.09	0.14	3.96	38.67	0.89	5.52
15%	46.75	1.08	7.02	8.70	0.20	5.66	55.45	1.28	7.92
Total OECD									
7%	603.51	0.76	5.71	197.88	0.25	14.73	801.39	1.01	7.01
10%	861.20	1.08	8.15	283.54	0.36	21.10	1,144.74	1.44	10.01
15%	1,291.28	1.62	12.22	428.26	0.54	31.87	1,719.53	2.16	15.04

bbl = barrels; mil.bbl = millions of barrels.
NOTE: 1983 consumption, production, trade, and stocks reflect precrisis market conditions. Consumption cutbacks + stock drawdowns = total supply cutbacks. EEC: Belgium, Denmark, France, Germany, Ireland, Italy, Luxembourg, the Netherlands, the United Kingdom. Other Europe: Austria, Finland, Greece, Iceland, Norway, Portugal, Spain, Sweden, Switzerland, Turkey. Other OECD: Australia, Canada, New Zealand.
SOURCE: Computed by author; see appendix A.

The first two assumptions overstate the benefits of oil sharing. Given the IEA's inability to coordinate "hypothetical paper transactions" during test runs, detailed administration of oil trades during an actual disruption seems unlikely. Administrative breakdowns seem inevitable. Similarly, the inconsistency in current accounting practices should produce stalemate until the Secretariat devises a coherent policy to balance the ledger between sales obligations and purchase rights.[57] In any event, these problems will introduce inflexibility into oil trading and allocation that would undoubtedly injure consumers.

The third assumption may understate the gains of oil sharing. Some analysts have argued that oil sharing may coordinate attempts by IEA member countries to exploit their collective monopsony power and thereby reduce world oil prices during a disruption.[58] But the treaty does not *require* that demand restraint be implemented before the transactions defined by oil sharing are completed. In fact, existing national demand restraint programs appear ineffective, if not counterproductive.[59] Moreover, past IEA attempts at coordinating consumption cutbacks have failed.[60] Finally, how can oil sharing administer a "buyers' cartel" if test runs have experienced significant operational difficulties? Although some would view this third assumption as pessimistic, actual experience suggests that it is prudent.

Qualitative effects. The successful administration of oil sharing requires national policies that enforce price disparities among national markets and create implicit income transfers among IEA countries. Economic inefficiencies would also be created in which the gains received by countries with purchase rights would be less than the losses suffered by countries with sales obligations.[61]

The necessity for complementary national policies arises from the conflict between the self-interest of individuals and their country's treaty obligations. The transactions mandated by oil sharing are intended to supplement normal commercial transactions. But an individual's demand for petroleum is not affected by oil sharing unless national policies link his decision about petroleum trade to *his* share of his country's purchase rights or sales obligations. In the absence of such policies, individuals would consume, at the world price, the quantity demanded in the absence of oil sharing. How can consumers in countries with purchase rights be induced to exercise their rights, and how can consumers in countries with sales obligations be induced to release oil to fulfill their countries' sales obligations?

Consider the case of a country with purchase rights. Its residents would have no economic incentive to exercise their rights if they must

47

pay the world price for oil. Instead, successful oil sharing requires a price subsidy equal to the difference between the world price and the price at which the quantity demanded equals the IEA consumption target. The gross transfer received from oil sharing equals that price subsidy multiplied by the oil purchased under oil sharing. The net gain, however, is less than the gross transfer because the additional oil purchased is valued at less than the world price. If the value of the oil were not lower, individuals would have purchased it without oil sharing.

Now consider the case of a country with sales obligations. Domestic oil prices must rise above world oil prices to induce its residents to release oil for sale under oil sharing. Residents in the country suffer two kinds of losses. First, they suffer a financial loss from the sale of petroleum at below world market prices. Second, the necessary reduction in consumption creates an economic inefficiency because the sacrificed uses will be valued at more than the world price. If these uses did not have a greater value, residents would not have acquired that oil in the absence of oil sharing.

The necessary price differentials among IEA countries must be defended by trade interventions. Private traders have an incentive to ship oil from countries with purchase rights to countries with sales obligations. Countries with purchase rights must impose export controls to defend domestic prices that are below world market prices. Countries with sales obligations must impose import controls to defend domestic prices above world market prices. National trade policies must be coordinated because domestic prices will deviate from world prices by different amounts, reflecting differences among countries in their targeted supplies, demand elasticities, and stockpiling policies.

Oil sharing inflicts a net loss on IEA countries as a group. Since the quantities of petroleum sold and purchased at below-market prices must be the same for the entire group, the gross income transfers between buying and selling countries must cancel. But the resource inefficiencies experienced in each country do not cancel. These losses constitute the economic cost of not allowing the marketplace to allocate available oil during a disruption. They are the cost that must be paid to achieve any equity goals that the income transfers under oil sharing are intended to create.

Quantitative effects. Table 2–10 summarizes regional information on the distribution of the gains and losses in national income from enforcement of the Emergency Sharing System.[62] Two major findings, based on country-by-country effects (not shown in the table), challenge the political viability of oil sharing.

TABLE 2-10
ESTIMATED DISTRIBUTION OF GAINS AND LOSSES FROM FORCED RETRADING UNDER EMERGENCY SHARING SYSTEM
(millions of dollars per year)

Country/ Shortfall	Income Transfer from Retrading	Resource Inefficiency	Net Gain
United States			
7%	−226.49	20.29	−246.78
10%	11.71	5.85	5.85
15%	26.41	13.21	13.21
Japan			
7%	100.88	50.44	50.44
10%	−4.67	0.03	−4.70
15%	1.22	0.61	0.61
EEC			
7%	229.73	711.27	−481.55
10%	176.20	2,075.73	−1,899.53
15%	536.72	5,675.60	−5,138.89
Other Europe			
7%	63.70	115.37	−51.67
10%	−41.62	436.12	−477.75
15%	−131.71	1,153.46	−1,285.17
Other OECD			
7%	−167.81	249.54	−417.35
10%	−141.61	215.64	−357.25
15%	−432.64	586.30	−1,018.94
Total IEA			
7%	0.00	1,146.91	−1,146,91
10%	0.00	2,733.37	−2,733.37
15%	0.00	7,429.19	−7,429.19

NOTE: 1983 consumption, production, trade, and stock levels reflect precrisis market conditions. EEC: Belgium, Denmark, France, Germany, Ireland, Italy, Luxembourg, the Netherlands, the United Kingdom. Other Europe: Austria, Finland, Greece, Iceland, Norway, Portugal, Spain, Sweden, Switzerland, Turkey. Other OECD: Australia, Canada, New Zealand.
SOURCE: Computed by author; see appendix A.

First, the total resource inefficiency due to oil sharing exceeds the gross income transfers between buying and selling countries. For the 7 percent supply disruption, the gross transfers of $767 million

49

are only 66 percent of the resource inefficiency of $1,147 million. While the gross income transfers are larger for the 10 and 15 percent supply disruptions, they do not grow as fast as the size of the resource inefficiency. For the 15 percent disruption, the gross transfers of $2.7 billion are only 37 percent of the resource inefficiency of $7.4 billion.

Second, none of the groups of countries are significant beneficiaries of oil sharing. The United States loses almost $250 million during the 7 percent disruption but virtually breaks even during the larger disruptions.[63] Oil sharing provides minimal gains to Japan. The EEC, other European countries, and other OECD countries experience significant economic losses from oil sharing.

The pattern of net gains from oil sharing among IEA members also illustrates the ineffectiveness of the Emergency Sharing System in achieving its implicit or explicit goals. This pattern is summarized by a regression analysis of the quantitative results, as reported in table 2–11. First, a country's net gain does not depend on its per capita

TABLE 2–11

REGRESSION COEFFICIENTS FROM ANALYSIS OF DETERMINANTS OF NET GAIN FROM OIL SHARING, BY SIZE OF SUPPLY DISRUPTION

Explanatory Variable	7 Percent	10 Percent	15 Percent
Intercept	0.685	0.644	18.70
	(0.15)	(0.60)	(0.68)
Per capita income (dollars)	0.0001	0.0009	0.0022
	(0.31)	(1.00)	(0.92)
Oil stocks/ consumption	−10.13	−51.06	−138.58
	(−0.82)	(−1.87)	(−1.84)
Net imports/ consumption	0.77	−0.36	−1.07
	(0.50)	(−0.11)	(−0.11)
EEC member	−0.89	−5.60	−15.81
	(−0.31)	(−0.90)	(−0.91)
Summary statistics R^2	0.053	0.257	0.252
Standard error of regression	6.20	13.62	37.67

NOTE: t-statistics are in parentheses.
SOURCE: Dependent variable computed by author; see appendix A for data sources of explanatory variables.

income.[64] Therefore, oil sharing would not solve any perceived equity problems by implementing a benevolent income transfer between rich and poor OECD countries. Second, the net gain does not depend on the extent of the country's dependency on imports.[65] So oil sharing does not help countries that are more dependent on net imports. Third, for the 10 and 15 percent supply disruptions, a country's net gain is inversely related to the level of its petroleum stocks.[66] The substantial policy and political implications are considered below.

Finally, EEC countries receive the same net gains from oil sharing as non-EEC countries.[67] The failure of the net gains from oil sharing to nurture this traditional political alignment is important because of the inevitable political controversy that will accompany successful implementation of the Emergency Sharing System.

Political Disputes Created by Oil Sharing. Full implementation of oil sharing would inflict economic losses on the IEA as a whole and on many of its members. Would the losers be willing to adopt the trade policies necessary to protect the inevitable price differentials among countries? Even if members honored their obligations under Article 66 of the treaty to "take the necessary measures, including any legislative measures, to implement this Agreement and decisions taken by the Governing Board," their divergent economic interests might generate political conflict within the IEA on how oil sharing is to be implemented.

The key political decisions in the IEA must be made within the framework established by the agreement. The Secretariat triggers and administers the oil-sharing program, provided that its actions are not overruled by the Governing Board. Given that existing pricing policy under oil sharing is ambiguous, new proposals about pricing may confront the board during a supply disruption if the Dispute Settlement Center proves incapable of resolving conflict between buyers and sellers. That such conflict will prove unresolvable under current rules seems likely, because the pricing of transferred oil at market prices is incompatible, on economic grounds, with the quantity goals of oil sharing. A choice must be made between the use of market prices and the achievement of the supply targets.

Whose policy positions are likely to prevail in the IEA? Do the beneficiaries or the losers from oil sharing possess sufficient voting power to overturn decisions taken by the IEA Secretariat? The answer provides insight into how much political autonomy the Secretariat enjoys. Do the beneficiaries or the losers possess sufficient voting power to control proposals taken up directly by the board?

These questions are studied by considering the pattern of gains

51

and losses that members experience under full implementation of oil sharing. Members that anticipate benefits would support the Secretariat's decisions to trigger and to implement the income transfers created under oil sharing. They would also support emphasis on the fair treatment clause of Article 10, implying adoption of the below-market pricing required to achieve supply targets. In contrast, members that anticipate losses from oil sharing may oppose the Secretariat's decisions and support emphasis on the comparable-commercial-transaction clause of Article 10.

Table 2–12 reports the net per capita gains that each member experiences from oil sharing for the three supply disruptions studied. The patterns suggest dividing the countries into three groups. First, six countries (Belgium, Denmark, Germany, Luxembourg, Sweden, and Switzerland) may be intense supporters of oil sharing because they consistently enjoy the largest per capita gains from full implementation. Second, four countries (Canada, Italy, the Netherlands, and the United Kingdom) may be intense opponents of oil sharing because they consistently suffer the largest per capita losses. Finally, the remaining voting members of the IEA (including Japan, the United States, and, except for relatively large disruptions, Spain and Turkey) would be relatively uninterested in the outcomes because they experience relatively small effects from oil sharing. The voting blocks implied by this pattern of net gains suggest two major conclusions about the policy positions likely to prevail in the IEA.

First, the Secretariat possesses a large degree of policy discretion that is unlikely to be overruled by the Governing Board. Therefore, the Secretariat can trigger oil sharing and make administrative decisions to implement the assumed oil-sharing programs. The Governing Board needs a special majority to overrule decisions by the Secretariat—that is, the support of at least eleven countries with ninety-six combined voting weights. As shown in table 2–13, the losers from oil sharing do not possess sufficient voting power to constitute a special majority. Therefore, the beneficiaries can block attempts to overrule the Secretariat.

In fact, the Governing Board is unlikely to overrule *any* decision by the Secretariat. Suppose that the Secretariat decided against triggering oil sharing or selected procedures that did not implement the income transfers during any of the supply disruptions. For the 7 percent and 10 percent disruptions, the supporters of oil sharing would not possess the 96 votes needed to overrule the Secretariat. Although it may appear that they have sufficient votes during the 15 percent disruption, 68 of their 112 votes represent Japan and the United States. Since both countries enjoy minimum gains from oil

TABLE 2–12
PER CAPITA NET GAINS FROM OIL SHARING, BY SIZE OF SUPPLY DISRUPTION
(dollars per year)

Country	7 Percent	10 Percent	15 Percent
Australia	0.07	1.11	3.09
Austria	0.52	0.30	0.62
Belgium	2.44	2.21	5.43
Canada	−16.81	−15.00	−42.55
Denmark	3.00	4.63	11.27
Germany	3.72	5.17	16.21
Greece	0.82	0.71	3.99
Ireland	0.08	−1.01	−3.79
Italy	−4.90	−22.83	−62.76
Japan	0.42	−0.04	0.01
Luxembourg	2.32	1.69	2.95
Netherlands	−17.06	−58.45	−161.09
New Zealand	0.05	−0.37	−2.06
Norway	0.35	2.79	6.96
Portugal	−0.41	−4.73	−9.81
Spain	−1.40	−7.48	−21.45
Sweden	2.28	1.91	4.71
Switzerland	4.70	6.63	17.39
Turkey	−1.20	−4.75	−12.52
United Kingdom	−4.02	−2.17	−5.56
United States	−1.05	0.02	0.06
Summary statistics			
Mean	−1.24	−4.26	−11.85
Standard deviation	5.70	14.14	38.95
Minimum	−17.06	−58.45	−161.09
Maximum	4.70	6.63	17.39

SOURCE: Computed by author; see appendix A.

sharing, the political alliance among supporters of oil sharing to overrule the Secretariat would rest on fragile economic foundations.

It is impossible for the Secretariat to ignore this power and operate on the basis of consensus. Any decision that promotes or impedes the implementation of oil sharing must split the membership. Almost an equal number of countries gain and lose from oil sharing. The Secretariat *must* exercise the policy discretion created by the voting

TABLE 2–13

DISTRIBUTION OF VOTING WEIGHTS,
BY STATUS OF GAINS FROM OIL SHARING

	Beneficiaries		Losers	
Disruption	Number	Combined voting weights	Number	Combined voting weights
7 percent	12	68	8	92
10 percent	10	94	10	66
15 percent	11	112	9	48

NOTE: Excludes the beneficiary Norway because it is a nonvoting member. To overrule the Secretariat or pass a resolution by special majority requires the support of eleven countries with at least 60 percent of the 160 combined voting weights, or 96 votes. To block override of the Secretariat or a resolution by special majority requires the support of either eleven countries or a smaller number of countries with at least 40 percent of the 160 combined voting weights, or 64 votes.
SOURCE: Computed by author.

rules. It has great power through its control over the agenda and when issues are raised and settled. As Robert Keohane has observed, "In practical terms, blocking (by the Governing Board) will not occur."[68]

The second major conclusion pertains to issues over which the Governing Board, not the Secretariat, has jurisdiction. The inevitable conflicts over pricing policy are likely to be addressed by the board. Other analysts have also concluded that the pricing issue remains an unresolved, potentially contentious issue.[69] The distribution of combined voting weights suggests that a stalemate is likely to occur on the pricing issue for the same reasons that the Governing Board is unlikely to overrule the Secretariat on any other issue.

Conclusion: Oil Sharing Creates Problems, Not Solutions. The probable economic consequences of oil sharing do not promote the stated goals of the international energy agreement. Oil sharing does not reduce but increases the economic losses inflicted on Western countries by supply disruptions. Nor does it achieve common equity goals. Its concentration on the proportionate equalization of supply cutbacks does not spread the losses in national income more evenly than the market does. Nor can oil sharing be defended on grounds that it effectively redistributes income from rich to poor OECD countries.

The inevitable, unresolved disputes about oil-sharing policies also do not diminish but enhance political conflict among IEA members.

54

During a supply disruption, stalemate and deadlock over centralized organization of the international oil market will heighten tensions among members. The de facto power of the Secretariat to establish policy, with little practical fear of veto by the Governing Board, promises to promote dissension as the fundamentals of the marketplace are transformed during a supply disruption. As Krapels observed:

> In a real supply crisis, the IEP (International Energy Program) allocation process will become in effect a multinational, multicorporate oil delivery schedule. . . . Under normal market conditions, the delivery of oil from source to market is a highly decentralized and flexible activity. The challenge to the IEP managers is to centralize this system and to subject it to a monthly accounting to determine if delivery targets have been met.[70]

International bureaucrats cannot trade off the political interests of different countries on technocratic grounds of centralized management without sparking conflict.

Even if unanimity could be reached on the rules of centralized management, oil sharing would promote additional political conflict. During a supply disruption countries will differ greatly in their views about the duration and future size of the disruption. Therefore, under any "coordinated" stock drawdown, countries that place a greater future value on their stocks are likely to find IEA membership burdensome.[71] Countries with large stockpiles, like Japan and the United States, may also be taxed for their foresight during a supply disruption.[72] Any such political conflicts during the disruption will deflect national leaders from addressing other international political issues.

Oil sharing also does not limit but extends the likely duration of supply disruptions. The four-month procedural protocol of IEA decision making casts a shadow over the international petroleum market. Will purchases on the international market this month reduce purchase rights in subsequent months? If so, an IEA member would have an incentive to limit its purchase of oil, even though forbearance would intensify the size and extend the duration of the disruption. Such responses exist in theory and have been considered by others during the analyses of hypothetical crises.[73] Furthermore, the ambiguities that surround existing policy create their own problems of delay. As Willrich and Conant observe: "Ambiguities seem to leave room for considerable debate, delay, and acrimony, although it has been claimed that one of the virtues of the IEP Agreement as a whole is the automaticity of the emergency activation procedures."[74]

These economic and political problems created by oil sharing do not enhance but diminish energy security. The fear is that OPEC governments, terrorists, or the Soviet Union may intentionally use supply disruptions to inflict harm on Western countries. Policy responses that increase the economic damage and create political disharmony among Western countries do not deter but encourage the likelihood of such disruptions.

Import Control and Consumption Restraint

Policies of import control and consumption restraint have been used by the IEA to achieve the stated objectives of the International Energy Program. Many analysts have supported such policies, at least in principle, because they seem to limit the economic problems associated with dependence on foreign oil. James Plummer has defined the oil import reduction premium as a measure of the economic benefits that accrue from the successful restraint of oil imports. In his words, that premium is

> the dollar economic benefit resulting from reducing oil imports by one barrel. The benefit arises from two different sources. First, lowering imports during normal (nondisruption) years results in some reduction in world oil prices, and thus a saving on the oil import bill. Second, having a lower level of oil imports at the onset of an oil supply disruption reduces the disruption losses because the oil price increases are paid on a lower volume of oil.[75]

Since private traders will ignore this premium when they import oil from OPEC countries, the premium represents the potential gains importing countries can capture from the imposition of judicious import restraint.

In principle, multilateral action by governments of importing countries will be more effective than unilateral action in restraining imports. With unilateral action each government will consider only the gains its residents will enjoy from import restraint, not the gains enjoyed by residents in other countries. The mutual interests of OECD countries in import restraint are sacrificed as governments free-ride on one another's efforts to reduce world oil prices. In theory, a multilateral agreement can coordinate the import restraints undertaken by all OECD governments and reduce world oil prices by more than would occur without the agreement. This potential gain from cooperation has been identified as the logic behind IEA policy.[76]

Has IEA policy in fact successfully implemented actions that achieve these theoretical advantages of import restraint and international cooperation? To answer this question, the following discussion considers three factors: problems of coordination under multilateral agreements; the economic implications of the structure of IEA import restraint policy; and evidence on the actual effects of IEA import ceilings and consumption restraint agreements.

Coordination Problems. A country will honor a multilateral agreement only if cooperating makes it better off than cheating. That the members as a group may benefit from an agreement does not guarantee that each member will find it in its interest to cooperate.

A fundamental problem of coordination confronts any multilateral agreement that seeks to reduce world oil prices: each country prefers that the other countries bear the burden of the policy. Suppose that national governments agree to restrain their net imports of oil from OPEC countries and that their efforts reduce the world price of oil. Each country would have an incentive not to restrain but to expand its use of petroleum because of the lower price. If all countries followed this temptation, no import restraint would occur. World oil prices would return to their levels in the absence of the agreement.

This problem can be solved by finding an incentive structure that makes it in the interest of each country to honor its commitments. Under the theory of self-enforcing agreements, cheating on an agreement today can be deterred only if it jeopardizes sufficiently large gains from future cooperation.[77] The gains from future cooperation can occur in two ways.

First, countries may engage in the import restraint as long as other countries honor their commitments. Under this tit-for-tat strategy—other countries honor the agreement if I do and cheat if I do not—a country that cheats today will understand that it destroys the gain from future import restraint. Not all multilateral agreements can be enforced by the concern for future cooperation. Self-enforcing agreements occur only when *each* member enjoys certain gains from future cooperation that are sufficiently large in relation to the current gains from cheating.[78] Making each country better off through the restraint agreement is a necessary, though not a sufficient, condition for an agreement to overcome the coordination problem.

Second, a country may honor an agreement on import restraint to preserve the good will of other countries. In effect, cooperation is linked with other multilateral agreements that would be jeopardized if the country cheated on its imports.

Not all multilateral agreements can be enforced by linkage to other agreements. Two conditions must be satisfied.[79] First, countries that link import restraint with other agreements must be made better off as a group by import restraint. It would not be credible for them to threaten termination of the other agreements to enforce an import

57

restraint policy that makes them worse off. Second, successful implementation of the import policy must raise the gains that the countries enjoy from the other, linked agreement. Otherwise, no country could credibly threaten to withdraw from the other agreement, because the failure of the import agreement would not reduce the gains from the linked agreement.[80] Successful linkage requires complementarity of issues, not independence.

If the coordination problem cannot be resolved, a country will not honor its obligations under a multilateral agreement. Agreements that fail, however, may be more than simply ineffective. Short-term cheating strategies may have a destabilizing influence on the marketplace. This point is illustrated by the following example.

Suppose that a country concludes that its interest is best served by ignoring its obligations under an import restraint agreement. It may anticipate that other countries will not predict its defection because they have incomplete and inaccurate information. The defecting country may therefore choose to import more oil than it would in the absence of the agreement to take advantage of the anticipated restraint by other countries. If a sufficient number of countries find themselves in this situation, their individually optimal cheating policies may put greater pressure on spot markets than would have occurred if no multilateral restraint agreement had been negotiated in the first place.

In summary, whether multilateral agreements to restrain imports or consumption can raise the national income of oil-importing countries depends on the answers to two questions. First, are the potential gains from cooperation plausible or illusory? If the latter, the prospects are slight that the agreements are self-enforcing. Second, have countries, in fact, honored the commitments specified in those agreements? If they have not, the agreements may have been ineffective and may have had a destabilizing influence on the marketplace.

The Mistaken Economic Logic of Oil Import Ceilings. IEA import ceilings suffer from many deficiencies that render them counterproductive in capturing any benefits envisioned by the oil import premium. The ceilings only accelerate the income losses from a reduced foreign oil supply; they do not mitigate the losses during a future supply disruption. They may *increase* world oil prices, not reduce them. These possibilities seriously throw into question whether IEA policy as implemented can achieve any of the theoretical gains from joint action by OECD countries.

Preparation for future disruptions. Some analysts have advocated import restraints as effective means of limiting income losses during

58

supply disruptions.[81] Initially, my analysis of this recommendation assumes that any import restraint, such as a quota, has no effect on world oil prices. This assumption allows the analysis to determine whether the second part of the oil import premium is illusory by comparing the income losses from future supply disruptions with and without the import ceiling. How import ceilings may affect OPEC pricing strategy is considered below.

Figure 2–2 presents the analysis. Before a supply disruption the world oil price is P_0 and the country whose supply and demand are S and D imports $(C_0 - Q_0)$ barrels of oil. Suppose that the national government imposes an import ceiling to limit imports to a smaller amount, say $(C_1 - Q_1)$. By limiting the supply of oil on the national market, the import ceiling would increase the domestic oil price to P_1.

The import ceiling affects three domestic interests that combine to determine the effect on national income. First, consumers pay higher prices for oil and suffer an income loss equal to the area P_1ABP_0. Second, domestic oil producers receive the higher oil price and enjoy an income gain equal to the area P_1EFP_0. Finally, the price differential

FIGURE 2–2

OIL IMPORT CEILINGS AND THE BURDEN OF SUPPLY DISRUPTIONS

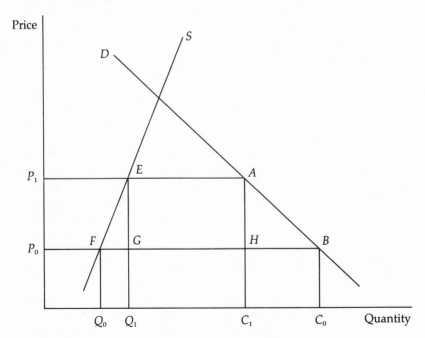

59

between domestic and foreign oil, $P_1 - P_0$, creates value for the rights to import oil. The means of allocation chosen by the government will dictate which parties (presumably domestic) benefit from the creation of this valuable import right. The value of those rights equals the area $EAHG$. From the viewpoint of national income, the losses of consumers exceed the gains of domestic producers and owners of the import rights for two reasons. Consumers sacrifice uses of oil whose value exceeds the world oil price—this cost is measured by the area ABH. Domestic producers expand their oil output and use resources whose value in alternative uses exceeds the value of the additional oil output—this cost is measured by the area EGF. These two areas together are the real resource costs of the import ceiling.

Now suppose that a supply disruption occurs that increases the world oil price to the domestic price, P_1. With the import ceiling, imports before and after the crisis are identical. Since the domestic price is unchanged, domestic production and consumption are also unaffected. The only additional income loss is the increased cost of oil imports: the area $EAHG$. The losers from the disruption are the owners of previously valuable rights to import oil. Their rights are now worthless because the disruption destroyed the differential between domestic and world prices.

Now compare the situation that would have prevailed if the national government had not imposed the import ceiling before the supply disruption. Higher world oil prices would have inflicted losses on consumers equal to the area P_1ABP_0. The increase in oil prices would have benefited domestic producers by the amount P_1EFP_0. The net loss in national income would equal the area $FEAB$.

On the surface it may appear that the loss of national income under the ceiling is less than the loss without the ceiling. The apparent gain equals areas EGF plus ABH. This result is illusory, however, because the ceilings had already inflicted those losses in national income. The import policy simply accelerated a portion of the income losses created by future supply disruptions.

The conclusion also holds if disruptions raise the world oil price above the initial domestic price. For the portion of the price increase above the initial domestic price, P_1, the income effects would be the same with or without import ceilings. Meanwhile, the analysis would still apply to that part of the increase in world prices that destroyed the differential between domestic and world prices originally created by the ceiling policy.

In summary, import ceilings that do not affect the world oil price cannot benefit oil-importing countries. The ceilings simply reduce national income before supply disruptions occur by an amount equal

60

to the resource inefficiencies created by the policy. This conclusion also holds even if consumers experience transition costs in responding to higher prices during supply disruptions.[82] The second part of the oil import premium, based on a lower volume of imports before a disruption, is negative. Without beneficial effects on world oil prices, IEA members cannot devise a self-enforcing agreement on import ceilings.

Import ceilings and OPEC pricing strategy. Whether import ceilings reduce the world oil price depends critically on the economic structure of OPEC oil supply. Figures 2–3 and 2–4 depict two possibilities. The first involves perfect competition in the supply of OPEC oil. That is, all thirteen members of OPEC operate independently of one another in setting their production, pricing, and export policies, and none of them, including Saudi Arabia, perceive that variations in the volume of their oil exports affect the world price. The second case involves imperfect competition or even collusion in the supply of OPEC oil. The exact structure is not important. OPEC may be an effective cartel, a cartel with intermittent problems, or a producing entity dominated by a large country, such as Saudi Arabia, which acknowledges that its volume of exports affects the world price of oil.

Figure 2–3 presents the analysis for the case of competition. Before import ceilings, demand and supply jointly determine the world price

FIGURE 2–3
OIL IMPORT CEILINGS AND OPEC PRICING STRATEGY:
COMPETITIVE SUPPLY

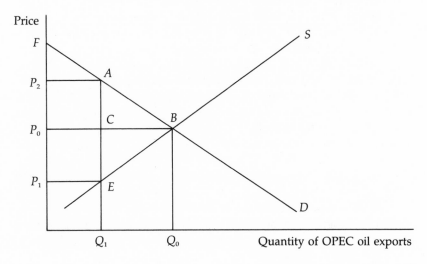

FIGURE 2–4
OIL IMPORT CEILINGS AND OPEC PRICING STRATEGY: NONCOMPETITIVE SUPPLY

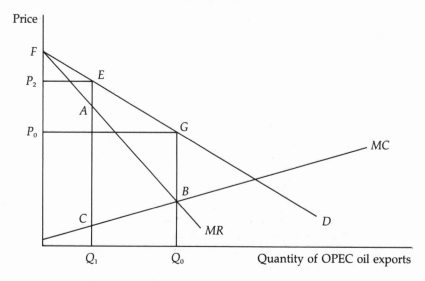

(P_0) and the volume of oil exports (Q_0) from OPEC countries. Consider an IEA import ceiling policy that restricts the quantity demanded to Q_1, below the level that prevailed before the policy. The demand for OPEC exports becomes the kinked curve FAQ_1. For any price below P_2, the quantity demanded is smaller than it was before the policy. This shift in demand reduces the world oil price to P_1.

The ceiling policy has three distinct income effects. First, the oil price in importing countries must increase, because the ceiling policy restricts the supply of oil in those markets. The domestic price rises to P_2 and generates an income loss equal to the area P_2ABP_0. Second, the rights to import oil in the IEA countries have economic value, because the quota scheme creates a differential between domestic and world oil prices. The total value of those rights equals the area P_2AEP_1. Which parties receive these benefits depends on the allocation mechanism employed by IEA member governments. Finally, the reduction in world oil prices inflicts an income loss on OPEC countries equal to the area P_0BEP_1.

In principle, oil-importing countries can select quotas so that the value of the import rights created by import ceilings exceeds the income losses from higher domestic oil prices. In this case, there would be a logical link between IEA policy actions and stated policy goals.

62

If the supply of OPEC oil is not competitive, however, the import ceiling policy need not benefit IEA countries, as shown in figure 2–4. Before the ceiling policy, suppose that the rate of exports was determined jointly by the marginal revenue curve MR and the marginal cost of OPEC production, MC. The imposition of the ceiling program creates a kinked demand curve, FEQ_1. The marginal revenue curve becomes the kinked curve FAQ_1, because there is no additional revenue to be obtained from attempting to export more oil than allowed by the ceiling. The best response of the exporting countries, in which they equate MC to the altered MR curve, is to reduce their output to the allowed level of imports, Q_1, and let the importing countries bid the world price of oil up to P_2. The import ceiling program successfully restricts imports, but it increases, rather than reduces, world oil prices.[83] We must question, therefore, whether IEA import ceilings can achieve one of the basic goals of the International Energy Program—the development of countervailing market power to resist that of OPEC.[84]

Actual Effects of IEA Policies. The import ceilings of 1980 and the 5 percent consumption cutback agreement of 1979 attempted to impose import restraint. Were these actions effective in restraining imports and consumption? Either a strong or a weak criterion for policy evaluation can be used to answer this question.

The strong criterion would ask whether all IEA countries achieved their targets. Did each country limit its 1980 net oil imports to its ceiling? Did each country cut back its 1979 consumption by 5 percent? If countries imported more than their ceilings or cut back consumption by less than 5 percent, IEA policies would appear to have been widely violated. If countries imported less than their ceilings or cut back consumption by more than 5 percent, IEA policies were too generous and therefore not binding on members. That is, the strong criterion demands perfection by policy makers.

The weak criterion asks whether import ceilings reduced net oil imports and whether the 5 percent agreement reduced consumption by IEA members, though perhaps not by their full target amounts. This criterion demands only some effectiveness, not perfection, on the part of a policy in achieving its stated goals. My analysis applies the weak criterion because it seems more reasonable than the strong one.

A fundamental problem confronts the application of the weak criterion. IEA policy actions followed, rather than anticipated, market developments. Therefore, all IEA countries would have reduced their net oil imports during 1980 in the face of higher world oil prices, even in the absence of an agreement on import ceilings. With the planned

63

growth of North Sea oil production, the United Kingdom would also have reduced its net oil imports, and Norway would have increased its oil exports. Statistical analysis was used to determine whether IEA policy exerted an independent effect on net oil imports and petroleum consumption.

Net oil import ceilings. Table 2–14 reports 1980 import ceilings and net oil imports for IEA member countries. For each country, import ceilings and actual 1980 imports are expressed in relation to actual 1979 net imports. Expressing the ceiling in relative terms provides a

TABLE 2–14

IEA IMPORT CEILINGS AND NET OIL IMPORTS BY IEA MEMBERS, 1980

Country	1980 Import Ceilings		Actual 1980 Net Imports	
	Amount[a]	Percentage of 1979 imports	Amount[a]	Percentage of 1979 imports
Australia	13.5	142.21	8.19	86.22
Austria	11.5	102.64	11.14	99.45
Belgium	30.0	103.49	25.85	89.19
Canada	7.4	97.27	9.30	122.20
Denmark	16.5	107.11	13.12	85.15
Germany	143.0	98.72	130.36	89.99
Greece	14.8	113.93	13.11	100.95
Ireland	6.5	102.65	5.72	90.35
Italy	103.5	104.28	96.23	96.96
Japan	265.3	99.36	241.00	90.26
Luxembourg	1.5	113.98	1.08	82.14
Netherlands	42.0	99.58	37.70	89.38
New Zealand	4.2	109.95	3.87	101.34
Norway	−15.5	174.67	−14.42	162.50
Spain	51.0	100.27	50.59	99.46
Sweden	29.9	104.45	25.77	90.03
Switzerland	14.0	108.42	12.30	95.25
Turkey	17.0	n.a.	13.33	n.a.
United Kingdom	12.0	63.53	0.91	4.82
United States	437.2	107.68	323.07	79.57

NOTE: Negative number indicates net exports. Portugal joined IEA in May 1980 and was not assigned an import ceiling. n.a. = not available.
a. In million tons of oil equivalent.
SOURCES: *OECD Quarterly Oil Statistics* for annual net imports; and *Petroleum Intelligence Weekly* for net import ceilings.

measure of the potential stringency of a country's quota that is independent of the country's size. The lower a country's relative import ceiling, the greater the obligation of its government to intervene and restrain its imports.

A positive relation would exist between import ceilings and actual 1980 imports if countries with greater obligations to restrain their imports restricted their 1980 imports by more than countries with smaller obligations. One would expect deviations from this relation because of the uncertainty of import control, varying responses to higher world oil prices, and different changes in national income. Table 2–15 reports estimates of the relation between the stringency of import ceilings and the actual change in net oil imports, using the

TABLE 2–15

REGRESSION ANALYSIS OF THE RELATION BETWEEN GROWTH IN
NET OIL IMPORTS AND STRINGENCY OF IMPORT CEILINGS
(net imports $= a + b \times$ ceiling $+ c \times$ EEC $+ d \times$ EEC $\times$ ceiling)

Variable (coefficient)	Full Sample		Excluding Norway and United Kingdom	
	(1)	(2)	(3)	(4)
Intercept (a)	-13.98	30.79	124.32	136.27
	(-0.60)	(1.18)	(4.98)	(5.30)
Ceiling (b)	0.98	0.63	-0.29	-0.37
	(4.65)	(2.80)	(-1.24)	(-1.59)
EEC member (c)		-131.78		10.07
		(-2.70)		(0.13)
EEC member $\times$ ceiling (d)		1.18		-0.18
		(2.53)		(-0.24)
R^2	0.56	0.71	0.09	0.32
Mean squared error	367.11	271.92	93.89	82.72

NOTE: t-statistics are in parentheses. Net imports measured as 1980 actual net imports as a percentage of 1979 actual net imports. Ceiling measured as 1980 quota as a percentage of 1979 actual net imports. For non-EEC member countries, effect of stringency of quota on net imports equals the coefficient b in all four equations. For EEC member countries, effect of stringency of quota on net imports equals the coefficient b in equations 1 and 3 and the sum of coefficients b and d in equations 2 and 4. Dummy variable, EEC member, signifies membership in EEC.
SOURCE: See table 2–14.

data of table 2–14. Differences between EEC and non-EEC members in the degree of their cooperation with the quota scheme were examined because the quotas for EEC countries were negotiated within the context of EEC policy and later adopted by the IEA.[85]

The first two equations, reported in columns 1 and 2, seem to provide evidence that IEA import ceilings had an important effect on actual imports. The first equation, for which the ceiling-response coefficient is 0.98, suggests that the ratio of actual 1980 imports to actual 1979 imports increased by virtually the same amount as the ratio of the 1980 ceiling to actual 1979 imports. The second equation, which distinguishes between EEC members and nonmembers, suggests that 1980 imports for EEC countries were more responsive to the stringency of their quota than 1980 imports for non-EEC countries; a 1 percent increase in the ceiling relative to 1979 actual imports resulted in a 1.81 percent increase (0.63 + 1.18; see note to table 2–15) in actual 1980 imports over 1979 imports for EEC countries but only a 0.63 percent increase for non-EEC countries. Perhaps EEC members exhibited greater responsiveness to the quota scheme because their quotas originated in bargaining within the EEC.

Closer examination reveals, however, that these conclusions result from spurious correlation. The relative ceilings and 1980 import levels are quite different for Norway and the United Kingdom from what they are for the remaining countries. With their expanded production from the North Sea, Norway and the United Kingdom may exhibit different behavior from that of the other oil-importing members of the IEA. Columns 3 and 4 investigate this possibility by excluding those two countries from the sample.

The differences in results are striking. Equation 3 shows no relation between the stringency of a country's quota and the change in its net oil imports. Equation 4 shows statistically insignificant differences in coefficients between EEC and non-EEC countries. The strong prior support for the effectiveness of IEA import ceilings was illusory.

The exclusion of Norway and the United Kingdom can be defended on statistical grounds. The "best" model for the full sample has a mean squared prediction error (271.92) about 3.3 times greater than that (82.72) of the model estimated by excluding Norway and the United Kingdom. Therefore, we conclude that import ceilings had no effect on the change in imports during 1980.

Petroleum consumption. In addition to the study of the agreement to cut consumption by 5 percent, the analysis of total petroleum consumption patterns provides a cross-check on the study of import ceilings. Is it possible that import restraint was obscured by the effects

66

of higher oil prices and changes in national income? This possibility is investigated by estimating whether consumption was lower during the period covered by IEA actions, taking account of the effects of changes in world (not national) oil prices and in national income. For our purposes the specific policy actions, including pricing policies, that achieved the reductions in consumption are irrelevant.

Table 2–16 reports the results of this broader regression analysis of the effects of IEA policy actions on petroleum consumption in selected OECD countries.[86] For both the consumption cutbacks and the quota targets, petroleum consumption was either unchanged or

TABLE 2–16

ESTIMATED EFFECTS OF IEA RESTRAINT POLICIES ON PETROLEUM CONSUMPTION BY SELECTED OECD COUNTRIES, 1979–1980
(percentage of estimated consumption)

Country	Consumption Cutback[a]	Import Quota[b]	Country	Consumption Cutback[a]	Import Quota[b]
Austria	10.6 (2.09)	9.9 (2.09)	Japan	8.3 (1.78)	3.3 (0.87)
Belgium	9.2 (1.06)	14.4 (1.98)	Luxembourg	6.0 (1.08)	2.5 (0.54)
Canada	6.6 (1.37)	8.1 (1.89)	Netherlands	10.1 (1.63)	3.7 (1.04)
Denmark	14.2 (1.69)	13.8 (1.84)	Norway	27.3 (2.48)	11.2 (1.17)
Finland	13.7 (1.22)	17.6 (2.15)	Sweden	14.4 (1.58)	12.6 (1.66)
France	6.4 (1.12)	5.2 (1.15)	Switzerland	10.4 (1.69)	18.3 (2.68)
Germany	11.1 (3.13)	3.2 (1.05)	United Kingdom	−0.1 (0.01)	−3.0 (0.86)
Greece	−0.3 (0.03)	7.2 (1.82)	United States	6.6 (1.28)	5.3 (1.32)
Italy	4.1 (1.41)	3.3 (1.30)			

NOTE: t-statistics are in parentheses.
a. Second through fourth quarter of 1979.
b. 1980.
SOURCE: Computed by author; see appendix B.

67

higher—certainly not lower—than would have been anticipated given trend growth rates in consumption, national income, world oil prices, and regular patterns of seasonality. All but three of the deviations from estimated consumption and imports are positive and substantial. Rather than imposing effective restraint, the consumption cutback and import ceiling agreements appear to have been violated by significant cheating on the part of many countries. In fact, this may be interpreted as evidence that for some countries cheating took the form of *increasing* consumption by engaging in the destabilizing short-term strategies created by the coordination difficulties of multilateral agreements.

Consider the agreement to cut consumption by 5 percent. Austria, Germany, and Norway all displayed statistically significant, economically large "abnormal surges" in their petroleum consumption (their t-statistics are 2.09, 3.13, and 2.48, respectively). Denmark and Japan also increased their consumption, although the estimated magnitudes are only marginally significant (the t-statistics are 1.69 and 1.78, respectively) according to traditional standards of statistical inference. The remaining countries, including the United States, displayed no statistically significant tendency to increase their consumption during the consumption cutback agreement.

Even more countries appear to have increased their consumption during the import restraint program. Austria, Belgium, Sweden, and Switzerland all display statistically significant, economically large abnormal surges in petroleum consumption. Canada, Denmark, Finland, and Greece also had abnormal, though only marginally statistically significant, increases in consumption, which are only slightly smaller than the increases estimated for the former four countries. The other countries do not show significant increases in consumption.

Conclusion: Misguided, Ineffective, but Not Inconsequential. The import restraint policies of the IEA have not achieved the economic and political goals of the International Energy Program. The intellectual foundation for the case that the IEP generates obvious economic benefits for oil-importing nations rests on flawed arguments. The presumed superiority of multilateral over unilateral action ignores the coordination problems that face all international agreements. The evidence reviewed above suggests that both the agreement to cut consumption by 5 percent and the program of import ceilings were ineffective in lowering consumption below what it would have been in the absence of those agreements. That the agreements were ineffective does not suggest that they were inconsequential. The short-term destabilizing cheating strategies of some IEA members may have heightened political tensions during the 1979 and 1980 supply disruptions, as illustrated by the anecdotal evidence reviewed in the section "Informal Assessments of the IEA."

Oil Stockpiling

Economists and other analysts have advocated public management of oil stockpiles as an effective means of coping with supply disruptions.[87] The logic of stockpiling is based on an attractive economic prescription: purchase petroleum during normal market conditions when prices are low, and release it during crises when prices are high. During disruptions releases from stockpiles are an alternative source of supply, which limit both the increase in petroleum prices and the economic losses suffered by oil-importing countries.

The potential economic benefits of prudent stock management have been identified as an economic justification for a government role in emergency preparedness. For example, Plummer has defined the oil stockpile premium as measuring the economic benefits from storing an additional barrel of oil. In his words, that premium is

> the expected dollar economic benefit, in terms of lower losses in disruption years, of adding a barrel of oil to stockpiles during normal years. This premium is a net measure that takes account of the fact that filling the stockpile during normal years will cause somewhat higher world oil prices during those years.[88]

Since private storers will ignore the effect of their stockpiling decisions on market prices during normal years and disruptions, government intervention is believed essential to ensure that the optimal stockpile is accumulated to cope with the risk of future supply disruptions.

As with import restraint, multilateral action by governments is believed to be more effective than unilateral policies toward stockpiling. Releases from U.S. stockpiles, for example, reduce world petroleum prices paid by all consumers, not solely U.S. consumers. Therefore, stockpiling by any country helps its neighbors.[89] Unilateral policies toward stockpiling will ignore the benefits of other countries; multilateral policies can specify obligations for each country that take account of the external benefits provided to other countries.

Do the oil stockpile premium and the theoretical advantages of multilateral agreements justify IEA stock management policies? Have actual IEA stock policies successfully achieved the theoretical advantages? The answers to these questions are found from review of the economic principles of stock management, discussion of national stock

69

management policies before and after the 1973 oil embargo, and an empirical assessment of how informal IEA stock policy has affected the stocks held in IEA member countries.

The Economics of Stockpiling. With few exceptions analyses of petroleum stockpiling have neglected private storage.[90] Even in the absence of public stockpiles or multilateral agreements, private parties have economic incentives to accumulate petroleum stocks during normal market conditions and release them during supply disruptions. Therefore, analysis of public stock management policies must consider the oil stockpile premium in the context of storage undertaken simultaneously by private individuals and how government stock policies affect such storage.

A key policy question is whether the private sector will hold sufficient stocks to cope with supply disruptions. Economists have shown that the answer is yes, provided that two conditions are satisfied: market prices received by storers measure the social value of the stored good; and private interest rates reflect the social opportunity cost of capital.[91]

Not all sources of "market failure" in private storage imply that the private sector stores insufficient quantities of petroleum. The nature of the inefficiency depends critically on what causes the discrepancy between prices received and social values. The discussion concentrates on the two major considerations for energy policy: the prospect of price controls and alleged international externalities from storage.[92]

The prospect of price controls reduces the incentives for the private sector to stockpile petroleum. If price controls are expected during a future supply disruption, even if the probability is slight, the expected future gains from stockpiling would be reduced.[93]

This "market failure," however, need not justify substantial, multilateral intervention in stockpiling. If countries adhere to the IEA's third principle for energy policy—allow domestic prices to reach world market levels—the distorting effect of future price controls would be minimal. If IEA countries cannot adhere to that general principle, what prospect is there of IEA stock policy's fine-tuning the inadequacies in private stock holding that result from the IEA's ineffectiveness in implementing its policy principles?

Neither does the alleged international externality from storage necessarily justify governmental actions that increase total stockpiling. Since individual private storers lack market power, they will ignore the tendency of storage to increase the current price and to reduce prices during a future supply disruption. Private storers therefore understate both the societal costs and the benefits of storage to oil-importing countries. Whether their storage is "too high" or "too low" depends on which effect is greater.

Private stocks will be below the so-called socially optimal level only if the external benefits of storage exceed the external costs of storage. For net external benefits to be positive, the marginal downward price effect of stock drawdown in disruptions must exceed the upward price effect of stock buildup—by an amount sufficient to overcome the fact that in disruptions oil consumption is lower and hence of lesser quantitative weight.[94]

This condition was not satisfied by the model used in the Chao and Manne study, which computed optimal U.S. petroleum stockpiles under alternative assumptions about the likelihood of disruptions and the degree of U.S. market power over world prices.[95] For their case of low frequency of disruptions, the optimal stockpile (private plus public) is computed as 1.7 billion barrels when the United States exerts "low" market power over world prices and only 1.4 billion barrels when the United States exerts "high" market power. For their case of high frequency of disruptions, the optimal stockpile is computed as 4.9 billion barrels for low U.S. market power and only 2.7 billion barrels for high market power.[96] Therefore, concerns about external benefits and external costs of storage due to market power cannot in every case justify increased stocks beyond those held by the private sector.

The possibility that private stockpiling is too large from the social perspective seriously attenuates any self-enforcing multilateral agreement that would effectively increase the stockpiles held by IEA countries. If, as the Chao and Manne study implies, the external costs of storage exceed the external benefits, any obligations to increase stockpiles beyond levels selected by unilateral action would make IEA countries worse off. If countries do not benefit or even suffer losses from an agreement, they are unlikely to honor their commitments.

National Stockpiling Policies. All countries store sufficient quantities to meet their obligations to sustain consumption for at least ninety days without any net oil imports. For example, table 2–17 reports 1973 total stocks of oil and petroleum products held in IEA countries and regions. The definition of stocks used by *OECD Quarterly Oil Statistics* coincides with the definition used by the International Energy Program.[97] Since the agreement specifies that government-controlled stocks are to be actual stocks less 10 percent, multiplying the stocks in the table by 0.9 yields the stocks defined by the program.

The table displays considerable variation among countries and regions. The United States holds below-average stocks measured in

71

TABLE 2-17
TOTAL STOCKS OF OIL AND REFINED PRODUCTS FOR SELECTED IEA COUNTRIES AND REGIONS, 1983

Country/ Region	Quantity (thousands of metric tons of oil equivalent)	Days of Consumption	Days of Net Imports
United States	183,321	102.67	302.10
Japan	62,692	120.02	109.68
EEC	116,056	110.23	146.56
Other Europe	41,801	113.49	144.63
Other OECD	20,233	83.28	−2,785.26ª
Total	424,103	106.73	188.56

a. The large negative number reflects the fact that these countries are small net exporters.
SOURCE: *OECD Quarterly Oil Statistics.*

days of consumption but above-average stocks measured in days of net oil imports. Japan holds slightly greater stocks than Europe measured in days of consumption but less measured in days of net imports. The other OECD countries (Australia, Canada, New Zealand) hold the lowest stocks measured in days of consumption. Since they are net exporters of oil and petroleum products, their lower stocks can perhaps be explained by the fact that their national incomes rise during supply disruptions.[98]

Whether the IEA has been instrumental in countries' attaining these stock levels is difficult to assess. A review of national policies before and after the 1973 oil embargo fails to support the presumption that IEA policy actions have played a central role in stockpiling.

Europe. Before the 1973 oil embargo, the EEC required each member country to hold storage equal to ninety days' consumption.[99] For example, France followed this policy in 1972, although the French government held no segmented reserves. The oil companies maintained, owned, and financed the entire French national stockpile.[100]

Stockpiling policy has changed in Europe since the 1973 embargo, but the role of European governments in the generally large accumulation of stocks seems minor. Germany, for example, established a special storage corporation that held segregated emergency reserves for German companies. The corporation centralized the storage and financing of legislatively mandated stocks that predate the 1973 embargo.[101] By 1978 the reserve in this government-created program

72

totaled 48 million barrels, or about 20 percent of the total stocks held in Germany.[102] Given the small relative size of those stocks, which, in any event, reflect preembargo policy, it seems unlikely that IEA policies had a significant influence in Germany.

Policy developments in the Netherlands are similar to those in Germany. A 1976 law raised the stock obligations of companies to ninety days' inland sales. The stocks held did not increase because the companies already held stocks exceeding the requirements created by that law.[103] Because of this experience the Dutch government established a new storage institution to increase stocks. The plan allowed required private stocks, however, to be reduced on a one-for-one basis with the accumulation of public stocks. It is thus unlikely that the policy contributed to an increase in stocks held in the Netherlands.[104]

In summary, the stock targets specified by the International Energy Program (originally sixty and later ninety days' net oil imports) were below those specified by EEC policy before the 1973 oil embargo. Stock policies in Germany and the Netherlands since the embargo indicate that those governments have been cautious in mandating significant increases in the stocks held by their national oil companies. It is difficult to find support for any presumption that IEA policy actions have been important in European stock building since 1973.

Japan. Like all participants in the international oil market, Japan did not anticipate the political instability that caused higher world oil prices in 1973. In that year Japanese stocks barely exceeded thirty days' consumption. Within one year the Japanese had increased their stocks to seventy-two days' consumption. From 1975 to 1983 they engaged in significant stock accumulation that increased their stocks from 40.5 to 62.7 million metric tons of oil equivalent, or over 50 percent.[105]

The Japanese government has taken an active role in this accumulation. It maintains some segregated emergency reserves through the Japan National Oil Company. It also requires private traders to meet stock levels defined by the Petroleum Stockpiling Law of 1975. It offers loans for construction of storage facilities, loans and interest subsidies for the purchase of oil that enters storage, tax breaks on storage facilities, and accelerated depreciation on storage investment undertaken by the private sector. It has been estimated that all this special treatment defrays slightly less than 20 percent of the private costs of storage.[106]

Can the IEA claim credit for persuading the Japanese government to engage in these policies? It seems improbable that the Japanese government relied on guidance from its Western allies before it engaged in its aggressive stockpiling program. In fact, the Japanese began their accumulation of stockpiles before the protocols of the International Energy Program were finalized.

The United States. The United States is distinct from other OECD countries in that its government has taken a large, active role in the construction and financing of a separate emergency reserve of petroleum.[107] The strategic petroleum reserve (SPR) was established by the Energy Production and Conservation Act of 1975, which also extended domestic petroleum price controls and ratified U.S. participation in the International Energy Program.

It is difficult to assess the importance of IEA policy in the accumulation of U.S. petroleum stocks. The buildup of the SPR has lagged far behind the schedule established by the 1975 act. Significant accumulation did not occur until after the outbreak of the Iran-Iraq war.[108] From the viewpoint of IEA policy, the timing of this buildup is ironic because it coincided with attempts by the IEA to rely on stock drawdowns to cope with the supply disruption created by that war. Nevertheless, the U.S. policy of stock building during the Reagan administration has made the SPR a significant factor in U.S. petroleum storage. By 1984 the SPR accounted for about 33 percent of the total stock of oil and petroleum products stored in the United States.[109]

The size of the SPR, however, seriously overstates the effectiveness of public policy in increasing stockpiling in the United States. It would be inappropriate to conclude that each barrel of the SPR constitutes a net addition to U.S. petroleum stocks. Increased government stocks are offset, in part, by declines in private stocks, for two reasons. Government stockpiling raises current market prices as public stocks are accumulated and thereby increases the private cost of storage. Government stockpiling also lowers anticipated future prices when the release of public stocks occurs and thus reduces the private benefits of storage. An analysis of U.S. private stockpiling reveals that for each two barrels stored in the SPR, the private sector stores one barrel less for its own account.[110]

In summary, experience does not provide strong support for the belief that IEA stock policies were a significant factor in American stockpiling. Congressional approval of U.S. participation in the IEA did accompany plans for the SPR. But the subsequent record does not reveal any durable link between public stockpiling policies and IEA treaty commitments. The United States met its initial sixty-day stock requirement by declaring that private stocks were part of the U.S. reserve. The buildup of the SPR was delayed during the 1970s while IEA policy was extolling the virtues of stock accumulation. By

74

the time U.S. policy shifted toward building the SPR, IEA policy favored restraint in stock buildup to avoid pressure on international oil markets.

Informal IEA Stock Policy. Not all IEA stockpiling actions concentrated on the formal obligations negotiated under the treaty. With the outbreak of the Iran-Iraq war, the IEA engaged in an informal policy of encouraging member countries to jawbone their oil companies to draw down their inventories. The intent was to avoid repetition of the "panic buying" created by the Iranian revolution.

Two considerations undermine the presumption that informal IEA stock policy was a display of IEA effectiveness. First, the policy encouraged private parties to draw down the stocks whose earlier buildup was against the better judgment of the IEA. Second, as James Plummer and John Weyant observed, "Since private inventories were very high during 1980, it was much easier to persuade the companies."[111] Is it possible that the celebrated drawdown of stocks would have occurred without the informal IEA policy? This question is answered by determining whether stocks deviated from normal storage patterns during late 1980 and early 1981.

Table 2–18 reports estimated "abnormal" stock levels for OECD countries during selected time periods. The entries are the proportionate deviations from a storage rule that, for each country, relates the total stock of oil and petroleum products held to its seasonally adjusted total petroleum supply, real interest rates, and IEA policy actions.[112] Positive entries indicate unusual stock building; negative entries, unusual stock drawdowns. The time periods include the first full year after the Iranian revolution (the fourth quarter of 1978 through the third quarter of 1979), the next five years (the fourth quarter of 1979 through the third quarter of 1984), and the three quarters during which the IEA informal stock policy was allegedly in force (the fourth quarter of 1980 through the second quarter of 1981).

There is evidence that the storage rule for most OECD countries changed after the Iranian revolution. The stocks held were higher for any given total supply. But there is no evidence that any alleged panic buying that occurred during the early phases of the Iranian revolution was related to abnormal stock building. Nor is there evidence that informal IEA stock policy had any significant effects during the early months of the Iran-Iraq war.

Consider the findings for the first full year after the Iranian revolution (column 1). Evidence is slight, at best, that countries engaged in any of the abnormal stock building that preoccupied IEA policy

75

TABLE 2–18

DEVIATIONS FROM NORMAL STOCK LEVELS DURING SELECTED PERIODS
OF MARKET EVENTS AND IEA POLICY ACTIONS, 1978–1981
(proportionate change)

	Periods of Political Instability		Informal IEA Policy		
Country	1978: IV–1979: III (1)	1979: IV–1984: III (2)	1980: IV (3)	1981: I (4)	1981: II (5)
Australia	1.09	1.18	0.09	-0.02	0.05
	(9.62)	(9.47)	(0.83)	(-0.16)	(0.49)
Austria	0.26	0.61	0.01	-0.03	-0.14
	(2.53)	(4.99)	(0.10)	(-0.24)	(-1.11)
Belgium	-0.07	0.06	0.05	0.15	0.09
	(-1.84)	(1.92)	(0.74)	(2.29)	(1.22)
Canada	-0.08	-0.01	-0.01	-0.04	0.08
	(-2.41)	(-0.46)	(-0.19)	(-0.54)	(1.23)
Denmark	0.02	0.12	0.03	0.03	0.08
	(0.55)	(4.92)	(0.50)	(0.56)	(1.51)
Finland	-0.06	0.10	0.05	0.10	0.08
	(-1.48)	(2.65)	(0.58)	(1.38)	(0.95)
France	-0.05	0.09	-0.08	0.01	0.06
	(-2.11)	(4.27)	(-1.62)	(0.30)	(1.22)
Germany	0.05	0.21	0.01	0.05	0.06
	(1.41)	(9.13)	(0.26)	(0.83)	(1.12)
Greece	-0.14	-0.02	0.00	0.05	-0.01
	(-2.28)	(-0.33)	(0.01)	(0.50)	(-0.13)
Ireland	0.04	0.12	0.07	0.08	-0.03
	(0.74)	(3.85)	(0.76)	(0.92)	(-0.26)
Italy	-0.01	0.10	-0.05	-0.03	0.02
	(-0.18)	(5.67)	(-0.95)	(-0.67)	(0.49)
Japan	-0.03	0.12	-0.02	-0.04	0.02
	(-1.03)	(5.27)	(-0.33)	(-0.83)	(0.34)
Luxembourg	0.10	0.15	-0.03	0.16	0.11
	(0.76)	(1.27)	(-0.10)	(0.65)	(0.42)
Netherlands	-0.04	0.17	0.12	-0.01	0.12
	(-0.73)	(4.29)	(1.18)	(-0.08)	(1.29)
Norway	-0.02	0.08	-0.03	0.09	0.15
	(-0.35)	(1.84)	(-0.28)	(0.73)	(1.30)
Portugal	-0.02	0.22	0.26	0.05	0.12
	(-0.18)	(1.64)	(1.56)	(0.31)	(0.73)
Spain	0.16	0.29	-0.10	-0.08	0.24
	(2.17)	(5.84)	(-0.76)	(-0.58)	(1.83)

TABLE 2–18 (continued)

Country	Periods of Political Instability		Informal IEA Policy		
	1978: IV–1979: III (1)	1979 IV–1984: III (2)	1980: IV (3)	1981: I (4)	1981: II (5)
Sweden	−0.03	−0.06	0.08	0.27	0.04
	(−0.40)	(−1.06)	(0.72)	(2.54)	(0.37)
Switzerland	0.08	0.12	0.03	0.02	0.04
	(2.55)	(4.91)	(0.70)	(0.46)	(0.85)
United Kingdom	−0.03	0.06	0.10	0.16	0.08
	(−0.68)	(1.41)	(1.33)	(2.15)	(1.09)
United States	0.02	0.14	−0.02	0.05	0.00
	(0.64)	(6.23)	(−0.45)	(1.15)	(0.08)

NOTE: Entries are proportionate deviations from each country's stocks as given by historical storage rule. Positive deviations represent unusual stock building; negative deviations, ususual stock drawdowns; t-statistics are in parentheses.
SOURCE: Computed by author; see appendix B.

discussions. Only four countries (Australia, Austria, Spain, Switzerland) "abnormally" increased their stocks. Four other countries (Belgium, Canada, France, Greece) "abnormally" reduced their stocks. The thirteen other countries displayed no significant deviations from their normal storage rules.

The situation was different in the years following the Iranian revolution (see column 2). Sixteen of the twenty-one countries increased their stocks for any given level of their total petroleum supplies. This response would be expected if the deterioration in Iranian-American relations during late 1979 and the outbreak of the Iran-Iraq war raised the likelihood of future catastrophe in the Middle East.[113] In such circumstances private storers would build their stocks, not reduce them, in anticipation of even higher prices in future periods, even if the exact timing of the future disruption was uncertain.[114]

Informal IEA stock drawdown policy during late 1980 and early 1981 had no effect on the storage activity of OECD countries. In fact, more countries display abnormally high stocks during late 1980 and early 1981, although none of the effects would be considered significant by conventional standards of statistical inference. Any apparent success of IEA-inspired jawboning occurred because oil companies were not asked to deviate significantly from their stock management plans.

Conclusion: The Prospects for Effective Multilateral Stock Management. The ineffectiveness of IEA emergency reserve and informal stock management policies need not be lamented. The international external benefits of government stockpiling are probably less than the international external costs. Therefore, multilateral action on stockpiling cannot devise a self-enforcing agreement to increase stockpiling in oil-importing countries. Even though the prospect of future price controls deters the private sector from holding the theoretically socially optimal stockpile, the presumption that multilateral action can resolve the problem rests on tenuous logical and empirical grounds.

It is uncertain whether the 1984 accord on IEA stock policy is a significant departure from the IEA's tradition of good intentions but ineffective results. Given the absence of specific country obligations, the accord does not even attempt to establish any new operational policies for supply disruptions. At best it focuses IEA discussion on the issue of stock drawdown decisions, but it ignores the political problems that will be created by the different expectations of IEA members about the duration and size of a supply disruption. Countries that perceive a disruption as short-lived will advocate a different stock drawdown policy from those that perceive it as long-lived. The experience of informal stock management policies in 1981 suggests that countries will follow their individual stock management policies despite any discussion to the contrary by the Governing Board.

Informal Assessments of the IEA

The preceding discussion has relied on economic theory and formal statistical testing to evaluate the economic consequences of IEA policy actions. Those assessments have failed to support the ability of IEA policy actions to achieve their stated goals. In fact, some actions, such as oil sharing and import quotas, may even be counterproductive.

Actual episodes have demonstrated that the IEA has been unable to formulate meaningful measures of compliance with its policies. Mistrust among members has arisen during supply disruptions. Self-assessments by the IEA have foundered on their inability to distinguish between economic adjustments that would have occurred without an agreement and what IEA cooperative action has added to the response by members to higher world oil prices. These themes are developed by considering four areas of IEA action: demand restraint, import ceilings, stock drawdown policy, and research and development.

Demand Restraint. The IEA's experience with demand restraint provides eloquent testimony to confusion and dissent. Before the Iranian

78

revolution claims of ineffectiveness may be found in the IEA's own self-assessments:

> The critical point is that we should not repeat the experience of 1975–1978 when optimism prevailed and efforts to promote and accelerate structural change slackened. The result was that, when IEA economies recovered after 1975, oil demand grew at very rapid rates . . . leaving countries unnecessarily vulnerable to the 1979 oil supply disruption.[115]

During the Iranian revolution the attempted IEA coordination of consumption cutbacks in 1979 avoided making simple comparisons between 1979 and 1978 actual consumption. It was recognized that countries differ at least in the growth of their economies. U.S. officials noted that equal proportionate cutbacks among countries would neglect differences in targeted rates of consumption before the revolution. For example:

> Noting that at present neither West Germany nor Japan would have to reduce their oil use by as much as the U.S., Mr. Cooper (Under Secretary of State for Economic Affairs) said this reflected the desire by other industrial nations to avoid damaging the "relatively buoyant" economies of both Germany and Japan.[116]

In this context the IEA policy of "equitable sharing" of reduced world supplies is difficult, if not impossible, to define. When does a country's bidding in the oil market reflect ambitious growth targets tempered by restraint, and when does it reflect competitive scrambling? This imponderable question quickly surfaced as disputes arose about which countries cooperated with IEA consumption targets and which did not.

> Faced with complaints by smaller IEA member countries that they were being crowded out of the oil market, the (IEA) cabinet level meeting called for greater international cooperation and "equitable distribution of available oil" in implementing the voluntary programs that had been agreed on at the IEA meeting last March.[117]

Despite these pronouncements, concern about cohesion among IEA members persisted. The IEA attempted to defuse the issue by declining to discuss specific countries' performance in demand restraint. It experienced, at best, modest success. The following observation is informative:

> The U.S. apparently has reached its full demand restraint. . . . But Japan and other countries have shown increases in demand rather than declines. At a news conference after the

79

Governing Board meeting, officials were reluctant to give comparisons of members' results, saying they depend on different climatic conditions and economic growth rates.[118]

Suspicion continued about spot market purchases by members. Increased purchases of Iranian oil by Germany and Japan were viewed as evidence of poor solidarity among IEA countries.[119]

The IEA's self-assessment of the 1979 episode is remarkable, in light of the controversy that surrounded the attempt at coordinated consumption cutbacks. In the IEA's view, "The results through 1979 of the (consumption cutback) efforts were modest, but encouraging. . . . All countries took some actions, and many countries either introduced or strengthened energy conservation and fuel-switching measures in ways that will have a continuing impact for years."[120] The distinction between what would happen with and without IEA policy actions continued to be an alien concept in IEA self-assessment. The conclusion of modest success seems overstated, in light of the evidence reviewed here.

Other commentators have also concluded that IEA action was unsuccessful. Wilfrid Kohl observed that the 5 percent agreement fell apart when Germany, Sweden, and other countries sent missions to Arab states and engaged in "extensive" buying on the spot market.[121] James Plummer and John Weyant report that threats of "competitive scrambling" were wielded in IEA policy discussions:

> During the Iranian Revolution, Exxon reduced crude supplies to its Canadian subsidiary by 30,000 barrels per day, attempting to offset disproportionate reduction in imports elsewhere. *Despite its IEA membership,* the Canadian government argued vociferously that since Imperial Oil (Exxon's subsidiary) received no oil from Iran, there was no reason Canada should be affected by the worldwide shortage at all. It even *threatened* to purchase additional crude in a direct state-to-state deal with Venezuela.[122]

In addition to its flawed economic analysis, the posturing by the Canadian government showed that political allocation need not be as enlightened as IEA proponents have argued.

In summary, the attempted demand restraint policy illustrated that the IEA could not control the competitive scrambling that prompted the original agreement. The use of poorly specified international obligations only created confusion and added tension among IEA members.

Import Ceilings. The IEA itself seems confused about its policy on import ceilings. Its review of the ceilings negotiated at the Tokyo

80

summit states: "Net oil import forecasts also show a significant downward revision, partly as a result of the Tokyo Summit and IEA Ministerial commitments made during 1979, but also because of lower expected economic growth and greater expectations for energy conservation and fuel switching."[123] Given the sharp increases in world oil prices during that period, greater expectations of energy conservation and fuel switching would have arisen without IEA policy actions. So the self-assessment leaves the recurrent unanswered question of whether the reduced volume of imports reflected normal economic forces only or whether it also reflected IEA policies, measures, or exhortations.

I have argued that policy-induced import ceilings may create serious economic problems for oil-importing countries if foreign oil is supplied noncompetitively. Effective quotas would not reduce but increase world oil prices. This possibility has not escaped notice at the IEA: "Even in the short term, such emergency steps (ceilings) hardly provide adequate comfort to Western consumer nations when oil-producing states can readily cut off supplies and raise prices almost at will, *IEA Ministers conceded privately.*"[124] Such concern is based on strong economic foundations (see chapter 4). It appears that the IEA was formulating effective quota targets while wondering whether they might be counterproductive.

Stock Drawdown Policy. The informal policy of coordinated stock drawdowns in late 1980 and early 1981 followed IEA tradition. Self-assessment again failed to distinguish between outcomes that would inevitably have occurred without IEA action and those that are a result of IEA action. In its analysis of market events in 1980, the IEA stated:

> The fragile balance in the market was again put at risk towards the end of the year by the Iran-Iraq conflict, but significant further price increases did not result because of:
> — substantial declines in oil consumption in 1980 compared to 1979;
> — increased production by some OPEC countries;
> — better stock positions in late 1980 as well as prompt action by IEA countries, in October and December of 1980, to discourage undesirable oil purchases on the spot market and to draw from oil stocks to compensate for the supply shortfall.[125]

The preceding section indicated that stock drawdowns would have occurred without informal IEA stock policy. That the market would naturally have drawn down stocks was evidenced by the early response to the supply cutoffs in the Middle East:

For the moment, the Iraqi cutoff actually has its bright side, in that it allows oil-consuming nations to draw down some of the heavy reserves that are pressing storage capacity due to sluggish demand. As an official of a big Japanese trading house puts it: "If the supply suspension will be only two to three weeks, it will be much appreciated."[126]

Subsequent IEA policy actions were accompanied by bickering and lack of cooperation among members. "Ministers of the IEA failed to provide a real means of enforcing the oil demand-curbing and reallocation procedures they agreed on last week."[127] "The total goal (of IEA policy) was not split up among countries."[128] Nothing in the public domain indicates that the IEA did anything but record market responses to the Iran-Iraq war.

The ineffectiveness of informal management policies is exemplified by the IEA's abortive attempt to use informal oil sharing to help Turkey. The intentions of the policy were grand:

> The IEA said it was invoking a special oil sharing agreement to help restock Turkey . . . who becomes the first of the 21 IEA nations to receive emergency aid as a result of Iraq's suspension of oil supplies. . . . Turkey will receive 7.3 million barrels of oil during the current quarter, although IEA officials did not say how, whether, or when the financially pressed nation would pay for the oil.[129]

The actual outcome for Turkey was at odds with the announced policy. Other countries' failure to cooperate and apparent management problems made Turkey turn to the unregulated world petroleum market:

> IEA fails to cover shortfall, so Turkey lines up oil itself. 60 percent of Turkey's oil was cut off by the Iran-Iraq War leaving Turkey in a desperate fix by December 1980. Turkey lined up enough oil for the 1st quarter of 1981, getting the oil through its own efforts from trade suppliers in Iraq, Iran, and Libya. Turkey had called to the IEA for help but there was disagreement over their need, and when supply offers were made it was for small cargoes of either the wrong quality or too far away, often at prices *exceeding* those on the spot market.[130]

Research and Development. At the time the International Energy Program was negotiated, IEA sponsorship of cooperative R&D ventures was intended to facilitate the long-term objectives of the program. This is one area where IEA policies might be presumed to have been effective, since the long-term perspective of R&D is not subject to the same political obstacles as management of short-term energy supply problems. The IEA embarked on its R&D ventures with substantial optimism. A 1977 review by the Committee on Energy Research and Development found that "in a number of countries there is a substantial potential for additional participation in existing IEA projects."

Given that optimism, the record of R&D conducted by IEA-sponsored projects must be disappointing. Table 2–19 summarizes countries' R&D and IEA collaborative efforts for 1977–1980 in nonfission projects (the agreement forbids collaboration in the fission area). The most striking features of the record are the relatively low and recently declining fractions of national R&D budgets funneled through IEA projects.

Self-assessments by the Committee on Energy Research and Development, conducted annually according to the terms of the treaty, have reluctantly reached the conclusion that the IEA's effort has been unimportant. The 1978 review stated:

> The proportion of the national efforts which are in cooperative projects, however, remains on average low, indicating there is a large scope for further collaborative work for all countries. . . . Overall budget allocations have increased . . . in many individual countries; however, the increases have been modest, and in some cases, there have been reductions in real terms.

At that time the reviewers had no idea that they were commenting on the heyday of IEA collaboration. The 1980 review lamented:

TABLE 2–19

IEA MEMBERS' PARTICIPATION IN COLLABORATIVE R&D PROJECTS, 1977–1980

(millions of U.S. dollars)

Year	Total R&D Effort by Members	IEA Collaborative Effort	
		Amount	Percent[a]
1977	2,704.8	46.0	1.7
1978	950.2	52.3	5.5
1979	3,914.8	105.7	2.7
1980	6,100.0	152.5	2.5

a. Percentage of countries' efforts devoted to IEA-sponsored research.
SOURCE: *IEA Annual Review, Energy Research, Development, and Demonstration, 1977–1980.*

83

Participation in IEA collaborative projects, although increasing, still represents a significant untapped potential for achieving economies and risk-sharing through cooperative action, while recognizing that the number of such projects is less significant than their importance to national programmes and the scale of effort involved.[131]

By 1981 the committee stopped reporting data on the scale of IEA-sponsored projects.

Conclusion: Many Promises, Few Results. IEA policies—the consumption cutback scheme, import ceilings, stock management, informal sharing, sponsorship of joint R&D projects—have a poor performance record. The IEA has been a minor actor in the international energy situation. Rather than playing the role of director in the energy drama, the agency has been relegated to photographing market responses, tempered by independent national energy policies. This state of affairs may well have been fortunate for the energy security of the Western world, as well as for Western oil consumers.

Both theory and anecdotal and statistical evidence show little link between IEA's policy actions and its stated policy goals. Rather than mitigate the economic losses and political tensions of supply disruptions, the IEA oil-sharing plan promises to intensify losses of national income and magnify political tensions. Rather than develop countervailing market power, import ceilings have destabilized international markets in the short term as IEA member countries ignored their commitments and would have raised oil prices in the long term if member countries had actually honored their obligations. Senator Metzenbaum's initial assessment of the IEA was prophetic. The promise of enhanced energy security that accompanied the negotiation and ratification of the treaty was indeed "merely a mirage."

Appendix A: Analytic Framework

This appendix presents the mathematical structure of the model of supply disruptions and oil sharing. For convenience, the model analyzes a composite commodity ("petroleum"), which should be understood as an aggregation of crude oil and refined products. Readers should consult the text for economic interpretation and discussion of the model.

Supply Disruptions. The model uses one definition and two behavioral relations. Equation A–1 states that the sum of a country's ending stock of petroleum (S_{it}) and its consumption (C_{it}) equals the sum of its domestic production (Q_{it}), net imports (M_{it}), and beginning stock (S_{it-1}). Equation A–2 relates a country's consumption to the domestic price of petroleum (P_{it}) and its real national income (I_{it}), where η_i is the compensated own-price elasticity and σ_i is the income elasticity of demand by country i. Equation A–3 summarizes a country's storage rule, which relates ending stocks to total supply—the sum of domestic production, net imports, and beginning stocks. These relations provide the framework for studying the effect of supply disruptions on world petroleum prices and the levels of national income for OECD countries.

$$S_{it} + C_{it} = Q_{it} + M_{it} + S_{it-1} \tag{A-1}$$

$$C_{it} = A_i P_{it} \eta_i I_{it} \sigma_i \tag{A-2}$$

$$S_{it} = \lambda_{i0} + \lambda_{i1}\{Q_{it} + M_{it} + S_{it-1}\} \tag{A-3}$$

Income effects of higher petroleum prices. Consumers, domestic producers, and private storers experience different kinds of income effects from higher petroleum prices. Equation A–4 depicts the income effect for consumers in country i—dI_{iC}—which is the area under the income-compensated demand curve for the original level of national income (I_{i0}) and between the original and new petroleum price. Integration of the expression in (A–4) and rearrangement of terms yield the expression for consumer losses as a fraction of national income before the disruption—equation A–5.

$$dI_{iC} = -\int_{P_0}^{P_1} \{A_i P \eta_i I_{i0} \sigma_i\} \, dP \tag{A-4}$$

$$dI_{iC}/I_{i0} = \alpha_{i0}\{(P_1/P_0)\eta_{i+1} - 1\}/(\eta_i + 1) \tag{A-5}$$

where α_{i0} is the fraction of national income consumers in country i spent on petroleum before the increase in petroleum prices.

The expressions for the income effects for domestic producers and storers are simple. Given the assumption that domestic oil production does not increase during supply disruptions, the gain of domestic producers in country i (dI_{iP}) equals the price increase multiplied by domestic production before the disruption (Q_{i0})—see equation A–6. Private storers experience two income effects. First, they enjoy a capital gain on their beginning stock equal to the price increase multiplied by the initial stock (S_{it-1}). Second, they experience a loss (dI_{iS}) on their planned stock accumulation, which, by virtue of the country's storage rule, can be written as a function of initial domestic production and net imports—see equation A–7.

85

$$dI_{iP} = (P_1 - P_0)Q_{i0} \tag{A-6}$$

$$dI_{iS} = -(P_1 - P_0)\{\lambda_{i0} + \lambda_{i1}(Q_{i0} + M_{i0}) + (\lambda_{i1} - 1)S_{it-1}\} \tag{A-7}$$

Supply disruption and price increases. Given the assumption that international arbitrage will equalize spot oil prices in OECD countries, the world petroleum price satisfies the equilibrium condition given in equation A–8. The supply disruption is modeled as a reduction in net imports available to OECD countries. Because domestic production is assumed to be fixed and beginning stocks are determined before the disruption, world petroleum prices will increase so that the resulting change in ending stocks and final consumption satisfies the condition given in equation A–9.

$$\Sigma_i S_{it} + \Sigma_i C_{it} = \Sigma_i Q_{it} + \Sigma_i M_{it} + \Sigma_i S_{it-1} \tag{A-8}$$

$$\Sigma_i dS_{it} + \Sigma_i dC_{it} = -\mu\Sigma_i M_{it} \tag{A-9}$$

where μ is the proportionate reduction in net imports available to OECD countries. For a given disruption, the right-hand side of (A–9) is a constant, and the left-hand side is ultimately a function of the change in the world petroleum price.

The following solution strategy was followed. The demand curve given by equation A–2 implies that the change in final consumption in country i (dC_{it}) is given by equation A–10. The expression for the change in ending stocks in equation A–11 was obtained by the following argument: (a) equation A–1 implies that $dS_{it} + dC_{it} = dM_{it}$, while equation A–3 implies that $dS_{it} = \lambda_{i1}dM_{it}$; (b) these two equations can be solved to yield (A–11).

$$dC_{it} = C_{i0}\{\eta_i P^* + \sigma_i(dI_{iC} + dI_{iP} + dI_{iS})/I_{i0}\} \tag{A-10}$$

where C_{i0} is country i's predisruption consumption and $P^* = $ the proportionate change in the world petroleum price.

$$dS_{it} = \lambda_{i1}dC_{it}/(1 - \lambda_{i1}) \tag{A-11}$$

Substitution of equations A–10 and A–11 in equation A–9 yields an implicit equation for P^* as a function of the distribution of the initial levels of consumption (C_{i0}) and national income (I_{i0}), price elasticity (η_i), income elasticity (σ_i), storage rule parameters (λ_{i1}), and magnitude of the supply disruption (μ). Once the price increase is computed, the income effects for consumers, producers, and private storers can be measured by the application of equations A–5, A–6, and A–7. Consumption cutbacks and stock releases can be computed by evaluating the expressions in equations A–10 and A–11 at the equilibrium proportionate increase in the world oil price.

Oil Sharing. Oil sharing is modeled as forced retrading among IEA countries after individuals have adjusted to higher world oil prices. Moreover, purchase rights must be based on total supply, not consumption, to avoid the fundamental inconsistency in the IEA's accounting scheme.

Let $q_{i\tau}$ be country i's targeted level of supply, and q_{i0} be country i's actual supply after a disruption. For countries with a selling obligation, $q_{i0} > q_{i\tau}$; for countries with a buying right, $q_{i0} < q_{i\tau}$. Since domestic oil production is assumed constant, any changes in total supply must occur through changes in net imports: $dq_i = dM_{it}$. Equation A–12 expresses this change in total supply in terms of changes in final consumption, an expression that results from noting that $dS_{it} + dC_{it} = dM_{it}$ and that $dS_{it} = \lambda_{i1}dM_{it}$.

$$dq_i = q_{i\tau} - q_{i0} = dM_{it} = dC_{it}/(1 - \lambda_{i1}) \qquad \text{(A–12)}$$

Dividing both sides of (A–12) by initial total supply and rearranging terms yields the expression for the proportionate change in total supply that results from meeting the supply targets implicit in the IEA oil-sharing scheme—see equation A–13. The expression shows that changes in total supply are ultimately related to changes in final consumption. This expression provides an implicit equation for the proportionate difference between domestic and world oil prices as a function of the difference between IEA targets for supply and actual supply, demand elasticity, consumption, domestic production, net imports, and the storage rule parameter λ_{i1}.

$$dq_i/q_{i0} = \{dC_{it}/C_{i0}\} \{C_{i0}/(Q_{i0} + M_{i0})\} \{1/(1 - \lambda_{i1})\} \qquad \text{(A–13)}$$

Equation A–14 uses a standard approximation for the resource inefficiency in country i (L_i) due to the deviation of the domestic oil price (P_d) from the world oil price (P_w). Multiplying and dividing the right-hand side of A–14 by $P_w q_{i0}$—recalling that $\eta_i = \{dC_{it}/C_{i0}\}/\{(P_d - P_w)/P_w\}$—and rearranging terms yields equation A–15.

$$L_i = -.5 \{q_{i\tau} - q_{i0}\} \{P_d - P_w\} \qquad \text{(A–14)}$$

$$L_i = -.5 \{q_{i\tau}/q_{i0} - 1\}^2 P_w q_{i0}/\eta_{i\tau} \qquad \text{(A–15)}$$

where $\eta_{i\tau} = \eta_i \{C_{i0}/(Q_{i0} + M_{i0})\} \{1/(1 - \lambda_{i1})\}$.

Appendix B: Empirical Studies of Consumption and Stockpiling

The empirical studies of OECD consumption and stockpiling provide estimates of the key parameters used in the simulation of supply disruptions and oil sharing and allow decomposition of actual changes

87

TABLE B-1

REGRESSION COEFFICIENTS OF QUARTERLY PETROLEUM CONSUMPTION, SELECTED OECD COUNTRIES, 1974–1984

| Country | Constant | $Log\ C_{t-1}$ | $Log\ HP_{t-1}$ | $Log\ Y_t$ | Trend | Quarter Dummies | | | IEA Policy | |
						First	Second	Third	1979	1980
Austria	-1.263	0.046	-0.192	1.838	-0.009	0.177	-0.032	-0.018	0.106	0.099
	(-0.32)	(0.28)	(-3.00)	(2.43)	(-1.92)	(1.41)	(-0.43)	(-0.46)	(2.09)	(2.09)
Belgium	2.518	0.220	-0.234	1.276	-0.003	0.038	-0.204	-0.284	0.092	0.144
	(0.93)	(1.42)	(-2.72)	(2.20)	(-0.91)	(0.57)	(-2.80)	(-5.23)	(1.06)	(1.98)
Canada	-3.662	0.442	-0.071	1.712	-0.010	-0.076	-0.191	-0.103	0.066	0.081
	(-2.03)	(3.08)	(-1.06)	(3.81)	(-3.19)	(-3.08)	(-8.35)	(-4.96)	(1.37)	(1.89)
Denmark	8.413	0.117	-0.283	0.074	-0.005	0.037	-0.245	-0.308	0.142	0.138
	(3.35)	(0.56)	(-2.28)	(0.19)	(-1.49)	(0.44)	(-2.85)	(-6.91)	(1.69)	(1.84)
Finland	8.343	0.097	-0.287	0.052	0.001	-0.069	-0.299	-0.301	0.137	0.176
	(2.13)	(0.54)	(-1.35)	(0.05)	(0.15)	(-0.57)	(-3.36)	(-3.10)	(1.22)	(2.15)
France	-8.569	0.005	-0.065	2.477	-0.019	0.019	-0.185	-0.343	0.064	0.052
	(-1.53)	(0.03)	(-0.83)	(3.06)	(-3.16)	(0.28)	(-2.63)	(-8.69)	(1.12)	(1.15)
Germany	-4.109	-0.110	-0.188	2.279	-0.012	-0.006	-0.048	-0.023	0.111	0.032
	(-1.85)	(-0.68)	(-3.89)	(5.29)	(-5.00)	(-0.35)	(-3.04)	(-1.45)	(3.13)	(1.05)
Greece	2.820	0.242	-0.073	0.780	0.005	-0.024	-0.210	-0.046	-0.003	0.072
	(2.46)	(1.65)	(-1.16)	(3.96)	(2.33)	(-0.79)	(-8.44)	(-1.80)	(-0.08)	(1.82)
Italy	-3.924	-0.057	-0.034	1.195	-0.009	0.031	-0.197	-0.183	0.041	0.033
	(-0.91)	(-0.39)	(-0.57)	(2.92)	(-5.47)	(1.07)	(-5.71)	(-11.14)	(1.41)	(1.30)

88

Japan	-15.340	0.555	-0.095	1.747	-0.019	-0.039	-0.250	-0.121	0.083	0.033
	(-1.29)	(3.71)	(-1.80)	(1.61)	(-1.59)	(-1.24)	(-8.23)	(-5.65)	(1.78)	(0.87)
Luxembourg	5.562	0.135	-0.315	0.321	0.001	0.032	-0.088	-0.174	0.060	0.025
	(4.71)	(0.85)	(-4.09)	(1.49)	(0.43)	(0.62)	(-1.74)	(-4.50)	(1.08)	(0.54)
Netherlands	-4.240	0.408	-0.003	2.089	-0.006	-0.088	-0.174	-0.116	0.101	0.037
	(-1.83)	(2.87)	(-0.03)	(3.39)	(-1.73)	(-2.34)	(-4.92)	(-3.39)	(1.63)	(1.04)
Norway	6.495	-0.038	-0.308	0.630	0.001	-0.010	-0.153	-0.199	0.273	0.112
	(2.10)	(-0.22)	(-2.19)	(1.03)	(0.11)	(-0.14)	(-2.68)	(-3.93)	(2.48)	(1.17)
Sweden	0.804	0.195	-0.210	1.514	-0.010	0.147	-0.176	-0.101	0.144	0.126
	(0.15)	(1.11)	(-1.52)	(1.46)	(-2.32)	(1.22)	(-1.48)	(-0.51)	(1.58)	(1.66)
Switzerland	5.509	-0.167	-0.280	1.419	-0.000	-0.288	-0.025	0.060	0.104	0.153
	(2.62)	(-0.99)	(-3.02)	(2.32)	(-0.75)	(-0.74)	(-0.61)	(1.50)	(1.69)	(2.68)
United Kingdom	1.093	0.881	-0.097	0.116	0.001	-0.139	-0.277	-0.230	-0.001	-0.030
	(0.30)	(5.09)	(-0.64)	(0.14)	(0.23)	(-2.10)	(-3.64)	(-5.19)	(-0.01)	(-0.86)
United States	0.718	0.388	-0.160	0.932	-0.005	-0.018	-0.092	-0.056	0.066	0.053
	(0.47)	(2.09)	(-2.18)	(2.95)	(-2.66)	(-0.93)	(-5.63)	(-3.96)	(1.28)	(1.32)

NOTE: t-statistics in parentheses. Dependent variable = natural logarithm of quarterly consumption; log C_{t-1} = natural logarithm of quarterly consumption in previous quarter; log HP_{t-1} = natural logarithm of real spot market oil price in home currency; and log Y_t = natural logarithm of real gross domestic product (1980 prices). Estimated by instrumental variables, where instruments included all explanatory variables, except log HP_t, and the additional variables log HP_{t-1} and log HP_{t-2}.

Seven OECD countries were excluded from analysis because of data problems: Australia, New Zealand, and Turkey (missing oil consumption data); Iceland, Ireland, New Zealand, Portugal, and Spain (missing quarterly gross domestic product data).

SOURCE: See discussion in text.

89

in OECD consumption and stockpiling into two components: those due to normal economic forces and those due to IEA policy actions.

Data Sources. As in any study using international data, problems were encountered with missing observations, which precluded obtaining a consistent data series for all twenty-four OECD countries. The models discussed below required information on final consumption and stockpiling activity, world oil prices, and a variety of standard macroeconomic data. The sources were the following:

• Final consumption and stockpiling: *OECD Quarterly Oil Statistics.*
• World oil price: *Petroleum Intelligence Weekly* reports monthly and quarterly series for international spot market transactions in U.S. dollars per barrel.
• Price levels, exchange rates, interest rates, and gross domestic product: Exchange rates (market rather than official rates) were used to express world oil prices in the home country's currency. All nominal data series were deflated by the home country's consumer price index. The source of the data was *International Financial Statistics,* published by the International Monetary Fund.

Petroleum Consumption. Equation B–1 presents the models used to explain the quarterly variation in petroleum consumption for the seventeen OECD countries for which data were available. Seven variables were used to control for standard economic forces. Lagged values for consumption (C_{it-1}) were included to introduce a simple dynamic structure into the demand equations. The real spot market price in the home currency (HP_{it}) was included to estimate the country's compensated price elasticity. The real gross domestic product variable (Y_{it}) was included to estimate the country's income elasticity. A trend variable $(Time_t)$ was included to measure the trend growth or decline rate in consumption. Three seasonal dummy variables—S_{1t}, S_{2t}, S_{3t}—measured the proportionate deviations of final consumption in the first, second, and third quarters, respectively, from consumption in the fourth quarter, after controlling for prices, income, and trend growth in final consumption. Two IEA policy periods are represented by the dummy variables IEA_{1t} and IEA_{2t}, which signify the consumption cutback and import quota agreements, respectively. ϵ_{it} is the residual that summarizes how actual consumption randomly deviated from the value predicted by the estimated equation. The equation was estimated by instrumental variables to avoid the well-known simultaneity bias that results from estimating demand equations by ordinary least squares. Tables B–1 and B–2 report the estimation results:

TABLE B–2
SUMMARY STATISTICS FOR REGRESSION MODELS OF
QUARTERLY PETROLEUM CONSUMPTION

Country	R^2	Durbin-Watson	Standard Error of Regression
Austria	0.757	2.16	0.063
Belgium	0.766	1.99	0.115
Canada	0.888	1.98	0.045
Denmark	0.888	1.93	0.090
Finland	0.711	1.95	0.106
France	0.924	2.01	0.061
Germany	0.896	1.78	0.035
Greece	0.932	2.20	0.045
Italy	0.940	2.24	0.036
Japan	0.894	1.37	0.047
Luxembourg	0.853	2.00	0.080
Netherlands	0.843	1.85	0.078
Norway	0.532	2.12	0.113
Sweden	0.889	1.53	0.099
Switzerland	0.402	1.85	0.090
United Kingdom	0.860	1.91	0.066
United States	0.859	1.83	0.031

SOURCE: See discussion in text.

$$\log(C_{it}) = \alpha_i + \beta_{iC}\log(C_{it-1}) + \beta_{iP}\log(HP_{it}) + \beta_{iY}\log(Y_{it})$$
$$+ \beta_{it}Time_t + \gamma_1 S_{1t} + \gamma_2 S_{2t} + \gamma_3 S_{3t}$$
$$+ \kappa_1 IEA_{1t} + \kappa_2 IEA_{2t} + \epsilon_{it} \qquad (B-1)$$

The estimated coefficients in table B–1 conform to conventional expectations. All estimated price elasticities are negative, and all income elasticities are positive. Most of the price and income elasticities are statistically significant. There is some evidence that the coefficients for the lagged consumption variables are positive and that many countries have non-zero trend growth rates. The coefficients for the quarterly dummy variables indicate statistically and quantitatively significant seasonality in petroleum consumption. The coefficients for the IEA policy periods are discussed in the text.

Table B–2 reports summary statistics for the estimated regression models. The R^2 statistics illustrate that the models explain a large portion of the variation in petroleum consumption in the seventeen countries. The Durbin-Watson statistics indicate that the residuals are

91

TABLE B-3

REGRESSION COEFFICIENTS FOR QUARTERLY STOCKPILING ACTIVITY BY SELECTED OECD COUNTRIES, 1974–1984

Country	Constant	Log Supply	$Log (1 + r)$	Quarter Dummies			R^2	DW
				First	Second	Third		
Australia	−0.369	0.814	−0.578	0.184	0.021	0.041	0.969	2.51
	(−2.06)	(3.53)	(−0.91)	(2.52)	(0.30)	(0.62)		
Austria	2.513	0.535	3.161	0.248	0.203	0.190	0.930	1.76
	(3.20)	(1.39)	(2.53)	(2.83)	(3.07)	(3.09)		
Belgium	−2.755	1.214	−1.088	−0.068	0.113	0.148	0.897	2.40
	(−2.75)	(11.54)	(−1.94)	(−2.18)	(3.42)	(4.63)		
Canada	−0.543	0.983	0.113	−0.044	0.018	0.038	0.786	2.07
	(−0.38)	(7.25)	(0.23)	(−1.54)	(0.58)	(1.37)		
Denmark	−0.812	1.025	0.018	−0.075	0.027	0.107	0.876	1.85
	(−0.83)	(9.69)	(0.09)	(−3.08)	(0.99)	(4.26)		
Finland	−0.357	0.978	0.919	−0.098	0.091	0.047	0.923	2.25
	(−0.17)	(4.31)	(1.44)	(−1.32)	(0.96)	(1.04)		
France	−4.897	1.378	0.154	−0.043	0.092	0.195	0.954	2.09
	(−4.95)	(15.40)	(0.38)	(−1.96)	(3.42)	(8.06)		
Germany	−5.337	1.407	0.500	−0.009	0.022	0.011	0.958	1.55
	(−3.73)	(10.90)	(0.78)	(−0.31)	(0.85)	(0.51)		
Greece	−5.558	1.586	0.075	−0.038	0.103	0.059	0.927	1.31
	(−4.49)	(10.92)	(0.13)	(−0.67)	(1.98)	(0.54)		
Ireland	−1.399	1.052	−0.038	0.058	0.123	0.135	0.788	1.36
	(−1.37)	(8.03)	(−0.15)	(1.29)	(2.74)	(3.34)		

Italy	-3.158	1.217	0.136	-0.067	0.104	0.113	0.860	1.75
	(-1.63)	(6.76)	(0.76)	(-3.10)	(3.83)	(5.15)		
Japan	-8.262	1.635	1.265	-0.091	0.152	0.078	0.963	2.06
	(-5.57)	(12.82)	(4.73)	(-4.10)	(6.31)	(3.34)		
Luxembourg	7.971	-0.556	-0.243	-0.167	-0.265	-0.328	0.402	1.87
	(2.78)	(-1.18)	(-0.18)	(-1.50)	(-2.33)	(-2.58)		
Netherlands	4.284	0.505	-1.438	-0.013	-0.017	0.056	0.658	1.58
	(2.16)	(2.53)	(-1.88)	(-0.31)	(-0.44)	(1.35)		
Norway	2.647	0.604	-0.145	-0.057	-0.059	-0.032	0.583	1.78
	(2.34)	(4.43)	(-0.24)	(-0.99)	(-1.17)	(-0.64)		
Portugal	-1.325	1.049	-0.083	0.019	0.085	0.035	0.895	2.69
	(-0.61)	(3.81)	(-0.24)	(0.26)	(1.10)	(0.42)		
Spain	5.908	0.307	-1.106	-0.025	0.049	0.095	0.654	0.58
	(4.14)	(2.14)	(-1.97)	(-0.44)	(0.89)	(0.89)		
Sweden	1.281	0.809	0.286	-0.099	0.051	0.129	0.869	2.49
	(0.91)	(5.67)	(0.40)	(-1.39)	(0.78)	(2.35)		
Switzerland	-0.287	0.970	-0.328	0.002	-0.006	-0.025	0.921	1.08
	(-0.22)	(6.56)	(-1.00)	(0.08)	(-0.27)	(-1.18)		
United Kingdom	-2.841	1.194	-0.473	-0.040	0.024	0.093	0.848	0.97
	(-1.32)	(5.94)	(-1.19)	(-1.01)	(0.48)	(2.38)		

NOTE: t-statistics in parentheses. Dependent variable = natural logarithm of quarterly ending stocks; r = ex post real interest rate. Estimated by ordinary least squares.
SOURCE: See discussion in text.

serially uncorrelated. The estimated standard errors of the regression models suggest that the residual variation is relatively small, ranging from a 3.1 percent fluctuation of actual consumption for the United States to 11.5 percent for Belgium.

Stockpiling Activity. As pointed out in the text, the United States was the only OECD country with a commercially significant government stockpiling program. The empirical study of stockpiling therefore estimated different models for non-U.S. and U.S. stockpiling activity.

Equation B–2 presents the models used to explain the quarterly variation in stockpiling for twenty OECD countries. Following the economic theory of storage, the level of stocks (S_{it}) was related to the country's total supply $(Supply_{it})$, the real ex post interest rate (r_{it}), and three quarterly dummy variables. The equations also included the disruption and IEA policy period dummy variables discussed in the section "Oil Stockpiling": D_{1t} signifies the first full year of the Iranian revolution (the fourth quarter of 1978 through the third quarter of 1979); D_{2t} signifies the fourth quarter 1979 through the remainder of the estimation period; I_{1t}, I_{2t}, and I_{3t} are dummy variables for fourth quarter of 1980 and the first and second quarters of 1981, respectively, periods when the IEA engaged in an informal stock drawdown agreement. v_{it} is the residual, which summarizes how the actual stock level in the country deviated from that predicted by the estimated equation.

$$\log(S_{it}) = \lambda_0 + \lambda_1 \log(Supply_{it}) + \lambda_r \log(1 + r_{it}) + \lambda_{S_1} S_{it}$$
$$+ \lambda_{S_2} S_{2t} + \lambda_{S_3} S_{3t} + \lambda_{d_1} D_{1t} + \lambda_{d_2} D_{2t}$$
$$+ \lambda_{I_1} I_{1t} + \lambda_{I_2} I_{2t} + \lambda_{I_3} I_{3t} + v_{it} \tag{B-2}$$

Table B–3 reports the estimation results. The estimated coefficients for the disruption and IEA policy variables are reported in the text and are not repeated in the table. The estimates of the key storage parameter, λ_1, are statistically significant and vary among the OECD countries. The coefficients for the quarterly dummy variables suggest, as expected, that there is significant seasonality in the stocks held in OECD countries. The estimated coefficient for the ex post real interest rates varied among countries, being negative for half the countries and positive for the other half. The R^2 statistics indicate that the stockpiling model explains a large portion of the actual variation in stocks held in OECD countries. The Durbin-Watson statistics provide no strong evidence that the residuals are serially correlated.

A slightly different specification was used to model the privately owned stocks held in the United States—see equation B–3. The additional explanatory variable (SPR) measured the ratio of the strategic petroleum reserve to total private stocks held in the United States. Its coefficient indicates that a one-barrel increase in the strategic petroleum reserve results in a 0.47 barrel reduction in the stocks held by the private sector. As in table B–3, the estimated coefficients for the disruption and IEA policy period variables are not reported—see text for their values. The estimated coefficients for the other variables are comparable in magnitude to the results found for the other OECD countries.

$$\log(S_t) = 2.545 + (0.732)\log(Supply_t) - (0.470)SPR_t$$
$$(1.66) \quad (6.11) \quad\quad\quad (-4.60)$$
$$+ (0.437)\log(1 + r_t) - (0.045)S_{1t}$$
$$(1.78) \quad\quad\quad (-2.65)$$
$$+ (0.017)S_{2t} + (0.045)S_{3t}$$
$$(0.92) \quad\quad (2.72) \quad\quad\quad\quad (B-3)$$

(t-statistics in parentheses) $R^2 = 0.868$ DW = 2.20

Notes

1. Henry Kissinger, "The Necessity of Decision," *Department of State Bulletin*, vol. 72 (1975), p. 237.

2. Robert O. Keohane, "International Agencies and the Art of the Possible: The Case of the IEA," *Journal of Policy Analysis and Management*, vol. 1, no. 4 (1982), pp. 469–81, esp. p. 479.

3. Mason Willrich and Melvin A. Conant, "The International Energy Agency: An Interpretation and Assessment," *American Journal of International Law*, vol. 71 (1977), pp. 199–223, esp. p. 202.

4. Ibid., pp. 202–3.

5. Edward N. Krapels, *Oil Crisis Management: Strategic Stockpiling for International Security* (Baltimore: Johns Hopkins University Press, 1980), p. 3; and Keohane, "Case of the IEA," p. 470.

6. Robert J. Lieber, "Cohesion and Disruption in the Western Alliance," in Daniel Yergin and Martin Hillenbrand, eds., *Global Insecurity: A Strategy for Energy and Economic Survival* (Boston: Houghton Mifflin Co., 1982), p. 32.

7. Ibid.

8. James L. Plummer and John P. Weyant, "International Institutional Approaches to Energy Vulnerability Problems," in James L. Plummer, ed., *Energy Vulnerability* (Cambridge, Mass.: Ballinger Publishing Co., 1982), p. 260.

9. Willrich and Conant, "Interpretation and Assessment," p. 204.

10. Ibid., p. 220.

11. Computed from data reported in U.S. Department of Energy, *Monthly Energy Review* (December 1981).

12. Plummer and Weyant, "International Institutional Approaches," p. 261.

13. Ibid., pp. 261–62.

14. Organization for Economic Cooperation and Development, *Energy Policies and Programmes of IEA Countries, 1979 Review* (Paris: OECD, 1980), frontispiece.

15. All references to the treaty pertain to the document *Agreement on an International Energy Program (as Amended to 19th May 1980)*. This document contains four chapters and an annex.

16. Plummer and Weyant, "International Institutional Approaches," p. 261.

17. Willrich and Conant, "Interpretation and Assessment," p. 206.

18. Plummer and Weyant, "International Institutional Approaches," p. 263.

19. Ibid.

20. Willrich and Conant, "Interpretation and Assessment," p. 210.

21. Krapels, *Oil Crisis Management*, pp. 45–48.

22. Ibid., p. 48.

23. Willrich and Conant, "Interpretation and Assessment," p. 202.

24. See Comptroller General of the United States, *The United States Remains Unprepared for Oil Import Disruptions*, report to the Congress (Washington, D.C., 1981), esp. vol. 1, p. 41.

25. See OECD, *Energy Policies and Programmes, 1979 Review*.

26. *Wall Street Journal*, March 2, 1979.

27. Plummer and Weyant, "International Institutional Approaches," p. 265.

28. Lieber, "Cohesion and Disruption," p. 326.

29. Ibid., p. 325.

30. Keohane, "Case of the IEA," p. 476.

31. Lieber, "Cohesion and Disruption," p. 334.

32. Keohane, "Case of the IEA," p. 475.

33. See John P. Weyant, "Coordinated Stock Drawdowns: Pros and Cons," chap. 5 in this volume, for an analysis of alternative ways of implementing the July accord.

34. See U.S. General Accounting Office, "Status of U.S. Participation in the International Energy Agency's Emergency Sharing System," Report GAO/NSIAD-85-99 (Washington, D.C., June 1985).

35. See Daniel B. Badger, Jr., "International Cooperation during Oil Supply Disruptions: The Role of the International Energy Agency," chap. 1 in this volume.

36. Willrich and Conant, "Interpretation and Assessment," pp. 212–13.

37. Ibid.

38. Ibid., p. 214.

39. International Energy Agency, *Annual Review, Energy R&D, 1980/81* (Paris: IEA, 1981), p. 3.

40. Krapels, *Oil Crisis Management*, p. 21; and Plummer, *Energy Vulnerability*, p. 13.

41. Walter J. Levy, "Oil and the Decline of the West," *Foreign Affairs*, vol. 58, no. 5 (Summer 1980), pp. 999–1015.

42. Krapels, *Oil Crisis Management*, p. 5.

43. Ibid., p. 20.

44. Ibid., p. 25; and Robert S. Stobaugh, "The Oil Companies in Crisis," in Raymond Vernon, ed., "The Oil Crisis in Perspective," *Daedalus* (Fall 1975), p. 104.

45. Krapels, *Oil Crisis Management*, p. 22. A commonly held view is that the size of the 1973–1974 reduction of supply was negligible: after an initial dip, world oil output rose and, on net, was essentially constant during that period. As George Horwich has noted, however, the real measure of the disruption is the lapse from trend that occurred in 1973. From 1918 to 1973 world oil output rose 7 percent per year; from 1960 to 1973 the growth rate was 8 percent, reaching over 10 percent in the twelve months preceding September 1973. The effective loss of supply was thus 8 to 10 percent, which, given the daily world output in 1973 of 56 million barrels, was equivalent to 4.5 to 5.6 million barrels per day. See George Horwich, "Coping with Energy Emergencies: Governmental and Market Responses," Department of Energy Staff Review, May 1984.

46. The section "Oil Stockpiling" discusses private stock-management policies, including the effects of government policies and various justifications for government interventions designed to overcome stockpiling myopia by the private sector.

47. Krapels, *Oil Crisis Management*, pp. 31–32.

48. See "Oil Stockpiling."

49. The income loss suffered by consumers can be measured by the compensating variation of income: the amount of money income, at predisruption oil prices, that consumers could lose and be as poorly off as they are when the supply disruption increases world oil prices. See John R. Hicks, *Value and Capital* (Oxford: Oxford University Press, 1968), esp. pp. 40, 330–32. This concept of income loss has also been employed by Henry S. Rowen and John P. Weyant, "Reducing the Economic Impacts of Oil Supply Interruptions: An International Perspective," *Energy Journal*, vol. 3, no. 1 (January 1982), pp. 1–34.

50. As described in appendix A, the analysis assumes that domestic producers cannot expand their production to offset the decline in foreign oil supplies. Therefore, the analysis overstates the extent to which OECD oil producers can expand their production during a supply crisis.

51. The estimated consumer losses and home producer gains correspond to standard social surplus interpretations given to areas under supply and demand curves. See George Horwich and David Leo Weimer, *Oil Price Shocks, Market Response, and Contingency Planning* (Washington, D.C.: American Enterprise Institute, 1984), esp. pp. 11–15.

52. Consider the following regression, which explains the pattern of per capita income losses from the 15 percent supply disruption for the twenty-four OECD countries (the results for the other disruptions are similar):

$$Loss_i = -159.03 + 0.02\ I_i\ -163.11\ Stock_i\ +\ 371.03\ Import_i$$
$$(-2.89)\quad (5.17)\quad (-1.84)\quad\quad (24.82)$$
$$[0.86]\quad [-0.26]\quad\quad [1.33]$$
$$+\ 46.23\ EEC_i\ -39.22\ IEA_i\quad\quad R^2 = 0.976$$
$$(1.78)\quad (-1.03)$$
$$[0.24]\quad [-0.21]$$

where $Loss_i$ = per capita income loss (\$) for country i; I_i = per capita national income (\$) for country i; $Stock_i$ = ratio of oil stocks to petroleum consumption for country i; $Import_i$ = ratio of net oil imports to petroleum consumption for country i; EEC_i = dummy variable signifying member of EEC; and IEA_i = dummy variable signifying member of IEA. t-statistics are in parentheses; elasticity at sample means is in brackets for continuous explanatory variables; proportionate change in dependent variable at sample mean is in brackets for dummy variables.

53. Consider the following regression, which explains the variation across the twenty-four OECD countries in the supply cutback for the 15 percent supply disruption:

$$Cutback_i = 0.15 + 0.0002\ I_i + 1.056\ Stock_i + 0.438\ Import_i$$
$$(0.16)\quad (3.51)\quad\quad (0.70)\quad\quad (1.74)$$
$$[0.82]\quad\quad [0.14]\quad\quad [0.13]$$
$$+\ 0.113\ EEC_i\ -0.45\ IEA_i\quad\quad R^2 = 0.26$$
$$(0.26)\quad (-0.70)$$
$$[0.05]\quad [-0.20]$$

where $Cutback_i$ = per capita supply cutback for country i. See note 52 for definition of other variables and format for t-statistics and elasticities.

54. See Krapels, *Oil Crisis Management*, p. 49, for discussion of test runs where the IEA has not included prices or considered the integration of refined product trade with crude oil trade, as required by the protocols established under the treaty.

55. As described in the section "The Institutional Structure of the IEA," the IEA's accounting system is based on the assumption that total supply (defined as production plus net imports) equals final consumption. This "identity" ignores the change in stocks held by government and private parties. Before a supply disruption, total demand (the sum of final consumption, C^0, and the increase in stocks, I^0) must equal total supply (the sum of domestic production, Q^0, and net imports, M^0).

For a 7 percent supply disruption, total supply rights of IEA member countries would equal 93 percent of base period consumption: $0.93C^0$. The treaty would define actual supply as 93 percent of base period supply: $0.93(Q^0 + M^0)$. Therefore, supply rights would be less than actual supply by 93 percent of the increase in stocks that had occurred during the base period. For the 7 percent disruption studied, aggregate sales obligations would exceed aggregate purchase rights by 7.5 percent.

56. This assumption corresponds to the "complete information" case discussed by George Horwich, Hank Jenkins-Smith, and David Leo Weimer, "The International Energy Agency's Mandatory Oil-sharing Agreement: Tests of Efficiency, Equity, and Practicality," chap. 3 in this volume.

57. Two considerations suggest the following solution: have the IEA measure actual demand restraint by supply cutbacks, not reductions in final consumption. First, the philosophy of the original agreement concentrated on the sharing of physical supplies. Second, the IEA reporting procedures are more likely to measure physical supplies on a timely basis than private stockpiling activities, which must also be monitored if demand restraint were to be expressed in terms of final consumption during the base period.

58. See Badger, "International Cooperation."

59. See General Accounting Office, "Status of U.S. Participation."

60. See "The Institutional Structure of the IEA" for an analysis of the treaty, "IEA Policy Actions" for a description of past IEA attempts at coordination of consumption cutbacks, and "Import Control and Consumption Restraint" for an assessment of those attempts.

61. For a comparable analysis based on a more elaborate simulation model, see figure 2–1 and accompanying discussion in Horwich, Jenkins-Smith, and Weimer, "Mandatory Oil-sharing Agreement." For a graphical treatment of the efficiency losses of sharing, see Horwich and Weimer, *Oil Price Shocks*, pp. 182–85.

62. The analysis consolidates refined products and crude oil into the composite commodity petroleum and therefore ignores many potential problems that result from the IEA's not specifying the products demanded by home consumers.

The computations assumed that each country with purchase rights faced a price that would induce its consumers and private storers to purchase the additional quantity of oil defined by its rights. For countries with sales obligations, it was assumed that they would receive the weighted average of the purchase prices paid by countries with purchase rights. In effect, the aggregated financial losses from forced sales at below-market prices were distributed among selling countries in proportion to their obligated sales.

63. The United States fares better during large than during small disruptions because it receives relatively favorable treatment from the formula that allocates mandatory stock drawdowns among IEA member countries. This computation becomes relevant only during large disruptions. That the United States changes from a country with sales obligations in a 7 percent disruption to a country with (minor) purchase rights during a 10 percent shortfall explains why the overall gross income transfers are about the same for the 7 percent and 10 percent disruptions.

For a discussion of the allocation of mandatory stock drawdowns, see Alvin L. Alm, E. William Colglazier, and Barbara Kates-Garnick, "Coping with Interruptions," in David A. Deese and Joseph S. Nye, eds., *Energy and Security* (Cambridge, Mass.: Ballinger Publishing Co., 1981), pp. 318–22.

64. The estimated coefficient for the per capita income variable is statistically insignificant in all three regressions reported in table 2–11.

65. The estimated coefficient for the net import variable is statistically insignificant in all three regressions reported in table 2–11.

66. While the estimated coefficients for the oil stock variable are only marginally significant on statistical grounds, the estimated effects are significant on economic grounds. For example, suppose that two countries differed solely in the level of their petroleum stocks—country A stored sixty days' consumption, and country B stored ninety days' consumption. Country A's per capita net gain is estimated to be $5 greater for the 10 percent disruption and almost $14 greater for the 15 percent disruption than country B's net gain. These effects are of about the same magnitude as the average per capita net gain for IEA member countries.

67. The estimated coefficient for the dummy variable signifying EEC membership is not significant in any of the regressions reported in table 2–11.

68. See Keohane, "Case of the IEA," p. 471.

69. See Krapels, *Oil Crisis Management*, p. 116; and Keohane, "Case of the IEA," p. 475.

70. See Krapels, *Oil Crisis Management*, p. 45.

71. Ibid., p. 51.

72. Ibid., p. 110. Recall that the study of the distribution of net gains from oil sharing found that higher stocks were estimated to reduce a country's net gains.

73. Krapels, *Oil Crisis Management*, pp. 52–53. In the example Japan is concerned that additional oil it purchases from Iraq will become part of the oil shared among IEA member countries.

74. Willrich and Conant, "Interpretation and Assessment," p. 210.

75. James L. Plummer, "Energy Vulnerability Policy: Making It through the Next Few Years without Enormous Losses," in Plummer, *Energy Vulnerability*, p. 7.

76. Alan S. Manne, "The Potential Gains from Joint Action by Oil Importing Nations," in Plummer, *Energy Vulnerability*, p. 235.

77. See Lester G. Telser, "A Theory of Self-enforcing Agreements," *Journal of Business*, vol. 53 (January 1980), pp. 27–44; and Robert Axelrod, *The Evolution of Cooperation* (New York: Basic Books, 1984).

78. See Axelrod, *Evolution of Cooperation*, chap. 1.

79. See Rodney T. Smith, "An Economic Theory of Coalition Formation," Center for the Study of Law Structures, Claremont McKenna College, May 1985, section 5.

80. Ibid.

81. See Plummer, "Energy Vulnerability Policy," p. 6.

82. See Zvi Eckstein and Martin S. Eichenbaum, "Oil Supply Disruptions and the Optimal Tariff in a Dynamic Stochastic Equilibrium Model," in Thomas J. Sargent, ed., *Energy Foresight and Strategy* (Washington, D.C.: Resources for the Future, 1985), pp. 41–69.

83. For a more general analysis of import ceilings, see George Horwich and Bradley A. Miller, "Oil Import Quotas in the Context of the International

Energy Agency Sharing Agreement," chap. 4 in this volume. They show that the conclusions from the simple analysis in figure 2–3 hold for a wide range of market conditions.

84. See the section "Analytical Framework."

85. See the section "The Iranian Revolution."

86. See appendix B, equation B–1, for a full discussion of the estimation procedure and results.

87. Cabinet Task Force on Oil Import Control, *The Oil Import Question* (Washington, D.C., 1970); William D. Nordhaus, "Energy in the Economic Report," *American Economic Review*, vol. 64, no. 1 (January 1974), pp. 558–65; and National Petroleum Council, Committee on Emergency Preparedness, *Emergency Preparedness for Interruption of Petroleum Imports into the United States* (Washington, D.C.: National Petroleum Council, 1981).

88. Plummer, "Energy Vulnerability Policy," p. 7.

89. William W. Hogan, "Oil Stockpiling: Help Thy Neighbor," *Energy Journal*, vol. 4, no. 3 (July 1983), pp. 49–71.

90. Brian D. Wright and Jeffrey C. Williams, "The Role of Public and Private Storage in Managing Oil Import Disruptions," *Bell Journal of Economics*, vol. 13, no. 2 (Autumn 1982), pp. 341–53.

91. See James E. Meade, "Degrees of Competitive Speculation," *Review of Economic Studies*, vol. 17 (1949–1950), p. 44; and Robert L. Gustafson, *Carryover Levels for Grains*, Technical Bulletin No. 1178, U.S. Department of Agriculture (Washington, D.C., 1958).

92. For an extensive discussion of other policy considerations in the context of grain storage, see John P. Stein and Rodney T. Smith, *The Economics of Grain Stockpiling*, R-1861-CIEP (Santa Monica, Calif.: Rand Corporation, 1977); and John P. Stein, Emmett Keeler, and Rodney T. Smith, *U.S. Grain Reserves Policy: Objectives, Costs, and Distribution of Benefits*, R-2087-RC (Santa Monica, Calif.: Rand Corporation, 1977).

93. See Wright and Williams, "Role of Public and Private Storage."

94. For example, suppose that the marginal effect of storage on market prices is the same during normal periods and disruptions—that is, $b_t = b_{t+i} = b < 0$. Let the quantity of oil imported today be Q^t and the quantity imported during a disruption be Q^{t+i}. Then the difference between the external benefits and costs of storage would be (noting the difference in timing of gains and costs)

$$-b(Q^{t+i}/(1 + r) - Q^t)$$

This expression is less than zero if $Q^{t+i} < Q^t$ and $r > 0$.

95. Hung-Po Chao and Alan S. Manne, "An Integrated Analysis of U.S. Oil Stockpiling Policies," in Plummer, *Energy Vulnerability*.

96. Ibid., table 4–3, p. 72.

97. Compare the stock definition provided in *OECD Quarterly Oil Statistics*, no. 4 (1984), with the one provided in Article 1 of the annex.

98. See section "The Economic Consequences of Supply Disruptions and Oil Sharing."

99. Krapels, *Oil Crisis Management*, p. 69.

100. Ibid.

101. Ibid., pp. 65–68.

102. Ibid. According to OECD data, Germany held 32.3 million metric tons of stocks. Using the standard conversion factor of 7.33 barrels per metric ton, total stocks held in Germany were 236.8 million barrels. The 48 million barrels in the government program account for about 20 percent of that total.

103. Ibid., p. 73.

104. Ibid., p. 74.

105. Computed from *OECD Quarterly Oil Statistics*, various issues.

106. Krapels, *Oil Crisis Management*, pp. 63–64.

107. Ibid., p. 76. See also David L. Weimer, *The Strategic Petroleum Reserve: Planning, Implementation, and Analysis* (Westport, Conn.: Greenwood Press, 1982).

108. See data on stockpiling reported by U.S. Department of Energy, *Monthly Energy Review*.

109. Ibid.

110. See appendix B, table B–3.

111. Plummer and Weyant, "International Institutional Approaches," p. 269.

112. See appendix B, equation B–2, for discussion of the sample, specification of the model, and full reporting of empirical results.

113. Wilfrid L. Kohl, "Introduction: The Second Oil Crisis and the Western Energy Problem," in Wilfrid L. Kohl, ed., *After the Second Oil Crisis: Energy Policies in Europe, America, and Japan* (Lexington, Mass.: D.C. Heath and Co., 1982), p. 1.

114. See Stanley Black, "The Use of Rational Expectations in Models of Speculation," *Review of Economics and Statistics*, vol. 54, no. 2 (May 1972), pp. 161–65.

115. International Energy Agency, *1980 IEA Annual Review, Summary and Conclusions*.

116. *Wall Street Journal*, March 5, 1979.

117. *Wall Street Journal*, May 23, 1979.

118. *Petroleum Intelligence Weekly*, July 11, 1979.

119. *Wall Street Journal*, December 11, 1979.

120. International Energy Agency, *1979 Review, Overall Report*, p. 31.

121. Kohl, "Introduction," p. 2.

122. Plummer and Weyant, "International Institutional Approaches," p. 267 (emphasis added).

123. International Energy Agency, *IEA Review, 1979*, p. 28.

124. *Wall Street Journal*, May 23, 1980 (emphasis added).

125. International Energy Agency, *IEA Review, 1980*, p. 1.

126. *Wall Street Journal*, September 30, 1980.

127. *Petroleum Intelligence Weekly*, December 19, 1980.

128. "Still No Teeth in IEA Plans to Curb Crude Imports," *Petroleum Intelligence Weekly*, December 15, 1980.

129. *Wall Street Journal,* October 22, 1981.

130. *Petroleum Intelligence Weekly,* January 26, 1981 (emphasis added).

131. International Energy Agency, *CRD Summary Review, 1979 Energy Research, Development, and Demonstration in IEA Countries.*

3

The International Energy Agency's Mandatory Oil-sharing Agreement: Tests of Efficiency, Equity, and Practicality

George Horwich, Hank Jenkins-Smith, and David Leo Weimer

The International Energy Program agreement, which created the International Energy Agency (IEA) in November 1974, establishes a system for the mandatory sharing of petroleum during severe disruptions of oil supply. Development of the agreement was initiated by Secretary of State Henry Kissinger during the attempted embargo of oil shipments to the United States and the Netherlands by the Organization of Arab Petroleum Exporting Countries in 1973. Kissinger feared that the scramble for oil supplies would strain the Western alliance and contribute to a West European tilt toward the Arab position in the Middle East.[1] A new framework for international cooperation in the sharing of oil during oil embargoes and other supply disruptions seemed desirable; ensuring every country its "fair share" would help blunt the oil weapon. The governments of twenty-one countries, including the United States, Japan, and all the countries of Western Europe except France, affirmed this view through their membership in the IEA.

The mechanism intended to achieve "fair" distribution of petroleum during severe disruptions is the Emergency Sharing System (ESS). Once triggered, the ESS is intended to guide transactions among members leading to approximately proportional reductions in petroleum consumption. The rules take the form of calculated "supply rights," with reference to which members earn buying rights or incur

104

selling obligations. Uncertainty remains over the prices at which the transactions would be made. Critics of the ESS have argued that implementation cannot be effective unless accompanied by national price controls and trade restrictions that would cause severe economic losses.[2] One might also question the willingness and ability of the IEA and its major members to implement the ESS in the face of uncertain information and disparate domestic policies.[3]

Our evaluation of the ESS attempts to answer three questions: First, what would be the economic consequences for the United States and other IEA members if sharing were implemented as planned? Second, how do limitations in information and market control hinder its implementation? Third, in light of such impediments, what are likely to be the actual economic consequences of attempted implementation?

Our evaluation employs the oil trade model (OTM), a representation of petroleum transportation, refining, and consumption in and among regional markets of the world. The model provides estimates of the economic costs of implementing the ESS as compared with unconstrained market allocation. We simulate sharing on the basis of both complete and incomplete information about the global consumption pattern generated by the disruption and the market adjustment. We analyze both full implementation, in which members exercise their full rights to sharing, and partial implementation, in which members are constrained by, but do not necessarily invoke their full entitlement to oil under, the agreement. We try to place our use of the OTM in a realistic institutional context by reviewing past policies of the IEA and the results of ESS training exercises, including the recent allocation systems tests 4 and 5 (AST-4 and AST-5).

We believe our analysis is timely. In January 1986 the United States completed ten years of formal participation in the IEA. Having fulfilled the terms of the agreement, the United States may now withdraw after giving one year's notice. An evaluation of the ESS could, therefore, influence continued U.S. participation.

We begin with a description of the ESS, followed by a graphical representation of the welfare gains and losses.

Outline of the Emergency Sharing System

Allocation of petroleum under the ESS may be initiated by either the Secretariat or the Governing Board of the IEA whenever the collective membership or any individual member sustains or is expected to sustain a reduction of 7 percent or more in the average daily rate of petroleum consumption from that of the base year. (The base year is

105

a moving average of the four most recent quarters lagged by one quarter.) A decision by the Secretariat or the Governing Board to initiate the ESS can be overruled only by special majorities (more than simple majorities of voting weights) of the membership. (See chapter 2 for a more detailed description.)

Once initiated, the ESS requires the calculation of supply rights for each IEA member. The supply rights reflect the principle that members should reduce consumption from base-year levels by 7 to 10 percent through measures to restrain demand and that supply losses beyond those percentages should be shared in proportion to members' stockpile requirements, which are equal to 90 days' base-year net imports. The supply right of member country i can be stated algebraically as

$$r_i = (1 - DR)cb_i - [(1 - DR)CB - S](mb_i/MB) \tag{1}$$

where DR is the required demand reduction or restraint, fixed at 7 percent for estimated total IEA consumption shortfalls of 7 to 12 percent and at 10 percent for shortfalls greater than 12 percent; cb_i is the base-year consumption of petroleum products of country i; CB is the total base-year consumption of petroleum products of all IEA members; S is the total petroleum supply estimated to be available to IEA members; mb_i is the base-year net petroleum imports of country i; and MB is the total base-year net petroleum imports of all IEA members.

The determination of the buying right or selling obligation of member country i is made by comparing the supply right (r_i) with the actual supply available to country i (s_i). Actual supply is defined as the sum of normal domestic crude oil production and available petroleum imports. If the supply right is greater than the actual supply, country i has a buying right equal to the difference ($r_i - s_i$). If the actual supply is greater than the supply right, country i has a selling obligation equal to the difference ($s_i - r_i$).

While the ESS was in effect, the IEA would direct sales from countries with selling obligations to those with buying rights. The agreement requires members to take necessary measures, including legislation, to implement the directed sales. Although it states that sales should be based on "price conditions prevailing for comparable commercial transactions," the actual determination of prices could be made by the Secretariat, subject to overrule by special majority. In other words, it is possible for sharing to be mandated at prices lower than world market prices. We will argue in the next section, as Smith did in chapter 2, that it is unlikely that any country would choose to exercise its buying right unless the price were below the market price.

It is worth noting some of the practical difficulties facing the IEA because of limited information. The greatest difficulty is the estimation of actual supply (s_i) for each member. Although normal domestic production can easily be determined from historical data, current and future available imports must be based on assumptions about how the loss of crude oil supply from the world market will be distributed among the members. The determination is complicated by the fact that the domestic regulatory policies of members will influence the quantities of petroleum products actually available to them. Countries, for example, with price ceilings on petroleum products, including imported products, will suffer greater import losses than they would if they followed market pricing.

Determining the prices of directed sales will also be difficult if the IEA does not rely on spot market prices. It is not enough to determine a single crude oil price. The crude oil being transferred will vary in sulfur content, specific gravity, and other characteristics relevant to refining. Determining which types of crude oil should be transferred will be difficult in the absence of market price data. Without extensive and detailed information about the refining industry of each country, the IEA would have to rely on assessments of optimal use made by the refiners themselves. Those assessments, however, will reflect the refiners' self-interest in the face of IEA-determined prices, which will not necessarily lead to the efficient use of refining capacity that unconstrained market prices would tend to dictate.

Finally, even the use of base-year consumption and import data is potentially troublesome. These data will be influenced by economic activity and weather conditions that may be abnormal. A country that enjoyed mild weather or suffered a large number of strike days a year earlier may find itself at a disadvantage under the ESS during a disruption.

A Simple Model of Oil Sharing

The welfare losses from implementation of the ESS can be illustrated with the aid of a simple model of sharing between two oil-importing countries.[4] Figure 3–1, which plots the demand schedules of two IEA members, A and B, assumes the existence of a fixed total quantity of oil equal to the length of the horizontal axis between O_A and O_B. The quantity consumed by country A is measured from the origin on the left, O_A, with increasing quantities scaled from left to right. The quantity of oil consumed by country B is measured from right to left, starting at the origin on the right, O_B. The actual quantity available

107

FIGURE 3–1
A SIMPLE MODEL OF SHARING BETWEEN TWO IEA MEMBERS

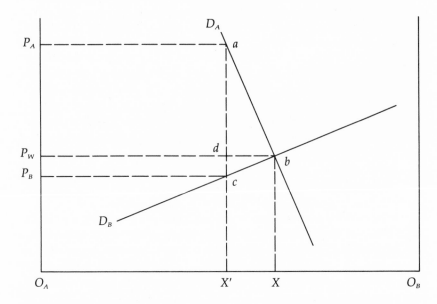

to B is the distance between the quantity consumed by A and O_B. D_A represents the demand schedule for A and D_B the demand schedule for B. The world price, P_W, is determined by the intersection of the two schedules, the distance between O_A and X representing the quantity consumed by A at the world price and the distance between X and O_B the amount consumed by B at the world price. The sum of consumption by A and B will just equal the total supply available, which is the length of the horizontal axis.

The picture of market equilibrium given in figure 3–1 may be interpreted as the free trade outcome of an earlier loss of supply. Assume that before the loss A and B consumed equal quantities of oil. After the loss A consumes more because its demand schedule is less elastic. A sharing formula, such as the ESS, that specifies sharing of losses roughly proportional to base-period consumption would require A to give oil to B so that each would again consume about the same quantity. If X' is the midpoint of the horizontal axis, A would have to transfer the quantity $X'X$ to B. The transfer from A to B, however, will raise the domestic price in A to P_A and lower the domestic price in B to P_B. The oil given up by country A thus has a domestic value equal to the area of the trapezoid $abXX'$, which represents the loss in consumer surplus in country A. In country B the

108

value of the oil received in terms of consumer surplus is given by the area of $cbXX'$. The result is a net loss in total consumer welfare represented by the area of triangle abc.

A return to free trade immediately after the transfer of oil from A to B under sharing would restore the presharing distribution. As long as P_A is greater than P_B, the consumers in both A and B could be made better off through sales from B to A. Such sales, which would continue until domestic prices returned to the presharing equilibrium level, P_W, would eliminate the losses in total joint welfare that resulted from sharing. The sharing, however, might well result in a net transfer of wealth from A to B. Assume that to induce B to buy the designated quantity of oil, A is forced to sell under sharing at a price below P_W. If, under the postsharing market response, A repurchases the oil at the market price, P_W, A will experience a net loss of wealth equal to the quantity transferred times the difference between P_W and the transfer price.

Our simple model also points to the problem that donor countries face in securing oil to meet their sharing obligations. The government of country A must offer its oil companies P_A, a price *above* the world market price, to get them to give up oil for transfer voluntarily. Government purchases at above-market prices are likely to generate domestic political opposition. An alternative would be to meet the selling obligation by drawing down previously accumulated government stocks. Inadequate government stocks or an unwillingness to use them might lead the government to expropriate privately owned oil and perhaps to allocate petroleum throughout the domestic economy.

The world is much more complicated than our simple model; various types of crude oil are transported to refineries where they are converted to products ultimately demanded by consumers. Attempts to allocate crude oil may interfere with the efficient use of refining capacity and the mix of products enjoyed by consumers. Moreover, demand restraint and sharing among IEA members will interact with the behavior of net petroleum importers who are not members. We can begin to take account of these complexities in our evaluation of the ESS using the oil trade model.

The Oil Trade Model

The OTM is a regional representation of world petroleum trade designed for the investigation of the short-run effects of oil supply disruptions.[5] The OTM divides the world into regions of supply, refining, and demand, all of which are linked by realistic geographical tanker routes and pipelines.[6] The supply regions produce specified quantities of six crude oils that vary in sulfur content and specific gravity and quantities of natural gas and natural gas liquids. The refining regions have various capacities and operating costs for seventy-six types of crude-oil distillation and downstream processing facilities that produce five petroleum products: high- and low-sulfur residual fuel oil, naphtha, distillates, and gasoline. Each consuming region has a constant-elasticity demand curve for each of the petroleum products.

A simulation using the OTM consists of finding the crude oil flows, refining activities, and pattern of petroleum product consumption that produce the largest total net economic surplus summed over all products and regions. The net economic surplus for each product is defined as the area under the demand curve from zero to the consumption level less the area under the supply schedule over the same range. This area equals the sum of producer and consumer surplus. The model solution resulting from maximization of total net economic surplus corresponds to the competitive equilibrium for fixed supplies of crude oil. A nonlinear programming algorithm is used to find OTM solutions.[7]

The starting point for our analysis is a base case representing a nondisrupted 1985 world oil market. (Sources for the data used in the base case are given in the appendix.) We determine the regional welfare implications, relative to the base case, of disruption scenarios with and without various degrees of ESS implementation. Our welfare measure is the change in regional consumer surplus in the petroleum product markets plus the change in the sum of regional crude oil revenues and refiner rents, an approximation to the change in producer surplus.

Simulations of Oil Sharing

We use the following procedure to evaluate the effects of implementing the ESS. First, we establish a predisruption base case using the OTM with supply, demand, and stockpile assumptions made by the Department of Energy for 1985. The base case provides the base-year consumption and net import data needed to calculate ESS supply rights. Second, we use the OTM to calculate consumption patterns and social surplus losses under an unconstrained market adjustment to a major reduction in supply from the Persian Gulf. The social surplus losses serve as a base line for evaluating the welfare effects of implementing the ESS. Third, we simulate the implementation of sharing and evaluate it under alternative calculations of supply rights.

We first calculate rights on the basis of the consumption generated by the unconstrained market response after the disruption. That is, the disruption is followed immediately by a full market adjustment, which produces consumption levels on which sharing is based and carried out. The IEA is assumed to know exactly what those consumption levels are. In a second scenario we calculate rights on the basis of consumption losses about which the IEA has imperfect information. The IEA simply assumes that the losses are those generated directly by the disruption, reflecting the pattern of trade between exporting and consuming countries before the disruption without market adjustments of any kind after the disruption.

In each case we use the OTM to calculate losses of social surplus resulting from the combined effect of the disruption and the sharing. We model full implementation of the ESS by restricting the consumption of IEA members to their supply rights and by providing cash consumption subsidies to ensure that countries with buying rights exercise their rights fully. Partial implementation prevents consumption of individual countries from exceeding their supply rights but does not require that consumption be raised to the supply right.

The Predisruption Base Case. Consumption of petroleum products and net petroleum imports under base assumptions are shown in table 3–1. IEA members are divided into six groups: Australia and New Zealand, Canada, Great Britain and Norway, Japan, the United States, and Western Europe.[8] Total quantities for the free world (that is, excluding Communist countries other than Yugoslavia) are also shown.[9] Under the base case total free world production of crude oil and natural gas liquids is 44.89 million barrels per day (mmb/d), total free world consumption of petroleum products is 44.69 mmb/d, and wellhead crude oil prices in the Persian Gulf range from $27.50 per barrel for heavy grades to $30.00 per barrel for lights.[10] U.S. consumption, for example, is 14.62 mmb/d, and U.S. net imports are 5.18 mmb/d. In contrast, Japan's consumption is only 4.09 mmb/d, but its net imports are 4.57 mmb/d.[11]

A Supply Disruption: Unconstrained Market Response. Our disruption scenario assumes the loss of 6 mmb/d of crude oil production in the Persian Gulf and a net stock drawdown of 1.125 mmb/d in the private sector of the free world.[12] The net loss of oil in world markets is thus 4.875 mmb/d. An unconstrained market response to the disruption is modeled by changing the base-case assumptions to reflect the production and stockpile changes and then allowing the OTM to find a new optimal solution. The disruption more than doubles crude

111

TABLE 3–1

PETROLEUM PRODUCT CONSUMPTION AND NET PETROLEUM IMPORTS:
PREDISRUPTION BASE CASE
(millions of barrels per day)

	Petroleum Product Consumption	Net Petroleum Imports	Persian Gulf Imports
Australia and New Zealand	0.66	0.45	0.39
Canada	1.54	0.08	0.00
Great Britain and Norway	1.53	−0.93	0.00
Japan[a]	4.09	4.57	2.89
United States	14.62	5.18	1.10
Western Europe[b]	8.27	8.23	5.56
Total IEA	30.71	18.69[c]	9.94
Total free world	44.69	n.a.	n.a.

n.a. = not available.
a. Net imports exceed consumption because of refinery loss and assumed stock additions.
b. As defined in note 8 (here and in all other tables).
c. Excludes net exports by Great Britain and Norway.

oil prices. For example, the price of Persian Gulf high-sulfur light rises from $30.00 per barrel in the base case to $87.28 per barrel in the disruption. Regional product prices also more than double. The price of gasoline in the U.S. Gulf Coast, for example, rises from $37.52 to $97.10 per barrel.

The reduction in consumption by region and the resulting losses of social surplus are presented in table 3–2. After market adjustment the IEA as a whole experiences a loss of petroleum product consumption of 3.33 mmb/d (non-IEA countries sustain the remaining reduction of world consumption, which, allowing for refinery loss, is 4.62 − 3.33 = 1.29 mmb/d).

The United States suffers a consumption loss of 1.84 mmb/d, which entails a loss of consumer surplus of $790 million per day. At the same time, U.S. oil producers and refiners receive a surplus of $582 million per day, yielding a net U.S. loss of social surplus of $208 million per day. Because Japan does not have significant domestic oil production, it suffers a similar loss of surplus even though its consumption is curtailed much less than that of the United States. The free world outside the IEA, which includes the major oil-exporting countries, enjoys a substantial gain in social surplus because of its net exports to IEA members. Of course, nonproducing non-IEA countries, who are net importers of petroleum, bear social welfare losses.

TABLE 3–2
REGIONAL DISTRIBUTION OF DISRUPTION COSTS UNDER UNCONSTRAINED MARKET RESPONSES

	Reduction in Petroleum Product Consumption		Change in Consumer Surplus	Change in Producer Surplus	Change in Social Surplus
	Quantity (mmb/d)	Percent	*(millions of dollars per day)*		
Australia and New Zealand	0.05	7.6	−37	12	−25
Canada	0.21	13.6	−84	88	4
Great Britain and Norway	0.14	9.2	−84	144	60
Japan	0.34	8.3	−226	−1	−227
United States	1.84	12.6	−790	582	−208
Western Europe	0.76	9.2	−457	23	−434
Total IEA	3.33	10.8	−1,678	848	−830
Rest of free world	1.29	9.2	−777	1,358	581

Great Britain and Norway enjoy welfare gains because they are net petroleum exporters. Canada also gains social surplus because it becomes a net exporter as a result of reductions in consumption caused by the higher disruption prices. The total net social surplus loss for the IEA is $830 million per day, or almost $303 billion per year.

Of the six IEA groups, the United States and Canada suffer the greatest percentage reduction in petroleum consumption, because they are assumed to have demand elasticities for petroleum products greater than those of the rest of the IEA. (Notice in table A–1 of the appendix that the geographical areas of the United States have demand elasticities equal to or greater than those of the other IEA regions for all products except distillates.) The difference in elasticities is especially pronounced for residual fuel oil because of U.S. flexibility in switching to natural gas and coal as boiler fuels. Canada has a similar advantage.

Calculation of Supply Rights. Petroleum supply rights under the ESS, calculated by equation 1, are presented in table 3–3. The left side of the table presents sharing allocations under the assumption that the consumption pattern after the disruption is determined by an unconstrained market response that is known to the IEA. The total available supply after the disruption (S in the sharing formula) is 28.60 mmb/

TABLE 3–3

PETROLEUM SUPPLY RIGHTS UNDER ALTERNATIVE ASSUMPTIONS
ABOUT AVAILABLE SUPPLY
(millions of barrels per day)

	Based on Full Market Information[a]			Based on Instantaneous Sharing[b]		
	s_i	r_i	$s_i - r_i$	s_i	r_i	$s_i - r_i$
Australia and New Zealand	0.62	0.59	0.03	0.57	0.60	−0.03
Canada	1.39	1.51	−0.12	1.63	1.51	0.12
Great Britain and Norway	1.51	1.52	−0.01	1.64	1.52	0.12
Japan	4.00	3.79	0.21	3.42	3.89	−0.47
United States	13.25	13.93	−0.68	15.23	14.05	1.18
Western Europe	7.83	7.27	0.56	6.54	7.45	−0.91
Total IEA	28.60	28.61	−0.01	29.03	29.02	0.01

a. Actual supply (s_i) and supply right (r_i) calculated after full market response to disruption.
b. Actual supplies estimated by assuming supply losses proportional to base-case imports of Persian Gulf petroleum. The supply rights differ from those based on full market information because total supply available to IEA members is greater in the immediate disruption aftermath, on which instantaneous sharing is based, than after the world market readjustment.

d, the sum of consumption by IEA members. The supply right (r_i) for each group can then be calculated and compared with actual consumption (s_i) under market response.

A surprising result, in the context of the public debate over the IEA, is that the United States in this case enjoys a buying right (0.68 mmb/d) under the formula. Japan and Western Europe each have an obligation to sell to the United States. There are three reasons for this outcome. One is the higher overall elasticity of petroleum demand in the United States than in other IEA countries. For given price increases under the free market response, the United States reduces its demand for oil more and hence has a lower supply available to it than the rest of the IEA. A second reason is the relatively smaller U.S. dependence on imports, which raises the supply right and increases in importance as the actual shortfall in supply becomes large in relation to specified levels of demand restraint.[13] Finally, the U.S. refining sector is more efficient in the sense that the volumetric ratio of petroleum product output to crude oil input exceeds that of most other IEA countries.

114

As a result, the loss of crude oil creates proportionately greater losses of product in the United States than elsewhere.[14]

The right side of table 3-3 presents an alternative calculation of supply rights based on imperfect or incomplete information. The IEA is assumed to implement the ESS without taking account of the market response to the disruption (which operates in this as in all cases). The IEA acts instantaneously on the assumption that all countries have suffered proportional losses of their predisruption Persian Gulf imports while enjoying the full benefits of their stock drawdowns. The total petroleum supply available to IEA members is 29.03 mmb/d, as determined by the assumed stock drawdown and proportionate losses of the interrupted supply without any market reallocation worldwide.

Under such instantaneous sharing the supply rights are quite similar to those of the post–market response case (in equation 1 only the S term is altered slightly owing to the absence of market-induced flows of oil between IEA and non-IEA countries after the disruption). But the regional distribution of buying rights and selling obligations to achieve those rights is necessarily quite different. The United States, with its low dependence on Persian Gulf oil, would have a large selling obligation, while Western Europe would have a large buying right. The instantaneous-response scenario corresponds to the world view most commonly encountered in policy debates about IEA sharing.

Market-based (Complete Information) Sharing. We begin our evaluation of the ESS by considering the distribution of costs and benefits resulting from full implementation of buying rights and selling obligations under the assumption that the IEA has complete knowledge of the unconstrained market response to the disruption. Given perfect information, the IEA fully implements the ESS so as to achieve the final distribution of petroleum consumption specified in the sharing formula. Members with selling obligations reduce consumption; members with buying rights increase consumption to equal their supply rights.

Full implementation of sharing. We model full implementation through a combination of consumption ceilings on members with selling obligations and cash subsidies to members with buying rights. The end effects of this procedure are domestic petroleum prices that implement the sharing illustrated in figure 3-1. Rather than being directly motivated by price increases, however, consumption in the model is physically constrained by the reduced supplies dictated by

115

the ceilings, which result in higher domestic prices. The subsidies are a de facto domestic price reduction but apply only to the incremental units of consumption.

Imposition of the consumption ceilings is straightforward. Regions that must reduce consumption below market response levels (Australia and New Zealand, Japan, and Western Europe, as indicated on the left side of table 3–3) are subjected to binding constraints on their total consumption consistent with their supply rights.[15] As supply is accordingly reduced in those regions, domestic prices simultaneously rise above market prices that prevail after the disruption and before sharing. Gasoline prices in West European members of the IEA, for example, increase about $13 per barrel above the price of gasoline in France, which is not an IEA member.

The consumption ceilings and higher prices in IEA countries will, of course, increase the losses of consumer surplus above those suffered under the unconstrained market response. Much of the loss is offset, however, by resulting simultaneous increases in either producers' rents or government revenue. If governments enforce their ceilings by imposing tariffs, the difference between domestic and world prices will accrue as government revenue on each barrel of imports and as producers' surplus on each barrel of domestic production. If the ceilings are enforced through import quotas, the difference will be realized as rents by domestic producers and importers. We will refer to these transfers from domestic consumers to their government and to domestic producers as "implied tariff revenues." Only the total of the transfers, of course, is relevant. The breakdown among receipts of governments, producers, and importers is a function of the actual use of tariffs and quotas, which is neither specified by our model nor material to our simulations.

Imposition of subsidies is somewhat more complicated. It is not possible to calculate appropriate sets of product subsidies directly from data from the case of unconstrained market response. Product subsidies must instead be found through an iterative procedure. Adjusting the subsidies in each region in proportion to the product prices that prevailed under market response, we eventually discover a complete set of product subsidies that result in the full exercise of all buying rights.

A key question, of course, is, Who pays the subsidies? Although the subsidies must be paid only on the additional quantities of consumption they induce,[16] the amounts involved can be substantial. We assume, in turn, each of two possibilities. One is that the subsidies are paid by the regions exercising the buying rights—the case if all directed sales under the ESS are made at world market prices. The total cost of the subsidies is then subtracted from the social surplus of the buying countries. The other possibility is that the subsidies are paid by the countries meeting their selling obligations. The subsidies are then treated as social surplus losses of those countries. We allocate the costs of the subsidies among the donor countries in proportion to their contributions to total directed sales under the agreement.

The distributional effects of full implementation of the ESS based on complete market information are presented in table 3–4. Notice that full implementation results in a net loss of social surplus of about $318 million per day to the IEA as a whole as compared with the unconstrained market response. This result is qualitatively consistent with the finding of Smith in chapter 2 based on a simple model of the crude oil market (ignoring the details of refining, distribution, and consumption). Our result suggests that full implementation would raise the costs of the disruption to the IEA by about $116 billion on an annual basis.

Notice also that the pattern of gainers and losers does not depend greatly on who pays the subsidies. Although Canada, Great Britain and Norway, and the United States—the oil-receiving countries—all do better if they receive subsidies (through directed sales at below-market prices) than if they pay them, only Canada's status switches from net loser ($4 million per day) when paying the subsidy to net gainer ($2 million per day) when receiving the subsidy. Only Great Britain and Norway, which are net exporters of petroleum, gain from full implementation of the ESS. Their gains result from the increased producer surplus due to an increase in total IEA consumption and in crude oil prices.[17]

Partial implementation of sharing. The picture changes dramatically when the subsidies are removed. Table 3–5 presents the distribution of changes in social surplus when supply rights are treated only as enforceable ceilings with no requirement that those with buying rights exercise them. Under such partial implementation of the ESS, the IEA as a whole gains about $57 million per day, or $21 billion per year, over the unconstrained market response. Even Australia and New Zealand, Japan, and Western Europe, which must reduce consumption under sharing (see the left side of table 3–3), are net gainers. The reason is that their consumption curtailments, unmatched by increases among other IEA countries, reduce total world demand for crude oil, depressing the world price below the unconstrained market price. (For example, the wellhead price of high-sulfur light crude oil from the Persian Gulf falls from $87.28 to $82.01 per barrel.) As a result, even though consumption in the constrained regions falls, the

117

TABLE 3-4

REGIONAL DISTRIBUTION OF COSTS UNDER FULL IMPLEMENTATION OF THE ESS
BASED ON COMPLETE MARKET INFORMATION, ALL SUPPLY RIGHTS FULLY ENFORCED

(millions of dollars per day except where noted)

	Reduction in Petroleum Consumption		Average Domestic Subsidy[a] ($/b)	Total Subsidy	Consumer Surplus Change from Base	Producer Surplus Change from Base	Implied Tariff Revenue	Social Surplus Change Excluding Subsidy	Social Surplus Change from Market Response	
	Quantity (mmb/d)	Percent							Donor subsidizes[b]	Recipient subsidizes[c]
Australia and New Zealand	0.07	10.6	—	—	−61	17	11	−33	−10	−8
Canada	0.11	7.1	57.50	6	−113	119	—	6	2	−4
Great Britain and Norway	0.14	9.2	19.92	1	−114	192	—	78	18	17
Japan	0.45	11.0	—	—	−342	0	41	−301	−87	−74
United States	1.27	8.7	47.58	39	−1,061	785	—	−276	−68	−107
Western Europe	1.02	12.3	—	—	−715	38	101	−576	−173	−142
Total IEA	3.06	10.0	—	46	−2,406	1,151	153	−1,102	−318	−318
Rest of free world	1.56	11.2	—	—	−1,046	1,855	—	809	−228	−228

a. Weighted average of product subsidies needed to increase domestic consumption to supply right.
b. Cost of subsidies distributed in proportion to donors' supply obligations.
c. Cost of subsidies borne by recipients.

118

TABLE 3-5

REGIONAL DISTRIBUTION OF COSTS UNDER PARTIAL IMPLEMENTATION OF THE ESS BASED ON COMPLETE MARKET INFORMATION, NO MINIMUM BOUNDS ON CONSUMPTION
(millions of dollars per day except where noted)

	Reduction in Petroleum Consumption		Consumer Surplus Change from Base	Producer Surplus Change from Base	Implied Tariff Revenue	Social Surplus Change from Base	Social Surplus Change from Market Response
	Quantity (mmb/d)	Percent					
Australia and New Zealand	0.06	9.1	−47	10	13	−24	1
Canada	0.19	12.3	−78	80	—	2	−2
Great Britain and Norway	0.14	9.2	−87	133	8	54	−6
Japan	0.39	9.5	−274	−1	66	−209	18
United States	1.74	11.9	−729	536	—	−193	15
Western Europe	0.86	10.4	−553	18	132	−403	31
Total IEA	3.38	11.0	−1,768	776	219	−773	57
Rest of free world	1.23	8.8	−718	1,244	—	526	−55

119

associated loss in consumer surplus is more than offset by reductions in the import bill of all IEA countries that are net importers. Canada and Great Britain and Norway, however, are net losers, relative to the free market, when sharing is unaccompanied by subsidies, because they are net exporters that suffer under the smaller increase in world prices after the disruption.

Before considering the implications of these findings in greater detail, we consider briefly how the ESS might operate without the benefit of complete information about market adjustment to the disruption.

Instantaneous (Incomplete Information) Sharing. The actual information available to the IEA during disruptions will be neither as comprehensive nor as timely as assumed in the simulations of market-based sharing. Because some oil companies will not participate in the IEA's information system, a complete picture of changing consumption and import patterns will not be available. In addition, the fact that reports are generally made monthly limits the speed at which the IEA can respond and the degree to which it can fine-tune implementation of the ESS.

To get a sense of how less than perfect information might affect implementation of the ESS, we go to the plausible alternative to market-based sharing referred to earlier. In the instantaneous sharing scenario, we assume that the IEA orders directed sales as if members were going to lose consumption in proportion to their imports from the Persian Gulf before the disruption. After market response, which occurs in this case as in that of perfect information, the resulting consumption levels are adjusted by the buying rights and selling obligations based on the instantaneously calculated losses to get new supply rights. We then calculate the distributional effects of full and partial implementation in the same way we did for market-based sharing with perfect information.

As we might expect, the aggregate IEA losses under full implementation of instantaneous sharing are somewhat larger than under market-based (complete information) sharing. They are larger because instantaneous sharing entails a greater reallocation of oil away from the actual market distribution after disruption than sharing under market-based (complete) information. As indicated in table 3–6, total IEA losses are about $373 million per day, or $136 billion per year, and only Great Britain and Norway gain in relation to the unconstrained market response.

The results of partial implementation under instantaneous (incomplete) information are displayed in table 3–7. As under market-

120

TABLE 3–6: REGIONAL DISTRIBUTION OF COSTS UNDER FULL IMPLEMENTATION OF THE ESS BASED ON INCOMPLETE (INSTANTANEOUS) INFORMATION, ALL SUPPLY RIGHTS FULLY ENFORCED
(millions of dollars per day except where noted)

	Reduction in Petroleum Consumption		Average Domestic Subsidy[a] ($/b)	Total Subsidy	Consumer Surplus Change from Base	Producer Surplus Change from Base	Implied Tariff Revenue	Social Surplus Change Excluding Subsidy	Social Surplus Change from Market Response	
	Quantity (mmb/d)	Percent							Donor subsidizes[b]	Recipient subsidizes[c]
Australia and New Zealand	0.03	4.6	48.95	1	−49	17	—	−32	−7	−8
Canada	0.29	18.8	—	—	−150	114	38	2	−10	−2
Great Britain and Norway	0.19	12.4	—	—	−139	191	28	80	15	20
Japan	−0.10[d]	−2.4	89.55	29	−299	0	—	−299	−72	−101
United States	2.67	18.3	—	—	−1,496	762	440	−294	−165	−86
Western Europe	−0.01[d]	0.0	80.64	62	−604	36	—	−568	−134	−196
Total IEA	3.07	10.0	—	92	−2,737	1,120	506	−1,111	−373	−373
Rest of free world	1.55	11.1	—	—	−1,032	1,828	—	796	215	—

a. Weighted average of product subsidies needed to increase domestic consumption to supply right.
b. Cost of subsidies distributed in proportion to donors' supply obligations.
c. Cost of subsidies borne by recipients.
d. Minus signs, denoting a negative reduction in consumption, indicate that sharing *raises* the consumption of countries with buying rights above the level generated by the free market after the disruption. This can only happen when sharing is based on incomplete information—that is, on the predisruption distribution of oil, as it is in this table. When, as in table 3–4, sharing is based on complete information (the known market-determined distribution of oil following the disruption), sharing can limit the reduction of, but not actually raise, the consumption of countries with buying rights.

121

TABLE 3-7
REGIONAL DISTRIBUTION OF COSTS UNDER PARTIAL IMPLEMENTATION OF THE ESS BASED ON INCOMPLETE (INSTANTANEOUS) INFORMATION, NO MINIMUM BOUNDS ON CONSUMPTION
(millions of dollars per day except where noted)

	Reduction in Petroleum Consumption		Consumer Surplus Change from Base	Producer Surplus Change from Base	Implied Tariff Revenue	Social Surplus Change from Base	Social Surplus Change from Market Response
	Quantity (mmb/d)	Percent					
Australia and New Zealand	0.04	6.1	−27	9	—	−18	7
Canada	0.28	18.2	−141	57	74	−10	−14
Great Britain and Norway	0.15	9.8	−96	102	33	39	−21
Japan	0.27	6.6	−168	1	—	−167	60
United States	2.32	15.9	−1,149	405	533	−211	−3
Western Europe	0.62	7.5	−341	23	—	−318	116
Total IEA	3.68	12.0	−1,922	597	640	−685	145
Rest of free world	1.07	7.6	−581	1,001	—	420	−161

122

based sharing, partial implementation yields net gains in social surplus for the IEA as a whole. In fact, because the fall in IEA consumption and the consequent decrease in the world price are both greater, total gains under instantaneous sharing exceed those under market-based sharing when supply rights are enforced only as ceilings rather than as both ceilings and targets. The fall in consumption is greater in the instantaneous case because, as noted, the reallocation of oil is greater, and the ceilings are therefore more constraining.

A comparison of tables 3–5 and 3–7 shows that the two cases of partial implementation lead to different regional distributions of costs and benefits. Under partial implementation of market-based (complete information) sharing, the United States, Western Europe, and Japan all make modest gains relative to the unconstrained market response. Under partial implementation of instantaneous (incomplete information) sharing, however, Western Europe and Japan make major gains, and the United States suffers a small loss. Similarly, Canada and Great Britain and Norway suffer substantially larger losses under instantaneous sharing. These comparisons, summarized in table 3–8, suggest that IEA members will not be indifferent to the assumptions that have to be made in the face of imperfect information.

Partial Implementation Reconsidered

Our analysis so far suggests that as long as the ESS is only partially implemented, with supply rights interpreted only as binding ceilings and not as enforceable targets, the IEA as a whole will do better than under the unconstrained market response. For at least three reasons this conclusion is highly unlikely to hold in practice.

First, the primary means of executing the ESS is the directed sale, which may be difficult to implement. If members declined to exercise their buying rights—as is all but inevitable when transactions are made at prevailing market prices—the curtailment of consumption in countries with selling obligations would have to be achieved by directed sales to the spot market. This would require such countries to bid petroleum away from their domestic consumers and sell it on the world market at a lower price, a politically dubious procedure at any time and especially in the wake of a disruption.

The directed sale is likely to occur only if companies in member countries with buying rights accept the oil and then simply reduce imports from other sources by an equal amount. Thus would partial implementation be preserved. But it appears more likely that governments would not allow private companies such complete autonomy. Instead, governments themselves are likely to exercise control

123

TABLE 3–8
GAINERS AND LOSERS UNDER THE ESS RELATIVE TO MARKET RESPONSE
(millions of dollars per day)

	No Lower Bounds on Consumption		Full Implementation, Full Market Information		Full Implementation, Instantaneous Distribution	
	Full market information	Instantaneous distribution	Recipient subsidizes	Donor subsidizes	Recipient subsidizes	Donor subsidizes
Australia and New Zealand	1	7	−8	−10	−8	−7
Canada	−2	−14	−4	2	−2	−10
Great Britain and Norway	−6	−21	17	18	20	15
Japan	18	60	−74	−87	−101	−72
United States	15	−3	−107	−68	−86	−165
Western Europe	31	116	−142	−173	−196	−134
Total IEA	57	145	−318	−318	−373	−373

124

over the incoming oil, adding it to stockpiles or allocating it at below-market price to refiners or distributors suffering "severe hardship." In this way the ESS would move toward full implementation and consequent efficiency losses for the IEA as a whole.

Second, the reduction in the world prices of crude oil resulting from partial implementation may not occur if petroleum exporters exercise market power. Under partial implementation members with selling obligations impose import quotas or tariffs to reduce their consumption so as not to exceed their supply rights. In general, their demand reductions produce an inward shift of the world demand schedule, which, coupled with our assumption of fixed quantities of crude oil supplies, results in lower world prices. If the demand reductions are achieved through quotas, however, petroleum exporters see a kinked demand curve in the world market that may offer price setters the opportunity to increase prices and profits by further reducing the quantities they supply. This phenomenon is described by Rodney Smith in chapter 2 (figures 2–3 and 2–4) and analyzed in considerable detail by George Horwich and Bradley Miller in chapter 4. The results of chapter 4 indicate that partial implementation of the ESS through import quotas could, under a wide range of assumptions, create higher crude oil prices in the world market. If this were to happen, partial implementation of the ESS would cause large losses for the IEA as a whole.

Third, our recorded social welfare losses understate the losses likely to be sustained in countries where, under demand restraints, domestic petroleum prices are raised above disruption levels by tariffs or quotas. That is, we have been reporting net losses or gains, ignoring the larger gross losses against which increased revenues to government (from tariffs) or to holders of import rights (under quotas) are netted. The larger gross losses, associated with the higher domestic prices, are a more accurate measure of the total costs incurred in moving from a predisruption to a postdisruption equilibrium. In particular, the gross loss and the absolute level of petroleum prices capture the full impact of the resource reallocation and hence the adjustment costs imposed by a disruption. For sizable price shocks, the adjustment or indirect costs are at least as large as the direct costs of the net loss of social surplus and perhaps larger.[18]

The adjustment costs result from structural rigidities that slow the movement to prices and wages consistent with economic efficiency at the higher oil prices, from the inability of the capital stock to adjust instantly to the new pattern of consumer demands, and from the possible short-run contraction of total demand as large transfers of money from petroleum consumers to foreign and domestic oil

125

producers are not immediately returned to the economy through purchases of investment and consumption goods.[19] Because indirect costs are likely to increase more than proportionately with the size of the price shock seen by consumers, such costs will not be fully offset by lower indirect costs elsewhere among IEA countries. Even if they were, they would make the ESS much more costly for members with selling obligations. Moreover, the political feasibility of raising consumer prices by quotas or tariffs during disruptions is questionable.

These considerations suggest to us that the predicted positive net benefits for the IEA as a whole from partial implementation of the ESS are unlikely to be realized in practice. Any net benefits would result from the incomplete exercise of supply rights rather than from total sharing as originally envisioned. A more direct way to reduce demand, however, would be through a system of disruption tariffs by selected IEA members. Attempting to reduce demand indirectly through partial implementation of the ESS runs the risk of a slide into full implementation, which would create substantial aggregate losses for the IEA.

Alternative Scenarios?

Whether sharing is based on complete or incomplete information and whether it is fully or partially implemented, over time it faces market forces that tend to counteract it. In the sharing case most compatible with the market solution, that of complete information and full implementation, the neglect in the sharing formula of national differences in demand elasticities alone ensures a continuing market tendency to undo ESS allocation of world supply. A full accounting of the sharing program should therefore address the character of the dynamic decision process as it unfolds in the months following a disruption.

We have made no attempt here to extend our simulations beyond the single-period horizon. To do so would be to undertake a complex task that the sharing agreement has never faced and for which its emergency manual offers no guidelines. It is safe to say, however, that immediately after an initial implementation, continued and vigorous reimplementation would be required to maintain any formula-determined distribution of oil.

The IEA might thus pursue various options. It might undertake an aggressive course of continuous implementation, during which individual countries might decide that domestic price controls and mandatory allocations were the only practical means of adhering to the prescribed, though constantly changing, supply rights. Even

126

without controls, full implementation would lock members into long-run inefficiencies. Under partial implementation, the first-order benefits could be overwhelmed by the continuing indirect costs of adjustment or by the emergence of the noncompetitive production tendencies that consumption quotas encourage.

Alternatively, the IEA could choose not to defend sharing against market forces. The problem then would be to devise methods of disengagement from the ESS.

Practical Problems of Implementation: AST-4

The IEA has conducted five major tests of the ESS. These tests were intended to acquaint key personnel in member countries with their responsibilities during actual emergencies. They were thus primarily training exercises designed to uncover administrative problems that might arise. Nevertheless, the tests can provide insight into some of the major policy issues that would have to be resolved during actual implementation of sharing.

The most publicized test, allocation system test 4 (AST-4), was conducted in the spring of 1983 and generated considerable controversy in the United States.[20] It was a retrospective simulation of a 10.6 mmb/d loss in world oil supply assumed to have occurred early in 1981. It was assumed that the United States suffered an initial loss of only 1.1 mmb/d and subsequently had to reduce consumption by an additional 1.2 mmb/d. (The disruption scenario used in the test is similar to our instantaneous response case.) The required reduction was accomplished by allowing the domestic price of crude oil to rise to $98 per barrel. Public and congressional criticism greeted a press release by the assistant secretary for environmental protection, safety, and emergency preparedness of the Department of Energy claiming that the test was a success. Although it was the high domestic price that attracted the most attention, the way the United States met its supply obligations to the IEA also came into question.

One objection was over the assumed role of the strategic petroleum reserve (SPR). At the time of the disruption the SPR would have held only about 120 million barrels, less than one-quarter its current size, but it was simultaneously receiving 500,000 barrels per day of imported oil. The administration did not want to conduct an exercise in which the president declared an energy emergency—a requirement for drawdown of the SPR or for diversion of the oil being used to fill it. Therefore, the test participants simply assumed that SPR suppliers, including the United Kingdom, an IEA member, exercised *force majeure* to stop deliveries. This reduced the supply available to the United States by 500,000 barrels per day and thus the U.S. supply obligation by the same amount.

More relevant to our consideration of the ESS was the controversy over the way the United States obtained voluntary offers from U.S. firms for sales of crude oil to IEA recipients. Firms were asked to make the offers without a clear indication of the prices at which the transfers would be made. Questions were raised about the willingness of firms to make the same voluntary offers during an actual disruption if transfer prices were below market prices.

Further, many of the firms that made voluntary offers did so under the assumption that a "fair sharing" program would be instituted to spread the burden of IEA sharing over the entire oil industry. The administration, correctly realizing that such a system could easily spread to an economywide system of petroleum price controls and allocations, assumed that fair sharing would not be necessary. If voluntary sharing were inadequate during an actual disruption, the United States would have a legal responsibility to order companies within its jurisdiction to sell oil to IEA recipients. Such directed sales might also lead to economywide regulation of petroleum. To avoid backing into domestic price controls and allocation in these ways, it is desirable that the United States meet its obligation with SPR drawdowns, now a viable option because of the larger size of the SPR. SPR oil might either be sold directly to IEA recipients or be used to compensate U.S. firms that made directed sales.

The very design of AST-4 and the recent AST-5, which also skirted the price issue, points to an unresolved policy question of fundamental importance: How will transfer prices be determined? The tests involved only quantities; there were no common assumptions about world market prices, domestic prices, or directed sale prices. During the planning of AST-4, the United States objected to the inclusion of price assumptions for fear that any artificial prices used might become standards for use in actual disruptions where they would be inappropriate.[21] Undoubtedly, fear of another political embarrassment added to the Department of Energy's resolve to block the inclusion of any price assumptions in AST-5. One must wonder whether it will be possible to agree on price during actual implementation of the ESS when it is not possible to do so for purposes of training exercises.

Conclusions

The Emergency Sharing System was an attempt to ensure that the burden of oil supply disruptions would be shared fairly among IEA members. Our analysis using the oil trade model provides several insights relevant to the policy debate over continued U.S. participation in the ESS.

First, it suggests that, contrary to the common assumption, the United States may be a net recipient of oil transfers under the ESS. If this result can be convincingly demonstrated, it may allow the United States to propose elimination of the ESS without harming its relations with other IEA members.

Second, full implementation of the ESS, in which rights to consumption are enforced by payment of subsidies, will entail substantial net costs for the IEA as a whole as well as for countries with selling obligations. Partial implementation with supply rights treated as ceilings (enforced by tariffs or quotas) but not enforced as targets may appear to lead to gains for the IEA relative to an unconstrained market response.

This conclusion has to be qualified by the general difficulties of implementing the ESS, by the possibility that partial implementation could, through the imposition of quotas, trigger noncompetitive producer behavior that would raise the world price and exacerbate the disruption costs, and by the fact that our measurements have ignored the very considerable adjustment costs due to the excess of the domestic price over the world price when tariffs or quotas are imposed. The selective use of petroleum tariffs could, moreover, accomplish the same moderating effect on postdisruption prices and costs without risking a slide into the disastrous consequences of full implementation.

Appendix

A description of the data base used in the contingency planning model (CPM) is provided in Sobotka & Co., Inc., "Documentation of Data Base for the World Oil Model," Washington, D.C., 1982. The most critical assumptions for our analysis are the regional demand elasticities for petroleum products. Table A–1 lists the elasticities used in our base case. They are based on review of the literature reported in Sobotka & Co., Inc., "Projected Price Elasticities of Demand for Use in the World Oil Model," Washington, D.C., 1982.

Projections of crude oil production by type and region for the 1985 base case were based on the data bank of the Bartlesville Energy Technology Center for Crude Oil Analysis. Other base-case data and assumptions about stock drawdowns during disruption scenarios were provided by the Energy Information Administration of the Department of Energy.

129

TABLE A–1

ASSUMED PRICE ELASTICITIES OF DEMAND

(absolute values)

	High-Sulfur Residual	Low-Sulfur Residual	Naphtha	Distillate	Gasoline
Persian Gulf and Africa	.08	.08	.10	.10	.10
Far East	.08	.08	.10	.13	.10
Australia and New Zealand	.08	.08	.10	.13	.10
Japan	.08	.08	.10	.17	.16
Latin America	.08	.08	.10	.13	.12
Great Britain and Norway	.08	.08	.10	.16	.16
France, Yugoslavia, and Finland	.08	.08	.10	.16	.16
Western Europe	.08	.08	.10	.16	.16
Eastern United States	.26	.26	.10	.14	.16
Gulf United States	.26	.26	.10	.11	.16
Western United States	.26	.26	.10	.11	.16
Canada	.22	.22	.10	.15	.16

Notes

The authors are grateful to Mohammad Amini of Southern Methodist University for computing assistance.

1. Wilfred L. Kohl, "The International Energy Agency: The Political Context," in J. C. Hurewitz, ed., *Oil, the Arab-Israeli Dispute, and the Industrial World* (Boulder, Colo.: Westview Press, 1976), pp. 246–57. Histories of the formation of the IEA can also be found in Charles F. Doran, *Myth, Oil, and Politics* (New York: Free Press, 1977), pp. 100–132; and in chapter 2, by Rodney T. Smith, in this volume.

2. George Horwich and David Leo Weimer, *Oil Price Shocks, Market Response, and Contingency Planning* (Washington, D.C.: American Enterprise Institute, 1984), pp. 181–89; and Stephen W. Salant, "The Design of a Self-enforcing Multilateral Agreement among Oil-importing Countries," *Contemporary Policy Issues*, no. 5 (March 1984), pp. 58–75.

3. It appears that the IEA has shown a preference for extensive informal negotiations rather than exercise of its formal emergency powers. See Robert O. Keohane, "International Agencies and the Art of the Possible: The Case of the IEA," *Journal of Policy Analysis and Management*, vol. 1, no. 4 (Summer 1982), pp. 469–81.

4. Our analysis is adapted from Horwich and Weimer, *Oil Price Shocks*, pp. 182–85.

5. The OTM was originally designed for use by the policy, planning, and evaluation staff of the Department of Energy by the authors, Lucian Pugliaresi, Jerry Blankenship, Steve Minihan, and Glen Sweetnam; Terry Higgins and William Johnson of Sobotka & Company; and Alan S. Manne, Constance R. Nelson, Kut C. So, and John P. Weyant of Stanford University. For a published version of the model, see Manne, Nelson, So, and Weyant, "CPM: A Contingency Planning Model of the International Oil Market," *Applications of Management Science*, vol. 14 (1985), pp. 1–35.

6. The structure is as follows. Supply regions: Persian Gulf, North Africa, West Africa, Far East, Australia/New Zealand, Latin America, Great Britain/ Norway, France/Finland/Yugoslavia, the rest of Western Europe, eastern United States, western United States, Alaska, and Canada. Refining regions: Persian Gulf, Africa, Far East, Latin America, Caribbean, Great Britain/Norway, the rest of Western Europe, eastern United States, Gulf Coast United States, central United States, western United States, Canada, Japan, Puerto Rico/Virgin Islands. Demand regions: Persian Gulf/Africa, Far East, Australia/ New Zealand, Japan, Latin America, Great Britain/Norway, France/Finland/ Yugoslavia, the rest of Western Europe, eastern United States, Gulf Coast United States, western United States, and Canada. Sea transport is by either large or small tanker.

7. The algorithm is described in B. A. Murtagh and M. A. Saunders, "Minos: A Large-Scale Non-linear Programming System," Technical Report SOL 77-9, Department of Operations Research, Stanford University, February 1977.

8. Western Europe excludes France, Finland, and Yugoslavia, which are not IEA members, and Britain and Norway, which are set out as a separate region because of their status as net petroleum exporters. Hereafter the designation "Western Europe" will include the group as defined here.

9. The Soviet Union, the People's Republic of China, and Eastern bloc countries are not dealt with in detail in the model. Rather, they account for fixed quantities of petroleum imports from, and exports to, the world market.

10. Wellhead crude oil prices are determined by the shadow price in the OTM associated with the supply constraint for each type of crude oil produced in each of the thirteen supply regions.

11. Net petroleum imports exceed consumption by the 0.18 mmb/d used by Japan in the refining process and the assumed addition to stocks of 0.30 mmb/d.

12. The loss consists of 3.87 mmb/d of high-sulfur light, 1.96 mmb/d of high-sulfur medium, and 0.17 mmb/d of high-sulfur heavy. The private sector drawdown consists of 0.19 mmb/d of crude oil and 0.26 mmb/d of petroleum products. This stock drawdown during the disruption contrasts with a stock buildup during the base period of 0.675 mmb/d to yield a net drawdown of 1.125 mmb/d. Publicly held stocks, such as the U.S. strategic petroleum reserve, are not drawn down in these simulations.

13. The gap between reductions due to demand restraint and the actual loss in IEA supply is allocated in proportion to base period imports. Because

131

the United States imports a smaller fraction of consumption than Japan or Western Europe, it bears less responsibility for reducing consumption during large disruptions.

14. The higher U.S. ratio of refined product output to crude oil input is due to two circumstances: (1) the U.S. product slate is lighter on the average and hence volumetrically greater than that of other countries; (2) the United States relies less exclusively on crude oil as refinery fuel; natural gas is also widely used. This, of course, also minimizes refinery crude oil loss.

Our simulations assume, as noted, that the United States does not draw down the strategic petroleum reserve (SPR). If the United States were to draw down the SPR faster than other IEA members draw down their national reserves, the U.S. position would be even more favorable under the ESS, because the SPR drawdowns would count in the calculation of total supply available to the IEA but not in the calculation of supply available to the United States.

David Henderson shows that the non-U.S. price elasticity of demand for oil would have to exceed that of the United States by at least 19 percent for the United States to have a supply obligation under the sharing formula. This difference, he calculates, is what is required for the market-driven reduction in consumption to reduce non-U.S. supplies sufficiently to overcome the tendency to a U.S. supply right provided by the lower U.S. dependence on imports. David R. Henderson, "The IEA Oil-sharing Plan: Who Shares with Whom?" Naval Postgraduate School, November 1986.

15. The IEA sets constraints in terms of metric tons rather than barrels. Our constraints reflect the IEA conversion rules—one metric ton of crude oil equals 7.26 barrels, one ton of residual fuel oil equals 6.66 barrels, one ton of gasoline equals 8.53 barrels, one ton of distillates equals 7.46 barrels, and one ton of naphtha equals 8.22 barrels.

16. This assumption implies that the subsidies can be targeted perfectly to induce marginal consumption without paying subsidies on the inframarginal units. Such targeting may not be practical because of limitations in information about the marginal valuations of additional consumption by individual consumers. To the extent that perfect targeting was not achieved, the subsidies would spill over to inframarginal consumption. Our analysis would then underestimate the wealth transfer effects of fully implementing the ESS.

17. The rise in total IEA consumption under full implementation is explained by differences in units of measurement between the IEA agreement and the specification of our model. OTM quantities are in volumetric units—millions of barrels per day. The ESS and our simulation of it express quantities of oil and oil products in units of weight—long tons. This stimulates countries whose supply rights require them to give up a given tonnage of oil to shift out of heavier products, such as residual fuel oil, and into lighter ones, such as gasoline. While meeting their ESS tonnage requirement, they are thus simultaneously able to raise their allowable volume of oil. The net effect is that IEA volumetric consumption rises as a result of sharing, drawing oil away from the rest of the world and thereby raising world prices.

18. For a summary of the empirical evidence on disruption costs, see Horwich and Weimer, *Oil Price Shocks*, pp. 45–47.

19. For a discussion of the adjustment process, see ibid., pp. 18–56.

20. Documents and testimony on AST-4 can be found in U.S. Congress, Senate, "Energy Preparedness Act Amendments of 1983; and the International Energy Agency Program," *Hearing before the Committee on Energy and Natural Resources*, 98th Congress, 1st session, October 19, 1983. See also William A. Vaughan, "This Is for Test Purposes Only and Has No Relationship to Real World Events," *Inside Energy*, October 31, 1983; and James T. Bruce, "Oil Games," *Inside Energy*, October 31, 1983.

21. See General Accounting Office, "Determination of Oil Price in the International Emergency Sharing System—An Unresolved Issue," GAO/ID-83-15, November 12, 1982.

4
Oil Import Quotas in the Context of the International Energy Agency Sharing Agreement

George Horwich and Bradley A. Miller

The oil-sharing agreement of the International Energy Agency (IEA) requires countries whose actual oil supplies exceed their supply rights during disruptions to eliminate the gap by reducing consumption. If the reduction is achieved through an import quota, the resulting "kink" in the world demand for imports could, under noncompetitive market conditions, cause the world price of oil to rise.[1] No serious assessment of the emergency programs of the IEA can ignore this possible perverse outcome of oil sharing.

The Emergency Sharing System (ESS) does not require countries to stay below their supply rights by imposing quotas. Tariffs, the major alternative means of limiting imports, are equally acceptable. But in conforming to a supply limitation prescribed by the ESS, countries will almost inevitably be forced to employ quotas rather than tariffs, because the supply right is expressed as a quantitative limit on consumption. The natural policy response is thus to specify the quantitative import ceiling that exactly meets the limit. A tariff, of course, is an addition to price that may or may not reduce imports exactly to the desired level. Altering the tariff in a trial-and-error attempt to bring imports precisely to the ceiling is almost certainly not feasible.

Governments will have a second reason for preferring quotas to tariffs. In the first instance both instruments will raise the effective domestic price of oil—tariffs simply by being added to the prevailing price, quotas by creating a value in the right or license to import oil. A rise in the effective price of oil will always be unpopular, but particularly so in the context of a disruption and the price rise already

134

associated with it. An effective further price rise reflecting the right to import oil under a quota, however, is less likely to be associated by the public with past or present governmental policies than a direct further rise due to a tariff.

If markets are competitive, the economic distinction between a tariff and a quota is unimportant. Both tend to raise the domestic price of the commodity and thereby to reduce domestic demand and the world price to some degree. But in a market in which individual producers exercise market power, only a tariff can be counted on to exert downward pressure on the world price. A tariff shifts the effective demand for imports to the left at all prices and creates a lower optimum price for both competitive and noncompetitive producers. A quota alters the world import demand schedule by rotating it to the left and raising its absolute slope at all prices below the kink price. For noncompetitive producers the new position of the schedule could create a higher optimum price, achieved by lowering production by an amount greater than or equal to the quota-mandated reduction.

This chapter explores the effect of quotas in a numerical simulation of the world oil market. The simulation is carried out under a broad range of assumptions about the size of quotas imposed by both the United States and other IEA countries, the elasticities of underlying supply and demand schedules, the size of an assumed oligopolistic core of oil producers, and the size of oil supply disruptions in the context of which the quotas are imposed.

The simulations yield four principal conclusions: (1) Even very small mandated reductions of imports, as little as 250,000 or 500,000 barrels per day by an individual country or a group of IEA countries, can cause the world price of oil to rise significantly. (2) Quota-mandated import reductions raise prices only up to a critical reduction level; thereafter, even in an oligopoly market, they tend to lower the world price. (3) A noncompetitive core producing as few as 2 million barrels per day and willing to reduce its output by as little as several hundred thousand barrels per day is sufficient to enable import quotas to result in price increases. (4) The greater the core size, the greater the increase in price resulting from given quota-mandated import reductions—up to a critical size of core. Beyond that critical size, which is relatively moderate, particularly during disruptions, oligopolistic solutions are unattainable.

Before proceeding to the model and the simulation, we call the reader's attention to the two occasions on which import quotas played a role in U.S. energy policy. The most important was the period of the Mandatory Oil Import Program, 1959 to 1972, during which quotas

135

limited oil imports until the world price reached the U.S. domestic wellhead price in the early 1970s.[2] While the quotas raised the effective domestic price by creating a substantial value in the import rights, there is no documented evidence that oligopoly forces succeeded in raising the world price in response to the quotas. Since the early 1970s the world oil market has, of course, changed significantly, with individual oil-producing nations, both inside and outside the Organization of Petroleum Exporting Countries (OPEC), exercising control over exports far exceeding that of any individual companies in the 1959–1972 era.

The other occasion when quotas were called into use was in July 1979, when President Jimmy Carter announced that quotas would be imposed to limit oil imports to a daily average of 8.2 million barrels in 1979, 8.5 million barrels in 1980, and 4.5 million barrels by 1990.[3] Because the world oil market then contained a number of producers who possessed and on occasion employed significant market power, economists in the Department of Energy's policy office strongly advised against implementing the president's announced import ceiling.[4] This advice appears to have been taken seriously, although natural market responses to higher prices soon reduced imports below the critical level and rendered the issue of import quotas moot.[5]

The Model

The analytical model that drives our simulation is a simple price-leader or dominant-firm formulation of the world oil market. The model's components, shown in figure 4–1, are the world demand for oil, represented by the schedule D; the supply of oil produced by price takers, or simply the competitive supply, appearing as the rising schedule S; and the marginal cost—the change in total cost per unit change in output—of price setters or noncompetitive producers, assumed to be constant, which is the horizontal schedule MC. The demand facing the noncompetitive producers, or "core" as we call them, is the portion of total demand that is not met by the competitive supply. The demand that competitive supply does not satisfy is the horizontal difference between the schedules D and S, designated the residual demand:

$$D_R = D - S \qquad (1)$$

D_R is, of course, flatter than D owing to the subtraction from D of S, a rising function.

136

FIGURE 4–1
DERIVATION OF RESIDUAL DEMAND
FACING THE NONCOMPETITIVE PRODUCING CORE
IN THE WORLD OIL MARKET

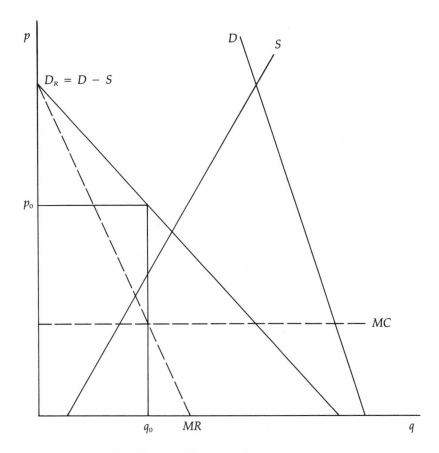

Because price setters will take account of the effect of their production levels on the market price, the relevant schedule for determining their optimum output is D_R's marginal revenue, labeled MR in the figure. MR plots the change in total revenue generated by the price-quantity combinations that lie along the D_R schedule. The intersection of MR and MC determines the profit-maximizing output of the noncompetitive core, q_0. Quantities to the right of q_0 are nonoptimal because, relative to q_0, they add more to costs than to revenues (MC lies above MR); quantities to the left of q_0 are nonoptimal because, relative to q_0, they reduce revenues more than they reduce costs (MR

137

lies above MC). At q_0 the market price, given by D_R, is p_0. At p_0 the output of competitive producers is $S(p_0)$, which, when added to q_0, will exactly equal total demand. This can be seen by reference to equation 1:

$$q_0 = D_R(p_0) = D(p_0) - S(p_0)$$
$$q_0 + S(p_0) = D(p_0)$$

A Binding Quota on Imports

We assume that a consuming nation in the model above imposes a quantity limit on its purchases that is below its current purchases. The resulting quota is analyzed first on the assumption that the imposing country is the only consumer of oil and second on the assumption that it is only one of a number of consumers. We also describe the case in which quotas are imposed simultaneously by two consuming entities.

To focus on the response of the core, we show the effect of quotas in a graphical representation of the world oil market as derived in figure 4–1. Because most actual and potential noncompetitive petroleum output is exported, the residual or net demand in the figure is directed essentially at imports and will be so characterized in what follows. In principle, however, noncompetitive output could be located in net importing countries, such as the United States, that have domestic production but negative net exports. The reference to net world demand as a demand for imports should not therefore be understood as necessarily precluding a broader interpretation.

One Buyer in the World Market. The single-buyer case is diagrammed in figure 4–2.[6] Demand D_0, a net demand for imports supplied by noncompetitive producers, corresponds to the residual demand (D_R) of figure 4–1. MR_0 is the marginal revenue associated with D_0. Before the imposition of an import restraint, imports are q_0, determined by the intersection of MR_0 and MC_0, the core's marginal cost. The world price, given by the demand schedule at q_0, is p_0.

The quota on imports is set at q_1, below q_0. The quota affects the demand for imports by preventing it from rising above q_1. The postquota demand schedule, D_1, thus coincides with D_0 up to the quantity q_1, at which D_1 becomes a vertical line. The new marginal revenue corresponding to D_1 is the prequota schedule, MR_0, up to the quantity q_1 and, since the quantity purchased cannot exceed q_1, is thereafter D_1 itself over the vertical portion. The postquota demand and marginal revenue are drawn in boldface.

138

FIGURE 4–2
IMPOSITION OF A BINDING OIL IMPORT QUOTA
IN A SINGLE-BUYER MARKET

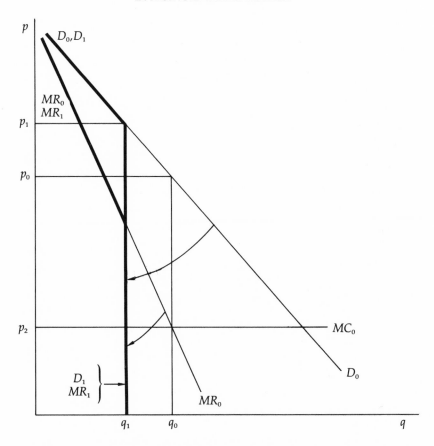

The new equilibrium, given by the intersection of the postquota marginal revenue, MR_1, with MC_0, is q_1, at which the price, given by D_1, is p_1. The price p_1 is located on D_1 at the kink—the point at which the schedule undergoes a sharp angular bend[7]—since a price-setting oligopoly, such as the core, has the option of choosing the highest price along any vertical demand segment. The effect of reducing imports through a quota or quantity restraint in a dominant-firm single-buyer model is thus to raise the price of oil received by producers from p_0 to p_1.[8]

Note that if the market were competitive and MC_0 were the competitive supply schedule, the equilibrium quantity would remain q_1, but competitive behavior would drive the price received by producers

139

down to p_2, at the height of the MC_0 schedule. The effective price to consumers, however, would still be p_1, where $p_1 - p_2$ is the market-determined value of the right to import a barrel of oil. The difference between the competitive and noncompetitive outcomes is thus not in the price to consumers but in who captures the value of the import right in oil—whether the government by its authority to issue and sell licenses, individuals to whom the government grants licenses or who manage independently to gain access to imports, or producers who exercise market power.

Multiple Buyers in the World Market. The case in which the quota-imposing country is not the only consuming country in the world is slightly more complicated but much more realistic in the price outcomes. In particular, the postquota price in an oligopoly market need no longer be at the kink price. We consider, in order, cases in which the postquota price is at the kink and below the kink, including the case in which the final price is below the prequota price.

Prices at the kink. In figure 4–3 the imposing country, assumed to be the United States, has a prequota demand of D_0^{US} net of domestic production. D_0^{US} is only a part of the total world residual demand, the initial schedule of which is D_0^T. The marginal revenue associated with D_0^T is MR_0, which meets MC_0, the marginal cost of the noncompetitive core, at quantity q_0. The price on D_0^T corresponding to q_0 is p_0.

The United States imposes a binding import quota, q_2. The postquota U.S. demand schedule, D_1^{US}, thus coincides with the prequota schedule, D_0^{US}, for quantities up to q_2 and at q_2 coincides with the vertical segment drawn there. The kink price at which D_1^{US} becomes vertical is p_1.

The world residual demand reflects the shift of the component U.S. demand by shifting an equal amount. At prices of p_1 and below, D^T rotates leftward by horizontal distances equal to those between D_0^{US} and D_1^{US}. This places D^T, a flatter schedule of much greater magnitude than D^{US}, in a leftward, but nonvertical, position for prices below p_1. The postquota schedule, drawn in boldface, coincides with D_0^T for prices above p_1 and occupies the designated position D_1^T for prices below p_1.

The marginal revenue, MR_1, associated with D_1^T coincides with MR_0 until the quantity q_1, which corresponds to p_1 on D_0^T, is reached. To the right of q_1, the lower and steeper marginal revenue corresponding to D_1^T is relevant. The two segments of the postquota marginal revenue, MR_0 for quantities up to q_1 and the lower marginal

140

FIGURE 4-3
Imposition of an Oil Import Quota by a Single Buyer in a Multiple-Buyer Market

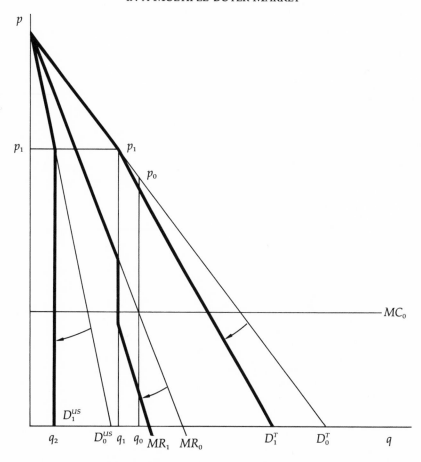

revenue schedule beyond q_1, are linked by a vertical segment. All three segments of MR_1 are drawn in boldface.

The MC_0 schedule intersects the postquota marginal revenue, MR_1, along its vertical segment. The new equilibrium is thus at the kink price, p_1, and the corresponding quantity, q_1. This is the same outcome we observed in figure 4-2, where the quota-imposing country was the only consuming unit for the commodity in question.[9] Here, however, where the quota is imposed by only one of several consuming entities, the postquota equilibrium price could be below the kink price, p_1, and even below the prequota price, p_0. The former possibility is illustrated in figure 4-4, the latter in figure 4-5.

141

FIGURE 4–4
A HIGHER WORLD OIL PRICE BELOW THE KINK PRICE
AFTER IMPOSITION OF AN IMPORT QUOTA

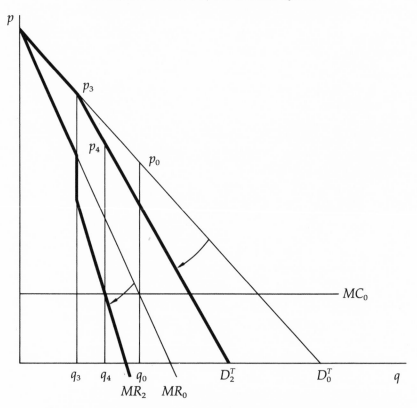

Prices below the kink. Figure 4–4 reproduces figure 4–3's prequota world demand and marginal cost schedules and their equilibrium at q_0 and p_0. Now, however, the U.S. import reduction (not shown directly in figure 4–4) is assumed to be larger than in figure 4–3, creating a kink price, p_3, in figure 4–4 greater than p_1 in figure 4–3. At the same time D^T shifts from D_0^T to D_2^T, farther than its previous shift to D_1^T. The intersection in figure 4–4 of MC_0 and MR_2, the marginal revenue schedule for D_2^T, creates a postquota equilibrium along the lower downward segment of MR_2 at a quantity q_4 and a corresponding price p_4. Although p_4 is above the prequota price, p_0, it is below the kink price, p_3.

The major difference between the schedules of figure 4–5 and figure 4–4 is that the schedules of the former are nonlinear. The portrayal of the market in figure 4–5 thereby conforms to the actual

142

FIGURE 4–5
DECREASE OF THE WORLD PRICE RESULTING FROM IMPOSITION OF AN OIL IMPORT QUOTA

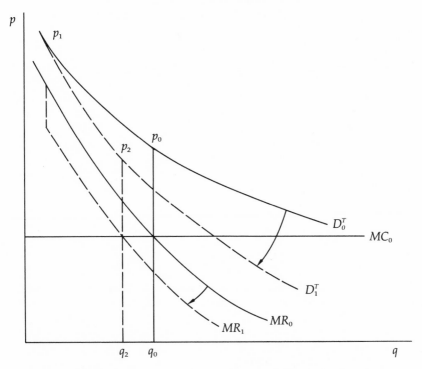

formulation of the simulation model as described in the appendix.[10] Now an initial equilibrium at p_0 and q_0 is upset by the imposition of an import quota, which creates a kink at p_1 on the initial net demand schedule, D_0^T, and generates a new quota-constrained demand, D_1^T. The new marginal revenue is MR_1, lying below or to the left of the initial schedule, MR_0, and intersecting the given marginal cost, MC_0, at q_2. When projected to D_1^T, the quantity q_2 corresponds to a new market price, p_2, below p_0.

As we shall learn from our simulations below, price reductions following quota-mandated import curtailments occur when a sufficiently large, critical size of curtailment is reached. The smaller the core size and any supply disruptions occurring just before the import restriction and the greater the absolute elasticity of residual or net demand, the smaller is the critical size of curtailment.

In intuitive terms the price falls when the mandated import reduction is so great as to create a sufficiently high kink price and thereby,

143

in the vicinity of the prequota equilibrium, a leftward horizontal shift that dominates the increased absolute slope of the curve (as in figure 4–5). The opposite case of a price increase results from a kink price nearer to the prequota price and a demand shift in which the increased absolute slope of the curve is not overwhelmed by its leftward horizontal movement (as in figures 4–3 and 4–4).

Note in figure 4–5 that the reduction in core output from q_0 to q_2 is *less* than the quota-mandated reduction in imports, which is equal to the horizontal distance between the demand schedules D_0^T and D_1^T at the initial price, p_0. When the quota raises the world price in a multiple-buyer market, however, the core cutback *exceeds* the mandated import reduction. This can be seen in figures 4–3 and 4–4, where, at the initial price, p_0, the mandated reduction is the horizontal distance between the initial demand schedule, D_0^T, and D_1^T and D_2^T, respectively. The core cutback is the distance between the beginning and ending output, $q_0 - q_1$ in figure 4–3 and $q_0 - q_4$ in figure 4–4, both of which exceed the demand shift. As one would expect, given a leftward shift of demand, the underlying reduction of the supply quantity must exceed the demand shift if price is to rise and conversely if price is to fall.

Numerical Example of an Import Quota in a Multiple-Buyer Noncompetitive Market. We turn now to a numerical illustration of the effects of a quota-mandated reduction in world imports on the profits and production of noncompetitive producers and thereby on the world price of oil. The hypothetical data, presented in table 4–1, are drawn from our numerical simulations, described below.

The first line in the table presents prequota equilibrium data for the world oil market.[11] The total profits in column 8 are the product of 0.365 and the entries in columns 5 and 7. The assumed price elasticities of the underlying supply and demand are characteristic of short-run behavior: the elasticity of aggregate demand is -0.15, that of competitive supply zero. These translate into a price elasticity of residual demand of -1.66 at the beginning equilibrium price and quantity (see appendix, equation A–3).

We illustrate the effect of a U.S. quota-mandated reduction in imports of 500,000 barrels per day. The second line of entries in the table shows the effect in the absence of any supply response by the core producers and hence in total world output. The reduction in U.S. imports from 4.50 to 4.00 million barrels per day, world output remaining constant, forces imports of all other consuming countries to rise by an equal amount. The net effect is essentially that of the competitive model, where a fall in demand is traced along a vertical

144

TABLE 4-1

EXAMPLE OF THE EFFECT OF A U.S. QUOTA-MANDATED IMPORT REDUCTION OF 500,000 BARRELS PER DAY IN A NONCOMPETITIVE WORLD OIL MARKET

| | Price (p) ($/barrel) (1) | Imports (mmb/d) | | | Exports (mmb/d) (5) | Noncompetitive Producers | | |
		United States (2)	Other (3)	Total (4)		Marginal cost (MC) ($/barrel) (6)	Profit (p) – (MC) ($/barrel) (7)	Profits[a] ($ billions per year) (8)
Pre–U.S. quota	29.00	4.50	10.90	15.40	4.00	11.58	17.42	25.43
Post–U.S. quota								
Total output constant	25.94	4.00	11.40	15.40	4.00	11.58	14.36	20.97
−1.15 mmb/d	33.57	4.00	10.32	14.32	2.85	11.58	21.99	22.91
				$(-1.08)^b$	(−1.15)			(+1.94)

NOTE: mmb/d = millions of barrels per day.

a. Based on nonrounded underlying data.

b. Total world output is reduced by 1.15 mmb/d, which is the core's cutback in production (see column 5), but world exports and hence imports fall by only 1.08 mmb/d. The smaller reduction in exports and imports is due to a 0.06 mmb/d reduction in consumption by OPEC countries in response to the quota-induced price rise (the difference between [1.15 − 0.06] and 1.08 is due to rounding). The reduction in consumption increases available exports equally because, apart from the core's contraction, OPEC output and world output are constant.

SOURCE: Authors' computer simulation of model as described in text and appendix.

145

aggregate supply schedule. The world market-clearing price falls to $25.94, and core profits drop to $14.36 per barrel and to $20.97 billion per year.

Facing a leftward rotation of both its demand and its marginal revenue schedules, however, the core reduces its exports and output by 1.15 million barrels per day (see, for example, in figure 4–4 the output contraction from q_0 to q_4).[12] The third row of the table shows that the drop in output raises the world price to $33.57 per barrel and the increase in price reduces non-U.S. imports to 10.32 million barrels per day. With core exports down but the profit margin up, the core's total profits are $22.91 billion per year—9.3 percent higher than they were before the core curtailed its exports.

Two Simultaneous Import Quotas in a Multiple-Buyer Market. Our simulations of import restrictions in the world oil market feature, as a general case, the imposition of quotas by two consuming countries (or groups of countries) simultaneously. Countries tend, of course, to have different consumption levels, different supply rights, and different import reduction goals. Countries restricting imports thereby tend to create different kink prices in their individual demands. The import quotas of two component countries are thus reflected in the market demand schedule in two kinks, one each at the height of the kink price of each quota-imposing country.

The economic effect of two simultaneous binding import quotas is derived mathematically in the appendix. In geometric terms, as constructed in figure 4–6, the two countries' kink prices (p_1 and p_2), when projected onto the demand schedule facing the core, divide that schedule into three segments, two of which are to the left of the original (prequota) schedule. The uppermost segment, above and to the left of the higher of the two kinks, p_1, is a section of the original demand schedule, D_0^T. Moving down and to the right, a second postquota demand segment lies on the demand curve D_1^T, formed when the country having the higher kink imposes its quota. The third segment begins at the lower kink price, p_2, and lies on D_2^T, which differs from D_0^T by the horizontal subtraction of the import reductions of both quota-imposing countries.

The marginal revenue corresponding to this segmented postquota demand itself has three downward-sloping segments. Each successive pair of marginal revenue segments (the first and second and the second and third) is connected by vertical lines.

Market equilibrium is determined by the intersection of the core's marginal cost, MC_0, with the postquota marginal revenue. That inter-section can occur at any quantity at or to the right of the uppermost

FIGURE 4-6
Simultaneous Imposition of Oil Import Quotas by Two Consuming Entities

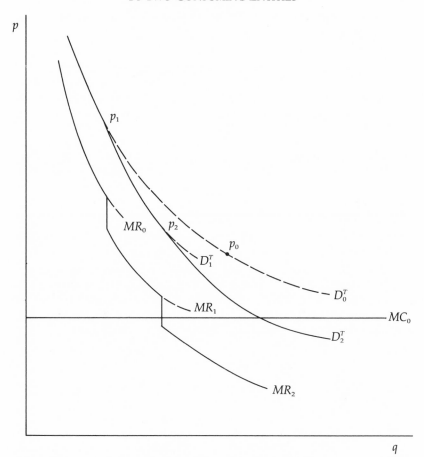

kink on either of the marginal revenue's two vertical or two lower downward segments. In the figure MC_0 meets the marginal revenue on its lower vertical section, for which the market price is p_2.

Do Oil-receiving Countries Offset the Kinked Demand Curve? A final question we address is whether countries that receive oil under the sharing program may respond in such a way as to offset the rotation and kink in the world import demand schedule introduced by quota-imposing donor countries. Such an offset will not occur because oil received either will meet, at the prevailing price, demand

147

that existed but was unsatisfied (owing, say, to market imperfections) or will be sold at an appropriately lower price, reflecting a movement down along the existing previously satisfied demand. In neither case is the world demand schedule moved or dislodged; it retains the kink and rotation imposed by the quota-mandated import reductions of donor countries.

Specification of the Model

The model described in general terms in figures 4–1 though 4–6 is specified for the numerical simulations as follows.

Sectors, Quantities, Prices. The world oil market, defined as excluding the Communist countries, is divided into five sectors. Three of them—the United States, other IEA countries, and the rest of the world outside OPEC and the IEA—are consumers, producers, and net importers of oil, as indicated in table 4–2. OPEC, which includes a subsector, the noncompetitive core, is a consumer, producer, and net exporter. The core is a producer and exporter but does not consume any oil.

Total world consumption and production of 44.4 million barrels per day are divided among the sectors as shown in the table. The United States consumes slightly more than all other IEA members but produces more and imports less. The rest of the world, outside IEA

TABLE 4–2

INITIAL CONSUMPTION, PRODUCTION, AND NET IMPORTS OR EXPORTS
FOR MAJOR REGIONS OF THE WORLD-OIL-MARKET SIMULATION MODEL
(millions of barrels per day)

	Consumption	Production	Net[a]
United States	14.7	10.2	4.5
Rest of IEA	14.1	6.0	8.1
OPEC total	2.9	18.3	−15.4
Core[b]	—	2, 4, or 6	−2, −4, or −6
Rest of the world	12.7	9.9	2.8
Total	44.4	44.4	0.0

a. Imports, if positive; exports, if negative.
b. Core (noncompetitive) production of 2, 4, or 6 million barrels per day is assumed to come entirely out of OPEC production. All core output is assumed to be exported.
SOURCE: Authors' assumptions.

and OPEC, is a relatively small net importer. The consumption of OPEC is small. Its total production, 18.3 million barrels per day, is divided between a competitive supply and the noncompetitive core, which is assumed to produce and export—in alternative prequota scenarios—2, 4, and 6 million barrels per day. This places the initial competitive output of OPEC at 16.3, 14.3, and 12.3 million barrels per day, respectively, and its initial competitive exports at 13.4, 11.4, and 9.4 million barrels per day.

In the simulations all demands, net of competitive supply, are summed to yield the net demand facing the core. The initial market quantity will be 2, 4, or 6 million barrels per day, equal, in each case, to the assumed size of the core. In all cases the initial predisruption, prequota price is $29.00 per barrel. The marginal cost is taken as equal to the value of the marginal revenue implied by the beginning price-output equilibrium. For example, if the core size is 2 million barrels per day, marginal cost will be set equal to the value of the marginal revenue at that quantity. In the absence of disruptions of world supply, marginal cost, its value so determined, will remain constant at all other quantities in response to quota-induced import-demand reductions.

All sector demands are assumed to be price-isoelastic, taking on elasticities of -0.10, -0.15, and -0.20 in alternative scenarios. All sector demand elasticities are the same in any simulation. Competitive supplies are also price-isoelastic and the same, in any simulation, for all sectors. Alternative supply elasticities are 0.00, 0.05, and 0.22.

Disruptions. In addition to describing import quotas in a nondisruption base case, the simulations carry out import restrictions under alternative disruptions in world supply of 3, 5, and 8 million barrels per day. These losses are assumed to come entirely out of the competitive component of OPEC supply and to reflect the ex post reduction in the world total after allowing for competitive supply responses to the resulting price increases. In terms of the basic model in figure 4–1, the disruption can be thought of as a leftward shift of the competitive supply, causing the residual demand (the demand facing the core) to shift upward or to the right. Marginal revenue will also tend to shift upward or to the right of its position before the disruption. Because our demand and competitive supply are isoelastic and not linear, however, the slopes of the demand schedules will change after a disruption, causing marginal revenue in some cases to shift downward or to the left of its predisruption position and in some instances to become negative. We return to this possibility in our discussion of alternative elasticities below.

The core size is assumed to be unaffected by disruptions. Holding core size constant facilitates our analysis of the price effects of other variables. But it means that the core's marginal cost must also shift after a disruption, taking on the value of the marginal revenue after the disruption at the unchanged core size. In all but a few cases marginal cost, like marginal revenue, will thus rise after a disruption, though remaining constant thereafter at its higher level in response to quota-mandated import curtailments.

Although the change in marginal cost is a mechanical outcome of the functioning of the model, any increase in marginal cost after a disruption can be rationalized economically in either of two ways: (1) We can assume that the disruption in fact affects both competitive and core OPEC production but that the core is reconstituted to its predisruption size by adding the production of other OPEC producers whose marginal costs increase with increasing output. This replacement core output leaves the core as a whole with higher marginal costs. (2) Alternatively, we can assume that the higher price of oil after a disruption is expected to persist indefinitely. The user-cost component, which is that part of marginal cost reflecting the opportunity cost of producing an exhaustible resource in the present instead of the future, accordingly pushes marginal cost upward.

Those few cases in which the disruption lowers marginal revenue at the core size are assumed, as in all other cases, to affect marginal cost equally.[13] We make no attempt to justify this postdisruption fall in cost economically. We incorporate it mechanically as a useful simplifying assumption that facilitates our analysis of quota-mandated import reductions. Whether core marginal cost rises or falls as a result of a disruption, we assume it remains constant in response to subsequent import quotas.

Simulation Results

We begin our simulations by examining the effect of import restrictions in the nondisrupted world market. Table 4–3 presents the world price of oil resulting from quota-mandated reductions in imports imposed alone, as well as simultaneously, by the United States and by all other IEA members acting collectively. Import curtailments proceed from zero to 2.5 million barrels per day by increments of 0.25 million barrels per day (except for the last 0.50 million barrels). Each cell, defined by a pair of import reductions, records the optimum or profit-maximizing world price of oil occurring under each of three assumed prequota core sizes and the given import restrictions. The

150

prequota price is $29.00 per barrel for all three core sizes of 2, 4, and 6 million barrels per day.

All regional demands, and hence aggregate demand, have price elasticities of -0.15; all competitive supply elasticities are 0.00. These are short-run elasticities that we take as our base case. They imply an elasticity of the demand facing the core at the initial equilibrium price and quantity of -3.33, -1.66, and -1.11 for core sizes of 2, 4, and 6 million barrels per day, respectively.[14] While the absolute demand elasticity in table 4–3 is greater than the lowest demand elasticity in our simulations, -0.10, we consider -0.15 a somewhat more realistic approximation to the elasticity prevailing in the several months following a disruption, when IEA sharing is likely to be introduced. The greater demand elasticity may also be regarded as incorporating some positive elasticity of competitive supply and the effect of stock drawdown, both of which raise the elasticity of the residual, or net, demand curve.

Single-Country Import Reductions. If only the United States imposes a quota reducing imports 0.25 million barrels per day, the world price of oil rises to $30.70, $32.51, and $32.51 again for each of the successively larger prequota core sizes. These prices result from decreases in core output in response to the quota-induced shift of demand and marginal revenue. The postquota core production or export levels at which marginal cost is equal to the reduced marginal revenue are 1.50, 3.25, and 5.25 million barrels per day for the prequota cores of 2, 4, and 6 million barrels per day, respectively.

A U.S. import reduction of 0.50 million barrels per day, while other countries continue not to impose a quota, creates a lower optimum world price of $29.65 for the core size of 2 million barrels per day. The cores of 4 and 6 million barrels per day, however, yield prices of $33.57 and $36.53 per barrel, respectively, which are higher than the prices for the smaller import curtailment. Postquota core outputs for the cores of 2, 4, and 6 million barrels per day are, in order, 1.40, 2.85, and 4.49 million barrels per day.

For the core of 2 million barrels per day, the price continues to fall as imports are further restricted. At an import reduction of 0.75 million barrels per day, the price is $28.66, below the $29.00 prequota price. For the core of 4 million barrels per day, the price peaks at $33.57 at a restriction of 0.50 million barrels per day but remains above the prequota level until the restriction is 1.50 million barrels per day (and the price is $28.15). When core size is 6 million barrels per day, the highest price reached is $39.11 in response to an import reduction of 0.75 million barrels per day.

151

TABLE 4–3

SIMULATED WORLD PRICE OF OIL RESULTING FROM MANDATED IMPORT REDUCTIONS BY THE UNITED STATES AND OTHER IEA COUNTRIES, WORLD OIL SUPPLY NONDISRUPTED

(dollars per barrel)

U.S. Mandated Import Reduction[a]	Core Size[a]	Rest of IEA Mandated Import Reduction[a]									
		0.00	0.25	0.50	0.75	1.00	1.25	1.50	1.75	2.00	2.50
0.00	2.00	29.00	30.55	29.53	28.56	27.65	26.78	25.95	25.17	24.43	23.05
	4.00	29.00	32.67	33.15	31.71	30.36	29.10	27.91	26.80	25.75	23.83
	6.00	29.00	32.67	36.89	38.11	35.86	33.78	31.85	30.05	28.38	25.38
0.25	2.00	30.70	32.51	32.51	31.37	29.36	27.54	25.91	24.43	23.08	20.75
	4.00	32.51	32.67	33.15	32.51	32.51	32.51	32.51	32.51	32.51	27.58
	6.00	32.51	32.67	36.89	38.11	35.86	33.78	32.51	32.51	32.51	32.51
0.50	2.00	29.65	32.67	31.37	29.36	27.54	25.91	24.43	23.08	21.86	—
	4.00	33.57	33.57	36.53	36.53	36.53	36.53	35.56	32.56	29.92	25.52
	6.00	36.53	36.53	36.89	38.11	36.53	36.53	36.53	36.53	36.53	36.53
0.75	2.00	28.66	31.37	29.36	27.54	25.91	24.43	23.08	21.86	20.75	—
	4.00	32.08	32.67	36.89	41.12	38.98	35.56	32.56	29.92	27.58	23.67
	6.00	39.11	39.11	39.11	41.12	41.12	41.12	41.12	41.12	41.12	38.97

1.00	2.00	27.72	29.36	27.54	25.91	24.43	23.08	21.86	20.75	—	—
	4.00	30.68	32.67	36.89	38.98	35.56	32.56	29.92	27.58	25.52	22.03
	6.00	36.75	36.75	36.89	41.75	46.39	46.39	46.39	46.39	43.99	34.64
1.25	2.00	26.83	27.54	25.91	24.43	23.08	21.86	20.75	—	—	—
	4.00	29.37	32.67	36.89	35.56	32.56	29.92	27.58	25.52	23.67	20.56
	6.00	34.56	34.56	36.89	41.75	47.36	52.44	49.84	43.99	38.97	30.90
1.50	2.00	25.99	25.91	24.43	23.08	21.86	20.75	—	—	—	—
	4.00	28.15	32.67	35.56	32.56	29.92	27.58	25.52	23.67	22.03	19.24
	6.00	32.54	32.67	36.89	41.75	47.36	49.84	43.99	38.97	34.64	27.65
1.75	2.00	25.19	24.43	23.08	21.86	20.75	—	—	—	—	—
	4.00	27.00	32.67	32.56	29.92	27.58	25.52	23.67	22.03	20.56	18.05
	6.00	30.65	32.67	36.89	41.75	47.36	43.99	38.97	34.64	30.90	24.83
2.00	2.00	24.43	23.08	21.86	20.75	—	—	—	—	—	—
	4.00	25.91	32.56	29.92	27.58	25.52	23.67	22.03	20.56	19.24	16.97
	6.00	28.91	32.67	36.89	41.75	43.99	38.97	34.64	30.90	27.65	22.36
2.50	2.00	23.02	20.75	—	—	—	—	—	—	—	—
	4.00	23.94	27.58	25.52	23.67	22.03	20.56	19.24	18.05	16.97	15.11
	6.00	25.78	32.67	36.89	38.97	34.64	30.90	27.65	24.83	22.36	18.31

NOTE: Dashes indicate an unattainable equilibrium. All prices assume elasticity of demand of −0.15; of supply, 0.00.

a. Millions of barrels per day.

SOURCE: Computer simulation of model.

153

A pattern similar to that created by the United States, though tending to slightly lower prices, emerges from import curtailments imposed by all other IEA countries acting as a unit.[15] When the United States imposes no restraints on imports, import restrictions by other IEA countries create maximum prices of $30.55, $33.15, and $38.11 under core sizes of 2, 4, and 6 million barrels per day, respectively (table 4–3). The respective core outputs at these prices are 1.51, 2.90, and 4.03 million barrels per day.

Joint Import Quotas. When both the United States and the other IEA countries simultaneously restrict imports, significantly higher prices may result. The table indicates a maximum price of $52.44 for the entire table when both sectors reduce imports by 1.25 million barrels per day against a core size of 6 million barrels per day. Additional import cutbacks for the same core size create prices that are lower than the peak but still above the prequota price of $29.00, until import curtailments of 2 million barrels per day by each sector are reached. For a core size of 4 million barrels per day, a maximum price of $41.12 is produced by equal import reductions of 0.75 million barrels per day. For a core of 2 million barrels per day, the maximum price, $32.67, occurs at a reduction of 0.50 million barrels per day by the United States and 0.25 million barrels per day by the other IEA countries. Thereafter larger import restraints depress the price to a low of $20.75 for various restraint combinations. Whenever import reductions by both sectors totaling 3 million barrels per day or more are imposed on the core of 2 million barrels per day, the new equilibrium requires the core to reduce output by 2 million barrels per day or more and hence is unattainable. The entries in the table for those cases are dashes. The market price in these situations, essentially competitively determined, would be the price at which the demand facing the core went to zero.

Alternative Elasticities. The ability of given import reductions to raise the world price depends on the elasticity of the demand facing the core. At a given demand price and quantity, the greater the absolute elasticity, the flatter will be the demand schedule—both prequota and postquota—and the less will given import curtailments succeed in raising the world price.

Our base-case elasticity of -0.15 for aggregate demand and 0.00 for competitive supply is intended as an approximation to price-induced behavioral responses occurring in a time interval relevant to oil sharing under the ESS. As time passes, however, absolute supply and

154

demand elasticities can both be expected to rise, raising the absolute elasticity of residual (core) demand and dampening the price increases attributable to given import cutbacks. In shorter periods of, say, less than two months, the lower demand elasticity of -0.10 might be relevant. This is particularly likely if the postdisruption response is characterized by buildup, rather than drawdown, of stocks. Adding to stocks shifts the demand schedule to the right, creating a steeper and less elastic demand path between successively higher prices.

Net demand elasticity. The entries of table 4–4 show, for all possible combinations of our assumed competitive supply and aggregate demand elasticities and for each disruption size, the elasticity of residual or net demand facing each core size at the beginning price and quantity equilibrium. For given core and disruption size, the greater the sum of the assumed absolute supply and demand elasticities, the greater the resulting net demand elasticity into whose determination the component elasticities enter additively (see appendix, equation A–3). The top three rows of the table, in which import quotas are imposed on the nondisrupted world market, constitute the case we have been analyzing thus far.

The table indicates that the absolute net demand elasticity varies inversely with both core size and disruption size. This can be seen directly in appendix equation A–3, the net demand elasticity expression. I, the net import demand quantity, which is equal to core size, enters the denominator and thus affects the absolute elasticity inversely.[16] S, the magnitude of competitive supply, out of which disruptions come, affects the absolute elasticity positively, implying that disruption size, with which S varies inversely, also has an inverse effect on the absolute elasticity.[17]

In the somewhat more intuitive terms of the market picture of figure 4–1, both an increase in core size and a disruption of supply are reflected in a leftward shift of competitive supply accompanied by an equal rightward shift of residual demand. Because supply, by assumption, retains its given elasticity after any such shift, the elasticity expression indicates that the slope of the schedule must increase since its quantities are less than they were before the shift.[18] Net demand reflects this change in competitive supply and itself becomes steeper.[19] Prescribed reductions in imports are thus traced along a steeper postquota demand schedule, causing greater price increases than occur under smaller core or disruption sizes. While our simulations show that lower elasticity and steeper demand do not ensure that price *declines* resulting from given quotas are less than under greater elasticity, the *spread* between the high and low prices—for the

155

TABLE 4–4
Net Import Demand Elasticities for Various Sizes of Noncompetitive Producing Core and Supply Disruptions
(elasticities at postdisruption, prequota equilibrium price)

					Demand Elasticity						
		Core size 2[a]			Core size 4[a]			Core size 6[a]			
Disruption Size[a]	Supply Elasticity	-0.10	-0.15	-0.20	-0.10	-0.15	-0.20	-0.10	-0.15	-0.20	
0	0.00	-2.22	-3.33	-4.44	-1.11	-1.66	-2.22	-0.74	-1.11	-1.48	
	0.05	-3.28	-4.39	-5.50	-1.61	-2.17	-2.72	-1.06	-1.43	-1.80	
	0.22	-6.88	-7.99	-9.10	-3.33	-3.89	-4.44	-2.15	-2.52	-2.89	
3	0.00	-2.07	-3.10	-4.14	-1.03	-1.55	-2.07	-0.69	-1.03	-1.38	
	0.05	-3.05	-4.09	-5.12	-1.50	-2.02	-2.54	-0.98	-1.33	-1.67	
	0.22	-6.40	-7.44	-8.47	-3.09	-3.61	-4.13	-1.99	-2.33	-2.68	
5	0.00	-1.97	-2.95	-3.94	-0.98	-1.48	-1.97	-0.66	-0.98	-1.31	
	0.05	-2.90	-3.89	-4.87	-1.43	-1.92	-2.41	-0.93	-1.26	-1.59	
	0.22	-6.08	-7.07	-8.05	-2.93	-3.42	-3.92	-1.88	-2.21	-2.54	
8	0.00	-1.82	-2.73	-3.64	-0.91	-1.36	-1.82	-0.61	-0.91	-1.21	
	0.05	-2.68	-3.59	-4.50	-1.31	-1.77	-2.22	-0.86	-1.16	-1.47	
	0.22	-5.60	-6.51	-7.42	-2.69	-3.15	-3.60	-1.72	-2.02	-2.33	

a. Millions of barrels per day.
Source: Computer simulation of model.

same size of core, disruption, and quotas—is invariably reduced as net demand elasticity increases.

Negative marginal revenue and the limitation on core size. All but 11 of the 108 net demand elasticities in table 4–4 are greater (in absolute value) than one; some are much greater, especially for smaller core sizes. Thus even while competitive supply and aggregate demand elasticities in the world oil market may be quite low, the net demand elasticity facing noncompetitive core producers may be quite high.[20] Indeed, unless the absolute net demand elasticity exceeds unity, marginal revenue is negative, and an equilibrium for noncompetitive producers does not exist.[21]

Since marginal revenue is a declining function, the cases of negative marginal revenue will tend to be generated not only by low elasticities of net demand and hence of competitive supply and aggregate demand but by larger core sizes. Nine of the eleven cases of inelastic net demand and negative marginal revenue in table 4–4 occur under our largest core size, 6, in combination with the lower range of demand elasticities (-0.10 and -0.15) and supply elasticities (0.00 and 0.05) in both disrupted and nondisrupted markets. Two cases of negative marginal revenue occur under core size 4 and the lowest combination of demand and supply elasticities (-0.10, 0.00) at the two highest disruption levels (5 and 8 million barrels per day). We conclude that noncompetitive producers must remain below a relatively small maximum size if, under plausible short-term elasticities, they are to be viable players in the world oil market.

Summary Tables of Postquota Prices. The next four tables summarize the effect on price of import quotas under all our elasticity combinations, core sizes, and disruption sizes. For each combination the tables show the highest and lowest price resulting from import reductions imposed separately (but simultaneously) by the United States and other IEA countries. We limit the import curtailments to a maximum of 1.5 million barrels per day, because larger curtailments create a high percentage of cases (1) in which the cutback exceeds the total imports of our quota-imposing sectors (after sizable disruptions) or (2) that require negative core production at a new equilibrium (for small and intermediate core size). In the simulations of oil sharing in chapter 3, moreover, where the gross disruption was 6 million barrels per day, 1.5 million barrels was at the upper range of discrepancies between supply rights and actual supplies and hence of the extent to which imports had to be reduced. A maximum import quota of 1.5 million barrels per day thus captures the overwhelming majority of

157

TABLE 4–5

HIGH AND LOW WORLD OIL PRICES GENERATED BY IMPORT QUOTAS
UNDER ALTERNATIVE ELASTICITIES AND CORE SIZE,
NONDISRUPTED WORLD OIL SUPPLY
(prices in dollars per barrel; import reductions and core size in millions of
barrels per day)

	Supply Elasticity					
	0.00		0.05		0.22	
	High price	Low price	High price	Low price	High price	Low price
Demand Elasticity = -0.10, Prequota Price = 29.00						
Core size 2	34.68	17.02	32.92	20.33	29.94	25.02
U.S. import reduction	(0.50)	(1.50)	(0.25)	(1.50)	(0.25)	(1.50)
Other IEA import reduction	(0.25)	(1.25)	(0.25)	(1.50)	(0.25)	(1.50)
Core size 4	50.09	22.57	38.64	24.12	31.77	26.56
U.S. import reduction	(1.00)	(1.50)	(0.75)	(1.50)	(0.50)	(1.50)
Other IEA import reduction	(0.75)	(1.50)	(0.50)	(1.50)	(0.25)	(1.50)
Core size 6	—	—	48.44	32.92	34.42	29.00
U.S. import reduction	—	—	(1.00)	(0.25)	(0.75)	(1.50)
Other IEA import reduction	—	—	(1.00)	(1.25)	(0.50)	(1.50)
Demand Elasticity = -0.15, Prequota Price = 29.00						
Core size 2	32.67	20.75	31.81	23.02	29.94	25.49
U.S. import reduction	(0.50)	(1.50)	(0.25)	(1.50)	(0.25)	(1.50)
Other IEA import reduction	(0.25)	(1.25)	(0.25)	(1.25)	(0.25)	(1.50)
Core size 4	41.12	25.52	35.77	25.82	31.31	27.01
U.S. import reduction	(0.75)	(1.50)	(0.75)	(1.50)	(0.50)	(1.50)

TABLE 4–5 (continued)

	Supply Elasticity					
	0.00		0.05		0.22	
	High price	Low price	High price	Low price	High price	Low price
Other IEA import reduction	(0.75)	(1.50)	(0.50)	(1.50)	(0.50)	(1.50)
Core size 6	52.44	32.51	42.24	31.81	33.55	29.32
U.S. import reduction	(1.25)	(0.25)	(1.00)	(0.25)	(0.75)	(1.50)
Other IEA import reduction	(1.25)	(1.50)	(1.00)	(1.00)	(0.50)	(1.50)
Demand Elasticity = −0.20, Prequota Price = 29.00						
Core size 2	31.71	22.70	31.19	24.13	29.92	25.86
U.S. import reduction	(0.50)	(1.50)	(0.25)	(1.50)	(0.25)	(1.50)
Other IEA import reduction	(0.25)	(1.25)	(0.25)	(1.25)	(0.25)	(1.50)
Core size 4	37.64	26.60	34.12	26.67	31.22	27.34
U.S. import reduction	(0.75)	(1.50)	(0.75)	(1.50)	(0.50)	(1.50)
Other IEA import reduction	(0.75)	(1.50)	(0.50)	(1.50)	(0.50)	(1.50)
Core size 6	43.93	31.60	39.02	31.19	33.08	29.50
U.S. import reduction	(1.25)	(0.25)	(1.00)	(0.25)	(0.75)	(1.50)
Other IEA import reduction	(1.25)	(1.50)	(1.00)	(1.00)	(0.75)	(1.50)

NOTE: Dashes indicate an unattainable equilibrium.
SOURCE: Computer simulation of model.

realistic and feasible cases generated by our simulations. The maximum prices, moreover, are not affected by the upper quota limit of 1.5 million barrels per day, since they are all produced by quotas at or below that level.

Price ranges in a nondisrupted market. Table 4–5 is the price-range summary for the zero disruption case that we have hitherto focused on. Each of the three parts of the table is identified by a particular aggregate demand elasticity. The columns are designated for each of the three competitive supply elasticities. The first two columns of the second part are defined by an elasticity of -0.15 for demand and 0.00 for supply, the same base-case combination underlying the prices reported in table 4–3.

The entries in those columns inform us that, starting with a pre-quota price of $29.00 per barrel, the imposition of import restraints ranging from zero to 1.5 million barrels per day against a core size of 2 million barrels per day creates a high price of $32.67 and a low price of $20.75. The parenthetical entries under each price indicate that the high price is produced by a U.S. import reduction of 0.50 million barrels per day simultaneous with a reduction of 0.25 million barrels per day by the other IEA countries; the low price is generated by U.S. and non-U.S. curtailments of 1.50 and 1.25 million barrels per day. When the core size is increased to 4 and then 6 million barrels per day, the price ranges are $41.12 to $25.52 and $52.44 to $32.51, respectively.

Table 4–5 confirms that higher absolute elasticities dampen the price increases, as do smaller core sizes at all elasticities. Even under the highest-valued pair of elasticities, however— -0.20 for demand and 0.22 for supply—import reductions can still raise the price by as much as $0.92 for a joint restriction of 0.25 million barrels per day each against the 2-million-barrel core and $4.08 for a joint restriction of 0.75 million barrels per day each against the 6-million-barrel core.[22]

Price ranges in disrupted markets. The results of table 4–5, in which binding import ceilings are imposed on a nondisrupted world oil supply, are essentially a reference case for the only relevant context for ESS-imposed ceilings, a disrupted world supply. Tables 4–6 through 4–8 summarize the simulations in which imports are reduced by quotas after successive world supply losses of 3, 5, and 8 million barrels per day. In each case the postdisruption, prequota price is independent of the competitive supply elasticity, varying (inversely) only with the absolute elasticity of aggregate demand. This follows from our requirement that the disruption equal the designated amount (3, 5, or 8 million barrels per day) *after* allowing for the competitive supply response to the accompanying price increase. As a result, the supply response, reflecting its underlying elasticity, has no bearing on the net loss of supply or the rise in price.[23] This assumption, like that of constant core size before and after a disruption, reflects our belief that restricting core size and disruption size to a controlled amount of

160

variation facilitates the analysis and comparison of the effects of import ceilings.

The beginning predisruption price continues to be $29.00 per barrel. In table 4–6 the postdisruption, prequota price after a loss of 3 million barrels per day in world supply is $58.37, $46.23, and $41.14 for successive aggregate demand elasticities of -0.10, -0.15, and -0.20. The general pattern of prices in table 4–6, in relation to the prequota prices, is the same as the pattern underlying table 4–5, the nondisruption case. Increasing quota-mandated import reductions after a disruption raise the world price to a critical point of import restriction, after which the price falls, eventually even below the prequota price. The greater the core size and the lower the underlying absolute elasticities, the higher the peak price and the import restriction under which it occurs.

Because any loss of world supply causes net demand, at any given price and quantity, to become a less elastic and steeper schedule, given import reductions create greater price increases after a disruption than in the nondisrupted oil market. This tendency is apparent not only in the summary data of table 4–6 but to an even greater extent in tables 4–7 and 4–8, where the disruptions are greater. Although the prices vary considerably, for the same size of quota the modal percentage increase of postquota over prequota prices (postdisruption in tables 4–6 to 4–8) is greater in the series underlying tables 4–6, 4–7, and 4–8 than in those of table 4–5 by roughly 8–10 percent, 13–15 percent, and 23–25 percent, respectively.[24]

The ability of quotas to raise the price of oil in disrupted circumstances is formidable. Under the base-case elasticities, -0.15 for demand and 0.00 for supply, a disruption of 3 million barrels per day initially raises the world price from $29.00 to $46.23 per barrel (table 4–6). Subsequent joint import cutbacks create maximum prices of $52.55, $67.28, and $87.46 for successively larger core sizes. After a world supply loss of 5 million barrels per day (table 4–7), binding quotas in the base case raise the price from $64.31 to a high of $73.58 and $95.44 for core sizes of 2 and 4 million barrels, respectively. (Under the base-case elasticities, the 6-million-barrel core has a negative marginal revenue for both the 5- and the 8-million-barrel disruptions and is not viable.) A loss of 8 million barrels per day (table 4–8) raises the price in the base case to $109.05, after which quotas produce maximum prices of $126.16 and $167.36.

Even under our maximum elasticities of -0.20 for demand and 0.22 for supply, which should capture the full force of effective public and private stock drawdown, IEA-mandated demand restraint, and competitive supply response, binding import quotas can elevate prices significantly. From an initial postdisruption price of $52.70, quotas

161

TABLE 4–6

HIGH AND LOW WORLD OIL PRICES GENERATED BY IMPORT QUOTAS
UNDER ALTERNATIVE ELASTICITIES AND CORE SIZE,
WORLD OIL SUPPLY DISRUPTED BY 3 MILLION BARRELS PER DAY
(prices in dollars per barrel; import reductions and core size in millions of
barrels per day)

| | Supply Elasticity | | | | | |
| | 0.00 | | 0.05 | | 0.22 | |
	High price	Low price	High price	Low price	High price	Low price
Demand Elasticity = −0.10, Prequota Price = 58.37						
Core size 2	70.73	32.69	66.62	39.51	61.45	49.26
U.S. import reduction	(0.50)	(1.50)	(0.25)	(1.50)	(0.25)	(1.50)
Other IEA import reduction	(0.25)	(1.25)	(0.25)	(1.50)	(0.25)	(1.50)
Core size 4	105.03	43.63	79.67	48.03	66.11	53.77
U.S. import reduction	(1.00)	(1.50)	(0.75)	(1.50)	(0.50)	(1.50)
Other IEA import reduction	(0.75)	(1.50)	(0.50)	(1.50)	(0.50)	(1.50)
Core size 6	—	—	—	—	72.44	61.73
U.S. import reduction	—	—	—	—	(1.00)	(1.50)
Other IEA import reduction	—	—	—	—	(0.75)	(1.50)
Demand Elasticity = −0.15, Prequota Price = 46.23						
Core size 2	52.55	32.20	50.97	35.94	48.33	40.73
U.S. import reduction	(0.50)	(1.50)	(0.25)	(1.50)	(0.25)	(1.50)
Other IEA import reduction	(0.25)	(1.25)	(0.25)	(1.25)	(0.25)	(1.25)
Core size 4	67.28	40.09	57.75	40.89	51.54	43.14
U.S. import reduction	(0.75)	(1.50)	(0.75)	(1.50)	(0.50)	(1.50)

TABLE 4-6 (continued)

	Supply Elasticity					
	0.00		0.05		0.22	
	High price	*Low price*	*High price*	*Low price*	*High price*	*Low price*
Other IEA import reduction	(0.75)	(1.50)	(0.50)	(1.50)	(0.50)	(1.50)
Core size 6	87.46	52.27	69.17	50.97	55.11	48.29
U.S. import reduction	(1.25)	(0.25)	(1.25)	(0.25)	(1.00)	(1.50)
Other IEA import reduction	(1.25)	(1.50)	(1.00)	(1.25)	(0.75)	(1.50)
Demand Elasticity = −0.20, Prequota Price = 41.14						
Core size 2	45.29	31.60	44.44	33.69	42.85	36.81
U.S. import reduction	(0.50)	(1.50)	(0.25)	(1.50)	(0.25)	(1.50)
Other IEA import reduction	(0.25)	(1.25)	(0.25)	(1.25)	(0.25)	(1.25)
Core size 4	54.51	37.41	48.91	37.65	45.33	38.80
U.S. import reduction	(0.75)	(1.50)	(0.75)	(1.50)	(0.50)	(1.50)
Other IEA import reduction	(0.75)	(1.50)	(0.50)	(1.50)	(0.50)	(1.50)
Core size 6	65.89	45.11	56.35	44.44	48.00	42.81
U.S. import reduction	(1.25)	(0.25)	(1.00)	(0.25)	(1.00)	(1.50)
Other IEA import reduction	(1.25)	(1.50)	(1.00)	(1.25)	(0.75)	(1.50)

NOTE: Dashes indicate an unattainable equilibrium.
SOURCE: Computer simulation of model.

after a 5-million-barrel-per-day disruption produce maximum prices of $55.31, $58.10, and $63.59 at increasing core sizes (table 4–7).[25]

At the other end of the elasticity spectrum, our lowest absolute

163

TABLE 4-7
HIGH AND LOW WORLD OIL PRICES GENERATED BY IMPORT QUOTAS
UNDER ALTERNATIVE ELASTICITIES AND CORE SIZE,
WORLD OIL SUPPLY DISRUPTED BY 5 MILLION BARRELS PER DAY
(prices in dollars per barrel; import reductions and core size in millions of
barrels per day)

	Supply Elasticity					
	0.00		0.05		0.22	
	High price	Low price	High price	Low price	High price	Low price
Demand Elasticity = -0.10, Prequota Price = 95.78						
Core size 2	117.20	47.42	109.73	63.05	—	—
U.S. import reduction	(0.50)	(1.50)	(0.25)	(1.50)	—	—
Other IEA import reduction	(0.25)	(1.50)	(0.25)	(1.50)	—	—
Core size 4	—	—	132.18	78.26	—	—
U.S. import reduction	—	—	(0.75)	(1.50)	—	—
Other IEA import reduction	—	—	(0.50)	(1.50)	—	—
Core size 6	—	—	—	—	—	—
U.S. import reduction	—	—	—	—	—	—
Other IEA import reduction	—	—	—	—	—	—
Demand Elasticity = -0.15, Prequota Price = 64.31						
Core size 2	73.58	43.88	71.15	49.19	67.88	58.42
U.S. import reduction	(0.50)	(1.50)	(0.25)	(1.50)	(0.25)	(0.75)
Other IEA import reduction	(0.25)	(1.25)	(0.25)	(1.25)	(0.25)	(1.50)
Core size 4	95.44	55.13	81.08	56.63	72.21	65.04
U.S. import reduction	(0.75)	(1.50)	(0.75)	(1.50)	(0.75)	(0.75)

164

TABLE 4-7 (continued)

	Supply Elasticity					
	0.00		0.05		0.22	
	High price	Low price	High price	Low price	High price	Low price
Other IEA import reduction	(0.75)	(1.50)	(0.50)	(1.50)	(0.50)	(1.50)
Core size 6	—	—	102.72	71.15	75.56	67.88
U.S. import reduction	—	—	(1.25)	(0.25)	(0.75)	(0.25)
Other IEA import reduction	—	—	(1.00)	(1.25)	(0.75)	(0.75)
Demand Elasticity = −0.20, Prequota Price = 52.70						
Core size 2	58.30	39.90	57.11	42.63	55.31	46.72
U.S. import reduction	(0.50)	(1.50)	(0.25)	(1.50)	(0.25)	(1.25)
Other IEA import reduction	(0.25)	(1.25)	(0.25)	(1.25)	(0.25)	(1.50)
Core size 4	70.86	47.60	63.13	48.07	58.10	50.86
U.S. import reduction	(0.75)	(1.50)	(0.75)	(1.50)	(0.75)	(1.25)
Other IEA import reduction	(0.75)	(1.50)	(0.50)	(1.50)	(0.50)	(1.50)
Core size 6	87.21	58.06	74.53	57.11	63.59	55.31
U.S. import reduction	(1.25)	(0.25)	(1.25)	(0.25)	(1.00)	(0.25)
Other IEA import reduction	(1.25)	(1.50)	(1.00)	(1.25)	(0.75)	(0.75)

NOTE: Dashes indicate an unattainable equilibrium.
SOURCE: Computer simulation of model.

elasticities pose a severe threat to oil sharing's price-stabilizing goals, even under modest import curtailments in the wake of small supply disruptions. This can be seen in computer printouts not reported in

165

TABLE 4-8

HIGH AND LOW WORLD PRICES GENERATED BY IMPORT QUOTAS
UNDER ALTERNATIVE ELASTICITIES AND CORE SIZE,
WORLD OIL SUPPLY DISRUPTED BY 8 MILLION BARRELS PER DAY
(prices in dollars per barrel; import reductions and core size in millions of
barrels per day)

| | Supply Elasticity | | | | | |
| | 0.00 | | 0.05 | | 0.22 | |
	High price	Low price	High price	Low price	High price	Low price
Demand Elasticity = −0.10, Prequota Price = 211.45						
Core size 2	263.13	97.42	243.69	158.97	—	—
U.S. import reduction	(0.50)	(1.50)	(0.25)	(0.75)	—	—
Other IEA import reduction	(0.25)	(1.50)	(0.25)	(1.50)	—	—
Core size 4	—	—	323.08	232.43	—	—
U.S. import reduction	—	—	(0.75)	(0.75)	—	—
Other IEA import reduction	—	—	(0.75)	(1.50)	—	—
Core size 6	—	—	—	—	—	—
U.S. import reduction	—	—	—	—	—	—
Other IEA import reduction	—	—	—	—	—	—
Demand Elasticity = −0.15, Prequota Price = 109.05						
Core size 2	126.16	71.81	121.34	84.80	—	—
U.S. import reduction	(0.50)	(1.50)	(0.25)	(1.00)	—	—
Other IEA import reduction	(0.25)	(1.25)	(0.25)	(1.50)	—	—
Core size 4	167.36	91.47	144.85	108.75	—	—
U.S. import reduction	(0.75)	(1.50)	(0.75)	(1.00)	—	—

166

TABLE 4–8 (continued)

	Supply Elasticity					
	0.00		0.05		0.22	
	High price	*Low price*	*High price*	*Low price*	*High price*	*Low price*
Other IEA import reduction	(0.75)	(1.50)	(0.75)	(1.50)	—	—
Core size 6	—	—	168.41	121.34	—	—
U.S. import reduction	—	—	(1.00)	(0.25)	—	—
Other IEA import reduction	—	—	(1.00)	(1.25)	—	—
Demand Elasticity = −0.20, Prequota Price = 78.31						
Core size 2	87.35	57.84	85.29	62.01	—	—
U.S. import reduction	(0.50)	(1.50)	(0.25)	(1.25)	—	—
Other IEA import reduction	(0.25)	(1.25)	(0.25)	(1.50)	—	—
Core size 4	107.98	69.86	97.12	74.57	—	—
U.S. import reduction	(0.75)	(1.50)	(0.75)	(1.25)	—	—
Other IEA import reduction	(0.75)	(1.50)	(0.75)	(1.50)	—	—
Core size 6	135.39	86.96	116.06	85.29	—	—
U.S. import reduction	(1.25)	(0.25)	(1.25)	(0.25)	—	—
Other IEA import reduction	(1.25)	(1.50)	(1.00)	(1.25)	—	—

NOTE: Dashes indicate an unattainable equilibrium.
SOURCE: Computer simulation of model.

the tables published here. In the aftermath of a 3-million-barrel-per-day loss of world supply, which drives the price to $58.37, elasticities of −0.10 for demand and 0.00 for supply imply that a joint U.S.–

167

non-U.S. curtailment of 0.25 million barrels raises price further to $70.17 and $70.73 for the cores of 2 and 4 million barrels, respectively.[26] A joint restriction of 0.50 million barrels creates prices of $67.41 for the core size of 2 and $84.65 for the core size of 4. Even allowing for a supply elasticity of 0.05, the -0.10 demand elasticity following joint import curtailments of 0.25 and 0.50 million barrels, respectively, establishes prices of $66.62 and $60.52 for the core size of 2 and $67.74 and $76.11 for the core size of 4 (the postdisruption, prequota price is unchanged at $58.37). The maximum prices produced by all three sizes of disruption under these low elasticities are shown in tables 4–6 through 4–8.

Conclusion

Binding import quotas imposed in a model of the world oil market containing a core of noncompetitive producers are shown to exert a significant upward effect on the world price. The price increases are particularly striking for noncompetitive core sizes of 4 million and 6 million barrels per day but are present and nontrivial for a core as small as 2 million barrels per day. The price effects are also greater for low absolute price elasticities of supply and demand and after disruptions in the world oil supply. These, of course, are the circumstances in which the ESS would be implemented, requiring IEA members whose supply rights fall below their de facto supply of oil to curtail imports accordingly.

After a loss of 5 million barrels per day (11 percent) of world supply under low (but not the lowest) base-case elasticities, import curtailments of as little as 250,000 barrels per day by a single country employing a quota can raise the world price from 7 to 14 percent, depending on the core size. If two countries jointly reduce imports by 250,000 barrels per day, the world price will rise 14 percent for any viable core. For curtailments of 500,000 barrels per day by one country, the price increase is 3 to 19 percent, and by two countries 10 to 30 percent, for the alternative core sizes.

As the size of the import reduction increases, a point is reached at which the world price decreases. Under postdisruption, base-case elasticity conditions, however, import cutbacks by one country must exceed 1 million barrels per day or, by two countries acting jointly, must exceed 1.5 or 2 million barrels per day before the price decline is significant—except against the smallest core size.

An interesting and somewhat unexpected finding is that the ability of the noncompetitive core to raise prices is constrained by both upper and lower limits on its size. Although binding import quotas may create small price increases when the core size is small (2 million

168

barrels per day), a core size as large as 6 million barrels per day, particularly under disruption circumstances, frequently encounters inelastic net world demand, at which marginal revenue is negative and equilibrium is unattainable. Only by reducing daily output below 6 million barrels will the core in such cases find an elastic demand segment whose marginal revenue is positive and along which it can operate.

It is often suggested that the major noncompetitive producers are located in the area of the Persian Gulf and would totally disappear if that region were disrupted. But it would not take a great deal of collusion among producers outside the gulf to form a critical size of alternative noncompetitive production. Even a single producer of as little as 2 million barrels per day could be an effective oligopolist in a postdisruption market. Such a producer might be a passive price taker in a world market without binding import constraints, but the imposition of IEA quota-mandated reductions after a disruption would create strong incentives for price-setting behavior, as described in our simulations.

There is, of course, no reason why oligopoly behavior, under the right incentives, cannot spring up among individual producers or combinations of producers anywhere in OPEC or outside OPEC, including even IEA producers or the Soviet Union. These producers might discover, inadvertently or otherwise, that deliberate or "accidental" production delays and cutbacks may yield an enormous gain.

Appendix: Mathematical Formulation of the Model

The following regions or sectors, with their corresponding subscript characters, are treated separately in computing the consumption and production effects of import quotas:

u: United States
r: rest of IEA members
n: OPEC producers not in the noncompetitive core
c: OPEC producers in the noncompetitive core
w: rest of the world

Supply and demand curves are assumed to be isoelastic, with the same supply elasticities and the same demand elasticities for all regions except the core producers.

The input parameters to the model are the initial world price, initial consumption and production for each region, demand and supply elasticities, disruption size, core size (core exports before the imposition of quotas), and postdisruption mandated import reductions by the United States and the rest of the IEA countries.

169

Prices, marginal cost, and marginal revenue are in dollars per barrel, quantities are in millions of barrels per day, and core profits are in billions of dollars per year.

Initial Conditions. The U.S. net demand for imports is given by

$$I_{u0} = D_{u0} - S_{u0} = A_u p_0^a - B_u p_0^b$$

where a is the demand elasticity, b is the supply elasticity, p_0 is the initial price, and A_u and B_u are determined from initial U.S. consumption (D_{u0}) and production (S_{u0}). Similarly, for other regions outside the core:

$$I_{r0} = D_{r0} - S_{r0} = A_r p_0^a - B_r p_0^b$$

$$I_{n0} = D_{n0} - S_{n0} = A_n p_0^a - B_{n0} p_0^b$$

$$I_{w0} = D_{w0} - S_{w0} = A_w p_0^a - B_w p_0^b$$

There is a zero subscript on B_n because the supply curve for OPEC producers not in the core shifts in a disruption. Initial total net import demand (equal to core size) is given by

$$I_{T0} = D_{T0} - S_{T0} = A p_0^a - B_0 p_0^b$$

where $A = A_u + A_r + A_n + A_w$; and $B_0 = B_u + B_r + B_{n0} + B_w$. Core size $Q_c = I_{T0}$.

The core is assumed to produce at a level where marginal cost equals the marginal revenue it faces. Total revenue (R) and marginal revenue (MR) as functions of price (that is, the marginal willingness to pay) are given in general by

$$R(p) = p I_T = A p^{a+1} - B p^{b+1}$$

$$MR(p) = [dR/dp][dp/dI_T]$$

$$dR/dp = (a + 1)A p^a - (b + 1)B p^b$$

$$dI_T/dp = a A p^{a-1} - b B p^{b-1}$$

$$MR(p) = \frac{(a + 1)A p^a - (b + 1)B p^b}{a A p^{a-1} - b B p^{b-1}} \tag{A-1}$$

Initial core marginal cost (MC_0) is assumed to be constant and is computed using $MC_0 = MR(p_0)$, A from above, and $B = B_0$ from above. Core profit (in billions of dollars per year) is then given by $(0.365)(p_0 - MC_0)Q_c$.

Postdisruption, Prequota Relationships. The net disruption size is defined as the quantity of predisruption equilibrium world supply

170

minus the quantity of postdisruption equilibrium world supply. Thus the price (p_d) resulting from a net disruption of size Q_d is given by

$$p_d = [(S_{T0} + Q_c - Q_d)/A]^{1/a}$$

To analyze the effects of import quotas for policy purposes, relevant comparisons among the various cases can be made when the core size is unchanged before and after the disruption. Thus, given a core size of Q_c before and after the disruption, the aggregate supply curve after the disruption for producers outside the core is given by

$$S_{Td} = B_d p_d^b$$

where $S_{Td} = Ap_d^a - Q_c$; $B_d = B_u + B_r + B_{nd} + B_w$; and B_u, B_r, and B_w are the constants determined from the initial conditions above.

The postdisruption supply curve for OPEC producers not in the core is determined once B_{nd} is computed:

$$B_{nd} = (Ap_d^a - Q_c)/p_d^b - B_u - B_r - B_w$$

The postdisruption net demand for imports by each region is then given by

$$I_{ud} = A_u p_d^a - B_u p_d^b$$

$$I_{rd} = A_r p_d^a - B_r p_d^b$$

$$I_{nd} = A_n p_d^a - B_{nd} p_d^b$$

$$I_{wd} = A_w p_d^a - B_w p_d^b$$

During the disruption the core still produces at a level where marginal cost equals marginal revenue. Thus the postdisruption marginal cost, which is assumed to be constant, is given by

$$MC_d = MR_d(p_d) = \frac{(a+1)Ap_d^a - (b+1)B_d p_d^b}{aAp_d^{a-1} - bB_d p_d^{b-1}} \qquad (A\text{-}2)$$

Core profit now is given by (0.365) $(p_d - MC_d)Q_c$.

Underlying our various assumptions about domestic demand and supply elasticities, core size, and disruption size is a wide range of resulting net import demand elasticities. This elasticity, at the postdisruption, prequota equilibrium, is given by

$$e_I = [dI/dp][p/I] = [dD/dp - dS/dp][p/I] = [e_d D - e_s S]/I \quad (A\text{-}3)$$

where $e_d = a$ and $e_s = b$ are demand and supply elasticities, respectively; D and S are aggregate demand and supply, respectively; and I is aggregate net import demand, or $D - S$.

171

Postdisruption, Postquota Relationships. U.S. and rest-of-IEA quotas are determined by mandated import reductions, which are input parameters to the model. The quota is given by the region's postdisruption, prequota imports minus its mandated import reduction. Thus, with an import reduction of R_u, the U.S. quota is

$$Q_u = A_u p_d^a - B_u p_d^b - R_u$$

Similarly, the quota for the rest of the IEA countries is

$$Q_r = A_r p_d^a - B_r p_d^b - R_r$$

The kink price for a region with a quota is the price below which the quota is binding for that region (that is, the region has excess demand for imports). The kink prices for the United States (p_u) and the rest of the IEA countries (p_r) are found by solving for p_u and p_r numerically from the following equations:

$$0 = A_u p_u^a - B_u p_u^b - Q_u$$
$$0 = A_r p_r^a - B_r p_r^b - Q_r$$

At prices where one or both quotas are binding—that is, at prices below one or both kink prices—equation A–1 must be modified to reflect the constant term introduced by the quotas. The marginal revenue faced by the core when quotas are binding is given in general by

$$MR_q(p;A_q,B_q,C_q) = \frac{(a+1)A_q p^a - (b+1)B_q p^b + C_q}{aA_q p^{a-1} - bB_q p^{b-1}} \qquad \text{(A–4)}$$

After quotas are imposed, the core still produces at a level where marginal cost equals marginal revenue. But the presence of quotas generates kinks in the net demand curve and hence vertical segments (discontinuities) in the marginal revenue "curve." If the core's marginal cost intersects one of the vertical segments of the marginal revenue curve, the postdisruption, postquota price (p_q) is given directly by the corresponding kink price associated with the vertical segment. If, however, the core's marginal cost intersects a downward-sloping segment of the marginal revenue curve, p_q must be computed numerically by solving the following equation for p_q:

$$0 = MC_d - MR_q(p_q;A_q,B_q,C_q) \qquad \text{(A–5)}$$

where MC_d is given by equation A–2 and $MR_q(p_q;A_q,B_q,C_q)$ is given by equation A–4 with $p = p_q$. The values taken on by A_q, B_q, and C_q depend on which regions, if any, impose quotas and where the resulting kink prices occur on the net demand curve.

172

Let

$$A_q^0 = A_u + A_r + A_n + A_w$$
$$B_q^0 = B_u + B_r + B_{nd} + B_w$$
$$C_q^0 = 0$$
$$A_q^1 = A_r + A_n + A_w$$
$$B_q^1 = B_r + B_{nd} + B_w$$
$$C_q^1 = Q_u$$
$$A_q^2 = A_u + A_n + A_w$$
$$B_q^2 = B_u + B_{nd} + B_w$$
$$C_q^2 = Q_r$$
$$A_q^3 = A_n + A_w$$
$$B_q^3 = B_{nd} + B_w$$
$$C_q^3 = Q_u + Q_r$$

Then p_q is determined either directly or numerically using equation A–5 with A_q, B_q, and C_q taking on the specified values, according to the following quota cases and conditions.

Case I. No import quotas are imposed.

- $p_q = p_d$.

Case II. Only the United States imposes an import quota.

- If $MC_d - MR_q(p_u; A_q^0, B_q^0, C_q^0) \geq 0$, then $p_q = p_d$.
- If $MC_d - MR_q(p_u; A_q^1, B_q^1, C_q^1) < 0$, then

$$A_q = A_q^1$$
$$B_q = B_q^1$$
$$C_q = C_q^1$$

- If $MR_q(p_u; A_q^1, B_q^1, C_q^1) \leq MC_d < MR_q(p_u; A_q^0, B_q^0, C_q^0)$, then $p_q = p_u$.

Case III. Only the rest of the IEA countries impose an import quota.

- If $MC_d - MR_q(p_r; A_q^0, B_q^0, C_q^0) \geq 0$, then $p_q = p_d$.
- If $MC_d - MR_q(p_r; A_q^2, B_q^2, C_q^2) < 0$, then

$$A_q = A_q^2$$
$$B_q = B_q^2$$
$$C_q = C_q^2$$

- If $MR_q(p_r; A_q^1, B_q^1, C_q^1) \leq MC_d < MR_q(p_r; A_q^0, B_q^0, C_q^0)$, then $p_q = p_r$.

173

Case IV. Both the United States and the rest of the IEA countries impose quotas.

If $p_u \geq p_r$:

- If $MC_d - MR_q(p_u; A_q^0, B_q^0, C_q^0) \geq 0$, then $p_q = p_d$.
- If $MR_q(p_u; A_q^1, B_q^1, C_q^1) \leq MC_d < MR_q(p_u; A_q^0, B_q^0, C_q^0)$, then $p_q = p_u$.
- If $MR_q(p_r; A_q^1, B_q^1, C_q^1) \leq MC_d < MR_q(p_u; A_q^1, B_q^1, C_q^1)$, then $A_q = A_q^1$, $B_q = B_q^1$, $C_q = C_q^1$.
- If $MR_q(p_r; A_q^3, B_q^3, C_q^3) \leq MC_d < MR_q(p_r; A_q^1, B_q^1, C_q^1)$, then $p_q = p_r$.
- If $MC_d - MR_q(p_r; A_q^3, B_q^3, C_q^3) < 0$, then $A_q = A_q^3$, $B_q = B_q^3$, $C_q = C_q^3$.

If $p_r \geq p_u$:

- If $MC_d - MR_q(p_r; A_q^0, B_q^0, C_q^0) \geq 0$, then $p_q = p_d$.
- If $MR_q(p_r; A_q^2, B_q^2, C_q^2) \leq MC_d < MR_q(p_r; A_q^0, B_q^0, C_q^0)$, then $p_q = p_r$.
- If $MR_q(p_u; A_q^2, B_q^2, C_q^2) \leq MC_d < MR_q(p_r; A_q^2, B_q^2, C_q^2)$, then $A_q = A_q^2$, $B_q = B_q^2$, $C_q = C_q^2$.
- If $MR_q(p_u; A_q^3, B_q^3, C_q^3) \leq MC_d < MR_q(p_u; A_q^2, B_q^2, C_q^2)$, then $p_q = p_u$.
- If $MC_d - MR_q(p_u; A_q^3, B_q^3, C_q^3) < 0$, then $A_q = A_q^3$, $B_q = B_q^3$, $C_q = C_q^3$.

Once it is determined, the postdisruption, postquota price, p_q, is substituted in the demand and supply equations for each region to yield the quantity effects of the quotas, including the postdisruption, postquota core exports, Q_{qc}. Core profit is then given by (0.365) $(p_q - MC_d)Q_{qc}$.

Finally, this profit is compared with the core's profit if the core does not cut back its exports when import quotas are imposed. The difference between the two profits is a measure of the incentive for the core to cut back production and raise the world price when import quotas are imposed.

Core profit if the core does not cut back production is given by (0.365) $(p_N - MC_d)Q_c$, where the aggregate net import demand curve (including the import quotas) is used to determine the price, p_N, at which Q_c (the initial core size) of net imports is demanded when import quotas are imposed. As a result of the kinks in the net import demand curve, a number of steps (similar to those in the determination of p_q above) are carried out to determine p_N directly or numerically.

Notes

We are grateful to Eric Petersen of the policy office of the Department of Energy for computer assistance in carrying out the simulations.

1. For most IEA member countries, which produce little or no oil, the restriction of consumption is necessarily a restriction of imports. Countries such as the United States that have significant domestic production could, in principle, reduce consumption without limiting imports. In meeting IEA supply limits, however, oil-producing countries that happen to be in surplus under the sharing agreement will find that restricting aggregate consumption is much more complex than restricting imports only and is also more difficult to measure, to monitor, and ultimately to control.

2. For a detailed history and analysis of the 1959–1974 import control program, see Douglas R. Bohi and Milton Russell, *Limiting Oil Imports* (Baltimore: Johns Hopkins University Press, 1978).

3. Department of Energy officials believed that imports in the first half of 1979 had been sharply reduced by the Iranian disruption. From 1980 to 1990 quotas were to reduce imports monotonically. See *Wall Street Journal*, July 17, 1979, p. 1.

4. A memorandum, "Oil Import Quota Policy Decisions" (August 2, 1979), written by Jerry Blankenship, Michael Barron, Thomas Neville, and others warned against imposition of an import ceiling on the grounds that the resulting kinked demand could induce a rise in the world price of oil.

5. A more recent attempt to limit oil imports was defeated by the U.S. Senate in July 1987 by the not overwhelming vote of 55–41. The Energy Security Act of 1987 (S. 694) would have required the president to take action to prevent imports from exceeding 50 percent of petroleum consumption. Although quotas were not specified as the control mechanism, it is difficult to see how the president could have avoided them. The bill required the president to submit to Congress a precise plan indicating how imports were to be held to the 50 percent limit for any year in which he had projected they would rise above that level. Given the uncertainty of the quantitative effect of tariffs on imports and recalling the lack of support for President Gerald Ford's $2-per-barrel tariff in 1975, a president today would have little choice but to impose quotas when and as the 50 percent ceiling was breached.

6. The analysis in this section corresponds to the treatment by Rodney Smith in chap. 2 of this volume; see, in particular, fig. 2–4. For the general theoretical treatment of quotas in both competitive and noncompetitive markets, see Jagdish Bhagwati, "On the Equivalence of Tariffs and Quotas," in Robert E. Baldwin et al., *Trade, Growth, and the Balance of Payments: Essays in Honor of Gottfried Haberler* (Chicago: Rand McNally & Co., 1965), pp. 53–67.

7. More technically, a kink on a curve is a point at which there is no first derivative.

8. The existence and response of competitive supply moderate, but do not, of course, prevent, a rise in price. The upward movement along D_0 from (p_0, q_0) to (p_1, q_1) entails simultaneous upward movements along aggregate demand D and competitive supply S (see figure 4–1 for the relations among D, S, and residual demand).

9. There is no requirement in this analysis of the multiple-buyer market that the quota-imposing buyer actually be receiving oil from the noncompetitive core. If the buyer were being supplied entirely from competitive

sources, the initial effect of an import-reducing quota, world output remaining constant, would be to depress the world price. But, given the fluidity of the world oil market and the configuration of world demand pictured in figure 4-3, noncompetitive producers would soon discover that reducing output would cause a sustainable rise both in the world price and in their profits, even though their particular buyers were not the ones imposing the quota. Cf. the numerical example summarized in table 4-1 and the accompanying discussion.

10. The main source of nonlinearity is our assumption that the underlying demand and competitive supply are isoelastic in price. Component linear schedules, which, unlike those pictured in figures 4-3 and 4-4, do not have a common vertical intercept, will have kinks in their horizontal sum or aggregate market demand schedules. Such kinks are not commonly observed in competitive demand schedules not constrained by special government policies, such as quotas.

11. Marginal cost is the sum of extraction costs plus user cost, which is the opportunity cost of a depletable resource: the value of forgone future production due to present production. See Shantayanan Devarajan and Anthony C. Fisher, "Hotelling's 'Economics of Exhaustible Resources': Fifty Years Later," *Journal of Economic Literature*, vol. 19, no. 1 (March 1981), pp. 65–73.

12. In this instance the intersection of marginal cost and marginal revenue is to the right of the vertical segment, as in figure 4-4. The resulting price is thus below the kink price.

13. While marginal revenue, and hence marginal cost, may fall after a disruption, only those cases in which marginal cost remains positive at the core export quantity are retained in our simulations.

14. See the complete set of net demand elasticities, as related to the elasticities of aggregate demand and competitive supply, in table 4-4.

15. The fact that a given import reduction by the United States creates a greater price rise than the same reduction by other IEA countries has the following geometric interpretation. Each country's or sector's demand has, by assumption, the same elasticity. The U.S. demand, however, has a smaller magnitude and therefore is a steeper schedule (see n. 18 for the parallel argument in connection with supply schedules). Equal mandated import reductions will thereby create a higher kink price along the U.S. demand than along the non-U.S. demand. This implies that a U.S. quota, compared with one imposed by non-U.S. buyers, will create a postquota net market-demand segment that is longer and steeper, extending from the common prequota price to a higher kink price. The simulations indicate that this geometric outcome invariably yields a higher price in response to U.S. import curtailments than to equal cutbacks by non-U.S. buyers.

16. Taking de_t/dI in appendix equation A-3 and substituting $dD/dI = 1$ and $dS/dI = -1$, we obtain $(e_s D - e_d S)/I^2 > 0$, indicating that raising I, the core size, raises the algebraic elasticity and lowers the absolute elasticity of demand.

17. Substituting $dI/dS = -1$ in de_t/dS in appendix equation A-3, we obtain $(e_t - e_s)/I < 0$, which indicates that absolute net demand elasticity varies positively with S and inversely with disruption size.

176

18. The elasticity of supply is $(dS/dp)(p/S)$. To maintain a constant elasticity, a decrease in S, the supply quantity, requires that dS/dp, the slope of supply with respect to the vertical (price) axis, decrease. A decrease in the slope of supply with respect to the vertical axis implies, of course, an increase in slope relative to the horizontal (quantity) axis.

19. With reference to equation 1 above, the slope of net demand with respect to the horizontal axis is

$$dp/dD_R = dp/dD - dp/dS$$

An increase in dp/dS, dp/dD remaining constant, requires a decrease in the left-side term of the equation, which, since it is a negative number, implies an increase in its absolute value.

20. In the 1970s Saudi Arabia was often credited with voluntary restraint in not raising its price to the maximum that inelastic world demand seemed to justify. The effective demand the Saudis faced was, of course, the residual, or net, demand, a price-elastic schedule at the equilibrium price and quantity, obtained by subtracting competitive supply. Net demand placed severe constraints on price-raising behavior.

21. This can be seen from the basic relationship, $MR = p(1 + 1/\eta)$, where MR is marginal revenue, p is demand price, and η is demand-price elasticity in algebraic terms. The condition $MR > 0$ implies, in the expression above, $\eta < -1$ (that is, that demand is elastic).

22. Dashes in table 4–5 correspond to the case in which the lowest pair of demand and supply elasticities (-0.10, 0.00) in the nondisrupted market generate a net demand elasticity below unity (see the entry, so defined, in table 4–4). Marginal revenue is thus negative, and there are no attainable equilibria under these parameters in the noncompetitive world oil market.

23. Whenever supply (S) is a rising schedule (that is, its price elasticity is greater than zero), a disruption is assumed to shift it to the left (at the predisruption equilibrium price) by more than the assumed disruption size. The supply response to the accompanying price increase then brings the net supply loss to exactly the assumed amount.

24. Dashes in table 4–6 again represent the unattainable cases of negative marginal revenue for core size 6 (see n. 22). In table 4–7 dashes under the columns for supply elasticities 0.00 and 0.05 are also due to negative marginal revenue, for cores of both 4 and 6 (cf. the corresponding net demand elasticities whose absolute value is less than unity in table 4–4).

Dashes under the column for supply elasticity 0.22 in table 4–7 reflect the tendency of huge price increases in disrupted markets to transform importer nations into net exporters, because of the high supply response and the resulting substantial increase in domestic production. With major importers becoming exporters after the disruption, market equilibrium under our characterization of the model breaks down. (Note that the price increases in tables 4–6 to 4–8 due to a given disruption size depend on the demand elasticity only and do not vary with supply elasticity. See discussion in text above.)

The dashes in table 4–8 are explained in exactly the same way as those in the corresponding columns of table 4–7.

177

25. The quota-induced price increases for this maximum elasticity case are also nontrivial in the wake of a disruption of 3 million barrels per day (see table 4–6). A disruption of 8 million barrels per day, however, wipes out the entire simulation for these high elasticities by converting the United States or other consuming sectors into net exporters and OPEC (excluding the core) into net importers (see n. 24).

26. The core of 6 million barrels per day is inoperable under these low elasticities for all disruption levels and the nondisrupted market as well, owing to negative marginal revenue at the 6-million-barrel import level.

5
Coordinated Stock Drawdowns: Pros and Cons

John P. Weyant

Slack world oil markets have clouded our recollections of the sudden increases in oil prices, the long gasoline lines, and the economic stagflation that punctuated the 1970s and decreased the international prestige of our country and its allies. To many, the collapse of oil prices in early 1986 brought down the curtain on an isolated thirteen-year sequence of unpleasant events associated with the operation of the world oil market. Some warn, however, that these events could occur again, especially if we fail to plan ahead.[1] Given the political instability of the world's most prolific oil-producing regions, another oil supply interruption could occur, and oil prices could shoot up once again. Moreover, lower oil prices now could be hastening our return to oil market turmoil in the not-too-distant future.

There is one significant difference, however, between the oil market today and that of the 1970s. The amount of oil now in government-mandated and government-held stockpiles is large enough to mitigate the sudden price increases and other adverse effects of oil supply interruptions.[2] Stockpiled oil can be substituted for the lost oil supply and, consequently, can counteract the upward pressure on oil prices. This makes oil stockpiles highly credible policy tools.

To be effective, it is important for large stock releases to occur as soon after a major oil supply interruption begins as possible.[3] This creates the need for international coordination. The fungible nature of oil guarantees that oil released anywhere reduces the effective size of any shortfall, decreasing the price paid for oil everywhere. If one country releases stocks, it reduces the price of oil to all countries buying oil on the world market; if other countries release stocks as well, the price of oil to the first country will be further reduced.

Total government-mandated and government-held stocks in the industrialized free market countries currently amount to about 1,500

179

million barrels of oil, making the potential value of coordinated stockpile releases considerable.[4] Because oil consumption in these countries is approximately 45 million barrels a day, a 10 percent interruption in supply could be completely replaced by stock releases for nearly a year. While larger and longer shortfalls are certainly conceivable, larger ones seem less likely, and smaller ones could be completely offset for a period longer than a year. Thus, many conceivable oil supply interruptions could be completely offset by the available publicly controlled oil stocks, if they are used in a timely manner.

Unfortunately, the existence of significant stocks of oil does not guarantee that they will be used effectively when an oil supply interruption occurs. Policy makers may be hesitant to require their use, either out of fear that the situation could well get worse before it gets better or because they believe that others ought to and will release their stocks first.[5] This concern led to the July 1984 agreement of the International Energy Agency (IEA) member governments to "coordinate" stock drawdowns when a shortfall occurs.[6] As promising as this pronouncement was, it was not a formal treaty. Although the intent to cooperate has been established, the means to ensure cooperation have not been. The potential benefits of formalizing oil stockpile coordination are the main concern in this chapter. The advantages of coordination in stock drawdowns are assessed in order to evaluate specific means of securing the desired degree of cooperation. I conclude with a discussion of the desirability of increasing stock levels worldwide.

Costs of Oil Supply Interruptions

Oil supply interruption has several costs: short- and long-run losses of welfare and gross national product[7] and strategic, political, and military costs.[8] Oil importers bear two major types of economic costs: (1) the direct welfare loss, which includes the loss of consumers' and producers' surplus, as well as the wealth transfer to the oil exporters, and (2) the indirect macroeconomic adjustment costs that derive from the increased unemployment of capital and labor that follows sudden increases in oil prices.[9]

Several observations regarding the nature of these costs are relevant to the design of any plan for coordinating stock drawdowns.[10] First, the longer the time between a disruption and stock drawdowns, the less important are the indirect adjustment costs and the more important the direct welfare costs.[11] Second, even for a permanent loss of oil supply, the increased price will stimulate reduced consumption and the development of alternative sources over time,

180

reducing the direct costs as well.[12] Because the most significant losses associated with an oil supply interruption occur during the first year or two, it is hard to imagine drawing stocks down too fast or too soon.[13] Minimizing the short-run costs of sudden oil supply interruptions ought to be the major objective of both cooperative and unilateral stock drawdown policies.[14]

Benefits of Oil Stock Drawdowns

Oil stockpiles can be used as substitutes for interrupted oil supplies. This substitution process preempts part of the increase in oil prices and reduces the direct and indirect economic costs associated with oil supply interruptions. In addition to the benefits of a reduced world oil price, which accrue to all who import oil, those who make stock releases will generally be able to sell the oil for a much higher price than prevailed when it was purchased, creating a capital gain. In fact, at the time of release, the acquisition, storage, and holding costs of the stocks are sunk, so that the relevant value of each barrel becomes the prevailing world oil price.

Lower Oil Prices. Although there is some debate about whether the indirect adjustment costs associated with a sudden oil price increase are proportional to oil imports or to total oil consumption, there is no question that smaller price increases are associated with lower economic costs. And with lower economic costs the accompanying political and military costs are certain to be less as well.[15]

Finally, a lower oil price at the onset of a disruption limits the extent to which oil prices will ratchet up to higher-than-competitive levels for extended periods of time. In the past, the oil market has entered disruptions with a few low-cost producers restricting their production below competitive levels to maintain prices substantially above their production costs while all other producers behaved more or less competitively. During the initial phases of a disruption, difficulty in making rapid supply and demand adjustments leads to excess demand for oil and very high prices. As the supply and demand adjustments are made, however, downward pressure on prices ultimately emerges. By restricting production still further, the low-cost producers can slow the inevitable price decline. This process can go on for quite some time as the low-cost producers can initially derive higher net revenues at lower output levels.

Capital Gains. Even while world oil prices decline, those actually releasing oil from their stockpiles will realize a capital gain. At the

181

time a barrel of oil is released, it has zero cost and displaces an expensive barrel of imported oil. Thus, even if domestic prices are controlled during an interruption, each barrel released from public stockpiles displaces an expensive imported barrel on the margin. At the time it was put into storage, a barrel of oil may have been expected to produce a low or even negative capital gain. At the time it is released, however, it can be a very valuable asset. This asset value of stockpiled oil makes international cooperation in drawdowns of oil stock less subject to strategic bias and "free riding" than would be the case if price reductions on the world market were its only benefit.

Advantages of Coordinated Stock Drawdowns

Some stock drawdown during an oil supply interruption is beneficial, but more is even better. A primary benefit of stock releases is that they buffer oil price increases during oil supply interruptions, and the more released the greater the effect. But because public stocks are now held by several countries, some coordination of stockpile releases may be required to ensure large aggregate drawdowns.

The more oil released from stockpiles during an oil supply interruption, the smaller should be the resulting price increase.[16] In the extreme, if enough stocks are available, the interrupted supplies can be completely replaced, and no price increase occurs. Of course, this result would depend on consumers' believing that the stock releases can be maintained until the interrupted supplies are restored or until they can adjust their demand patterns to offset a more permanent loss.

Strategic Interactions. Much has been written on the effects of strategic interaction among oil importers.[17] The primacy of oil stockpiles in the debate on energy security policy has focused attention on strategic interaction problems in cooperative stockpiling agreements. In general, these studies help explain some of the reluctance of oil importers to build significant stocks. Because the benefits of stock releases are widely shared and the costs are imposed only on those who hold the stocks, there is a disincentive for individual countries to hold stocks if they believe other countries will do so.

Two observations can be made about this important research. First, the argument that you should not build stocks because others will build enough for both themselves and you pales over time if others do not, in fact, build such stocks. One cannot rely on stocks that should have been built, but have not, to mitigate the price effects of an oil supply interruption. If others are not building the stocks

182

required, they must be forming different conclusions or experiencing difficulty persuading those in charge to do what is demonstrably in their own best interest. In any case, it makes little sense to forgo doing what is in one's interest because others are not doing what is in theirs.

A second observation about the literature on strategic interaction relative to oil stockpiling is that it focuses on the incentives for countries to build stocks, not on their incentives to release already existing stocks. What countries avoid in free-riding on the stockpile capabilities of others are the costs of acquiring, holding, and storing oil. Once the time comes to release oil that is already in storage, these costs should not enter into the decision on whether or not to release it. Thus, the strategic interaction calculations for the release of already existing stocks should be much different from those for the building of such stocks.

Although the acquisition, holding, and storage costs of stocks should be considered sunk costs when the release of those stocks is at issue, there is one cost that is not a sunk cost, and it is one to which policy makers are sure to give heavy weight. If oil is released now, it cannot be released again in the future when oil market conditions could be worse rather than better.[18] There is an opportunity cost incurred whenever stockpiled oil is released, equal to its expected future value. If the conditions under which public stocks are to be released are set judiciously, the value of present use will exceed the present value of future use. Nevertheless, although achieving international cooperation in drawing down public stocks is a formidable challenge, it should not be as difficult to negotiate as cooperation on international stock building.

Private Sector Interaction. Another concern that has frequently been voiced in discussions of public stockpiling is its effect on private stockpiling. The most extreme manifestation of this concern is the possibility that each barrel of oil placed in public stocks results in one less barrel in private stockpiles. This view is somewhat dubious because the level of public stocks is now larger than the level of privately held *emergency* stocks. Moreover, most careful studies have concluded that additional public stock building does not reduce the propensity of the private sector to stockpile.[19] In addition, the incentives for private and public stockpiling are dramatically different. For example, the macroeconomic adjustment costs associated with oil supply interruptions are not typically taken into account in private stockpiling decisions, but ideally they should be given heavy weight in public stockpiling decisions. Although the influence of public stock behavior on private stock responses should be taken into account in designing

183

stock programs, it need not paralyze and dominate decision making on public stock acquisition and drawdown. For example, a system designed so that the value of releasing oil early in a crisis is greater than the expected value of releasing it later should be at least as effective in stimulating early private stock releases as it is in stimulating early public releases.[20]

Exporter Retaliation. Another concern regarding public stock acquisition and drawdown is the possible retaliation by oil exporters who may feel that stock releases are designed to undercut their natural market advantage.[21] By now, however, the exporters are as keenly aware of the adverse effects of sudden oil price increases on the economies of the importers and on the exporters' own oil revenues as are the importers. A stock coordination program designed to focus on avoiding sudden oil price increases, rather than appearing to be an instrument for long-run price manipulation, should not elicit serious objections from the exporters. Moreover, if the exporters preferred to use any of their available spare capacity in lieu of stock releases by others, so much the better.

Having described the general concerns that are relevant to designing a cooperative policy of stockpile drawdown, let us take a closer look now at some specific proposals.

Specific Proposals for IEA Cooperation

A number of proposals for coordination of stock drawdowns by IEA member countries have been put forth, and the July 1984 accord should stimulate more proposals in this area.[22] The healthy level of stocks now held in publicly controlled stockpiles and the way the IEA has evolved (as summarized in chapters 1 and 2) create opportunities for cooperation on what is now undeniably the membership's first line of defense against future oil supply interruptions. In fact, the elements that are essential for the successful implementation of such a plan lie at the heart of the IEA's strength—information dissemination, rapid communication, and the corresponding ability to put transgovernmental political pressure on member governments in an area of great mutual interest.[23] Thus, although more work needs to be done on the design of the program and on convincing the member governments of its desirability, there is cause for optimism about the success of those necessary first steps.

Status Quo. Before the July 1984 accord, it was assumed that the IEA's first line of defense was standby demand restraint programs for each

184

country. When the total supply of oil to member nations is reduced by 7 percent, each country is obliged to reduce its demand for oil by 7 percent. Stock releases could be used to offset some of the demand restraint obligation of each country, but this has been viewed by many member governments as the option of last resort.[24]

The plan has several problems, as noted in chapters 2 and 3. First, almost no one feels that any of the member countries' demand restraint programs will actually work. In fact, a number of analysts who reviewed a preliminary U.S. plan concluded that it may actually increase rather than decrease oil demand. Second, it will be difficult to determine the success of these plans for many critical months after the onset of the shortfall. Finally, it may ultimately take higher oil prices rather than a government program to accomplish the demand reduction.[25]

The description of the emergency sharing program contained in chapter 2 (of which the demand restraint program is but one component) points out that the program is designed to ensure an equitable sharing of available supplies among IEA members rather than to reduce the upward pressure on oil prices experienced by the members. This clear statement of objectives invites two important observations: (1) the commitment to demand restraint is only part of the calculation of each country's "supply right" under the sharing agreement and, as such, is really not a demand reduction program at all, and (2) there is no intent in the design of the sharing agreement to limit the price increases that might occur. In other words, demand must be restrained, but the reduction in demand could result from higher prices rather than from any explicit success in limiting demand beyond the market response. Only if the spread among IEA importers of the market-driven reduction in imports differs from the way it is spelled out in the sharing rule would any additional action be required. In short, it is not so much what the program is designed to do that concerns those who have looked at it carefully as what people may be expecting from it. It appears to them that many observers and policy makers are eschewing programs designed to relieve upward pressure on oil prices during an oil supply interruption on the mistaken impression that the IEA's sharing program is, in fact, designed primarily to prevent sudden oil price increases.

These concerns undoubtedly led to the July 1984 IEA accord on coordinated stock drawdowns. The accord establishes that oil stockpile releases are the first line of defense against the sudden price increases brought about by interruptions in oil supply. And although stock levels are not as great as most analysts would like, there is now enough oil stockpiled to make a big difference if it is used wisely.

185

Surprisingly, analysts have expressed some concerns about coordinated stock drawdowns. The dominant concern seems to be that one country will release its stocks only to have another country or private sector speculators buy them up immediately. Such a fear seems unfounded for several reasons. First, if governments or speculators were inclined to add to their stockpiles at the onset of a shortfall, they would be bidding up the spot price even more if others were not releasing their stocks. Further, releases stockpiled by others can be used to augment total available oil supplies in the future. Finally, if the trigger for the stock drawdown program is chosen judiciously, speculative behavior can be made to look relatively unattractive.

We now turn to the design and implementation of a specific cooperative stock drawdown program.

More Formal Cooperative Drawdown Agreements. The IEA can easily identify and chastise those who are not cooperating with an agreement, and a small group of major oil importers can create the right incentives for other members and nonmembers to cooperate.

One of the most comprehensive discussions of the elements involved in designing a cooperative stock drawdown agreement is found in a report by Christopher Gibson.[26] This report touches on virtually all aspects of the negotiation of a coordinated stock drawdown agreement. In particular, it recommends, at least as a starting point, a carefully designed agreement between the three biggest oil importers who are IEA members—the United States, Japan, and West Germany. In addition, it suggests that the negotiations be handled through the use of a single negotiating document (SND) to allow revisions to be proposed and reviewed sequentially by the three signatories.

This is the best available statement of goals and objectives for such a cooperative agreement; its only liability may be that the procedure that is proposed may be too ambitious and complicated to bring to fruition. Indeed, a starting point for the negotiations might well be identifying what actually needs to be negotiated. Nonetheless, because this is the best available proposal, a slightly revised version of it will be used as a prototype in what follows.

A Specific Proposal for Cooperation in Stock Drawdowns. One of the strengths of the Gibson proposal is the use of changes in the spot price of oil rather than changes in oil availability as a trigger mechanism for the implementation of the program. The spot price is easy to measure, monitor, and agree upon; and because sudden price increases are really the major problem caused by reduced oil supplies, focusing on them attacks that problem more directly. The question

186

of how high spot prices should go before the cooperative agreement is triggered is at once complicated and critically important. If the spot-price trigger is set too low relative to the available level of stocks, it is bound to encourage rather than discourage speculative stock holding (and stock building) at the onset of a shortfall. If it is set too high, though, most of the economic and foreign policy damage caused by the price increase could materialize before any stocks are released at all. The indirect adjustment costs are particularly sensitive to the size of the initial oil price shock.

The proposal put forward here would be to trigger the cooperative drawdown plan any time the spot price of oil rises more than 50 percent above its average value in the most recently completed quarter. This level of price increase would cause noticeable economic hardship, particularly if it persisted for months or years, but would cause decidedly less than that experienced in 1973–1974 and 1979–1980. In addition, the drawdown might have a reasonable chance for success if available stocks were used first and other available measures over the longer term.

Of course, circumstances could cause large numbers of oil market participants to expect the price ceiling not to be defended in the long run. This expectation could still induce speculative stock holding. Such circumstances, however, would probably be dire enough to require more than just energy cooperation. In addition, a much greater danger exists: without an agreement of the type described here, oil might not be released when it would be most useful.

The agreement would be deactivated after the first quarter in which the average spot price of oil drops to 25 percent or less above its pre-trigger-quarter average. Thus exporters would see that the agreement was not designed to manipulate long-term price trends, and speculators would question the desirability of holding oil once the 50 percent trigger is reached.

The second design criterion for the program (also discussed in the Gibson proposal) is the amount of oil that should be released. It is probably more important to agree on a reasonable drawdown rate that would be effectively activated upon reaching the trigger than to agonize at length over the optimal level, leaving open the option to adjust drawdown levels after the plan has been put into action. The level of drawdown needs to be large enough to make the 50 percent cap on price increases credible in the short run, but small enough so that it can be maintained for as long as necessary to limit the oil price increase credibly in the future.

One thing that will help accomplish the latter is the now credible expectation that if oil consumers believe that even a 25 percent price increase is likely to persist for a long period of time, they will reduce

187

their consumption accordingly. In fact, given the dual-fired boiler and other fuel-switching capabilities that now exist and a one-year demand elasticity of, say, -0.25, a price increase of 25 percent (or more) will lead to a demand reduction of 6.25 percent ($0.25 \times 0.25 = 0.0625$). Six and a quarter percent multiplied by 46 million barrels per day would equal 2.9 million barrels per day worldwide by the end of a one-year period. If the full 50 percent price increase is expected to persist, oil demand might decline by as much as 6 million barrels per day within a one-year period. Thus, the stock releases can be used to buy time for consumers to adjust to higher prices. Consequently, if the trigger were used to initiate a stock drawdown of 3 million barrels per day for one year and prices remained 25 percent or more above their pretrigger level, price-induced demand responses would, by the end of a year, have reduced aggregate oil demand by at least 3 million barrels per day, or about 7 percent of pretrigger consumption. In addition, one-third of the available public stocks would still remain.

Three million barrels per day of new supply would help reduce the price increase caused by any interruption and, coupled with the 50 percent trigger rule, would provide a powerful incentive for producers with spare capacity and speculators with extra stocks to take advantage of the 25–50 percent disruption profits.[27]

Another advantage of an initial drawdown rate of 3 million barrers per day is that only a few of the largest importers (currently the United States, Japan, and West Germany) could cover it themselves for a long time (in fact, U.S. stockpiles can reportedly be drawn down at 3.0 million barrels per day), which would put economic and political pressure on other IEA members and nonmembers to participate. Their participation would not diminish the desirability of deciding on a sharing agreement in advance; it would merely make the situation more self-correcting, particularly given the asset value of stored oil, which only those who release it can realize.

Because a sharing agreement based on preinterruption oil consumption shares favors Japan and Western Europe and one based on preinterruption import shares favors the United States, almost any choice between the two should be agreeable, particularly because the penalty for "overcommitting" might well be a healthy dose of capital gains that could be used to combat the stagflation to which all importers would be exposed.

Two examples of the operation of the proposed system. Results for two hypothetical examples of the operation of this system are shown in tables 5–1 and 5–2. For simplicity it is assumed that the price of oil would average $16 per barrel with very minor fluctuations over the 1987–1991 period in the absence of any supply interruptions. Each example considers a net loss of 6 million barrels per day in oil supply starting in the first quarter of 1988. In the first example, the oil supply is lost for one year only; in the second, it is lost permanently. Three assumptions regarding government stock activity are considered: (1) no stock releases, (2) a release of 1 million barrels per day from the U.S. strategic petroleum reserve (SPR), and (3) a release of 3 million barrels per day in IEA stocks as in the modified Gibson plan proposed here.

After the temporary interruption (see table 5–1), the world oil price does not return to its original level of $16 per barrel immediately. The major oil exporters have historically increased prices faster as they approach their production capacity than they have decreased them in response to decreases in the demand for their oil. This "ratchet effect" is reflected in the price trajectories shown in table 5–1. Before the interruption occurs, the exporters are producing at their desired level of capacity utilization (about 80 percent). When the interruption occurs, capacity utilization increases dramatically, and prices shoot up to clear the market. When supplies are restored, however, prices decline only gradually toward $16 per barrel. Insofar as stock releases preempt part of the initial price increase, the return to the equilibrium price is therefore more rapid.

In the case of a permanent interruption (see table 5–2), a similar price response mechanism operates. During the first year of the interruption the price dynamics are identical to those for the temporary (one-year) disruption. In subsequent years prices decline gradually, but toward a higher equilibrium price (about $18 per barrel), reflecting the long-run adjustment of IEA oil supply and demand to the reduced level of non-IEA supply. Again, the stock releases preempt part of the ratchet effect by reducing the magnitude of the initial price increase.

The cost and benefit numbers shown in tables 5–1 and 5–2 are for the entire IEA membership, except the capital gains for the U.S. SPR release, which accrue only to the United States. The U.S. share of the other costs and benefits shown is roughly one-third of the IEA total. Interestingly, during the first year of either disruption, if the United States releases SPR oil on its own, the capital gains it makes on those releases are about equal to all the other economic benefits it receives.

In both examples the trigger, a 50 percent increase in the spot price, is achieved early in 1988. After the initial price shock, oil prices decline gradually as supply and demand adjust to the new level of prices. During a temporary disruption, prices would drop further when the interrupted supplies are restored at the beginning of 1989.

189

TABLE 5-1
EXAMPLE 1: ECONOMIC EFFECTS ON IEA COUNTRIES OF A TEMPORARY OIL SUPPLY INTERRUPTION OF 6 MILLION BARRELS PER DAY UNDER ALTERNATIVE STOCK RELEASE ASSUMPTIONS
(billions of 1985 dollars)

	No Stock Draw				U.S. SPR Releases of 1 Million Barrels per Day					IEA Stock Releases of 3 Million Barrels per Day			
Year/ Quarter	Average price	Welfare loss	Indirect costs	Average price	Reduction in IEA welfare loss[a]	Reduction in IEA indirect costs[a]	U.S. capital gains[b]	Average price	Reduction in IEA welfare loss[a]	Reduction in IEA indirect costs[a]	IEA capital gains[b]
1987: I	16										
II	17										
III	15										
IV	16										
1988: I	35	34	34	32	5	5	3	26	16	16	7
II	32	29	29	30	4	4	3	24	14	14	7
III	30	25	25	28	4	4	3	23	13	13	6
IV	29	23	23	26	5	5	2	22	13	13	6

190

1989: I	24	14	7	22	4	2	2	18	11	5	5
II	24	14	7	22	4	2	—	18	11	5	—
III	24	14	7	22	4	2	—	18	11	5	—
IV	24	14	7	22	4	2	—	18	11	5	—
1990: I	20	7	2	19	2	0	—	17	5	1	—
II	20	7	2	19	2	0	—	17	5	1	—
III	20	7	2	19	2	0	—	17	5	1	—
IV	20	7	2	19	2	0	—	17	5	1	—
1991: I	18	4	0	17	2	0	—	16	4	0	—
II	18	4	0	17	2	0	—	16	4	0	—
III	18	4	0	17	2	0	—	16	4	0	—
IV	18	4	0	17	2	0	—	16	4	0	—

NOTE: SPR = strategic petroleum reserve.
a. Welfare losses begin at the start of the disruption, the first quarter of 1988.
b. Capital gains on the U.S. SPR and IEA stocks materialize only during the course of the drawdown, the first quarter of 1988 through the first quarter of 1989.
SOURCE: Author.

TABLE 5–2

EXAMPLE 2: ECONOMIC EFFECTS ON IEA COUNTRIES OF A PERMANENT OIL SUPPLY INTERRUPTION OF 6 MILLION BARRELS PER DAY UNDER ALTERNATIVE STOCK RELEASE ASSUMPTIONS
(billions of 1985 dollars)

Year/ Quarter	No Stock Draw				U.S. SPR Releases of 1 Million Barrels per Day					IEA Stock Releases of 3 Million Barrels per Day			
	Average price	Welfare loss	Indirect costs	Average price	Reduction in IEA welfare loss[a]	Reduction in IEA indirect costs[a]	U.S. capital gains[b]	Average price	Reduction in IEA welfare loss[a]	Reduction in IEA indirect costs[a]	IEA capital gains[b]
1987: I	16											
II	17											
III	15											
IV	16											
1988: I	35	34	34	32	5	5	3	26	16	16	7
II	32	29	29	30	4	4	3	24	14	14	7
III	30	25	25	28	4	4	3	23	13	13	6
IV	29	23	23	26	5	5	2	22	13	13	6

192

1989: I	26	18	9	24	4	3	2	20	11	5	5
II	26	18	9	24	4	3	—	20	11	5	—
III	26	18	9	24	4	3	—	20	11	5	—
IV	26	18	9	24	4	3	—	20	11	5	—
1990: I	24	14	4	22	4	1	—	19	9	2	—
II	24	14	4	22	4	1	—	19	9	2	—
III	24	14	4	22	4	1	—	19	9	2	—
IV	24	14	4	22	4	1	—	19	9	2	—
1991: I	22	11	0	21	2	0	—	18	7	0	—
II	22	11	0	21	2	0	—	18	7	0	—
III	22	11	0	21	2	0	—	18	7	0	—
IV	22	11	0	21	2	0	—	18	7	0	—

NOTE: SPR = strategic petroleum reserve.

a. Welfare losses begin at the start of the disruption, the first quarter of 1988.

b. Capital gains on the U.S. SPR and IEA stocks materialize only during the course of the drawdown, the first quarter of 1988 through the first quarter of 1989.

SOURCE: Author.

The 1 million barrels per day of U.S. stock drawdown is assumed to continue for five quarters, at which point there would be only about 50 million barrels left in the SPR. If 3 million barrels per day of IEA stocks were released over the same period, the average spot price during the first quarter of 1989 would drop to $18 per barrel in the temporary disruption and to $20 per barrel under the permanent supply shortfall. These prices are both within 25 percent of the pre-trigger price ($16 × 1.25 = $20), which would automatically terminate the cooperative drawdown plan.

The stock releases preempt a large portion of the price increases that would otherwise have occurred. The 50 percent price cap does not hold in the first quarter of the cooperative IEA plan but does hold in the second quarter and thereafter. These price reductions reduce the welfare losses and the indirect costs of the supply disruptions in each year. In addition, without stock releases, oil prices would take much longer to return to their normal level in the temporary disruption case and to fall to their new long-run level in the permanent disruption case. Thus the benefits of the stockpile releases would continue after the drawdown stopped.

Several messages emerge from these illustrative calculations: (1) the biggest economic effects of both the temporary and the permanent disruptions occur in the first year or two after they start; (2) stockpile releases can significantly reduce the immediate effects of oil supply interruptions; (3) the more stocks are released, the more the IEA countries are insulated from the debilitating effects of the oil supply interruptions; and (4) those countries actually releasing stocks receive significant capital gains. A release of 1 million barrels per day from the U.S. SPR would result in a $32 billion reduction in welfare loss and indirect costs during 1988 that is shared by all IEA importers, with the U.S. share approximately $10 billion. In addition, however, the United States would receive another $10 billion from the sale of oil from the strategic reserve.

Except in the most extreme circumstances, world oil stocks are now sufficient to limit oil price increases to a maximum of 50 percent in any single year. The option of building more stocks is appealing because additional stocks would reduce the level of spot price triggers for drawdowns and ease the hardship caused by even more catastrophic oil supply interruptions.

The Case for Building More Stocks

The plan just described has a good chance of succeeding because public stocks of oil are now large enough to make a difference during an oil supply interruption. Unfortunately, a 50 percent oil price increase

194

is still quite large for so basic and important an input to the world economy, and there is no guarantee that any strategy for limiting the price increase even to 50 percent will work. But one thing seems certain: the more oil held in stockpiles before an oil price shock, the more likely it is that a strategy like that described in the preceding section will be successful.

Most careful analyses of oil stockpile levels put the optimal amount for the combined IEA members at approximately double the current levels, or about 3 billion barrels.[28] Here, though, the concerns about free riders are more serious. Because the benefits of oil stockpile releases are widely shared and the costs of building stocks are narrowly imposed, some major importers still hesitate to build more stocks on the grounds that others will be doing so and thereby providing them with the necessary coverage. The fact is, however, that the others are not doing so year after year, despite calculations made by Hogan and by others showing the small cost of building stocks relative to the large costs of mistakenly expecting that others will build them.[29] And if the military and political costs of building more stocks are factored in as well, the case for building additional stocks becomes even stronger. Adding 200–300 million barrels a year to the IEA's stocks through the 1980s seems not only justifiable but absolutely vital to the common interests of the member countries.

Conclusions

The current world oil glut has helped provide us with temporary and much-needed relief from the debilitating effects of oil supply interruptions. But the glut will not last forever. Rather than using it as an excuse not to build additional oil stocks, the IEA members should regard it as providing a tremendous opportunity to buy oil for their stockpiles when it is cheap in anticipation of using it when it is dear. Such use can be based either on an oil supply interruption or, preferably, on a slow and steady increase in the price of oil over a number of years so that capital gains can safely be taken on it. Either way, such investments continue to be among the wisest public investments available.

The oil glut also provides us the time necessary to work out an agreement for cooperating in drawing down stocks during a supply interruption. It would be useful to agree as early as possible when stocks should be used, how much should be used, and who should do the drawing down. Given the long lead times necessary for working out international agreements of this magnitude, the "flexibility" that one gains by failing to work out these critical dimensions of a cooperative stock drawdown program amounts to flexibility in the choice of methods for dealing with a mountain of economic and foreign policy losses if another interruption occurs. Public oil stockpiles can now be used significantly to reduce price increases induced by oil supply interruptions and the attendant wealth-transfer and macroeconomic and noneconomic costs. But these benefits will not be captured if the stocks are not used wisely. In fact, many fear—not without reason—that they will never be used at all or that the full benefits of their use will never be realized.

From a U.S. perspective, there is no creditable argument against early and significant use of the SPR. And the same can be said about the use of the available stocks of other IEA member nations. Early use of the SPR can preempt much of the macroeconomic adjustment losses that were responsible for the oil shock–related recessions of the past decade. Some nations and private stockholders, however, will be reluctant to use their stocks if they believe that additional price increases are likely to occur. Therefore, cooperative stock-use agreements should focus directly on changing such expectations by including an oil-price-increase trigger and total IEA drawdown rate that influence those not party to the agreement to draw down their stocks sooner rather than later.

The United States can accomplish a great deal on its own, but cooperation from Japan, West Germany, and other large oil-importing nations will make the strategy even more effective and help silence domestic critics of early and vigorous use of the SPR. It is not necessary for the agreement to be completely self-enforcing for all individual IEA members. All that is required is for a small number of large importers to realize that, by acting together to draw down stocks in a visible way, they can significantly influence everyone's expectations regarding the future trajectory of world oil prices, thereby helping themselves and their longstanding allies as well. In this policy area U.S. leadership should prove both inexpensive and highly effective.

Notes

The author gratefully acknowledges helpful suggestions by Richard Cooper, William Hogan, George Horwich, Hillard Huntington, Alan Manne, Henry Rowen, Dorothy Sheffield, Jim Sweeney, Michael Toman, David Weimer, and Robert Weiner.

1. See, for example, John P. Weyant, "The Continuing Threat of Oil Supply Interruptions," *Journal of Policy Analysis and Management*, vol. 3, no. 3 (1984), pp. 393–405.

2. See, for example, Thomas J. Teisberg, "A Dynamic Programming Model of the U.S. Strategic Petroleum Reserve," *Bell Journal of Economics*, vol. 12, no. 2 (Autumn 1981), pp. 526–46; Glen Sweetnam, "Stockpile Policies for

196

Coping with Oil-Supply Disruptions," in George Horwich and Edward J. Mitchell, eds., *Policies for Coping with Oil-Supply Disruptions* (Washington, D.C.: American Enterprise Institute, 1982), pp. 82–98; Hung-po Chao and Alan Manne, "An Integrated Analysis of U.S. Stockpiling Policies," in James L. Plummer, ed., *Energy Vulnerability* (Cambridge, Mass.: Ballinger Publishing Co., 1983); Henry S. Rowen and John P. Weyant, "Reducing the Economic Impacts of Oil Supply Interruptions: An International Perspective," *Energy Journal*, vol. 3, no. 1 (January 1982), pp. 1–34; and W. W. Hogan, "Oil Stockpiling: Help Thy Neighbor," *Energy Journal*, vol. 4, no. 3 (July 1983), pp. 49–72.

3. For an illuminating discussion of this phenomenon, see Phillip K. Verleger, *Oil Markets in Turmoil* (Cambridge, Mass.: Ballinger Publishing Co., 1982).

4. See chapter 2 of this volume for a rundown on current stock levels in the IEA countries. There is some ambiguity regarding the amount of publicly mandated but privately held stocks that could be drawn down expeditiously. Since these stocks constitute over one-third of the total government "controlled stocks," ensuring positive control of them by member governments is thus the highest-priority option for short-term oil stockpiling.

5. If, for equity or military reasons, stocks are allocated in an inefficient manner, rather than through, say, market mechanisms, they may not be effective in reducing price because individuals who would not buy oil at the prevailing market price would consume it.

6. See chapter 2 for a discussion of the July 1984 IEA stock drawdown coordination accord.

7. George Horwich and David Leo Weimer, *Oil Price Shocks, Market Response, and Contingency Planning* (Washington, D.C.: American Enterprise Institute, 1984), p. 12.

8. See Henry S. Rowen and John P. Weyant, "Tradeoffs between Military Policies and Vulnerability Policies," in Plummer, *Energy Vulnerability*; see also Charles K. Ebinger, *The Critical Link: Energy and National Security in the 1980s* (Cambridge, Mass.: Ballinger Publishing Co., 1983); and Paul E. Gallis, "The NATO Allies, Japan, and the Persian Gulf," Congressional Research Service, Report DS 270, November 8, 1984.

9. For good overviews of the macroeconomic effects of energy shocks, see Knut Anton Mork, ed., *Energy Prices, Inflation, and Economic Activity* (Cambridge, Mass.: Ballinger Publishing Co., 1981); George Horwich, "Government Contingency Planning for Petroleum Supply Interruptions: A Macroperspective," in Horwich and Mitchell, *Policies for Coping with Oil-Supply Disruptions*, pp. 33–65; U.S. General Accounting Office, "Oil Supply Disruptions: Their Price and Economic Effects," Report GAO/RCED-83-135, May 20, 1983; and Energy Modeling Forum, "Macroeconomic Impacts of Energy Shocks: A Summary of Key Results," in Bert G. Hickman, Hillard G. Huntington, and James L. Sweeney, *Macroeconomic Impacts of Energy Shocks* (Amsterdam: North-Holland, 1987).

10. Hillard G. Huntington and Joseph Eschbach, "Energy Policy Issues and Macroeconomic Models," in Hickman, Huntington, and Sweeney, *Macroeconomic Impacts*.

11. Energy Modeling Forum, "Macroeconomic Impacts of Energy Shocks." Richard Cooper has pointed out that the tremendous foreign debt problems that oil-importing developing countries experience during an oil supply shock may not dissipate so rapidly, so that the total costs of an oil supply interruption may not be quite as peaked as a U.S. macroeconomic model would project. This in itself should not lessen the argument for early stockpile releases, because a good way to limit the foreign debt problem would be to limit the initial oil price increase.

12. There have been several excellent attempts to analyze the costs of oil supply interruption using integrated oil market/macroeconomy models. See, for example, Knut A. Mork and Robert E. Hall, "Macroeconomic Analysis of Energy Price Shocks and Off-setting Policies: An Integrated Approach," in Mork, *Energy Prices*; or R. Glenn Hubbard and Robert C. Fry, Jr., "The Macroeconomic Impacts of Oil Supply Interruptions," Energy and Environmental Policy Center, Discussion Paper E-81-07, Kennedy School of Government, Harvard University, 1982.

13. Energy Modeling Forum, "Macroeconomic Impacts of Energy Shocks."

14. See, for example, Verleger, *Oil Markets in Turmoil*.

15. Rowen and Weyant, "Tradeoffs between Military Policies and Vulnerability Policies."

16. Rowen and Weyant, "Reducing the Economic Impacts of Oil Supply Interruptions."

17. See Hogan, "Oil Stockpiling"; R. Glenn Hubbard and Robert J. Weiner, "Government Stockpiles in a Multicountry World: Coordination versus Competition," in Alvin L. Alm and Robert J. Weiner, eds., *Oil Shock: Policy Response and Implementation* (Cambridge, Mass.: Ballinger Publishing Co., 1984), pp. 197–218; and Frederic H. Murphy, Michael A. Toman, and Harold J. Weiss, "International Cooperation in Stockpiles and Tariffs for Coping with Oil Supply Disruptions," Discussion Paper, Resources for the Future, June 1985.

18. Of course, the cost of building storage capacity for the oil need not be repeated, but it would be necessary to buy more oil.

19. See, for example, Hubbard and Weiner, "Government Stockpiles in a Multicountry World"; or Frederic H. Murphy, Michael A. Toman, and Mark J. Goldstein, "Strategic Oil Stocks and Public-Private Interactions: A Dynamic Game Analysis," Discussion Paper, Resources for the Future, April 1984.

20. Hubbard and Weiner, "Government Stockpiles in a Multicountry World," p. 45.

21. For a discussion of how such concerns have affected U.S. stockpile policy in the past as well as a complete history and evaluation of the strategic petroleum reserve (SPR) program, see David L. Weimer, *The Strategic Petroleum Reserve: Planning, Implementation, and Analysis* (Westport, Conn.: Greenwood Press, 1982). For a review and assessment of current plans for using the SPR, see U.S. General Accounting Office, "Evaluation of the Department of Energy's Plan to Sell Oil from the Strategic Petroleum Reserve," Report GAO/RCED-85-80, June 5, 1985.

22. Hubbard and Weiner, "Government Stockpiles in a Multicountry World"; Christopher S. Gibson, "Creative Oil Stockpiling: Evaluating a Three Country

Agreement and Designing a Negotiating Strategy," Energy and Environmental Policy Center, Discussion Paper H-84-03, Harvard University, November 1984; and Douglas R. Bohi and Michael A. Toman, "Restructuring the IEA Crisis Management Program to Serve Members' Interests Better," this volume, chap. 6.

23. See Robert O. Keohane, "International Agencies and the Art of the Possible: The Case of the IEA," *Journal of Policy Analysis and Management*, vol. 1, no. 4 (Summer 1982), pp. 469–81.

24. See Bohi and Toman, this volume, chap. 6. Additional descriptions and assessments of IEA programs by IEA officials can be found in Ulf Lantzke, "Energy Policies in the Industrialized Countries: An Evaluation of the Past Decade," *Journal of Energy and Development*, vol. 9, no. 1 (Autumn 1983), pp. 11–18; Herman T. Franssen, "International Energy Agency Strategies to Cope with Energy Uncertainties," *Journal of Energy and Development*, vol. 10, no. 1 (Autumn 1984), pp. 13–28; and Helga Steeg, "Surveying a Decade of Energetic Activity," interview reported in *OPEC Bulletin*, vol. 15, no. 10 (December 1984/January 1985), pp. 7–10.

25. For a more thorough critique of the IEA Emergency Sharing System, see U.S. General Accounting Office, "Status of U.S. Participation in the International Energy Agency's Emergency Sharing System," Report GAO/NSIAD-85-99, June 13, 1985. For an extended simulation of the sharing system, see George Horwich, Hank Jenkins-Smith, and David Leo Weimer, "The International Energy Agency's Mandatory Oil-sharing Agreement: Tests of Efficiency, Equity, and Practicality," this volume, chap. 3.

26. Gibson, "Creative Oil Stockpiling."

27. R. Glenn Hubbard and Robert J. Weiner, "Managing the Strategic Petroleum Reserve: Energy Policy in a Market Setting," *Annual Review of Energy*, 1985.

28. See references given in note 2.

29. Hogan, "Oil Stockpiling."

6
Restructuring the IEA Crisis Management Program to Serve Members' Interests Better

Douglas R. Bohi and Michael A. Toman

The International Energy Agency (IEA) program for responding to disruptions of oil imports calls for restraints on import demand, the use of accumulated oil reserves, and implementation of a plan for sharing available oil to equalize the burden of supply interruptions. Although these provisions have not been tested in a crisis,[1] many observers would agree that (1) the oil-sharing plan is likely to be ineffective in altering private market outcomes, particularly given the changes in the structure and performance of the oil market during the past few years, and (2) the provisions for demand restraint and oil reserves are vague exhortations rather than concrete guidelines for action and, as such, may be ineffective and inconsistent with the interests of member countries.[2]

Most studies directed at strengthening international energy cooperation have focused on expanding the size of strategic stocks held by the IEA or, to minimize coordination problems, by the United States, Japan, and West Germany—the three largest importers—together with agreements for coordinating the use of those stocks in a crisis.[3] Typically, the gains from cooperation in these analyses are measured by increases in economic well-being over a situation in which governments take independent and uncoordinated actions to improve their individual economic positions. An almost universal finding is that, measured in this fashion, the gains from stockpile coordination are substantial.

We do not dispute in broad terms the findings of these studies that stockpile cooperation offers large *potential* benefits (in fact, our own modeling analysis supports a variant of this conclusion.) A large gap remains, however, between these analytical findings and the

200

actual behavior of governments in oil-consuming countries. As discussed further in the next section, all the IEA countries appear to agree on the importance of cooperation, but they do not agree on how this aim is to be achieved other than by continued participation in the existing IEA program. The United States has argued strongly for expanded and coordinated stockpiling and has opposed the use of demand restraints (including tariffs, other taxes, and quotas); other IEA members prefer demand restraints and regard stockpiling (beyond private sector inventories) as either a last resort or not worthwhile. Consequently, little concrete improvement of the IEA agreement has been achieved.

If one accepts (as we do) that governments pursue their own *perceived* interests in formulating policies for energy security, what is to be made of the gap between analytical findings about the benefits of stockpile cooperation and actual practice? The answer, in our view, is not that the models referred to above are incorrect but that they are incomplete. Analytical models have inherent limitations even in their description of strategic interactions among utilitarian actors pursuing narrow, aggregate economic ends (that is, maximizing social surplus). Just as significant, this stylized description of interactions does not include other important concerns that must be considered in a full evaluation of how to enhance cooperation. Thus, although the models have an important normative content and can profitably be used to inform the process of policy analysis and policy determination, they cannot be relied on alone to provide definitive answers.

In this chapter we take the broader perspective suggested by the comments in the previous paragraph to consider both stockpile coordination and other options for strengthening international cooperation among IEA members. To carry out this task, we begin in sections two and three by assessing the current policy positions of the IEA and of its three largest oil-importing members—the United States, West Germany, and Japan. Our primary focus is on these three nations because of their importance in the IEA and because they are the only IEA members with sufficient quantities of public stocks to participate in an agreement to coordinate stockpiles. The information on these countries' positions allows us to make tentative rankings of policy options for cooperation and noncooperation on the basis of the perceived interests of the United States and other IEA members.

In section four we contrast these "revealed preference" rankings with the ordering implied by a variant of Hogan's dynamic programming model[4] that includes demand restraint as an alternative to stockpiling, along with updated input assumptions to reflect recent changes in the oil market. The model results both corroborate the findings of earlier studies in indicating that stockpile coordination is a dominant strategy for the United States and other IEA members and question the desirability of demand restraint in a crisis. This sharp gap between model predictions and the apparent perceptions of self-interest by IEA members leads us into a consideration of what elements are missing from the stylized "utilitarian actor" approach to analyzing cooperation. The model outcomes also provide useful information in the search for more immediately practical alternatives to stockpile coordination.

In the fifth and concluding section we draw together the strands of our analysis to formulate a practical recommendation for improving on the current IEA system for international energy security. While recognizing the ultimate desirability of expanding stockpile coordination (particularly as regards the size and availability of reserves), we conclude that a mixed approach—with primary emphasis on stock use by the United States and primary reliance on demand restraint by other IEA members—is the best current option. It is not first best from a narrow economic perspective, but it has the best prospect for acceptance given the disparate interests of IEA members. Moreover, it offers the prospect of avoiding substantial costs from a breakdown in cooperation.

Before proceeding with these arguments, it is useful to recall that since the formation of the IEA in 1974, the international oil market has experienced important changes that alter the potential benefits of cooperation and that shape the policy positions of members.[5] Worldwide demand for oil has declined in the face of past price increases, despite a resurgence in economic activity, and has become more flexible as consumers have adapted to price uncertainty. The share of the market supplied by the Organization of Petroleum Exporting Countries (OPEC) has also declined with the increased availability of both non-OPEC oil and competing fuels. These developments imply an attenuation of OPEC's ability to control oil prices because demand for its output is more elastic. With more volatile oil earnings, OPEC as a group would probably suffer from actions that raise oil prices. Now, in contrast to the past, OPEC as a group appears to have an interest in oil price stability that is more consistent with the interests of importers, rather than an interest in permanently elevating base oil prices.

In addition, the stability and efficiency of the oil market have increased markedly with the growth of spot markets and the introduction of futures trading. The spot market is now more likely to be a viable source of incremental supplies in a crisis, rather than drying up as in the past; and futures trading provides a convenient way to hedge risks.[6] Thus private inventories can be expected to show far more stable behavior in future disruptions than in past crises, when small or negligible supply shocks led to large price shocks because of "panic" buying.[7] When coupled with the substantial increase in stocks controlled by governments, these observations suggest that the appropriate objectives of cooperation have changed greatly since the IEA was formed. With the greater flexibility of the oil market, the objectives of countering targeted embargoes (as with the oil-sharing plan), of attenuating upward ratchets in base oil prices, and of fore-stalling panic buying become less important than dampening short-term price fluctuations (as traditionally encountered in agricultural commodity markets). By the same token, while early release of stra-tegic stocks may be desirable, a massive early sale to hold down the floor price of oil or to offset panic is less likely to be warranted.

Policy Positions within the IEA: Demand Restraint versus Stocks

We begin by considering the current policy positions of the United States and other IEA members, which clearly have a strong bearing on the practical possibilities and limits of cooperation. We should state at the outset that the hard evidence on this subject is rather thin; certainly it is not sufficient for a thorough evaluation of political forces influencing the behavior of individual IEA members or coalitions.[8] Nevertheless, this material illustrates the sharp divergence in interests and positions among IEA members that must be confronted in assess-ing how more effective and practical agreements on cooperation can be designed. It further offers some clues to the underlying sources of these problems and ways in which they might be addressed.

With a sizable strategic petroleum reserve (SPR), the United States has taken the lead in attempting to forge a new agreement among IEA countries to cooperate in building and using government-owned stocks early in a crisis. Secretary of Energy Donald Hodel testified before the House Subcommittee on Fossil and Synthetic Fuels on February 21, 1984, that

> in a major disruption, the early sale of SPR oil in large vol-umes ordinarily is the best policy for SPR use. . . . The mar-ketplace needs to know in advance that this is our general policy . . . and I have no hesitancy in declaring our willing-ness and intention ordinarily to use it to optimum advantage early in a serious oil supply interruption.

203

At the same time the United States has expressed its opposition to a strategy of applying demand restraints early in a crisis instead of drawing on stocks.[9]

The United States has encountered strong resistance from other IEA countries over the strategy of using oil reserves as the first line of defense.[10] Most countries are unwilling to accept the financial burden of building government-owned stocks and see themselves as too small a part of the market to make much difference. Germany and Japan, though holding some stocks, have no indigenous sources of oil to speak of and are more inclined than the United States to save their reserves as a last line of defense.[11]

The official IEA position remains that stock drawdowns and demand restraints are substitutes for each other.[12] This decision, and the debate leading up to it, provide the most concrete evidence of other IEA members' preference for demand restraint, in contrast to the U.S. position.

The possibility that other countries will free-ride on the United States by failing to take action or, worse yet, will actually negate a U.S. stock drawdown by simultaneously allowing their private sectors to accumulate reserves is a major fear that could lead to failure by the United States to follow its preferred course of action even though that would be detrimental to its economic interests. As Secretary Hodel has stated,

> The thing that concerns us is that our reserves are comparable to the reserves maintained by our allies. Otherwise we get into this difficult situation that, come a crunch where we say we're going to draw . . . and they're reluctant to draw, we'd be making a partial gift to them. We're not inclined to do that.[13]

U.S. concerns about free riding are exacerbated by the perception that the nonmarket demand restraints many other countries seem to prefer would be of limited value and difficult to monitor. These restraints seldom call for stringent and observable measures such as tariffs on oil imports or taxes on domestic consumption of petroleum products. Instead, they frequently refer to nonmarket restrictions on petroleum consumption, such as allocation controls, or restraints on activities that consume petroleum, such as driving restrictions. These nonmarket instruments of control are not only less effective than taxes or tariffs but also difficult to verify and evaluate.

Little public information is available about the credibility of the U.S. position in the eyes of Japan or Germany (or other IEA members).

It seems plausible to assume, however, that the erratic U.S. commitment to the SPR (past and present) diminishes confidence in its being used decisively and effectively in a crisis. In the past, budgetary battles have impeded the filling of the SPR, and concerns persist that legal and political constraints will stymie drawdowns in a disruption.[14] Logistical problems continue to plague the distribution system.[15] The budget battle has recently been rejoined with the Reagan administration's call for a moratorium on filling the SPR. Finally, Japan, Germany, and other IEA members seem to place greater emphasis than the United States on the need for cooperation and the role of the IEA in sustaining positive responses by individual countries.

Implications for Policy Preferences

The information presented in the previous section can be used to form tentative judgments of how IEA members rank policy options according to their own perceived interests. These "revealed preference" rankings are summarized in table 6–1. Three alternative policy options—denoted by N, S, and T—are considered. The no-action option, N, represents a relatively weak unilateral response (through stocks or demand restraint) to a crisis; the stockpile use option, S, means a more aggressive use of strategic reserves to reap both individual and joint benefits; the demand restraint option, T, represents effective and verifiable demand restraint in a crisis through taxes or

TABLE 6–1

APPARENT PREFERENCES FOR ALTERNATIVE POLICIES

United States	Other IEA Members		
	S	T	N
S	a_1/b_1	a_2/b_2	a_3/b_3
N	a_4/b_4	a_5/b_5	0/0

- U.S. policy ranking: $a_1 > a_4 > 0$; $a_2 > a_5 > 0$; $a_3 < 0$ (assurance)
- Rankings by other IEA members:
  $b_2 > \max \{b_1, b_3\} > 0 > \max \{b_4, b_5\}$ (assurance)
  $b_3 > \max \{b_1, b_2\} > 0 > \max \{b_4, b_5\}$ (free rider)

NOTE: S = stockpile use; T = demand restraint; N = no action; see text for more precise interpretations. The a_i and b_i refer to gains (or losses) *relative* to the no-action outcome (N,N).
SOURCE: Authors.

205

similar measures. In the payoff matrix the a entries represent net gains to the United States and the b entries net gains to other IEA members, *relative* to the joint no-action outcome (N,N).[16]

The U.S. position suggests a policy ranking given by the inequalities

$$a_1 > a_4 > 0; a_2 > a_5 > 0; a_3 < 0 \qquad (1)$$

In other words, a strong stockpile response is preferred if other countries also take positive action (S or T), but in the event of a weak response by those countries (response N), the U.S. response to a crisis would also be limited ($a_3 < 0$).[17] Thus (1) is an "assurance" ranking: positive actions evoke positive actions; negative actions evoke negative actions.[18]

Two alternative policy rankings can be posited for other IEA members, particularly for Germany and Japan. The first is another assurance ranking but with a preference for demand restraint:

$$b_2 > \max \{b_1, b_3\} > 0 > \max \{b_4, b_5\} \qquad (2)$$

This ranking implies that the preferred response by these countries to aggressive U.S. stockpile use is effective demand restraint but that the response to a weaker U.S. action would also be limited. Such a ranking is suggested not only by the relative preference of non-U.S. IEA members for demand restraint but also by their emphasis on the need for cooperation to make individual responses effective.

An alternative (and more cynical) evaluation of these preferences is that, notwithstanding diplomatic pronouncements on the subject, the true ranking of policies by other IEA members is that the no-action option N (as we have defined it) is a dominant strategy.[19] In symbols this free-rider ranking is given by[20]

$$b_3 > \max \{b_1, b_2\} > 0 > \max \{b_4, b_5\} \qquad (3)$$

Such a ranking may be plausible for smaller IEA members but somewhat less likely for Germany and Japan, each of which has more to lose from a weak response to a crisis and has shown greater willingness to strengthen its policies on energy security.

If both sides have the assurance rankings indicated by (1) and (2), the policy participation game in table 6–1 has two Nash equilibria:[21] mutually weak actions (N,N) and the outcome (S,T), where aggressive U.S. use of the SPR is coupled with effective demand restraint by other IEA members. Moreover, (S,T) is "Pareto superior" to (N,N)—that is, all parties prefer the former outcome—so that self-interested governments would be expected to negotiate an agreement to pursue (S,T) fairly easily.

206

If IEA members other than the United States have the free-rider ranking (3) rather than (2), however, the only Nash equilibrium in table 6-1 is (N,N).[22] Nevertheless, this negative finding about the prospects for cooperation is not the end of the story. To begin with, the Nash hypothesis is only one plausible characterization of strategic interactions and expectations among independent actors.[23] Moreover, the outcome (S,T) remains Pareto superior to (N,N). Thus the United States could be persuaded to play strategy S rather than N if it had reason to expect effective demand restraint by other IEA members, and the other countries could be induced to play T rather than N if they conjectured that failure to do so would result in defection by the United States from S to N.

This argument is strengthened by the recognition that decisions on energy policy are not just the one-shot game reflected in table 6-1 but are a repeated game where Pareto-superior outcomes can be sustained by mutual promises and "threats."[24] In principle, the same reasoning could be applied to argue for the viability of the joint stockpiling outcome (S,S). On practical grounds, however, this argument is much weaker than the argument for the (S,T) outcome, given the strong divergence of positions on stockpiling between the United States and other IEA members.

In summary, prospects for international cooperation on energy security may be hindered but are not negated by discord and preferences for free riding. Achieving cooperation in such circumstances, however, is likely to require more than a narrow exercise of national self-interest; negotiation and communication to establish mutual expectations of cooperation are also needed. Moreover, the larger the perceived gains from cooperation, the better are the prospects for cooperation. The analysis in the next section sheds some light on the potential economic gains from cooperation and also highlights the limitations of a tightly circumscribed economic evaluation.

Dynamic Simulation Analysis

In this section we present numerical policy evaluation results from a dynamic programming model of policy interactions that is an extension and refinement of the framework in Hogan.[25] The model considers noncooperative and cooperative stockpiling decisions by two actors: the United States and an aggregate representing West Germany and Japan.[26] Significantly, the model assumes that these two players in the game behave as "utilitarian actors," with the objective of minimizing the expected present value of the aggregate economic costs of oil supply disruptions. These costs are the larger transfers of

207

wealth to oil exporters in a crisis and the macroeconomic dislocations caused by oil price shocks with sticky product and factor prices (particularly wage rates) in the economy.[27]

The logic of the dynamic programming model for optimal stockpile management by a single country or a cooperating group of countries may be summarized as follows. Given (perhaps subjective) probabilities of oil market crises with different severities occurring or persisting from period to period, the stockpile manager can postulate alternative scenarios for the oil market over time and the (compound) probabilities of each scenario's emerging. Further, given expectations about the behavior of oil supply and prices and about macroeconomic dislocations in both disrupted and undisrupted market "states," the manager can calculate the discounted net savings in disruption costs from alternative stockpile policies for each market scenario. By combining these calculations, a stockpile management *rule* can be derived that minimizes the expected present value of disruption costs. The dynamic programming algorithm greatly simplifies this potentially complex optimization problem and allows for stockpile fill or release decisions to be updated with changes in inventory size and market state.

When multiple uncoordinated stockpilers are brought into the analysis, the derivation of optimal decision rules becomes more complex because of the interdependence of individual decision rules: in calculating for different market scenarios the discounted net savings in disruption costs from alternative policies, each country's stockpile manager must take into account how the behavior of market oil prices will be altered by other nations' policies. This complication is addressed in the model through the Nash hypothesis discussed above. Under this hypothesis each stockpile manager calculates an optimal policy given expectations of other countries' decision rules. The calculations are then repeated until the policy expectations are consistent with the actual outcome of the game.

In addition to strategic stockpile interactions, the model can be used to simulate and evaluate restraints on oil demand in a crisis. Demand restraint is represented in the model by a tariff on oil imports, but the results are easily reinterpreted in terms of an import quota or domestic excise taxes. Generally, our input assumptions for the model are consistent with those in Hogan and in Chao and Manne.[28] We do, however, assume somewhat greater responsiveness of oil supply and demands and lower risks of disruption to reflect the recent changes in the oil market discussed at the beginning of the chapter.[29]

To present model results that are comparable to table 6–1 and the discussion following it, we must settle on more precise definitions for model implementation of the strategies S, T, and N in that table. Part of the definitional problem arises in distinguishing between stockpile size and stockpile use. For example, we could define the no-action option to include positive but noncooperative stockpiling, rather than cooperative stockpiling. A comparison of these two scenarios, however, indicates almost no difference between them either in the pattern of stock use during a crisis or in the magnitude of avoided costs.[30] In any event, such a comparison does not seem to be in keeping with the analysis in the previous section, where the focus was on "corner solutions" concerning stockpile sizes—for example, the willingness of IEA members to create and maintain available stocks.

Accordingly, in presenting the model results, we define the strategy options N, T, and S in the following way:

• The no-action option, N, is defined as literally doing nothing— neither restraining demand nor *creating* a strategic reserve for use in a crisis. Note that this definition overstates the gains from participation reflected in table 6–1, where N was defined more broadly to include limited unilateral actions.[31]

• The demand restraint option, T, for the Japan-Germany aggregate is defined as imposition of a $2 per barrel tariff on oil imports (and thus consumption) in a crisis.

• If the other side does nothing (option N), the stockpile option, S, for each side is defined as implementing a unilateral strategy of stockpile fill and release that minimizes disruption costs, subject to a capacity constraint. When Japan-plus-Germany restrains demand (option T), strategy S by the United States involves stockpile use to minimize aggregate disruption losses experienced by the three countries. Finally, if both countries stockpile—the outcome (S,S)—it is assumed that inventories are coordinated by choosing an aggregate stock change policy (fill and release) that minimizes aggregate losses and then apportioning those stock changes to the two sides in proportion to their inventory capacities.[32] The inventory capacity for the United States is set at 750 million barrels (the current target size of the SPR), the combined German-Japanese capacity at 400 million barrels.[33]

Table 6–2 summarizes the rankings of these policy options implied by the model in terms of the expected present value of avoided disruption costs (in billions of 1983 dollars). Because of the numerous simplifications of reality involved in the model, the actual magnitudes of the entries are not of great importance, but their ordinal relationships are.[34] Note first that, according to the model, cooperative

209

TABLE 6–2
ECONOMIC RANKINGS OF POLICY OPTIONS
(billions of 1983 dollars)

United States	Japan/Germany		
	S	T	N
S	434/331	367/233	337/249
N	214/169	13/−34	0/0

NOTE: S = stockpile use; T = demand restraint; N = no action (including acquisition and storage of strategic reserve); see text for more precise interpretations and contrasts with table 6–1. Entries represent the expected present value of avoided disruption costs for various policy combinations.
SOURCE: Dynamic simulation model developed by the authors.

stockpiling is a dominant strategy for both the United States and Japan-Germany. Demand restraint is inferior for Germany and Japan, however, to both stockpile use and doing nothing, regardless of the U.S. action.

The sharp contrast between these model predictions and the apparent policy preferences of IEA members, as summarized in table 6–1, illustrates the limitations of a narrow economic benefit-cost comparison for evaluating the current behavior of IEA members and the prospects for cooperation (as opposed to the use of the model in drawing broader normative inferences).[35] To be sure, some "mechanical" arguments related to our application of the model may explain part of the disparity. As noted, for example, our specification of policy options in table 6–2 probably overstates the benefits of cooperation. At the margin the dominance of the stockpiling strategy is not so pronounced.[36] Nor is the demand restraint option necessarily as unfavorable as indicated above.[37]

At bottom, however, the contrasts between tables 6–1 and 6–2 seem to reflect a fundamental gap between the apparent interests of IEA members and the "utilitarian actor" interests described by the economic evaluations in the model. Part of this gap no doubt reflects economic concerns not reflected in the model.[38] But it also seems plausible that the gap arises from the effects on the process of policy formation of concerns about free riding and the need for assurance.

One conclusion of the model that is consistent with the policy rankings in table 6–1 concerns the viability of the policy approach (S,T). Although this policy combination is neither first best nor, at first glance, even credible according to table 6–2, both sides would

210

prefer it even on narrow economic grounds to the no-action outcome (N,N). This observation plays an important role in our recommendation for restructuring the current IEA crisis management program, to which we now turn.

Conclusion and Recommendation

IEA members agree that cooperation is desirable in responding to energy emergencies but do not effectively agree on how this aim can be achieved beyond the current, deficient IEA crisis management system. Economic analyses of different policy combinations under various strategic and coalitional configurations can contribute much to informing this debate, particularly over longer periods when an accumulation of such analytical evidence may lead to at least some shifting of governmental policy preferences.[39] But these studies do not seem to yield policy predictions consistent with the positions of IEA members on either unilateral or cooperative measures to increase energy security.

One important implication of these observations is that recommendations for greater stockpile coordination based on narrow economic analyses must be tempered by a realization of the immediate practical difficulties posed by the disparate current interests and expectations of IEA members. We do not doubt the ultimate gains from such cooperation (although our analysis suggests that it would be more important in expanding inventory sizes than in coordinating their use). For the time being, however, international agreement to coordinate stocks seems difficult if not impossible to achieve, given the widely varying positions of IEA members on the role of stocks.

In view of the substantial costs (economic and other) that would result from a no-action outcome in the event of another oil crisis and the apparent risk of such an outcome's actually occurring given the current state of IEA preparedness, we believe that both individual IEA members and the IEA itself should consider other measures for enhancing cooperation to avoid that outcome. Our analysis has focused on a mixed approach, with the United States relying primarily on aggressive use of its SPR and other IEA members relying primarily on effective, market-oriented demand restraints. This approach, though not first best in a narrow economic sense, has several commendable features.

First, both the United States and other IEA members would experience net economic gains under the plan over an outcome with ineffectual or even nugatory policy responses. Particularly from the U.S. point of view, demand restraints by other oil-consuming nations have

211

the same effects on world oil supplies and prices as releases of stocks by those countries. The United States thus has no economic rationale to be opposed to such restraints per se.

Second, a credible commitment to such restraints would address any assurance problem that impedes an effective U.S. stockpile response. The credibility of a professed commitment by other IEA members to demand restraints is not immediately apparent, given the economic costs of such restraints in a crisis. The problem for these countries may also be one of assurance, but their incentives may run nominally in the direction of free riding. Even in this case, however, important expectational factors—such as concern over evoking a weak policy response by the United States—may militate against this deleterious outcome. The important point is that because the mixed policy approach is tailored to the disparity of interests of IEA members, it seems unambiguously more credible a priori than alternatives—like stockpile coordination—that do not reflect that disparity.

This assertion is not intended to suggest that achieving such an agreement would be easy or that success is guaranteed. Other IEA members would face the burden of making their demand restraint policies credible, but the United States would face a similar burden given its fitful commitment to the SPR. Problems also arise in monitoring compliance with policy measures during a crisis, when accurate and timely information about market conditions is difficult to obtain.[40] As both a gatherer of information and a forum for consultation and establishment of expectations, the IEA could play an important role in addressing these issues.[41]

Notes

The authors gratefully acknowledge helpful discussions with Jaime Marquez and Knut Mork. Partial financial support for this research was provided by the U.S. Department of Energy. Responsibility for errors and opinions is the authors' alone.

1. After the 1979 price shock, first Sweden and later Turkey requested initiation of the oil-sharing system to relieve local shortages, but both were unwilling to pay going market prices. See Robert O. Keohane, "International Agencies and the Art of the Possible: The Case of the IEA," *Journal of Policy Analysis and Management*, vol. 1, no. 4 (Summer 1982), pp. 469–81.

2. See, for example, Mason Willrich and Melvin A. Conant, "The International Energy Agency: An Interpretation and Assessment," *American Journal of International Law*, vol. 71, no. 2 (April 1977), pp. 199–223; Stephen W. Salant, "The Design of a Self-enforcing Multilateral Agreement among Oil-importing Countries," *Contemporary Policy Issues*, no. 5 (March 1984), pp. 58–75; George Horwich and David Leo Weimer, *Oil Price Shocks, Market Response,*

and Contingency Planning (Washington, D.C.: American Enterprise Institute, 1984); and Douglas R. Bohi and Michael A. Toman, "Oil Supply Disruptions and the Role of the International Energy Agency," *Energy Journal*, vol. 7, no. 2 (April 1986), pp. 211–24.

3. See, for example, William W. Hogan, "Oil Stockpiling: Help Thy Neighbor," *Energy Journal*, vol. 4, no. 3 (July 1983), pp. 49–72; Shantayanan Devarajan, R. Glenn Hubbard, and Robert Weiner, "The Coordination of Worldwide Stockpiles of Oil" (Paper presented at the Fifth Annual Research Conference of the Association for Public Policy and Management, Philadelphia, October 1983); Salant, "Design of a Self-enforcing Multilateral Agreement"; R. Glenn Hubbard, Jaime Marquez, and Robert J. Weiner, "Oil and the OECD Economies: Measuring Stockpile Coordination Benefits" (Paper presented at the International Association of Energy Economists International Conference, Bonn, June 1985). How coordinated long-run tariff policies by importers also yield joint benefits is examined in Hung-po Chao and Stephen Peck, "Coordination of OECD Oil Import Policies: A Gaming Approach," *Energy—The International Journal*, vol. 7, no. 2 (February 1982), pp. 214–20. Attempts to measure gains from coordinated disruption tariffs are reported in Alan S. Manne, "The Potential Gains from Joint Action by Oil Importing Nations," in James Plummer, ed., *Energy Vulnerability* (Cambridge, Mass.: Ballinger, 1982); and Henry S. Rowen and John P. Weyant, "Reducing the Economic Impacts of Oil Supply Interruptions: An International Perspective," *Energy Journal*, vol. 3, no. 1 (January 1982), pp. 1–34. The cost of oil price shocks in these studies, however, includes only the increased cost of oil imports. The joint application of demand restraint and stockpiles is considered by Frederic H. Murphy, Michael A. Toman, and Howard J. Weiss, "International Cooperation in Stockpiles and Tariffs for Coping with Oil Supply Disruptions," *Journal of Policy Modeling*, vol. 7, no. 4 (Winter 1985), pp. 649–72.

4. Hogan, "Oil Stockpiling."

5. For further discussion of these issues, see Douglas R. Bohi and William B. Quandt, *Energy Security in the 1980s: Economic and Political Perspectives*, Brookings Institution Staff Paper (Washington, D.C.: Brookings Institution, 1984).

6. See Douglas R. Bohi and Michael A. Toman, "Futures Trading and Oil Market Conditions," *Journal of Futures Markets*, vol. 7, no. 2 (April 1987), pp. 203–21.

7. See also Douglas R. Bohi, "What Causes Oil Price Shocks?" Discussion Paper D-82S, Resources for the Future, 1983; and Bohi and Toman, "Oil Supply Disruptions."

8. As one might expect, given the sensitivity of the subject, government perceptions and stances do not receive extensive public discussion; nor are policy-level deliberations within the IEA a part of the public record. (We have found that even private discussions with IEA staff or individual country representatives tend to elicit very guarded responses.) Moreover, since the provisions of the current IEA agreement have never been tested in a crisis and conditions in the oil market have changed in any event, there is little in the way of a historical record to which one can turn. The information that is

213

available consists primarily of a few public pronouncements by U.S. officials along with secondary sources cited in the trade press.

9. See E. Allan Wendt, "International Energy Security: The Continuing Challenge," Current Policy Paper no. 612, U.S. Department of State, 1984, pp. 3–4.

10. "U.S., Allies Disagree on Use of Oil Stocks," Inside Energy/with Federal Lands, June 4, 1984, p. 4.

11. See Christopher S. Gibson, "Creative Oil Stockpiling: Evaluating a Three-Country Agreement and Designing a Negotiation Strategy," Energy and Environmental Policy Center Discussion Paper H-84-03, Harvard University, November 1984, p. 22. There is also a presumption that other IEA members are generally more concerned with equity and have a greater distrust of the market than the United States. These factors reinforce their predisposition toward demand restraints.

12. International Energy Agency (IEA), IEA Press Release 84(9) (Paris, October 10, 1984), p. 3.

13. "Pearlman, Wendt Parley in France over Use of Oil Stocks in an Emergency," Inside Energy/with Federal Lands, May 28, 1984, p. 4.

14. See David L. Weimer, The Strategic Petroleum Reserve: Planning, Implementation, and Analysis (Westport, Conn.: Greenwood Press, 1982); Horwich and Weimer, Oil Price Shocks; and Steven Kelman, "Allocating SPR Oil: An Analysis of the Options Alternative," Energy and Environmental Policy Center Discussion Paper H-84-01, Harvard University, March 1984.

15. See General Accounting Office (GAO), Additional Improvements Needed in Logistics Support for the Strategic Petroleum Reserve, Document no. GAO/ RCED-84-12 (Washington, D.C., 1984); and U.S. Congress, House of Representatives, Problems with Distribution of Oil from the Strategic Petroleum Reserve (Hearing before the Subcommittee on Environment, Energy, and Natural Resources, Committee on Government Operations, May 10, 1984).

16. The policy option T for the United States is not included in table 6–1 because the U.S. public position suggests that this option is dominated by both S and N, regardless of other countries' actions.

17. Note that the inequalities (1) do not provide a complete ordering of the policy options in table 6–1. It is reasonable to assume further that $a_4 >$ a_5, given U.S. distaste for demand restraint. The relationship between a_2 and a_4 is not so clear, however. Note also that an alternative U.S. ranking is $a_1 >$ $a_4 > a_5 > a_2 > 0 > a_3$. This ranking differs from (1) in that only a strong stockpile response evokes a similar action by the United States. As noted further below, this ranking has a negative implication for the prospects for cooperation. It also seems less plausible than (1), however, because it implies a complete discounting by the United States of the economic gains from even the most effective demand restraints by other IEA members.

18. For recent discussions of the assurance problem, see C. Ford Runge, "Common Property Externalities: Isolation, Assurance, and Resource Depletion in a Traditional Grazing Context," American Journal of Agricultural Economics, vol. 63, no. 4 (November 1981), pp. 595–606; and Runge, "The Fallacy

214

of 'Privatization,'" *Journal of Contemporary Studies*, vol. 7, no. 1 (Winter 1984), pp. 3–18.

19. In other words, N is the optimal response regardless of U.S. actions.

20. For a classic discussion of the free-rider problem, see Mancur Olson and Richard Zeckhauser, "An Economic Theory of Alliances," *Review of Economics and Statistics*, vol. 48, no. 3 (August 1966), pp. 266–79.

21. Roughly speaking, the Nash hypothesis for a noncooperative game posits that each "player" chooses actions that best serve its interests, given expectations of other players' actions; in equilibrium, these expectations are borne out by the actual behavior of other players. Note that this hypothesis does *not* assume inherently myopic or naive behavior, contrary to some discussions of it in the literature. For a more formal treatment of this and other noncooperative equilibrium concepts, see James Friedman, *Oligopoly and the Theory of Games* (Amsterdam: North-Holland, 1977). One alternative concept that has been used in the oil security literature is the so-called Stackelberg leader-follower equilibrium, in which one player (the leader) makes choices taking into account the reactions of others. We have avoided this equilibrium concept here because, in our view, the choice of leader in the context of international energy security is not so clear-cut.

22. The same is true, along with the caution about this finding noted below, if U.S. aversion to demand restraint leads to the policy ranking $a_1 > a_4 > a_5 > a_2 > 0 > a_3$, rather than (1).

23. For a general discussion of alternative noncooperative "conjectural variation" equilibria in externality situations, see Richard Cornes and Todd Sandler, "Externalities, Expectations, and Pigouvan Taxes," *Journal of Environmental Economics and Management*, vol. 12, no. 1 (March 1985), pp. 1–13.

24. See Thomas Schelling, *The Strategy of Conflict* (Cambridge, Mass.: Harvard University Press, 1960); Friedman, *Oligopoly*; and Russell Hardin, *Collective Action* (Washington, D.C.: Resources for the Future, 1982). The standard argument here is that cooperation can be sustained if decision makers do not discount the future too heavily, so that transient gains from defection are exceeded in the long run by the costs of noncooperation.

25. See Hogan, "Oil Stockpiling." Because the model is similar to Hogan's, our discussion of it here is brief. A more complete description of model structure and assumptions is contained in Murphy, Toman, and Weiss, "International Cooperation in Stockpiles and Tariffs."

26. Such a bilateral specification of interests is common to the dynamic programming approach but is an obvious drawback, since it requires us to assume more homogeneity of interests and cooperation among IEA members other than the United States than is realistic, while ignoring the role of private inventory behavior. This and other weaknesses of the model are discussed further below. Public-private inventory interactions for a single stockpiling nation are examined in Brian D. Wright and Jeffrey C. Williams, "The Roles of Public and Private Storage in Managing Oil Import Disruptions," *Bell Journal of Economics*, vol. 13, no. 2 (Autumn 1982), pp. 341–53; and Frederic A. Murphy, Michael A. Toman, and Howard J. Weiss, "An Integrated Analysis of

U.S. Oil Security Policies," *Energy Journal*, vol. 7, no. 3 (July 1986), pp. 67–81.

27. For further discussion of these costs, see, for example, Douglas R. Bohi and W. David Montgomery, *Oil Prices, Energy Security, and Import Policy* (Washington, D.C.: Resources for the Future, 1982); and Richard J. Gilbert and Knut A. Mork, "Will Oil Markets Tighten Again? A Survey of Policies to Manage Possible Oil Supply Disruptions," *Journal of Policy Modeling*, vol. 6, no. 1 (Spring 1984), pp. 111–42. Note that the macroeconomic disruption costs we focus on here are "relative price problems," as described in Gilbert and Mork, rather than problems of inflation and aggregate demand insufficiency, which are more amenable to standard macroeconomic stabilization policies. International cooperation in addressing the latter problems is discussed, for example, in Matthew B. Canzoneri and Jo Anna Gray, "Two Essays on Monetary Policy in an Interdependent World," International Finance Discussion Paper 219, Federal Reserve Board of Governors, February 1983.

28. Hogan, "Oil Stockpiling"; and Hung-po Chao and Alan S. Manne, "An Integrated Analysis of U.S. Oil Stockpiling Policies," in Plummer, *Energy Vulnerability*.

29. Specifically, our "base case" assumptions include a 15 percent chance of a "moderate" crisis (one resulting in about a $10 per barrel increase in the world price of oil) and a 5 percent chance of a "severe" crisis (with about a $30 per barrel price increase). In contrast, the base case probabilities in Hogan, "Oil Stockpiling," are 20 percent and 10 percent respectively. Another distinction between our model application and Hogan's is that in describing noncooperative outcomes where both sides stockpile, we use the Nash hypothesis, whereas Hogan used the Stackelberg leader-follower approach.

30. This comparison may not be very powerful because the model, like others of its type, assumes an annual decision period and thus may obscure important finer-grained distinctions between noncooperative and cooperative outcomes where both sides stockpile. The comparison should not be viewed as a refutation of theoretical results that indicate more rapid stock release under cooperation, such as those in Devarajan, Hubbard, and Weiner, "Coordination of Worldwide Stockpiles." For further discussion of this issue, see Murphy, Toman, and Weiss, "International Cooperation in Stockpiles and Tariffs"; and Michael A. Toman, "Policy Responses to Uncertainty," in Allen V. Kneese and James L. Sweeney, eds., *The Handbook of Natural Resource and Energy Economics*, vol. 3, *Economics of Energy and Minerals* (Amsterdam: North-Holland, forthcoming).

31. The definition understates the gains, however, by ignoring the costs of building but not using a strategic reserve. Other model results not reported here indicate that our qualitative conclusions would not be changed if we focused on expanding stock sizes rather than on the decision of whether or not to institute a strategic reserve policy.

32. This specification of cooperation is intended to mimic in broad terms the proposal for stockpile coordination in Devarajan, Hubbard, and Weiner, "Coordination of Worldwide Stockpiles"; and Gibson, "Creative Oil Stockpiling."

216

33. In the joint stockpiling outcome the U.S. capacity is set at 800 million barrels to make it an integer multiple of the Japanese-German capacity figure. These capacity limits are larger than current stock sizes but are binding constraints in the model, in that they are well below theoretically optimal inventory sizes. This is one potential explanation for the insignificant differences noted above between Nash outcomes (with both countries stockpiling) and the cooperative outcome.

34. These entries were generated with a single set of "base case" input assumptions. Except as noted below, however, the results are robust to a wide range of changes in assumptions. For details, see Murphy, Toman, and Weiss, "International Cooperation in Stockpiles and Tariffs."

35. We emphasize that this limitation applies not just to dynamic programming formulations but to the whole class of analyses that focus solely on an economic criterion of net benefits maximization for addressing these issues.

36. Our results also *assume* cooperation between Germany and Japan, however, and thus *understate* the potential benefits of cooperation in practice.

37. If the probabilities that crises linger are larger than assumed in table 6–2, so that the average duration of a disruption is longer, then the disruption tariff contributes more to recapturing rents from oil exporters and causes less macroeconomic damage (because crises are less frequent and private markets have more time to adjust to the tariff). Under these circumstances the tariff need not be inferior to no action for Japan and Germany, provided that the United States uses its reserve. Note also that with more countries than Germany and Japan participating in the demand restraint, the economic costs of restraint for each participant would be reduced.

38. These factors include risk aversion, the burdens of either localized shortages or long-term lack of access to oil supplies, doubts that crises will play out smoothly as in the stylized description by the model, and equity issues.

39. For a recent example of this involving the Law of the Sea Treaty, see James K. Sebenius, *Negotiating the Law of the Sea* (Cambridge, Mass.: Harvard University Press, 1984).

40. It is often argued—correctly—that demand restraint policies can be subverted with hidden subsidies. Given the IEA's current difficulties in establishing a meaningful definition and measures of available stocks, however, the monitoring problems with inventory policy seem no less serious in practice.

41. For a discussion of the role of institutions in overcoming assurance problems, see Runge, "Common Property Externalities," and "The Fallacy of 'Privatization.'" Gibson, "Creative Oil Stockpiling," describes an approach for achieving a stockpile coordination agreement based on the conflict resolution method in Howard Raiffa, *The Art and Science of Negotiation* (Cambridge, Mass.: Harvard University Press, 1982). Presumably this method could also be used for achieving agreement with a mixture of policy tools.

217

7
Empirical Analysis of World Oil Trade, 1967–1984

Joseph M. Anderson

The mandatory oil-sharing system is the centerpiece of the emergency program of the International Energy Agency (IEA). Economic justification of mandatory sharing must be premised on a concern that in future disruptions of oil supply the world oil market may not allocate oil efficiently, either because of institutional rigidities or because of the influence of important nonmarket forces, such as a targeted embargo.[1] A sharing agreement does not increase the supply of oil. If binding on any country, it simply redistributes the existing supply. Under normal market conditions, moreover, allocation by the sharing formula will compare unfavorably with the market's tendency to allocate petroleum so as to equalize the value of the marginal barrel in each consuming country.[2]

During a disruption, however, normal market forces may not operate. Temporary allocational distortions may arise because of rigidities in supply channels, such as those that result from contractual arrangements or historical buyer-seller relationships, or because of targeting actions by exporters. A sharing scheme, by offsetting such distortions, could serve to transfer oil from low-valued uses to higher-valued uses, albeit imperfectly.

In this chapter I attempt to evaluate the relative performance of the world oil market from 1967 to 1984 during periods of normal and disrupted supply. I first examine and compare import prices and quantities among major oil-importing countries to determine whether any country was disproportionately affected by supply disruptions. For this analysis I construct import price indexes adjusted for changes in the quality of oil. Second, I analyze the demand for oil imports to determine whether the imports of various countries during supply disruptions can be explained adequately by the same factors that operate during nondisrupted periods.

218

Prices and Quantities of Imported Petroleum

I begin my analysis with a descriptive review of data on import volumes and prices. Specifically, I consider data from major oil-importing countries—the United States, Japan, West Germany, the United Kingdom, France, Italy, and the Netherlands—over the period 1967–1984.[3] The data permit a cross-country comparison to determine whether the experiences of any particular countries seem to deviate substantially from the general experience.[4]

Import Quantities. Figure 7–1 shows the relative volume of petroleum imported by each of the seven countries over the period 1973–1974, using imports for the first quarter of 1970 as the base. In the first quarter of 1974, coinciding with the embargo by the Organization of Arab Petroleum Exporting Countries (OAPEC), U.S. oil imports declined absolutely and relatively to the imports of the other countries. Imports for the Netherlands, which was also a target, and for West Germany, which was not, also declined absolutely and relatively.[5] Imports of the United Kingdom, France, Italy, and Japan were more or less stable in the first half of 1974.

Figure 7–2, which covers the period 1978–1981, shows that U.S. petroleum imports were relatively stable in 1979 but began falling in 1980. Other importing countries exhibited a similar pattern, although the decline in U.S. imports in 1980 was greater.[6] The 1980 decline can be attributed to the steep price increase that occurred in 1979 and to the drawdown of inventories that were built up in 1979. Although prices increased sharply in 1979 after the disruption of Iranian supplies, imports appear to have been fairly stable until 1980. No country's imports seem to have been disproportionately affected by the disruption in Iran.

Figures 7–1 and 7–2 show that U.S. crude imports fell somewhat more than those of other major oil-importing countries in 1974:I and in 1980, though not in 1979. If the own-price elasticity of demand for oil imports is larger in the United States, imports would be expected to fall relatively more in response to an increase in oil prices. Because the United States is an oil producer as well as importer and can more easily substitute other fuels, we would expect its price elasticity of demand for imports to be greater. Consequently, data on import quantities alone do not establish conclusively whether one or more countries were affected by the disruptions of 1973–1974 or 1979–1981 other than by market forces.

Import Prices. A second source of information bearing on the func-

219

FIGURE 7-1
INDEX OF PETROLEUM IMPORTS,
UNITED STATES AND SIX OTHER COUNTRIES, 1973:I–1974:IV
(1970:I = 100)

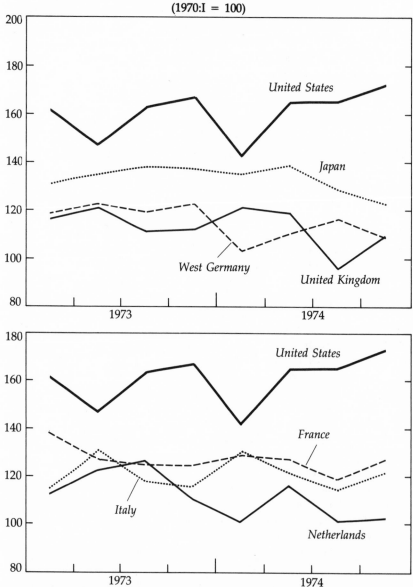

SOURCES: 1973: Bureau of Mines, *Petroleum Statement Monthly*; 1974–1984: Department of Energy, *Annual Energy Review, Monthly Energy Review*, various issues; and OECD, *Quarterly Oil Statistics, Provisional Oil Statistics*.

220

FIGURE 7–2
INDEX OF PETROLEUM IMPORTS,
UNITED STATES AND SIX OTHER COUNTRIES, 1978:I–1981:IV
$(1970:I = 100)$

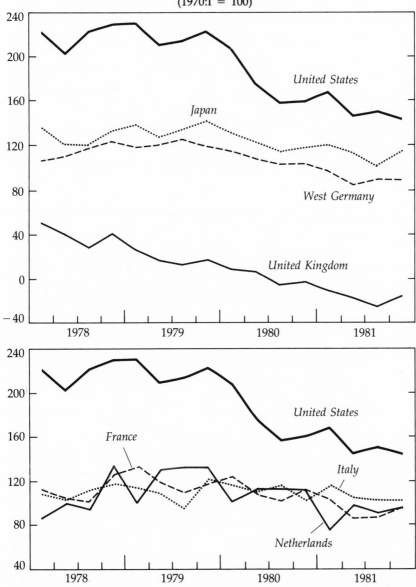

SOURCES: See figure 7–1.

221

TABLE 7-1
AVERAGE PRICE PAID FOR IMPORTED CRUDE OIL
BY SELECTED IMPORTING COUNTRIES, 1973–1984
(dollars per barrel)

	United States	Japan	West Germany	United Kingdom	France	Italy	Nether-lands	Total
1973[a]	6.85	4.15	5.59	4.76	3.88	4.52	3.69	4.75
1974	12.46	10.80	11.92	10.59	10.56	11.09	11.36	11.19
1975	12.63	11.95	12.64	11.70	12.66	11.98	12.23	12.26
1976	13.29	12.61	13.26	12.38	12.77	12.14	13.06	12.84
1977	14.34	13.68	14.38	13.79	13.72	13.31	13.87	13.94
1978	14.32	14.00	14.42	14.00	14.13	13.64	14.02	14.11
1979	21.47	18.64	20.85	18.37	18.33	18.13	19.93	19.67
1980	33.69	33.15	34.11	30.21	32.22	30.59	32.40	32.82
1981	36.49	37.19	37.41	34.22	36.69	35.69	36.19	36.57
1982	33.22	34.55	34.56	33.29	35.32	33.25	33.89	33.62
1983	29.03	30.80	30.98	30.06	31.36	29.65	30.47	30.24
1984	28.65	29.32	29.84	28.68	29.64	28.67	29.04	29.10

NOTE: Prices are average landed (cost, insurance, and freight—c.i.f.) prices in nominal (current) dollars per barrel, including transportation.
a. Price data for 1973 are available for the United States only for the fourth quarter; consequently, only fourth-quarter data are reported for other countries, except the Netherlands, for which only third-quarter data are available.
SOURCES: United States: Department of Energy, "Monthly Crude Oil Acquisition Report," EIA-856; EP Form 51; and predecessor reports. Others: Middle East Economic Survey, *International Crude Oil and Products Prices.*

tioning of the world petroleum market during periods of disruption is provided by data on prices paid for crude oil imports. A country targeted by an effective embargo or affected adversely by nonmarket forces during a disruption will experience prices above the world level.

Table 7-1 reports the average landed prices in nominal dollars per barrel paid by the United States and other major importing countries for imported crude oil each year during the period 1973–1984.[7] Table 7-2 records the ratio of each importing country's average price to the average price paid by all seven countries. Tables 7-3 and 7-4 show these prices and ratios quarterly. The prices paid by the United States in 1973, 1974, and 1979 averaged about 10 percent higher than those paid by other countries. The average prices paid by West Germany in those years were also somewhat higher, though less than the U.S. prices. The average prices paid by the Netherlands were about the same as those paid by other countries.[8]

222

TABLE 7-2
RATIO OF IMPORTING COUNTRY'S AVERAGE PRICE OF IMPORTED CRUDE
OIL TO SEVEN-COUNTRY AVERAGE PRICE, 1973–1984

	United States	Japan	West Germany	United Kingdom	France	Italy	Netherlands
1973[a]	1.44	0.88	1.18	1.00	0.82	0.95	1.03
1974	1.11	0.97	1.07	0.95	0.94	0.99	1.02
1975	1.03	0.97	1.03	0.95	1.03	0.98	1.00
1976	1.04	0.98	1.03	0.96	0.99	0.95	1.02
1977	1.03	0.98	1.03	0.99	0.98	0.95	0.99
1978	1.01	0.99	1.02	0.99	1.00	0.97	0.99
1979	1.09	0.95	1.06	0.93	0.93	0.92	1.01
1980	1.03	1.01	1.04	0.92	0.98	0.93	0.99
1981	1.00	1.02	1.02	0.94	1.00	0.98	0.99
1982	0.99	1.03	1.03	0.99	1.05	0.99	1.01
1983	0.96	1.02	1.02	0.99	1.04	0.98	1.01
1984	0.98	1.01	1.03	0.99	1.02	0.99	1.00

a. Fourth quarter only except the Netherlands. The Netherlands ratio is third-quarter Netherlands price to third-quarter average price of six importing countries, excluding the United States, for which third-quarter price data are unavailable.
SOURCE: Table 7–1.

Table 7–5 presents quarterly data on relative crude oil prices charged to the United States by each of the six exporting countries providing the largest share of U.S. oil imports over the 1973–1984 period.[9] The six are Saudi Arabia, Iran, Nigeria, Libya, Algeria, and Mexico. These data were assembled to determine whether any of the exporting countries appear to have discriminated against the United States in price, particularly during periods of disruption. The table shows the ratio of the average price paid by the United States for oil imported from each of the six countries to the average price paid by the five other largest importing countries.[10]

In 1974:I the United States paid 34 percent to 58 percent more for crude oil from Saudi Arabia, Iran, Libya, and Nigeria than the average of the five other major importing countries. The United States paid slightly more than other countries in 1974:II and 1974:III for oil from Saudi Arabia and Iran. The price to the United States for oil from Saudi Arabia, Iran, Libya, and Nigeria also rose more than the price to other importing countries in 1979. For most of the remainder of the period, U.S. prices were in line with prices charged to other importing countries. The average landed prices paid by the United

223

TABLE 7–3
AVERAGE PRICE PAID FOR IMPORTED CRUDE OIL,
SELECTED IMPORTING COUNTRIES, QUARTERLY, 1973–1985
(dollars per barrel)

	United States	Japan	West Germany	United Kingdom	France	Italy	Netherlands	Total
1973 I		2.82	3.42	3.19	3.20	2.98	3.06	3.07
II		3.01	3.75	3.43	3.46	3.19	3.37	3.31
III		3.25	4.18	3.65	3.56	3.68	3.69	3.59
IV	6.85	4.15	5.59	4.76	3.88	4.52		4.75
1974 I	12.80	9.03		8.72	8.19	9.73		9.47
II	12.90	11.29	11.64	11.31	10.82	11.25	11.13	11.52
III	12.20	11.32	11.63	11.06	11.26	11.66	11.25	11.52
IV	12.07	11.59	12.51	11.36	12.08	11.86	11.72	11.86
1975 I	12.23	11.97	12.71	12.04	12.76	12.01	12.58	12.25
II	12.43	11.69	12.15	11.37	12.55		11.89	12.00
III	12.47	11.61						12.00
IV	13.25	12.49	13.04			11.96		12.72
1976 I	13.23	12.67	13.32	12.84	12.83	11.31	12.92	12.77
II	13.24	12.63	13.04	12.08	12.77	12.38	12.82	12.78
III	13.30	12.70	13.29	12.47	12.65	12.50	13.25	12.92
IV	13.36	12.46	13.39	12.16	12.83	12.36	13.22	12.87
1977 I	14.21	13.28	14.10	13.38	13.23	12.90	13.37	13.61
II	14.34	13.62	14.27	13.70	13.70	13.33	14.09	13.92
III	14.39	13.65	14.42	13.85	13.81	13.36	13.92	13.99
IV	14.43	14.17	14.75	14.31	14.13	13.63	14.16	14.25
1978 I	14.34	14.17	14.73	13.99	14.04	13.69	14.17	14.19
II	14.24	14.00	14.21	13.78	14.25	13.65	13.95	14.07
III	14.22	14.34	14.34	14.24	14.17	13.72	14.01	14.18
IV	14.47	13.51	14.43	14.01	14.06	13.52	13.95	14.03
1979 I	15.67	13.98	15.62	14.51	14.35	14.32	15.10	14.81
II	19.38	16.15	18.89	16.58	16.40	16.36	17.66	17.59
III	23.68	20.29	23.01	20.42	20.20	20.02	22.36	21.74
IV	26.97	23.98	25.55	22.04	22.91	21.99	24.39	24.55
1980 I	31.89	30.42	31.97	26.71	29.29	27.08	30.12	30.29
II	33.63	33.50	34.30	30.43	32.12	31.24	32.12	32.98
III	34.60	34.18	35.13	31.80	33.38	31.98	33.39	33.89
IV	35.03	34.84	35.26	32.82	34.60	32.33	34.45	34.50
1981 I	38.03	37.00	38.86	34.51	36.24	35.29	36.65	37.06
II	36.95	38.00	37.74	34.34	37.88	36.39	37.35	37.27
III	35.30	37.09	36.21	32.53	36.54	35.84	35.28	35.93
IV	35.43	36.67	36.71	35.28	36.19	35.28	35.41	35.97
1982 I	34.57	35.28	35.90	34.88	36.46	34.71	34.81	35.24
II	33.00	34.46	33.62	32.19	35.19	32.41	33.07	33.60
III	32.71	34.21	34.23	32.93	34.63	32.76		31.76

TABLE 7–3 (continued)

		United States	Japan	West Germany	United Kingdom	France	Italy	Netherlands	Total
	IV	32.77	34.14	34.59	33.26	34.72	32.97	33.82	33.70
1983	I	29.61	33.72	33.03	31.71	34.27	32.22	32.98	32.61
	II	28.63	29.96	30.48	30.20	30.88	29.17	29.68	29.65
	III	29.14	29.53	29.99	29.32	30.25	28.60	29.62	29.42
	IV	28.93	29.79	30.46	29.17	30.25	28.74	29.81	29.54
1984	I	28.79	29.70	30.61	29.34	30.08	29.09	29.52	29.52
	II	28.98	29.27	30.26	29.14	29.90	28.87	29.53	29.33
	III	28.46	29.17	29.26	28.20	29.31	28.07	28.60	28.79
	IV	28.37	29.07	29.13	28.22	29.15	28.54	28.38	28.73
1985	I		28.86	28.63	27.45	28.37		28.11	28.53
	II					28.74			28.74

NOTE: Prices are average landed (cost, insurance, and freight—c.i.f.) prices in nominal (current) dollars per barrel, including transportation.
SOURCES: United States: Department of Energy, "Monthly Cruide Oil Acquisition Report," EIA-850, EP Form 51, and predecessor reports. Others: Middle East Economic Survey, *International Crude Oil and Products Prices.*

States for oil from Algeria and Mexico were generally lower than the prices paid by other importing countries. The lower price for oil from Mexico may reflect differences in transportation costs.

The price and quantity data presented in figures 7–1 and 7–2 and in tables 7–1 through 7–5 show that U.S. oil imports fell and prices increased more than those of other major importing countries during the 1973–1974 disruption. U.S. relative oil import prices also increased slightly in 1979. Because these data do not control for the quality of imported oil, however, they are not adequate to determine whether the United States suffered disproportionately during the oil supply disruptions of 1973–1974 and 1979–1981. An adjustment for quality is made in the following section.

Import Prices Adjusted for Quality. If the average quality of oil imported by a country changes systematically, data on the recorded price of imports will mask changes in the true cost of the oil. Differential changes in quality among countries, which change the real cost of oil, may indicate the influence of noncompetitive elements in the world market on the allocation of traded oil. To investigate whether such quality changes occurred and, if they did, to measure their effect on the true cost of oil, I carried out a comprehensive analysis of the price of U.S. oil imports.

225

TABLE 7-4
RATIO OF IMPORTING COUNTRY'S AVERAGE PRICE OF IMPORTED CRUDE OIL TO SEVEN-COUNTRY AVERAGE PRICE, QUARTERLY, 1973–1985

	United States	Japan	West Germany	United Kingdom	France	Italy	Netherlands
1973 I		0.92	1.12	1.04	1.04	0.97	1.00
II		0.91	1.13	1.04	1.04	0.96	1.02
III		0.91	1.16	1.01	0.99	1.02	1.03
IV	1.44	0.88	1.18	1.00	0.82	0.95	
1974 I	1.35	0.95		0.92	0.87	1.03	
II	1.12	0.98	1.01	0.98	0.94	0.98	0.97
III	1.06	0.98	1.01	0.96	0.98	1.01	0.98
IV	1.02	0.98	1.05	0.96	1.02	1.00	0.99
1975 I	1.00	0.98	1.04	0.98	1.04	0.98	1.03
II	1.04	0.97	1.01	0.95	1.05		0.99
III	1.04	0.97					
IV	1.04	0.98	1.02			0.94	
1976 I	1.04	0.99	1.04	1.01	1.00	0.89	1.01
II	1.04	0.99	1.02	0.94	1.00	0.97	1.00
III	1.03	0.98	1.03	0.97	0.98	0.97	1.03
IV	1.04	0.97	1.04	0.95	1.00	0.96	1.03
1977 I	1.04	0.98	1.04	0.98	0.97	0.95	0.98
II	1.03	0.98	1.03	0.98	0.98	0.96	1.01
III	1.03	0.98	1.03	0.99	0.99	0.95	0.99
IV	1.01	0.99	1.04	1.00	0.99	0.96	0.99
1978 I	1.01	1.00	1.04	0.99	0.99	0.96	1.00
II	1.01	1.00	1.01	0.98	1.01	0.97	0.99
III	1.00	1.01	1.01	1.00	1.00	0.97	0.99
IV	1.03	0.96	1.03	1.00	1.00	0.96	0.99
1979 I	1.06	0.94	1.05	0.98	0.97	0.97	1.02
II	1.10	0.92	1.07	0.94	0.93	0.93	1.00
III	1.09	0.93	1.06	0.94	0.93	0.92	1.03
IV	1.10	0.98	1.04	0.90	0.93	0.90	0.99
1980 I	1.05	1.00	1.06	0.88	0.97	0.89	0.99
II	1.02	1.02	1.04	0.92	0.97	0.95	0.97
III	1.02	1.01	1.04	0.94	0.98	0.94	0.99
IV	1.02	1.01	1.02	0.95	1.00	0.94	1.00
1981 I	1.03	1.00	1.05	0.93	0.98	0.95	0.99
II	0.99	1.02	1.01	0.92	1.02	0.98	1.00
III	0.98	1.03	1.01	0.91	1.02	1.00	0.98
IV	0.99	1.02	1.02	0.98	1.01	0.98	0.98
1982 I	0.98	1.00	1.02	0.99	1.03	0.98	0.99
II	0.98	1.03	1.00	0.96	1.05	0.96	0.98
III	1.03	1.08	1.08	1.04	1.09	1.03	
IV	0.97	1.01	1.03	0.99	1.03	0.98	1.00

226

TABLE 7–4 (continued)

	United States	Japan	West Germany	United Kingdom	France	Italy	Netherlands
1983 I	0.91	1.03	1.01	0.97	1.05	0.99	1.01
II	0.97	1.01	1.03	1.02	1.04	0.98	1.00
III	0.99	1.00	1.02	1.00	1.03	0.97	1.01
IV	0.98	1.01	1.03	0.99	1.02	0.97	1.01
1984 I	0.98	1.01	1.04	0.99	1.02	0.99	1.00
II	0.99	1.00	1.03	0.99	1.02	0.98	1.01
III	0.99	1.01	1.02	0.98	1.02	0.98	0.99
IV	0.99	1.01	1.01	0.98	1.01	0.99	0.99
1985 I		1.01	1.00	0.96	0.99		0.99
II					1.00		

SOURCE: Table 7–3.

The objective of this analysis was to provide a "constant-quality" crude oil price series by which the functioning of the world oil market could be assessed. I derived the series by estimating the relationship between the price of imported crude oil and its quality, as measured by American Petroleum Institute (API) gravity and sulfur content. For this purpose I used a Department of Energy data base containing almost 50,000 records, each of which contains, for each cargo of oil shipped to the United States, the price, country of origin, transaction type, contract terms, physical characteristics, and other data. With data covering the period 1973–1984, I estimated multiple regression equations relating the price of the oil in each quarter to its gravity, sulfur content, country of origin, transaction type, and other attributes. The details of the analysis are reported in appendix A.

The regression coefficients provided estimates, for each quarter, of the dollar-per-barrel reduction in price associated with a one-percentage-point increase in sulfur content and the dollar increase in price associated with an additional degree of API gravity. Virtually all the sulfur and gravity coefficients were highly significant statistically. The coefficients vary over the period, reflecting changes in the composition of demand for petroleum products, in refinery configurations, and in relative supplies of the various types of crude oil. At the end of 1984 each additional percentage point of sulfur content was associated with a reduction in the price per barrel of about $1.00, and an additional degree of API gravity corresponded to an increase in price of about four cents.

I used these estimated quality differential coefficients to adjust the average recorded price of U.S. crude oil imports in each quarter

TABLE 7–5
RATIO OF AVERAGE PRICE PAID BY UNITED STATES FOR OIL FROM
SELECTED COUNTRIES TO VOLUME-WEIGHTED AVERAGE PRICE PAID BY
FIVE OTHER MAJOR IMPORTERS, 1974–1984
(dollars per barrel)

		Saudi Arabia	Iran	Libya	Nigeria	Algeria	Mexico
1974	I	1.35	1.52	1.58	1.34	0.96	
	II	1.11	1.22	1.07	1.10	0.97	
	III	1.07	1.11	—	1.01	0.99	
	IV	1.05	1.09	0.95	0.96	0.98	
1975	I	1.02	1.05	0.95	0.95	1.02	
	II	1.06	1.12	1.00	1.01	1.06	
	III	1.08	1.09	0.97	1.00	—	
	IV	1.08	1.04	1.05	1.02	0.96	
1976	I	1.06	1.03	1.06	1.01	1.00	
	II	1.05	1.05	1.04	1.05	0.97	
	III	1.03	1.02	1.03	1.03	0.97	
	IV	1.04	1.02	1.04	1.03	0.97	
1977	I	1.04	1.03	1.04	1.06	0.98	
	II	1.03	1.03	1.03	1.04	0.97	
	III	1.04	1.02	1.01	1.04	0.97	
	IV	0.99	1.00	0.99	1.02	0.95	
1978	I	1.00	1.00	1.00	1.01	0.94	
	II	1.00	1.01	1.00	1.02	0.95	
	III	0.99	0.99	1.01	1.01	0.94	
	IV	1.03	1.02	1.03	1.06	0.96	
1979	I	1.07	1.10	1.05	1.07	0.97	
	II	1.15	1.10	1.05	1.15	0.99	
	III	1.09	1.17	1.08	1.11	0.99	
	IV	1.13	1.21	1.12	1.14	1.00	
1980	I	1.05	0.93	1.05	1.10	1.01	0.99
	II	1.00	—	1.00	1.04	0.98	0.94
	III	1.01	—	1.00	1.00	0.93	1.01
	IV	1.03	0.93	1.00	1.01	0.93	0.99
1981	I	1.00	—	1.00	1.05	0.96	1.10
	II	0.99	—	0.98	1.00	0.93	0.95
	III	0.99	—	0.96	0.97	0.94	1.01
	IV	1.01	—	0.96	1.03	0.90	1.02
1982	I	1.00	—	0.91	1.01	0.92	0.97
	II	1.02	1.05		1.00	0.90	0.96
	III	1.02	1.01		1.01	0.92	0.97
	IV	1.05	1.03		1.01	0.94	0.89
1983	I	1.03	1.17		0.92	0.91	0.90
	II	1.07	1.03		0.99	0.90	0.88

TABLE 7-5 (continued)

	Saudi Arabia	Iran	Libya	Nigeria	Algeria	Mexico
III	1.04	1.03		1.02	0.95	0.93
IV	1.00	1.02		1.02	0.91	0.96
1984 I	0.99	1.00		1.02	0.88	0.98
II	1.02	1.02		1.03	0.92	0.96
III	1.03	1.02		1.00	0.92	0.98
IV	0.99	1.02		1.03	0.94	0.95

NOTE: Prices are average landed (c.i.f.) prices in nominal (current) dollars per barrel. The five other major importers are Japan, West Germany, the United Kingdom, France, and Italy.
SOURCES: United States: Department of Energy, "Monthly Crude Oil Acquisition Report," EP Form 51, and predecessor reports. Others: Middle East Economic Survey, *International Crude Oil and Products Prices.*

for quality change. In this way I constructed a price index for crude oil imports of a constant quality. The base was the average quality, in gravity and sulfur content, of crude oil imported in 1977, a year when the world oil market was relatively calm. To construct the index I used the regression equation estimated for each quarter to predict what the average price of U.S. crude oil imports would have been in that quarter if the imports had had the average gravity and sulfur of crude oil imported in 1977 but in all other respects had been unchanged. Because higher quality commands a premium, the price index for any quarter in which the quality is below that of 1977 will exceed the actual recorded price of oil in that quarter. The converse is true for quarters in which the quality is above that of 1977. The difference between the index value for each quarter and the actual price shows approximately how much more or less the United States would have had to pay in that quarter for oil of the same quality it imported in 1977.

Figure 7-3 graphs the difference between the constant-quality index price and the recorded price of the crude oil actually imported over the period 1973:IV through 1984:IV. Throughout the 1970s the average quality of U.S. oil imports varied little, although a very slight deterioration occurred during the disruption of 1973:IV–1974:IV. The index price for those five quarters exceeds the actual price by about twenty-four cents (about 1 percent). The quality of U.S. oil imports began to deteriorate after the onset of the 1979 disruption. The maximum difference—$1.37 per barrel—was not reached until 1982, however, throwing doubt on the hypothesis that the deterioration was

229

FIGURE 7-3
DIFFERENCE BETWEEN CONSTANT-QUALITY INDEX PRICE
AND ACTUAL AVERAGE PRICE, 1973–1984
(1984 dollars per barrel)

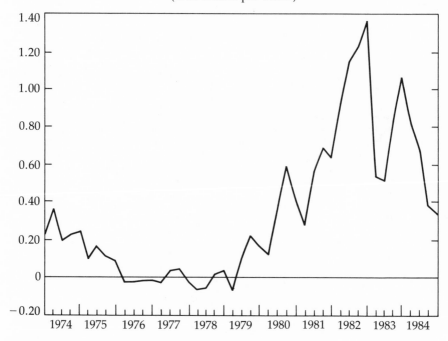

SOURCE: Appendix table A–2.

associated with the disruption. In any case, the effect of lower-quality imports was to understate the price increase associated with the disruption, but at most by sixty to seventy cents per barrel.

A question raised by this evidence is, Why did the United States import lower-quality oil? A plausible hypothesis is that the price differential associated with higher quality increased, reducing the demand for higher-quality crude relative to that for lower-quality crude. To explore the apparent changes in quality of U.S. crude oil imports further, I constructed a second index. That index takes the crude oil price regression equation estimated for each quarter, replaces the gravity and sulfur coefficients estimated for that quarter with the coefficients estimated for 1977, and uses the modified equation to predict what the price of U.S. crude oil imports would have been if the sulfur and gravity price differential of 1977 had obtained but everything else, including the sulfur and gravity content of imports, had been the same.

230

This second index can be considered a "constant-price-of-quality index," analogous to the constant-quality index described earlier. The only difference is that rather than holding quality constant at 1977 levels, it holds the price differentials associated with quality constant at 1977 levels. When the index exceeds the actual price in a given quarter, it means that the "price of quality"—the weighted average of the sulfur and gravity price differrentials—was greater in 1977 than in that quarter.[11]

Figure 7–4 displays the difference between the constant-price-of-quality index and the actual average prices by quarter. The price of quality rose sharply in both the 1973–1974 and the 1979–1980 disruptions. This rise had two possible causes. On the supply side high-quality crudes may have been disrupted more severely than low-quality crudes—the oil supply disruptions were accompanied by quality supply disruptions. On the demand side users of heavy petroleum products may have reduced consumption or switched to alternative fuels more than users of lighter products did, increasing the value of

FIGURE 7–4

DIFFERENCE BETWEEN CONSTANT-PRICE-OF-QUALITY INDEX PRICE
AND ACTUAL AVERAGE PRICE, 1973–1984
(1984 dollars per barrel)

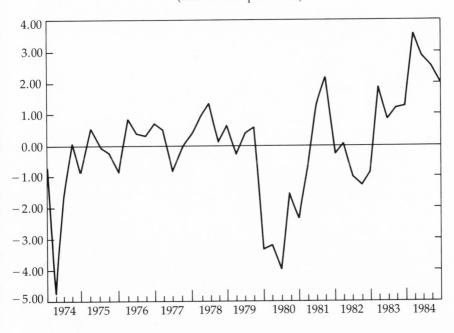

SOURCE: Appendix table A–2.

231

gasoline and other light products relative to that of heavier products. Because gasoline is taxed more heavily and gasoline taxes are usually specific (that is, specified in cents per gallon), the proportional change in gasoline prices to the consumer may be less than that of heavier fuels when crude oil prices change. As a consequence, the value of higher-quality crudes, which tend to yield more gasoline, rose in relation to the value of lower-quality crudes. Given the sharp increase in the price of quality, it is an open question why the quality of oil imported by the United States did not decline more than it did.

In 1984 the price differentials between high- and low-quality crudes were much less than in 1977. There are two possible causes for the decline. On the supply side OPEC was partially successful at enforcing production quotas on cartel members. It is generally more profitable to restrict production of lower-quality than of higher-quality crudes because the latter fetch higher prices and are no more costly to extract. Such a production strategy would in itself serve to reduce quality differentials.[12] On the demand side an extended coal strike in the United Kingdom, a large coal consumer, increased demand for heavy petroleum products (which are close substitutes for coal), pushing their prices up in relation to the price of gasoline. As a consequence, the value of lower-quality crudes relative to that of higher-quality crudes rose.

Summary of Data. The data on quantities, recorded prices, and quality-adjusted prices suggest that the 1973–1974 targeted embargo did affect U.S. oil imports and prices somewhat more than those of most other countries. The 1979 Iranian disruptions also had small effects on the relative price paid by the United States. During the 1980–1981 period of disruption associated with the Iran-Iraq war, all major importing nations appear to have fared about the same. If any importing country depended disproportionately on supplies from Iran or Iraq before 1979, its dependence does not appear to have affected the allocation of oil significantly after Iranian or Iraqi supplies were disrupted.

Tests for Structural Change in the World Oil Market

In this section I investigate the hypothesis that the quantities of oil imported by major importing countries can be explained by conventional determinants of import demand—oil prices, economic activity levels, weather, and other variables. Specifically, I test the hypothesis that the same factors and relationships explain import levels during periods of disruption as during nondisrupted periods—that is, that the basic allocational structure of the world oil market was unchanged during disruptions. If nonmarket allocative mechanisms or influences

232

played an important role during disruptions, we would expect that the observed oil imports during supply disruptions could not be adequately explained by the same determinants and relationships that exist during nondisrupted periods.

First I specify simple models of import demand, consumption of petroleum products, domestic production of crude oil, and inventories of products and crude. Next I statistically estimate the parameters of those models for several major oil-importing countries. Finally I use the estimates to test hypotheses concerning the behavior of the oil market during nondisrupted and disrupted periods.

The petroleum imports model, estimated equations, and statistical tests are described in appendix B. This section describes in general terms the estimation and test results.

For an oil-importing country that has some domestic production and refining, imports are determined by domestic production, consumption, inventory change, and refinery losses.[13]

$$M_c + M_p = C + \Delta S_{cd} + \Delta S_{pd} + \Delta R_d - Q_{cd}$$

where

M_c = crude oil imports

M_p = petroleum product imports

C = petroleum product consumption

ΔS_{cd} = change in domestic crude oil stocks

ΔS_{pd} = change in domestic product stocks

ΔR_d = domestic refinery losses (or gains)

Q_{cd} = domestic crude oil production

Consumption was specified to be a function of average real prices of products, economic activity levels, and heating degree days (the sum of the deviations of each day's mean temperature below 65 degrees Fahrenheit). I expected these variables to have a lagged effect on current-period consumption. To capture the lagged effects, I specified that consumption responds according to a Koyck-type partial adjustment model, estimated by including lagged consumption in the equation. Changes in stocks of crude oil and products were specified to be determined by previous stock levels, expected price changes, the interest rate, and seasonal variables. Production was specified to be a function of price, the interest rate, time, and lagged production. Refinery gains were assumed to be exogenous. In addition to estimating separate equations for each of the determinants of imports, I estimated a reduced-form equation for imports directly, as a function

233

of the explanatory variables in the individual equations for the determinants.

Detailed specification and estimation results are described in appendix B. Reasonably good estimates of consumption and imports equations were obtained for the United States, France, West Germany, and Japan. Because the United Kingdom moved from being a net importer to being a net exporter during the period as a result of the development of the North Sea oil fields, good estimates of import equations for the United Kingdom were not obtained. Table 7–6 displays estimates of short-run and long-run own-price elasticities of consumption and of imports derived from the estimated equations.

The import demand equations reported in appendix B were used to perform statistical tests of whether the quantities of oil imported by the major importing countries could be explained by the same underlying demand relationships during both normal periods and periods of disruption. Tests were conducted as follows. Equations for domestic consumption, production, crude stock changes, product stock changes, and total imports were estimated, using data only for quarters considered nondisrupted. The nondisrupted periods were defined as 1969:I–1973:III, 1975:I–1978:III, and 1982:I–1984:IV. The same equations were also estimated for the entire period 1969:I–1984:IV.

TABLE 7–6

PRICE ELASTICITIES OF PETROLEUM CONSUMPTION AND OF IMPORTS, MAJOR IMPORTING COUNTRIES

	Consumption		
Country	Short run[a]	Long run[b]	Imports, Short Run[a]
United States	$-.092*$	$-.094*$	$-.33*$
France	$-.15*$	$-.29*$	$-.26*$
United Kingdom	$-.11*$	$-.25*$	n.a.
West Germany	$-.11*$	$-.22*$	$-.25*$
Italy	$-.02$	$-.14$	$-.04$
Netherlands	$-.003$	$-.02$	$-.001$
Japan	$-.07*$	$-.22*$	$-.29*$

*Indicates estimate is significant at the .95 confidence level.
n.a. = not available.
a. Short-run elasticities are taken from regression coefficients on price terms in consumption and net import equations. See appendix B.
b. Long-run elasticities were calculated from estimated short-run elasticities using the relationship: long-run elasticity = short-run elasticity/(1 − adjustment coefficient).
SOURCE: Appendix B, tables B–1 and B–6 through B–11.

(Complete data are available only beginning in 1973:I for the six OECD countries other than the United States.) The sums of squared residuals for the nondisrupted periods and for the entire period, including the disrupted periods, were calculated.

To test the hypothesis that the same structure prevailed during both the disrupted and the nondisrupted periods, I constructed the following test statistic: the ratio of the change in the sum of squared residuals per degree of freedom resulting from including the disruption observations in the sample period to the sum of squared residuals per degree of freedom for the nondisrupted periods only.[14] This test statistic is distributed as F under the hypothesis of no structural change and can be compared with the value of an F-statistic with appropriate degrees of freedom to determine whether the hypothesis of no structural change can be rejected. Table 7–7 shows the value of the test statistic obtained from the equation for each determinant of imports and for the import equation itself for each of the major importing countries and the critical value of the F-statistic at a .95 confidence level. If the test statistic exceeds the critical value of the F-statistic, the hypothesis of no structural change during supply disruptions can be rejected.

For most equations the hypothesis cannot be rejected. The hypothesis is rejected at the .95 confidence level for the total imports equation for the United States, for the product stocks equation for the Netherlands, for the production equation for the United Kingdom (where rapid growth in North Sea output was not well explained by any of the estimated regression equations), for the crude stocks equation for West Germany, and for the total imports equation for Japan.[15]

Conclusion

The data and statistical tests reported in this chapter do not provide unambiguous conclusions about the relative performance of the world oil market during disrupted and nondisrupted periods. The data indicate that both prices and quantities of U.S. oil imports changed in relation to those of other major importing countries during the 1973–1974 oil supply disruption. In the 1979 disruption U.S. prices changed relatively to those of other importing countries, but imports did not change disproportionately. Imports of the Netherlands fell somewhat more during the 1973–1974 disruption than those of other countries. No other country appears to have been affected disproportionately in either prices or quantities. When import prices are adjusted for quality changes, no disproportionate effect associated with periods

235

TABLE 7-7

RESULTS OF TESTS OF NO STRUCTURAL CHANGE IN EQUATIONS FOR
IMPORT DEMAND AND DETERMINANTS OF IMPORT DEMAND
DURING OIL SUPPLY DISRUPTIONS

Country/Equation	Test Statistic	Critical Value[a]	Hypothesis Rejected
United States			
Consumption	.39	1.86	
Production	.26	1.87	
Crude stocks	1.67	1.93	
Product stocks	1.39	1.92	
Imports	1.95	1.90	*
Netherlands			
Consumption	.83	2.33	
Production	.52	2.15	
Crude stocks	.67	2.31	
Product stocks	2.60	2.22	*
Imports	1.63	2.46	
United Kingdom			
Consumption	.64	2.33	
Production	3.42	2.06	*
Crude stocks	.62	2.53	
Product stocks	1.07	2.53	
West Germany			
Consumption	1.41	2.17	
Production	1.62	2.12	
Crude stocks	5.17	2.13	*
Product stocks	1.54	2.18	
Imports	1.10	2.39	
France			
Consumption	1.09	2.12	
Production	1.04	2.22	
Crude stocks	1.09	2.48	
Product stocks	0.22	2.41	
Imports	1.44	3.50	
Japan			
Consumption	.97	2.07	
Crude stocks	1.61	2.17	
Product stocks	1.34	2.17	
Imports	2.98	2.18	*
Italy			
Consumption	1.23	2.17	
Production	1.41	2.17	
Crude stocks	1.16	2.13	
Product stocks	.82	2.18	
Imports	1.31	2.39	

a. 95 percent confidence level.
SOURCE: Appendix B.

236

of disruption appears, although the price premiums associated with quality increased during both periods.

I conducted statistical tests to investigate whether import levels could be explained by the same economic determinants during oil supply disruptions as under normal market conditions. For the United States and six other major oil-importing countries, hypotheses of no structural change could generally not be rejected, although the hypotheses were rejected for aggregate import equations for the United States and Japan.

Appendix A: Quality-adjusted Price Indexes for U.S. Crude Oil Imports

To develop price indexes for crude oil imports adjusted for quality changes, I estimated the relationship between the price of imported crude oil and its quality, as represented by sulfur content and API gravity. To obtain accurate estimates of the effects on price of these quality characteristics, it is necessary to control for other attributes of crude oil imports that may be correlated with quality.

The Data. The influence of quality and other characteristics of imported crude oil on its price was estimated by multiple regression analysis of a large data base on U.S. crude oil imports. The data are from the Department of Energy form EIA-856, "Monthly Crude Oil Acquisition Report"; EP form 51, "Monthly Foreign Crude Oil Transactions Report"; and their predecessor reports. All firms importing 500,000 barrels of foreign crude oil during a month must file form EIA-856. This data base has approximately 50,000 records, each of which provides data on the following fifteen variables for one cargo of oil:

- country of origin
- stream type of the oil
- gravity value
- loading date
- landing date
- purchased volume
- landed price
- purchase price
- other costs
- transportation price
- port of landing
- collection date
- contract type (spot transactions recorded since 1979)

237

- transaction type (purchase from affiliate, unaffiliated company, host government resale, and so on)
- days of credit for the purchase (recorded since 1979)

The stream type of a cargo of crude is the Department of Energy classification of that cargo by sulfur and gravity characteristics. I used a second Department of Energy data base that contained information on the sulfur content of each stream type from each country. Therefore, the record for each cargo had its appropriate sulfur content appended to it.

To compare prices over time, I deflated the landed price by a monthly implicit gross national product deflator. I estimated the monthly GNP deflator series by interpolating between the published quarterly GNP deflators according to the monthly changes in the consumer price index.

The Model. The influence on the price of U.S. crude oil imports of sulfur content, gravity, country of origin, contract terms, and other features was estimated using the following specification:

$$P_{ijks} = a + \sum_{j=1}^{40} c_j COUNTRY_i + \sum_{k=2}^{7} d_k TRNTYP_{ik} + e_s SPOT_i$$
$$+ f\, CRDDAYS_i + g\, SULFUR_i + h\, GRAVITY_i \qquad (A-1)$$

where

P_{ijks} = price of oil of cargo i, imported from country j, of transaction type k, and spot or contract value s

$COUNTRY$ = country dummy (1 if cargo i is from country j, 0 otherwise)

$TRNTYP$ = transaction type (buyer-seller relationship) dummy; $TRNTYP_{ik}$ = 1 if cargo i is of transaction type k and = 0 otherwise (k = affiliate, resale, host government, refiner-buyer, unknown, and arm's length)

$SPOT$ = spot or contract transaction dummy (1 if spot)

$CRDDAYS$ = days of credit

$SULFUR$ = sulfur content

$GRAVITY$ = API gravity level

Since the coefficients on the forty country dummies were constrained to sum to zero, each country's coefficient shows that country's average departure from the mean price for all countries during that quarter.

238

This equation was estimated separately for each quarter of the period 1973:IV–1984:IV. The coefficients of each of the forty-five quarterly equations were then used to create a constant-quality price index.

The results of the quarterly regressions are not reported in this appendix because of their length. To provide more concise results, which nevertheless demonstrate the magnitude and significance of the coefficients, I estimated the following equation, which is similar to equation A–1, pooling data of all four quarters in each year:

$$P_{ijksq} = a + \sum_{q=1}^{3} b_q QUARTER_i = \sum_{j=1}^{40} c_j COUNTRY_i$$

$$+ \sum_{k=2}^{7} d_k TRNTYP_{ik} + e_s SPOT_i + f\, CRDDAYS_i$$

$$+ \sum_{q=1}^{4} g_q SULFUR_{iq} + \sum_{q=1}^{4} h_q GRAVITY_{iq}$$

where

P_{ijksq} = price of oil of cargo i, imported from country j, of transaction type k, and spot or contract value s, in quarter q

$SULFUR_{iq}$ = sulfur content of cargo i imported in quarter q

$GRAVITY_{iq}$ = API gravity level of cargo i imported in quarter q

The country dummy coefficients were constrained in the same manner as in equation A–1.

The regression results for this specification are reported in table A–1. The quarterly sulfur and gravity coefficients of these annual equations are very similar to the sulfur and gravity coefficients in the quarterly equations.

Constant-Quality Crude Oil Price Index. To create a constant-quality price index, I used the estimated equation A–1 for each quarter to predict what the average price of U.S. crude oil imports would have been in that quarter if the imports had had the average gravity and sulfur content of crude oil imported in 1977 but in all other respects had been unchanged. I calculated a fitted value of equation A–1 for each crude oil cargo, using that cargo's actual characteristics but substituting the average sulfur and gravity values of 1977 imports for its actual sulfur and gravity. I averaged over these fitted values for all the cargoes imported in each quarter to calculate that quarter's constant-gravity index price.

TABLE A–1: ESTIMATED COEFFICIENTS OF U.S. OIL IMPORT PRICE EQUATION, 1973–1984
(results of annual regression with quarterly sulfur and gravity variables)

	1973		1974		1975		1976		1977		1978	
	Coefficient	t-statistic	Coefficient	t-statistic	Coefficient	t-statistic	Coefficient	t-statistic	Coefficient	t-statistic	Coefficient	t-statistic
Intercept	7.25	5.04	14.26	13.83	17.62	55.33	18.80	99.33	17.40	85.19	17.15	2.99
First quarter	0.00	0.00	4.70	3.24	0.22	0.55	-0.48	-1.88	1.94	8.47	1.46	7.23
Second quarter	0.00	0.00	6.20	5.12	0.29	0.74	-0.63	-2.66	1.55	6.85	0.47	2.40
Third quarter	0.00	0.00	3.30	2.87	-1.26	-3.18	-0.51	-2.29	0.29	1.26	-0.58	-2.95
Sulfur, QI	0.00	0.00	-1.00	-4.15	-0.49	-7.38	-0.38	-8.06	-0.70	17.30	-0.62	17.99
Sulfur, QII	0.00	0.00	-0.97	-5.25	-0.37	-5.90	-0.42	-9.38	-0.69	17.20	-0.45	13.88
Sulfur, QIII	0.00	0.00	-0.32	-1.87	-0.22	-3.45	-0.50	11.86	-0.38	-9.52	-0.40	12.77
Sulfur, QIV	-0.04	-0.13	0.48	2.50	-0.45	-7.22	-0.60	14.37	-0.24	-5.88	-0.57	18.45
Gravity, QI	0.00	0.00	0.14	4.58	0.09	11.06	0.09	15.70	0.08	16.86	0.07	16.71
Gravity, QII	0.00	0.00	0.09	3.63	0.07	9.06	0.09	17.81	0.09	18.71	0.08	18.99
Gravity, QIII	0.00	0.00	0.11	4.81	0.10	12.30	0.08	18.23	0.11	23.35	0.09	22.48
Gravity, QIV	0.10	2.88	0.16	6.29	0.10	12.74	0.07	14.53	0.11	21.68	0.08	18.42
Days of credit	0.00	0.00	0.00	0.00	0.00	0.00	0.00	0.00	0.00	0.00	0.00	0.00
Spot purchase	0.00	0.00	0.00	0.00	0.00	0.00	0.00	0.00	0.00	0.00	0.00	0.00
Affiliate	1.00	3.14	0.42	3.15	-0.07	-1.77	-0.27	10.43	-0.07	-3.51	-0.01	-0.65
Resale	0.64	1.25	2.31	11.39	0.21	3.44	-0.16	-4.59	-0.13	-5.00	-0.07	-3.50
Host government	0.45	0.66	3.49	11.99	0.02	0.26	-0.31	-7.88	-0.15	-5.10	0.02	0.75
Refiner-buyer	5.04	2.22	-3.35	14.75	-2.05	24.41	-0.59	-5.40	-0.16	-0.71	0.12	0.28
Unknown	0.00	0.00	0.00	0.00	0.00	0.00	0.00	0.00	0.00	0.00	0.00	0.00
Arm's length	0.00	0.00	0.00	0.00	0.00	0.00	0.00	0.00	1.21	21.09	1.17	16.90

240

	1979		1980		1981		1982		1983		1984	
	Coef-ficient	t-sta-tistic	Coef-ficient	t-sta-tistic	Coeff-icient	t-sta-tistic	Coef-ficient	t-sta-tistic	Coef-ficient	t-sta-tistic	Coef-ficient	t-sta-tistic
Intercept	31.07	21.95	33.14	32.23	32.15	45.34	30.53	53.37	28.85	48.87	27.41	81.23
First quarter	-15.14	-8.94	3.88	3.09	11.14	13.89	3.27	4.33	-1.75	-2.18	0.81	2.18
Second quarter	-6.66	-3.86	3.82	2.98	8.87	10.19	-0.27	-0.38	-1.40	-2.10	1.08	3.03
Third quarter	0.50	0.31	3.35	2.60	4.22	4.86	0.90	1.28	-0.59	-0.92	0.71	1.98
Sulfur, QI	0.19	0.69	-1.99	11.71	-2.22	18.53	-2.20	19.85	-1.08	-9.10	-1.34	26.68
Sulfur, QII	-1.19	-4.42	-2.01	11.86	-2.35	19.05	-1.83	17.97	-1.31	13.47	-1.34	28.69
Sulfur, QIII	-2.50	10.36	-1.54	-9.11	-1.73	13.91	-2.16	21.53	-1.35	14.29	-1.06	22.98
Sulfur, QIV	-2.00	-7.82	-0.71	-4.20	-0.90	-7.27	-2.15	21.67	-1.18	11.43	-0.98	15.73
Gravity, QI	0.17	5.05	0.16	6.33	0.05	3.44	0.16	9.48	0.16	9.20	0.05	7.97
Gravity, QII	0.10	2.71	0.20	7.69	0.08	4.37	0.20	13.03	0.09	7.46	0.04	7.30
Gravity, QIII	0.08	2.61	0.21	8.29	0.13	6.75	0.18	11.73	0.08	6.34	0.03	4.37
Gravity, QIV	0.19	5.41	0.27	10.60	0.20	11.49	0.18	12.34	0.05	3.08	0.04	4.68
Days of credit	-0.01	-5.42	-0.00	-3.68	0.00	0.69	-0.00	-0.90	-0.00	-1.75	0.00	3.87
Spot purchase	3.25	9.47	1.29	4.11	0.01	0.04	-0.37	-2.14	-0.09	-0.67	0.08	0.87
Affiliate	-2.43	11.61	-1.33	-8.35	-0.13	-1.18	-0.01	-0.06	0.12	1.10	-0.10	-1.87
Resale	-0.74	-3.23	0.08	0.46	0.33	2.42	-0.35	-2.57	-1.39	-3.12	0.31	0.38
Host government	-1.77	-5.31	-0.42	-1.83	0.35	2.01	-0.26	-1.78	-0.48	-3.65	-0.50	-7.56
Refiner-buyer	-2.42	-1.80	-0.21	-0.38	1.12	0.98	0.00	0.00	0.00	0.00	0.00	0.00
Unknown	-1.22	-3.44	0.00	0.00	0.00	0.00	0.00	0.00	0.00	0.00	0.00	0.00
Arm's length	-0.97	-2.16	-2.80	-1.79	-0.87	-1.08	0.97	2.06	0.38	0.74	0.22	0.94

NOTE: Model also included dummy variables for each exporting country; coefficients not shown for economy of presentation.
SOURCE: See appendix A.

241

TABLE A-2
ACTUAL, CONSTANT-QUALITY INDEX, AND CONSTANT-PRICE-OF-QUALITY INDEX PRICES, OIL IMPORTED BY UNITED STATES, 1973–1984
(1984 dollars per barrel)

Quarter	Actual		Constant Quality			Constant Price of Quality		
	Price	% change	Index	% change	Difference from base	Index	% change	Difference from base
1973 IV	11.25	—	11.47	—	0.22	10.53	—	−0.72
1974 I	23.31	107.2	23.66	106.3	0.35	18.45	75.3	−4.86
II	22.95	−1.5	23.14	−2.2	0.19	21.16	14.7	−1.79
III	21.22	−7.5	21.44	−7.3	0.22	21.34	0.8	0.12
IV	20.41	−3.8	20.65	−3.7	0.24	19.40	−9.1	−1.01
1975 I	20.24	−0.8	20.33	−1.5	0.09	20.81	7.3	0.57
II	20.03	−1.0	20.19	−0.7	0.16	19.94	−4.2	−0.09
III	19.45	−2.9	19.56	−3.1	0.11	19.23	−3.5	−0.22
IV	20.50	5.4	20.59	5.2	0.09	19.58	1.8	−0.92
1976 I	20.81	1.5	20.78	0.9	−0.03	21.64	10.5	0.83
II	20.75	−0.3	20.72	−0.3	−0.03	21.13	−2.4	0.38
III	20.58	−0.8	20.56	−0.8	−0.02	20.93	−0.9	0.35
IV	20.46	−0.6	20.44	−0.6	−0.02	21.17	1.1	0.71
1977 I	21.46	4.9	21.43	4.8	−0.03	21.91	3.5	0.45
II	21.32	−0.7	21.35	−0.4	0.03	20.41	−6.9	−0.91
III	21.24	−0.4	21.28	−0.3	0.04	21.24	4.1	0.00
IV	20.98	−1.2	20.95	−1.6	−0.03	21.31	0.3	0.33
1978 I	20.57	−2.0	20.50	−2.1	−0.07	21.46	0.7	0.89
II	19.91	−3.2	19.85	−3.2	−0.06	21.27	−0.9	1.36
III	19.47	−2.2	19.48	−1.9	0.01	19.53	−8.2	0.06
IV	19.23	−1.2	19.26	−1.1	0.03	19.87	1.7	0.64
1979 I	20.37	5.9	20.30	5.4	−0.07	19.99	0.6	−0.38
II	25.19	23.7	25.28	24.5	0.09	25.58	28.0	0.39
III	30.31	20.3	30.53	20.8	0.22	30.91	20.8	0.60
IV	34.03	12.3	34.20	12.0	0.17	30.69	−0.7	−3.34
1980 I	39.59	16.3	39.71	16.1	0.12	36.34	18.4	−3.25
II	40.86	3.2	41.24	3.9	0.38	36.85	1.4	−4.01
III	41.19	0.8	41.78	1.3	0.59	39.66	7.6	−1.53
IV	40.64	−1.3	41.03	−1.8	0.39	38.22	−3.6	−2.42
1981 I	42.94	5.7	43.22	5.3	0.28	42.41	11.0	−0.53
II	41.19	−4.1	41.75	−3.4	0.56	42.50	0.2	1.31
III	38.20	−7.3	38.89	−6.8	0.69	40.35	−5.1	2.15
IV	37.80	−1.0	38.44	−1.1	0.64	37.48	−7.1	−0.32

TABLE A–2 (continued)

Quarter		Actual		Constant Quality			Constant Price of Quality		
		Price	% change	Index	% change	Difference from base	Index	% change	Difference from base
1982	I	36.69	−2.9	37.62	−2.1	0.93	36.78	−1.9	0.09
	II	34.54	−5.9	35.69	−5.1	1.15	33.50	−8.9	−1.04
	III	34.01	−1.5	35.24	−1.3	1.23	32.70	−2.4	−1.31
	IV	33.18	−2.4	34.55	−2.0	1.37	32.37	−1.0	−0.81
1983	I	30.20	−9.0	30.74	−11.0	0.54	32.09	−0.9	1.89
	II	28.81	−4.6	29.33	−4.6	0.52	29.67	−7.5	0.86
	III	28.95	0.5	29.78	1.5	0.83	30.13	1.5	1.18
	IV	28.42	−1.8	29.49	−1.0	1.07	29.67	−1.5	1.25
1984	I	28.04	−1.3	28.85	−2.2	0.81	31.60	6.5	3.56
	II	28.00	−0.1	28.67	−0.6	0.67	30.85	−2.4	2.85
	III	27.54	−1.6	27.93	−2.6	0.39	30.13	−2.3	2.59
	IV	27.41	−0.5	27.75	−0.6	0.34	29.34	−2.6	1.93

SOURCE: See appendix A.

The constant-quality price index is displayed in table A–2. The quality did not undergo major changes over the period examined, but the quality of U.S. crude oil imports deteriorated somewhat after 1980.

Constant-Price-of-Quality Crude Oil Price Index. I calculated an index price designed to show what the price of crude oil imports would have been in each quarter if there had been no change in the quality price differentials from their 1977 values over the periods. I refer to this as a "constant-price-of-quality" index price. It is calculated analogously to the constant-quality index, using the results of the quarterly regression equation A–1.

I calculated the fitted value of estimated equation A–1 for each crude oil cargo, using that cargo's actual characteristics but substituting the average estimates of the sulfur and gravity coefficients in 1977 for the coefficient estimates of that quarter's equation. The fitted values for all cargoes in each quarter were averaged to obtain that quarter's constant-price-of-quality index price.

The index is displayed in table A–2. The actual price exceeded the constant-price-of-quality index price in 1974 and in 1979–1980, indicating that the price of quality—that is, the average of the sulfur and gravity regression coefficients in the equations for those quarters, weighted by the actual sulfur and gravity levels—increased sharply during those periods.

243

Appendix B: Analysis of Import Demand Equations and Tests of Hypotheses Concerning Structural Change for Major Importing Countries

In this appendix I describe my analysis of oil import demand for seven major importing countries. I first briefly describe a general model of petroleum import demand. From this model I derive equations explaining the determinants of petroleum imports. I next describe specifications of those equations and the results of statistical estimation of the parameters. Finally I use the estimated equations to test the hypothesis that the level and allocation of oil imports during periods of disruption can be explained in terms of the normal behavior of the world oil market—that is, that imports during disrupted periods can be explained adequately by the same factors and relationships as during nondisrupted periods. I test this hypothesis by performing specific statistical tests of structural change for each of the equations explaining the determinants of petroleum import levels.

Determination of Oil Import Levels. The level of oil imports in each quarter is specified to be determined by domestic consumption, domestic production, and changes in domestic stocks of crude and products, as follows:

$$M_C + M_P = C + \Delta S_C + \Delta S_P + \Delta R - Q_C \qquad (B\text{-}1)$$

where

M_C = imports of crude oil
M_P = imports of petroleum products
C = consumption of petroleum products
ΔS_C = changes in crude oil stocks
ΔS_P = changes in products stocks
ΔR = refinery losses
Q_C = crude oil production

Consumption. I specify that domestic consumption of petroleum in each country is determined by the level of economic activity, weather conditions, and petroleum product prices. These variables will affect consumption with a lag. To represent this, I specify a Koyck-type partial adjustment model, using the lagged value of consumption to estimate lagged adjustment effects.

Domestic economic activity is represented in the consumption equations for each country by GNP, gross domestic product (GDP), or an index of industrial production. Since complete data on GNP or

244

GDP are not available for some importing countries I investigated, I used an index of industrial production in those cases. Where data on both variables were available, the choice was based on goodness of fit. Real (relative) petroleum prices were represented by the domestic producers price index for petroleum products, deflated by the GDP deflator. Weather conditions were represented by heating degree days—the population-weighted national average for the United States and data for representative cities for other countries.

The following general functional specification was used:

$$C_t = C(P_{PDt}, Y_t, HDD_t, C_{t-1}) \qquad (B\text{--}2)$$

where

C_t = consumption of petroleum products in period t
P_{PDt} = real price of petroleum products in period t
Y_t = economic activity (GNP, GDP, or industrial production) in period t
HDD_t = heating degree days in period t

Domestic Crude Oil Production. I estimated a very simple model of aggregate crude oil production.[16] Drawing on the theory of optimal extraction of nonrenewable resources associated with Hotelling, I specify that U.S. crude oil production is related to the marginal price of crude oil, the real rate of interest, and geological and technological factors, which are proxied by a time trend.[17] These factors affect production with a lag, which is represented using a Koyck partial adjustment specification by the lagged value of production. The following general specification was used:

$$Q_{Ct} = Q(P_{Ct}, i_t, G(t), Q_{Ct-1}) \qquad (B\text{--}3)$$

where
i_t = real rate of interest
P_{Ct} = real price of domestic crude oil in period t
$G(t)$ = time trend proxy for resource depletion and technological change

Crude Oil Stock Changes. My models of crude oil and petroleum product inventory behavior draw on discussions in the economics literature of general inventory models and of models of petroleum inventories.[18] Oil inventories may be held as part of work in process, to smooth seasonal patterns of demand and asynchronous fluctuations in supply and demand, or for speculative motives. The first two motives suggest that inventory changes will be related positively to

245

long-term trends in consumption but may be related negatively to short-run deviations of consumption from long-term trends. Discussions of speculative demand for inventories note that the expected profit on the marginal barrel added to inventories in period t would be

$$[EP_{t+1}/(1 + i)] - P_t - k$$

where

EP_{t+1} = expected price in period $t + 1$
P_t = price of marginal barrel in period t
i = interest rate
k = marginal cost per barrel of holding inventories

In addition to influencing expected profits from holding stocks, the real interest rate may also influence the desired inventory-sales ratio for working inventories. Finally, because actual inventories may not adjust to the desired level within one period (quarter), this period's inventory change may be related negatively to the previous period's inventories. The following general functional specification was used:

$$\Delta S_{Ct} = \Delta S_C(\Delta \overline{C}_{Pt}, P_{Ct}, EP_{Ct+1}, i_t, S_{Ct-1}) \qquad \text{(B–4)}$$

where

$\Delta \overline{C}_{Pt}$ = change in the moving average of consumption of domestic petroleum products
P_{Ct} = real price of crude oil in period t
EP_{Ct+1} = expected real price of crude oil in period $t + 1$
i_t = real short-term interest rate
S_{Ct-1} = private stocks of crude oil in period $t - 1$

To represent the cost of acquiring crude oil to add to inventories, I used a data series on the marginal price of crude oil. To represent the expected price of crude one period in the future, I used the current period spot price. This choice was based on evidence that, over the time period studied, contract prices for crude followed spot prices with a lag.[19] Therefore, current spot prices were good predictors of future marginal prices.[20]

Petroleum Product Stock Changes. A similar conceptual model was used for petroleum product inventories. Because product stocks do not show a defined trend over the period since 1967, changes in product stocks and long-term trends in consumption were not significantly related. The general functional specification was as follows:

246

$$\Delta S_{Pt} = \Delta S_P (P_{Pt}, EP_{Pt+1}, i_t, S_{Pt-1}) \qquad (B-5)$$

where

P_{Pt} = price of petroleum products (to inventory holders) in period t

EP_{Pt+1} = expected price of products in period $t + 1$

S_{Pt-1} = stocks of products in period $t - 1$

To represent the cost of adding petroleum products to inventories, I used the marginal price of crude oil. To represent the expected price of products in the next period, I used this period's spot crude oil price.

Aggregate Stock Changes. I also estimated a model of aggregate stock changes, conceptually similar to those for crude oil and products. The results—not reported here—were similar to the results for the crude stock equation and the product stock equation. The estimates of the crude stock equation and the product stock equation differ somewhat, suggesting that it is useful to model the two separately.

Total Petroleum Imports. Substituting equations B–2 through B–5 into equation B–1 provides a general equation for net imports of crude oil and products:

$$M_C + M_P = C(P_P, Y, HDD, C_{t-1}) + \Delta S_C(\Delta \overline{C}_P, P_C, EP_{Ct+1}, i, S_{Ct-1})$$
$$+ \Delta S_P(P_P, EP_{Pt+1}, i, S_{Pt-1}) + \Delta R - Q(P_C, G(t), i, Q_{Ct-1})$$

Several expanatory variables influence more than one determinant of imports. (The real interest rate, for example, appears in the two stock change equations and the crude production equation.) Each variable that appears in more than one equation, however, has the same predicted direction of effect on imports in each equation. Consequently, a general specification of a net petroleum import equation can be written as follows:

$$M_C + M_P = M(P_P, Y, HDD, C_{t-1}, \Delta \overline{C}_P, P_C,$$
$$EP_{Ct+1}, i, S_{Ct-1}, EP_{Pt+1}, S_{Pt-1}, \Delta R, G(t), Q_{Ct-1})$$

Petroleum imports are defined as the sum of crude imports and product imports measured in barrels.

Estimation Equations. These general functional specifications were estimated as linear equations with all variables in logarithmic form. The following equations were estimated for the United States and

247

similar equations for the United Kingdom, France, West Germany, Italy, the Netherlands, and Japan.

Consumption

$$\ln C_t = a + b_1 \ln IN_t + b_2 \ln HDD_t + b_3 \ln C_{t-1} + b_4 \ln P_{Pt} \quad \text{(B-6)}$$

Domestic crude oil production

$$\ln Q_{Ct} = a + b_1 P_{Ct}^{marg} + b_2 \ln i_t + b_3 \ln T + b_4 \ln Q_{Ct-1} \quad \text{(B-7)}$$

Changes in stocks of crude oil

$$\ln\left(\frac{S_{Ct}}{S_{Ct-1}}\right) = a + b_1 \ln\left(\frac{\overline{C}_t}{\overline{C}_{t-1}}\right) + b_2 \ln S_{Ct-1} + b_3 \ln i_t$$
$$+ b_4 \ln P_{Ct}^{marg} + b_5 \ln P_{Ct}^{spot} + b_6 D1$$
$$+ b_7 D2 + b_8 D3 \quad \text{(B-8)}$$

Changes in stocks of petroleum products

$$\ln\left(\frac{S_{Pt}}{S_{Pt-1}}\right) = a + b_1 \ln S_{PT-1} + b_2 \ln i_t + b_3 \ln P_{Ct}^{marg}$$
$$+ b_4 \ln P_{Ct}^{spot} + b_5 D1 + b_6 D2 + b_7 D3 \quad \text{(B-9)}$$

Aggregate oil import equations. Because the net imports equation is somewhat more ad hoc than the equation for the determinants of imports, I estimated two specifications. The results are similar.

$$\ln(M_{Ct} + M_{Pt}) = a + b_1 \ln IN_t + b_2 \ln HDD_{t+1}$$
$$+ b_3 \ln C_{t-1} + b_4 \ln S_{Ct-1} + b_5 \ln i_t$$
$$+ b_6 \ln T + b_7 \ln P_{Ct} + b_8 \ln P_{CT}^{spot}$$

$$\ln(M_{Ct} + M_{Pt}) = a + b_1 \ln Y_t + b_2 \ln HDD_t + b_3 \ln C_{t-1}$$
$$+ b_4 \ln S_{Ct-1} + b_5 \ln i_t + b_6 \ln T$$
$$+ b_7 \ln P_{Ct}^{marg} + b_8 \ln P_{Ct}^{spot} + b_9 D1$$
$$+ b_{10} D2 + b_{11} D3 \quad \text{(B-10)}$$

where

M_{Ct} = U.S. imports of crude oil in period t
M_{Pt} = U.S. imports of petroleum products in period t
IN_t = index of industrial production in period t
Y_t = real GNP or GDP

HDD_t = average heating degree days in period t (United States, population-weighted national average; other countries, selected cities)

C_{t-1} = consumption of petroleum products in period $t-1$

S_{Ct-1} = U.S. private stocks of crude oil in period $t-1$

i_t = real short-term interest rate in period t

T = time, 1967:I = 1, 1967:II = 2, . . . , 1984:IV = 72

P_{Ct} = real average refiners' acquisition cost of crude oil (U.S. composite)

P_{Ct}^{spot} = real spot price of crude oil in period t

P_{Ct}^{marg} = real marginal price of crude oil to U.S. refiners in period t

$D1$ = 1 in quarter 1, 0 otherwise

$D2$ = 1 in quarter 2, 0 otherwise

$D3$ = 1 in quarter 3, 0 otherwise

Data. The equations were estimated using quarterly observations for the period 1969:I through 1984:IV. Where the data are reported monthly, quarterly observations were created by summing or averaging the monthly observations, as appropriate.

Data for U.S. consumption were from U.S. Bureau of Mines, *Mineral Industry Survey*, and OECD, *Quarterly Oil Statistics*. Production data were from *Petroleum Economist*. Inventory data were from *Mineral Industry Survey*; OECD, *Quarterly Oil Statistics*; and U.S. Department of Energy, *Monthly Energy Review*. Import data were from U.S. Bureau of the Census, FT135 reports; Bureau of Mines, *Petroleum Statement Monthly*; and OECD, *Quarterly Oil Statistics*. Data on heating degree days were from National Oceanographic and Atmospheric Administration (NOAA), *State, Regional, and National Monthly and Seasonal Heating Degree Days*. Price data were from Department of Energy, *Monthly Energy Review*; Bureau of Labor Statistics, *Producers Price Index*; and *Petroleum Intelligence Weekly*.

Data for Japan, France, West Germany, Italy, the Netherlands, and the United Kingdom were from OECD, *Quarterly Oil Statistics* and *Provisional Oil Statistics*; Middle East Economic Survey, *International Crude Oil and Product Prices*; and NOAA, *Monthly Climatic Data for the World*. Economic data were from OECD, *Main Economic Indicators, Historical Statistics: 1964–1983*, and *Main Economic Indicators*, various monthly issues.[21]

Real values of variables in the equations were calculated by deflating reported nominal values by an appropriate national price index (GNP or GDP deflator or consumer price index). Crude oil prices for

249

all countries are reported in dollars (prices for countries other than the United States are dollars per metric ton). All oil prices were converted to local currency using the current exchange rate and were then deflated by a domestic price index. Oil prices for West Germany, for example, were adjusted as follows:

P(1980 DM per ton)

$$= \frac{P \text{ (current dollars per ton)} \times \text{ exchange rate (DM per \$)}}{\text{GNP deflator (base: } 1980 \ = \ 100)}$$

Estimation Results and Hypothesis Tests. Equations B–6, B–7, B–8, B–9, and B–10 were estimated for each country by ordinary least squares. Tables B–1 through B–5 report the estimation results for the United States for the period 1969:I through 1984:IV. Tables B–6 through B–11 report estimation results for all five equations for each of the six other countries for 1973:I through 1984:IV.

To test hypotheses that the same basic structural demand relationships determined import levels of the major importing countries

---

TABLE B–1

U.S. OIL CONSUMPTION, RESULTS OF
ORDINARY LEAST SQUARES ESTIMATES, 1969:I–1984:IV
(t-statistics in parentheses)

	Constant	IN_t	HDD_t	C_{t-1}	P_{Pt}	R^2	DW
Equation B–6	5.01	.57	.03	.016	− .09	.38	.67
(entire period)	(11.23)	(4.19)	(3.61)	(1.44)	(− 2.49)		
	S.S.R = .3468		N = 64		RMSE = .0749		
Equation B–6	5.38	.47	.025	.015	− .08	.28	.63
(nondisrupted	(9.64)	(2.77)	(2.60)	(1.22)	(− 1.63)		
periods)[a]							
	S.S.R = .2958		N = 46		RMSE = .0802		

Test for change of structure during disrupted periods versus nondisrupted periods:

Test statistic = .39 $F_{.95}(18,41)$ = 1.86

RMSE of predicted values of disrupted periods using equation B–6 for nondisrupted periods versus actual values = .0593.

NOTE: S.S.R. = sum of squared residuals; RMSE = root mean square error; DW = Durbin-Watson statistic.
a. Nondisrupted periods defined as 1969:I–1973:III, 1975:I–1978:III, and 1982:I–1984:IV.

TABLE B-2

U.S. CRUDE OIL PRODUCTION, RESULTS OF
ORDINARY LEAST SQUARES ESTIMATES, 1969:I–1984:IV
(t-statistics in parentheses)

	Constant	P_{Ct}^{marg}	i_t	T	Q_{Ct-1}	R^2	DW
Equation B–7	.68	.003	.025	$-.01$	.90	.87	1.89
(entire period)	(1.66)	(.15)	(1.25)	$(-.57)$	(14.74)		
	S.S.R. $= .6969$		N $= 63$		RMSE $= .0343$		
Equation B–7	.71	.03	.015	$-.03$	.90	.85	1.74
(nondisrupted	(1.31)	(.85)	(.50)	(-1.15)	(11.05)		
periods)[a]							
	S.S.R. $= .6228$		N $= 45$		RMSE $= .0372$		

Test for change of structure during disrupted periods versus nondisrupted periods:

Test statistic $= .2640$ $F_{.95}$ (18,40) $= 1.87$

RMSE of predicted values of disrupted periods using equation B–7 for nondisrupted periods versus actual values $= .0256$.

NOTE: See note to table B–1.
a. For nondisrupted periods see table B–1.

during periods of oil supply disruption as during nondisrupted periods, I also estimated each of these equations over periods defined as nondisrupted, compared the estimates for the entire period with those for the nondisrupted periods, and applied a standard test for structural change. From a review of historical events and of oil price changes, I identified the periods of significant oil price disruption as 1973:IV–1974:IV and 1978:IV–1981:IV.[22] I therefore defined the nondisrupted periods as 1969:I–1973:III, 1975:I–1978:III, and 1982:I–1984:IV.

To test for structural change in each of the equations during periods of supply disruption, I calculated the sum of squared residuals for each equation estimated for nondisrupted periods. I compared this sum of squared residuals with the sum of squared residuals of the equation estimated for the entire period and calculated the increase in the sum of squared residuals resulting from adding observations of disrupted periods. Under the null hypothesis of no structural change, the ratio of the change in the sum of squared residuals per degree of freedom resulting from including the disruption observations in the sample to the sum of squared residuals per degree of freedom for the nondisrupted periods only has the distribution of an F-statistic. This test statistic can be compared with the critical values of an F-statistic

251

TABLE B-3

U.S. CRUDE OIL STOCK CHANGES, RESULTS OF ORDINARY LEAST SQUARES ESTIMATES, 1969:I–1984:IV

(t-statistics in parentheses)

	Constant	$\bar{C}_t/\bar{C}_{t-1}$	S_{Ct-1}	i_t	P_{Ct}^{in+s}	P_{Ct}^{s+t}	D1	D2	D3	R^2	DW
Equation B–8 (entire period)	.39 (1.56)	.26 (.52)	–.06 (–1.29)	–.007 (–.33)	–.03 (–.68)	.03 (1.30)	–0.1 (–.76)	.01 (.95)	–.04 (–2.61)	.29	2.11
Equation B–8 (nondisrupted periods)ᵃ	.19 (.49)	–.09 (–.16)	–.013 (–.17)	–.03 (–1.10)	–.03 (–.47)	.29 (.77)	–.012 (–.76)	.014 (.91)	–.041 (–2.56)	.40	2.20

S.S.R. = .7131   N = 60   RMSE = .0354

S.S.R. = .0373   N = 42   RMSE = .0298

Test for change of structure during disrupted periods versus nondisrupted periods:

Test statistic = 1.67 $F_{.95}(18,33) = 1.93$

RMSE of values for disrupted periods predicted using equation B–8 for nondisrupted periods versus actual values = .0460.

NOTE: See note to table B–1.
a. For nondisrupted periods see table B–1.

252

TABLE B-4

U.S. PETROLEUM PRODUCT STOCK CHANGES, RESULTS OF ORDINARY LEAST SQUARES ESTIMATES, 1969:I–1984:IV
(t-statistics in parentheses)

	Constant	i_t	S_{Pt-1}	P_{Ct}^{marg}	P_{Ct}^{spot}	$D1$	$D2$	$D3$	R^2	DW
Equation B–9 (entire period)	1.13 (2.70)	–.06 (–2.48)	–.15 (–2.42)	–.029 (–.74)	.028 (1.10)	–.03 (–9.10)	–.05 (–3.03)	.06 (4.15)	.82	1.90
		S.S.R. = .0797		N = 60	RMSE = .0395					
Equation B–9 (nondisrupted periods)[a]	1.84 (3.21)	–.09 (–2.92)	–.24 (–2.97)	–.07 (–.94)	.05 (1.21)	–.14 (–8.52)	–.06 (–3.40)	.06 (3.06)	.87	1.79
		S.S.R. = .0459		N = 42	RMSE = .0331					

Test for change of structure during disrupted periods versus nondisrupted periods:

Test statistic = 1.39 $F_{.95}(18,33) = 1.92$

RMSE of values for disrupted periods predicted using equation B–9 for nondisrupted periods versus actual values = .0514.

NOTE: See note to table B–1.
a. For nondisrupted periods see table B–1.

253

TABLE B-5
U.S. NET PETROLEUM IMPORTS, RESULTS OF ORDINARY LEAST SQUARES ESTIMATES, 1969:I–1984:IV
(t-statistics in parentheses)

	Constant	IN_t	HDD_t	C_{t-1}	S_{Ct-1}	i_t	T	P_{Ct}^{mc}	P_{Ct}^{spot}	R^2	DW
Equation B–10 (entire period)	−11.67 (−5.16)	.40 (1.18)	.08 (5.39)	2.31 (6.70)	−.18 (−.94)	−.10 (−1.12)	.05 (.45)	−.30 (−1.80)	.20 (2.64)	.88	1.65
			S.S.R. = .8645		N = 63	RMSE = .1171					
Equation B–10 (nondisrupted periods)[a]	−7.70 (−2.57)	.78 (2.22)	.07 (4.46)	1.88 (4.82)	−.41 (−1.63)	.07 (.63)	−.85 (−.65)	−1.02 (−4.11)	.57 (5.45)	.92	1.72
			S.S.R. = .4376		N = 45	RMSE = .0986					

Test for change of structure during disrupted periods vs. nondisrupted periods:

$$\text{Test statistic} = \frac{(.8645 - .4376)/18}{.4376/(45 - 9)} = 1.95 \qquad F_{.95}(18,36) = 1.90$$

RMSE of values for disrupted periods predicted using equation B–10 for nondisrupted periods versus actual values = .2472.

254

	Constant	Y_t	HDD_t	C_{t-1}	S_{Ct-1}	i_t	T	P_{Ct}^{marx}	P_{Ct}^{spot}	$D1$	$D2$	$D3$	R^2	DW
Alternative equation B-10 (entire period)	-9.96 (-2.39)	.20 (.34)	.06 (.53)	2.55 (7.50)	-.25 (-1.39)	-.05 (-.57)	.86 (.58)	-.33 (-1.99)	.31 (2.64)	-.21 (-3.27)	.14 (1.36)	.23 (.64)	.90	1.82
			S.S.R. = .7067		N = 63		RMSE = .1059							
Alternative equation B-10 (nondisrupted periods)[a]	-8.36 (-2.03)	.09 (.17)	.08 (.72)	1.94 (5.12)	.10 (.33)	.08 (.79)	-.14 (-.92)	-1.30 (-4.48)	.94 (5.39)	-.19 (-3.03)	-.18 (-1.31)	.24 (.70)	.94	1.97
			S.S.R. = .3359		N = 45		RMSE = .0864							

Test for change of structure during disrupted periods versus nondisrupted periods:

$$\text{Test statistic} = \frac{(.7067 - .3359)/18}{.3359/(45 - 12)} = 2.024 \quad F_{.95}(18,33) = 1.93$$

RMSE of values for disrupted periods predicted using alternative equation B-10 for nondisrupted periods versus actual values = .2408.

NOTE: See note to table B-1.
a. For nondisrupted periods see table B-1.

255

TABLE B-6
FRANCE, OIL IMPORT DEMAND, RESULTS OF ORDINARY LEAST SQUARES ESTIMATES, 1973:I–1984:IV

Imports	Constant	IN_t	C_{t-1}	SC_{t-1}	i_t	T	P_t^{imp}	P_t^{spot}	R^2	DW
Coefficient	7.59	1.03	.05	.02	–.00	–.55	–.26	.17	.97	1.86
t-statistic	(1.91)	(1.33)	(.20)	(.20)	(–.50)	(–2.53)	(–1.90)	(1.46)		

Consumption	Constant	C_{t-1}	HDD_t	IND_t	P_t^{imp}				R^2	DW
Coefficient	3.10	.48	.02	.69	–.15				.83	1.88
t-statistic	(1.92)	(3.89)	(8.14)	(4.44)	(–4.51)					

Crude Oil Production	Constant	$Prod_{t-1}$	i_t	T	P_t^{imp}				R^2	DW
Coefficient	.19	.88	–.01	.21	–.03				.98	1.82
t-statistic	(.79)	(12.7)	(–.24)	(2.32)	(–.97)					

Crude Oil Stocks	Constant	SC_{t-1}	$D1$	$D2$	$D3$	$Prof_t$			R^2	DW
Coefficient	.30	–.03	–.06	.09	–.06	.00			.32	1.96
t-statistic	(.46)	(–.45)	(–1.05)	(2.00)	(–1.14)	(1.94)				

Product Stocks	Constant	P_t^{spot}	$D1$	$D2$	$D3$	$Prof_t$			R^2	DW
Coefficient	–.21	.02	–.08	.02	.22	.00			.85	2.35
t-statistic	(–.52)	(.04)	(–2.14)	(.94)	(5.93)	(1.94)				

256

TABLE B-7
ITALY, OIL IMPORT DEMAND, RESULTS OF ORDINARY LEAST SQUARES ESTIMATES, 1973:I–1984:IV

Imports	Constant	IN_t	HDD_t	C_{t-1}	SC_{t-1}	i_t	T	P_{Ct}^{marg}	P_{Ct}^{spot}	R^2	DW
Coefficient	-4.51	1.77	.006	.12	-.28	.009	-.81	-.02	-.07	.73	1.68
t-statistic	(-.84)	(3.63)	(3.37)	(1.43)	(-2.63)	(1.66)	(-6.39)	(-.27)	(-.98)		

Consumption	Constant	C_{t-1}	IN_t	P_t^{imp}	D1	D2	D3	R^2	DW
Coefficient	1.56	.86	.03	-.02	-.11	-.38	-.14	.89	1.89
t-statistic	(1.38)	(8.20)	(.30)	(-.93)	(-2.97)	(-13.00)	(-3.84)		

Crude Oil Production	Constant	$Prod_{t-1}$	i_t	T	P_t^{imp}	R^2	DW
Coefficient	.99	.48	-.02	.81	-.07	.90	1.94
t-statistic	(1.24)	(4.66)	(-2.66)	(4.75)	(-1.03)		

Crude Oil Stocks	Constant	SC_{t-1}	i_t	P_t^{imp}	P_t^{spot}	HDD_t	R^2	DW
Coefficient	1.15	-.31	-.01	.14	-.00	-.01	.37	2.02
t-statistic	(1.00)	(-2.19)	(-1.97)	(1.20)	(-.04)	(-2.87)		

Product Stocks	Constant	SP_{t-1}	i_t	P_t^{imp}	P_t^{spot}	HDD_t	R^2	DW
Coefficient	1.32	-.15	-.00	.05	-.04	-.02	.65	1.98
t-statistic	(.87)	(-1.11)	(-.44)	(.51)	(-.50)	(-5.90)		

257

TABLE B-8
JAPAN, OIL IMPORT DEMAND, RESULTS OF ORDINARY LEAST SQUARES ESTIMATES, 1973:I–1984:IV

Imports	Constant	GDP_t	HDD_t	C_{t-1}	SC_{t-1}	i_t	T	P_t^{imp}	P_t^{spot}	R^2	DW
Coefficient	17.94	-.61	.01	.06	-.01	-.01	-.19	-.30	.21	.69	1.59
t-statistic	(3.25)	(-1.11)	(3.50)	(.64)	(-.90)	(-.63)	(-.67)	(-2.64)	(2.15)		

Consumption	Constant	C_{t-1}	HDD_t	IN_t	P_t^{imp}					R^2	DW
Coefficient	2.72	.70	.01	.09	-.07					.86	2.03
t-statistic	(2.00)	(7.09)	(11.70)	(1.06)	(-2.52)						

Crude Oil Stocks	Constant	SC_{t-1}	i_t	P_t^{imp}	P_t^{spot}	HDD_t				R^2	DW
Coefficient	.88	-.12	-.01	-.05	.10	-.00				.23	2.04
t-statistic	(2.60)	(-2.90)	(-.68)	(-.52)	(.96)	(-1.14)					

Product Stocks	Constant	SP_{t-1}	i_t	P_t^{imp}	P_t^{spot}	HDD_t				R^2	DW
Coefficient	.48	-.05	-.01	-.15	.17	-.02				.82	2.03
t-statistic	(.56)	(-.55)	(-1.40)	(-1.90)	(1.92)	(-10.22)					

TABLE B-9

Netherlands, Oil Import Demand, Results of Ordinary Least Squares Estimates, 1973:I–1984:IV

Imports	Constant	IN_t	HDD_t	C_{t-1}	SC_{t-1}	i_t	T	P_t^{imp}	P_t^{spot}	R^2	DW
Coefficient	−1.07	2.34	−.28	.34	.01	.01	−.41	.01	−.07	.74	2.02
t-statistic	(−.55)	(4.98)	(−5.71)	(2.72)	(.40)	(1.50)	(−3.20)	(1.03)	(−.84)		

Consumption	Constant	C_{t-1}	IN_t	P_t^{imp}	$D1$	$D2$	$D3$			R^2	DW
Coefficient	−1.53	.84	.65	.003	−.12	−.16	.00			.78	2.01
t-statistic	(−.87)	(9.39)	(1.66)	(.32)	(−3.37)	(−3.41)	(.00)				

Crude Oil Production	Constant	$Prod_{t-1}$	i_t	T	P_t^{imp}					R^2	DW
Coefficient	−.19	.98	−.002	.08	.002					.93	1.97
t-statistic	(−.63)	(15.93)	(−.46)	(1.41)	(.18)						

Crude Oil Stocks	Constant	SC_{t-1}	i_t	P_t^{imp}	P_t^{spot}	HDD_t				R^2	DW
Coefficient	1.95	−.24	.01	.03	−.04	.01				.19	1.99
t-statistic	(2.10)	(−2.19)	(1.59)	(1.10)	(−.63)	(.67)					

Product Stocks	Constant	SP_{t-1}	HDD_t	$Prof_t$						R^2	DW
Coefficient	2.65	−.29	−.01	−.00						.18	1.89
t-statistic	(2.54)	(−2.45)	(−1.23)	(−.07)							

259

TABLE B-10
UNITED KINGDOM, OIL IMPORT DEMAND, RESULTS OF ORDINARY LEAST SQUARES ESTIMATES, 1973:I–1984:IV

Consumption	Constant	C_{t-1}	IN_t	P^{imp}	$D1$	$D2$	$D3$	R^2	DW
Coefficient	2.41	.76	.10	-.07	-.13	-.27	-.24	.88	1.69
t-statistic	(1.48)	(7.50)	(.43)	(-1.66)	(-3.78)	(-7.55)	(-6.56)		

Crude Oil Production	Constant	$Prod_{t-1}$	i_t	T	P^{imp}			R^2	DW
Coefficient	1.00	1.05	.002	-.66	.27			.99	1.65
t-statistic	(1.36)	(26.83)	(.20)	(-1.90)	(1.88)				

Crude Oil Stocks	Constant	SC_{t-1}	i_t	P^{imp}	P^{spot}	$D1$	$D2$	$D3$	R^2	DW
Coefficient	1.77	-.16	.01	-.14	.06	-.02	.09	.03	.47	2.22
t-statistic	(2.01)	(-1.75)	(1.20)	(-2.60)	(1.03)	(-.49)	(2.98)	(.59)		

Product Stocks	Constant	SP_{t-1}	i_t	P^{imp}	P^{spot}	$D1$	$D2$	$D3$	R^2	DW
Coefficient	.78	-.06	-.01	-.15	.11	-.03	.05	.06	.50	2.14
t-statistic	(.89)	(-.90)	(-1.50)	(-2.35)	(1.88)	(-.90)	(2.07)	(2.13)		

TABLE B-11
WEST GERMANY, OIL IMPORT DEMAND, RESULTS OF ORDINARY LEAST SQUARES ESTIMATES, 1973:I–1984:IV

Imports	Constant	GDP_t	HDD_t	C_{t-1}	SC_{t-1}	i_t	T	P_t^{imp}	P_t^{spot}	R^2	DW
Coefficient	−4.5	2.74	−0.1	−.11	−.12	−.01	−1.04	−.32	.17	.90	1.88
t-statistic	(−.87)	(3.11)	(−.77)	(−.58)	(2.07)	(−1.07)	(−4.17)	(−3.03)	(1.98)		

Consumption	Constant	C_{t-1}	IN_t	P_t^{imp}	$D1$	$D2$	$D3$			R^2	DW
Coefficient	4.06	.51	.36	−.11	.01	−.05	.02			.84	2.14
t-statistic	(3.32)	(4.12)	(1.88)	(−3.82)	(.36)	(−2.41)	(.85)				

Crude Oil Production	Constant	$Prod_{t-1}$	i_t	T	P_t^{imp}					R^2	DW
Coefficient	.17	.97	.001	.01	.002					.95	1.89
t-statistic	(.38)	(18.11)	(.49)	(.64)	(.30)						

Crude Oil Stocks	Constant	SC_{t-1}	HDD_t	$Prof_t$						R^2	DW
Coefficient	.94	−.10	.01	.00						.13	2.43
t-statistic	(2.21)	(−2.29)	(.48)	.77							

Product Stocks	Constant	SP_{t-1}	i_t	P_t^{imp}	P_t^{spot}	HDD_t				R^2	DW
Coefficient	5.57	−5.6	.02	−.19	.16	−.01				.55	1.84
t-statistic	(4.55)	(−4.13)	(4.00)	(−2.89)	(2.61)	(−1.13)					

261

with appropriate degrees of freedom to determine whether the hypothesis of no structural change can be rejected.[23] The test statistics for the U.S. equations are shown in tables B–1 through B–5. All the test statistics for the equations reported here are displayed in table 7–7 in the main text. For most of the equations the hypothesis of no structural change cannot be rejected.

Notes

1. A sharing agreement may have a political justification—to demonstrate to oil-exporting countries that in a disruption importing countries will cooperate to maintain the established distribution of oil supplies, thereby removing or reducing the incentive to engage in a targeted embargo. This chapter does not consider the validity of this political justification for an agreement.

2. This is true even if petroleum is not supplied competitively. The existence of a functioning cartel could reduce the total quantity supplied and drive prices up, so that the marginal value in consumption would exceed the marginal cost. The IEA sharing agreement is not designed to increase supply in a disruption, nor is it an effort to use the potential monopsony power of the organization of consumers.

3. These include the major oil-consuming non-Communist countries. The Netherlands is included because it was a target of the 1973–1974 embargo by the Organization of Arab Petroleum Exporting Countries (OAPEC).

4. Detailed data on the prices and quantities of internationally traded oil are provided in Joseph M. Anderson, "The World Oil Market, 1967–1984: Prices and Quantities of Internationally Traded Oil," ICF Incorporated, Washington, D.C., November 1986. These data are the sources for the tables and figures in this section.

5. In the first quarter of 1974, U.S. imports of crude oil and products fell 15 percent from the previous quarter, West German imports fell 15 percent, and imports of the Netherlands fell 8 percent. Crude oil imports of the United Kingdom, West Germany, Italy, and the Netherlands declined significantly in 1975 with the onset of the recession.

6. U.S. imports dipped 8.2 percent in 1979:I, then recovered from 1979:II to 1979:IV. Japan, the United Kingdom, and the Netherlands showed a similar pattern. From 1979:IV to 1980:IV imports of the United States fell 28 percent; of Japan, 17 percent; of West Germany, 13 percent; of France, 13 percent; of Italy, 16 percent; and of the Netherlands, 15 percent. During this period the United States was phasing out the system of domestic crude oil price controls. The United Kingdom became a net exporter during this period as North Sea production began to come on stream.

7. F.o.b. (free on board) prices would be preferable for comparisons among countries to eliminate the effects of transportation costs, but complete series of f.o.b. prices are not available for all the importing countries examined.

8. Note that price data for the Netherlands are unavailable for 1973:IV, the first embargo quarter.

9. Prices were average landed prices in nominal dollars per barrel.

10. Japan, West Germany, the United Kingdom, France, and Italy.

11. The weights used to calculate the weighted average of the price differentials are the sulfur content and API gravity respectively.

12. During the 1982–1984 period, Saudi Arabia reduced production more than other OPEC members, perhaps increasing the average quality of OPEC crude.

13. Six of the seven importing countries have some domestic production. Japan has no significant production.

14. This is the test proposed by Gregory C. Chow, "Tests of Equality between Sets of Coefficients in Two Linear Regressions," *Econometrica*, vol. 28 (1960), pp. 591–605; and Franklin M. Fisher, "Tests of Equality between Sets of Coefficients in Two Linear Regressions: An Expository Note," *Econometrica*, vol. 38 (1970), pp. 361–66.

15. These test results should be interpreted with caution. Where poor estimation results were obtained—for example, for the consumption equations of Italy and the Netherlands—failure to reject the hypothesis based on statistics derived from these equations does not provide conclusive results.

16. No production equation was estimated for Japan, where production is negligible.

17. Harold Hotelling, "The Economics of Exhaustible Resources," *Journal of Political Economy*, vol. 39 (April 1931), pp. 137–75.

18. See, for example, R. Glenn Hubbard and Robert J. Weiner, "The 'Sub-Trigger' Crisis: An Economic Analysis of Flexible Stock Policies," *Energy Economics*, vol. 5 (1983), pp. 178–89; Hubbard and Weiner, "Inventory Optimization in the U.S. Petroleum Industry: Empirical Analysis and Implications for Energy Emergency Policy," *Management Science*, vol. 32, no. 7 (July 1986), pp. 773–90; and Phillip K. Verleger, *Oil Markets in Turmoil* (Cambridge, Mass.: Ballinger, 1982).

19. See Verleger, *Oil Markets*; and Hubbard and Weiner, " 'Sub-Trigger' Crisis."

20. Because the spot market for crude oil was thin during much of the period studied and most oil was sold under contracts, the spot price did not reflect the current marginal price.

21. Data sources for each variable, units of measurement, frequency of observation, period, and method of combining or constructing data series are described in detail in Joseph M. Anderson, "The Determinants of Petroleum Import Demand of Major Importing Countries," ICF Incorporated, Washington, D.C., November 1986.

22. The embargo and production cutback by OAPEC producers began in 1973:IV and officially ended in 1974:II. The U.S. price of imported crude oil increased from $3.60 in 1973:III to $12.90 in 1974:II. The strike of Iranian oil field workers occurred in October 1978, initiating a period of turmoil that resulted in the fall of the shah. The U.S. embassy was seized in November

263

1979. In late September 1980 war broke out between Iran and Iraq. The average price of imported crude oil to the United States increased from $14.47 in 1978:IV to $34.60 in 1980:III and to $38.03 in 1981:I and then declined to $35.43 in 1981:IV.

23. This is the test proposed by Chow, "Tests of Equality"; and Fisher, "Tests of Equality."

8
An Analysis of the International Energy Agency: Comments by a Sometime Practitioner

Richard N. Cooper

The papers of this volume include two, by Smith and by Badger, that offer an overall evaluation of the International Energy Agency (IEA). They offer radically different assessments. Smith is unremittingly hostile, arguing that the IEA did no good under any heading and strongly suggesting that it actually destabilized the oil market. Badger in contrast reasserts the traditional rationale for the IEA in terms of macroeconomic externalities, terms-of-trade effects, and the free-rider problem and gives a cautiously positive appraisal but with much less supporting analysis than Smith offers. I am closer to Badger in my appraisal, but Smith has provided a detailed analysis supporting his evaluation, and it deserves careful examination.

The remaining five papers are less broad in scope, each focusing on a particular aspect of international energy policy. Horwich, Jenkins-Smith, and Weimer provide a quantitative appraisal of a stylized oil-sharing scheme on the assumption of a given temporary shortfall in oil production and a given drawdown of oil stocks. They conclude that allowing the price to clear the market is superior to alternative methods of allocation, except when it can be expected that terms-of-trade gains will more than compensate for the efficiency losses caused by any nonprice allocation scheme. Their analysis is an excellent exercise in applied price theory, but in my judgment it is much too static and relies too heavily on equilibrium assumptions to be reliable as a guide to policy in an oil emergency. It is subject to the same kinds of weaknesses as some of Smith's analysis; these are discussed in more detail below.

265

Horwich and Miller analyze the introduction of oil import quotas to restrain demand when the oil market is governed by an oligopoly. They conclude that quotas not only are inferior to tariffs for restraining import demand but are positively dangerous in that they would stimulate an astute oligopolist to raise oil prices even further and thus worsen the terms of trade of the quota-imposing countries. This analytical conclusion is surely correct, and import quotas should generally be avoided. They should not be confused with target import ceilings, however, a topic taken up further below. And before we can draw firm policy conclusions, we must clearly understand the nature and the interests of the oligopoly in question—also discussed further below.

Weyant argues in favor of a coordinated drawdown of oil stocks as early as possible after a disruption of the oil market and offers quantitative evidence for his conclusion based on simulations both of a temporary and of a permanent disturbance of the oil market. This policy conclusion is also surely correct in general, although a stock drawdown should be sensitive to the detailed features of the disturbance and the role of the continuing suppliers of oil. A coordinated and highly visible drawdown would not make much sense, for instance, if it induced a barrel-for-barrel cut in oil production.

Bohi and Toman also assert the superiority of a stock drawdown to alternative methods of dealing with a disturbance of the oil market, but they observe that many Europeans markedly prefer measures to restrain demand. Their preference perhaps arises because they do not want to incur the initial budgetary outlays required to build sufficiently large stocks and perhaps also because, West Germany apart, they do not share the ideological objections of many Americans to the introduction of nonmarket demand restraint measures. Bohi and Toman suggest a "second-best" solution of a mixed response, combining stock drawdowns by those who are able and willing to undertake them with equivalent demand restraint by other members of the coalition of consuming countries. Again, their suggestion on this matter is probably correct—the practical alternative may be no action at all. But if this solution is to be workable in the context of burden sharing, a satisfactory equivalence must be worked out between stock drawdowns, which are intrinsically once for all, and demand restraint measures, some of which may be readily reversible but some not.

Joseph Anderson provides the valuable service of looking closely at the data on the oil market, with a view to discovering whether the United States was put at a special disadvantage during the Arab oil embargo of 1973–1974 and whether the periods of substantial turbulence in world markets demonstrate structural characteristics in terms of oil consumption, production, stock building, and imports that differ significantly from those in nonturbulent periods. In examining the first question, Anderson draws on a large pool of import price data to correct for changes in the quality mix of oil imported by the United States, a desirable step since the mix has shifted toward heavier, lower-priced crudes. He finds some evidence of a greater than average increase in the (quality-adjusted) price paid by the United States during the Arab oil embargo of 1973-1974 and a decline in imports into both the United States and the Netherlands, but the effects were not great.

In examining the second question, Anderson finds that the hypothesis that no structural change took place in the oil markets of seven countries during periods of market disruption cannot be formally rejected in many instances, although the results must be interpreted with caution since the fitted equations are not always of high explanatory power. Moreover, in several important instances—imports into Japan and the United States and stockbuilding in Germany and the Netherlands—the data suggest that structural change did take place during periods of disruption.

The Origins of the IEA

I will come back to some of these points below. But before evaluating the IEA, one must understand its origins by putting it into its political and historical context. The IEA was an outcome of the Washington Energy Conference of February 1974, which was called to deal with the crisis created by (1) an Arab embargo on oil sales to the United States and the Netherlands—a deliberately political act in response to the resupply of Israel by those countries during the Yom Kippur War of October 1973—and (2) the nearly fourfold oil price increase decided by the Organization of Petroleum Exporting Countries (OPEC) in December 1973, a deliberate economic act led by the shah of Iran and building on the shift from output to price adjustment in the world oil market that had begun tentatively in 1970. There was much talk at the time of extensive use of the "oil weapon," not only by politically aggressive OPEC countries such as Algeria and Venezuela but also, paradoxically, by many oil-importing developing countries that were economically hurt by the oil price increase but hoped that at last developing countries as a group had found a method, in the threat to reduce oil supplies, to redress real and imagined grievances against the industrialized countries.

In this environment the United States under President Richard Nixon and Secretary of State Henry Kissinger felt that it would be tactically unwise for the industrialized countries either to remain

267

passive or to respond piecemeal and in disarray to the embargo and the sharp price increase. The Washington Energy Conference was the immediate effort to introduce some cohesion among the industrialized countries. It must be seen as a tactical move in a situation that resembled bilateral monopoly but with each side made up of loose coalitions. Developing countries also took steps during this period to increase their cohesion, despite the intrinsic division of interest between oil-exporting and oil-importing countries on the question of oil prices. The United Nations became a principal forum reflecting the division between developing and developed countries.

The Americans envisaged from the outset of the Washington conference the creation of a mechanism for cooperation among consumer countries, and they persuaded Europeans despite strong French objections. The most urgent problem that the Washington conference was designed to address was that of the already proliferating bilateral deals by individual European and other countries to secure oil supplies, including a willingness to sell arms or political favors for oil, in ways that both tended to keep upward pressure on the world oil market and ran the risk of undermining the Nixon-Kissinger peace strategy in the Middle East.

In opening the conference, Kissinger outlined seven tasks for energy cooperation among the participants: conservation, development of alternative energy sources, research and development, emergency sharing of oil, international financial cooperation with respect to the balance-of-payments problems created by the sharp increase in oil prices, help for the poor developing countries for the same reason, and producer-consumer relations.[1] The U.S. administration envisaged the need for an organization to carry out these cooperative tasks, and the IEA formally received the required support in November 1974. Its very existence was designed to convey the impression of cohesion among industrial oil-importing nations, providing a forum both for discussion and for action and thus creating the possibility of concerted action in the event of any further steps by OPEC, whether politically or economically motivated, to exploit its short-run monopoly on incremental supplies of oil.

The IEA was thus seen from the beginning as a move in a larger strategic game vis-à-vis OPEC, whose function lay as much in its potentialities as in its actual modalities. But of course any agency must have some concrete assignment. It cannot merely exist and be staffed successfully as a looming eminence. Moreover, the immediately antecedent experience suggested some concrete tasks: collecting and analyzing information on the oil market, on oil use, and on national oil policies, so that each country would know what the others

268

were doing, with a view to discouraging uncoordinated bilateral negotiation; encouraging oil conservation in member nations; and establishing an emergency oil-sharing scheme to be triggered in the event of another oil embargo. The tasks of international cooperation to deal with balance-of-payments problems and help for the poor developing countries were taken up in other forums, notably the Organization for Economic Cooperation and Development (OECD) and the International Monetary Fund. Furtherance of producer-consumer relations, by which many outside the United States meant negotiation, took place both within the context of the United Nations and in a special French-initiated forum, the Conference on International Economic Cooperation, which lasted from 1975 to mid-1977.

The IEA held out to nervous consumers the possibility of constructive collective action, and it suggested to OPEC producers that the consuming countries could respond collectively to future OPEC moves, whether or not politically motivated. The process of creation brought home to all consuming nations (except France) the disadvantages of isolated national action, and it created a forum for exchanging information, anxieties, and proposals for separate or joint action.

So the creation of the IEA served a useful purpose in a difficult time. Now that that time has passed, should the IEA be abandoned? Has its usefulness been exhausted? That is a question committed officials do not like to ask. Government, including its international appendages, is highly inertial. It takes considerable effort to close an operation gracefully, almost as much as to create one, but without the satisfaction that comes from creation. It is difficult to arouse much enthusiasm for destruction. Closings are usually brought about only after a prolonged period of lack of interest leading to atrophy, followed by an acute need for budgetary savings, or by the arrival of directors—one or more of the supporting governments—with such a deep hostility to the activity of the agency that destruction of the agency itself becomes a creative mission.

It would undoubtedly be useful to require a periodic formal review of most organizations, say once a decade, to reaffirm their value and suitability in a world undergoing continuous change. How that examination would come out for an agency like the IEA would depend in part on prognostication of future developments in world energy. Obviously the examination must address prospective as well as current usefulness. But if the energy market were expected to be soft for the indefinite future, with no major disturbances conceivable, presumably the rationale for continuing the IEA would be weak. Its data-gathering and monitoring functions could be absorbed into the OECD.

269

How the examination would come out would also depend on the usefulness of a forum for consideration of collective action in the event of some disturbance of the world energy market. If it were felt that any disturbance could best be handled by allowing unimpeded market response or market response reinforced by uncoordinated national action, presumably also the IEA would be unnecessary, for it would have no apparent role beyond data gathering. The judgment was made at the time of its creation that this was not the case, and that judgment was all but universally shared by the governments involved.[2] If, after ten years, that judgment is reversed, therefore, a burden of proof must be met to show why conditions have changed to reverse the earlier judgment or to show what new experience suggests that the original judgment was erroneous.

Another, more subtle judgment must be made as well: that the nature and magnitude of any disturbances of the world energy market are not themselves ameliorated by the very existence of the IEA. An agency does not have to take action to affect the environment. The mere possibility of its taking action may deter unwanted actions by others. If, for example, in some future Middle Eastern squabble, the Arab oil producers perceived the likelihood or even the serious possibility of a collective response by industrialized oil-consuming countries in a direction that might blunt the impact of their actions, they might desist. Or they might lose through disagreement a cohesion that they might otherwise have achieved. In this respect the IEA does not have to be confrontational in its statements or its actions; it merely needs to exist to provide a forum for serious discussion that holds out the possibility of collective action. Ambiguity and vagueness about what the collective action will be may actually enhance the deterrent role. But, of course, the IEA would then be open to the charge that it did not have an exact plan of action in an emergency.

So the IEA does have a plan of action for an emergency, focusing on the definition of the emergency and a scheme for sharing the limited supply of oil. The existence of this scheme and periodic testing of it in dry runs apprise energy officials of at least some of the practical problems that would arise in an emergency, although very likely some unforeseen problems would arise from the nature of the actual disturbance. But the existence of a formal scheme also allows intellectual scrutiny of its consistency, its likely effectiveness, and its likely efficiency as compared with alternative allocative mechanisms—or at least it allows these comparisons in stylized versions of the emergency sharing scheme and its alternatives, as reflected in the papers of this volume. So we turn to the process of evaluation and the appropriate framework for carrying it out. It is, however, worth noting here the

270

finding by political scientist Robert Keohane that the IEA as a forum for discussion and as a means of executing decisions informally has been and is likely in the future to be far more important than its formal mechanisms, whether for targeting or for emergency sharing.[3]

The Analytical Framework

When economists take on an analytical assignment involving the allocation of resources, they all but invariably reach the conclusion that any interference with allocation through flexible "market-determined" prices will lead to an inefficient use of resources or worse. Exceptions concern the presence of genuine externalities, which many economists concede may theoretically exist, or the effort by a nation to exploit its possible influence on its international terms of trade. "Worse" refers to the bureaucracy that nonprice allocation typically entails and the venality that it encourages.

The economists are generally correct: nonprice allocation does generally lead to allocational inefficiencies. And allocation by price will also serve to discipline those who wish to monopolize. Some economists confidently predicted the collapse of OPEC in 1974, on the grounds that no attempt to hold commodity prices above competitive levels through cartel action had hitherto survived. Sure enough, twelve years and two major recessions later the world price of oil fell sharply, to about twice what it had been in 1973 in real terms. In the meantime the price levels of the major industrial countries had doubled or trebled, and the world had lost over $1 trillion in output by failing to produce at its potential.

The typical economic analysis focuses on the long-run allocational effects while being shockingly unclear on how long the long run is. Moreover, it neglects two factors that may overwhelm the allocational inefficiencies in their effects on real incomes: (1) the macroeconomic consequences, including governmental responses to the disturbance; and (2) a dynamics of adjustment to a disturbance that may lead to enduring changes in the behavior of economic agents and thus alter the economic structure that is typically assumed unchanged in an analysis of allocational efficiency. Keynes's famous comment on the long-run comparative static analysis of classical economics was that "in the long run, we are all dead." This did not necessarily imply a shorter time horizon than in classical analysis—although it might do so—but rather that in the long run appropriate to classical economics, adjustment turbulence may result in such structural change in behavior as to render the long-run comparative static analysis irrelevant for policy.

271

These observations are pertinent to policy for dealing with disturbances in the world oil market. The IEA emergency sharing scheme is designed to cope with emergencies, not to provide the basis for long-run allocation of oil. The adjustment dynamics are therefore crucial in assessing the value of the scheme, and the long-run allocational effects are relevant only insofar as the incentives they reveal affect the dynamics of adjustment.

Furthermore, in their search for a determinate solution economists have been driven to assume either many "atomistic" economic agents (who need not be perfect competitors) or a pure monopoly. The intermediate cases are known to involve a range of indeterminacy in output and prices, a range that is narrowed to a single outcome in reality by such fuzzy factors as negotiating skill, bargaining power, or advertising appeal, which neither economists nor others have mastered analytically. Yet world oil production involves precisely such a messy structure, neither purely monopolistic nor containing atomistic agents but rather consisting of uneven coalitions of households and firms in nations and uncertain coalitions of nations in international groups such as OPEC and the IEA. Equilibrium analysis based on well-defined demand and supply schedules drawn from atomistic agents should be suspect from the start in this kind of structure.

Equilibrium Analysis and Oil Sharing

The core of Smith's analysis is predicated on the existence of a single market-clearing price at which all potential buyers of oil can purchase as much oil as they choose, no matter what the source or nature of the disturbance. Is *that* what an oil disruption looks like? More likely, the designers of the IEA had in mind a situation in which most oil is purchased under contractual arrangements at contract prices. Then some of the contracts are broken by the sellers as a result of the supply disruption, whatever its source. In the first instance oil continues to flow under the unbroken contracts at the prices stipulated in the contracts. Those found without oil supplies must go to the spot market and in the process bid up the spot price above the contract price. Under Le Chatelier's principle, the spot market price will rise *above* a uniform market-clearing price.[4] The spot price, highly visible, may then lead to a revision of contract prices to that level, above the market-clearing price at available supplies, but in a market structure that leads to reductions in output to sustain the new contract price, whatever it be.

Applying Smith's analysis, which excludes market dynamics altogether, to this situation would suggest that oil sharing by those still getting low-priced contract oil with those who have been cut off from

272

contract oil will not lead to the efficiency losses that he identifies. On the contrary, it will lead to efficiency gains if the oil is sold at the price above the contract price that will clear the market, thereby avoiding the spike in the spot price by keeping the acquirers of shared oil out of the spot market. In this way oil sharing will also lead to an improvement in the terms of trade of the IEA countries with OPEC over what they would otherwise be. All IEA countries could be made better off than they would be under the alternative of a market split between spot and contract sales, both because of efficiency gains of the kind that Smith emphasizes and because of better terms of trade.

Which of these very different situations best characterizes the actual oil market after an unexpected disruption? That is an important question, since an evaluation of the efficiency of the IEA emergency oil-sharing scheme hinges on it. Anderson's paper provides some indirect evidence on the homogeneity of crude oil prices during periods of disruption. His tables 7–1 and 7–2 show the variation in average crude oil import prices among countries. Such prices may be expected to differ somewhat because of the differing average quality of imported oil and differing geographic locations in relation to foreign sources of oil. What is of special interest here, however, is that the variation of import prices among countries was much higher in the turbulent years of 1974 and 1979–1980 than in the relatively quiet years of 1978 and 1984, for instance.

This observation is confirmed by looking at import prices in the United States. Using invoice data on oil imports into the United States, Anderson attempts through cross-section regression equations to control for differences in oil quality (sulfur content and volatility), country of origin of the oil, nature of the contract (spot, between affiliates, and so on), and several other factors, quarter by quarter from late 1973 through 1984. The residuals to these fitted equations thus offer a rough indicator of the quality-corrected deviation from a single market-clearing price for oil imported by the United States. Figure 8–1 shows the standard error of estimate of these quarterly equations, measured in 1982 U.S. cents per barrel. Even in quiet years such as 1976–1978 there was a standard deviation on prices of 2–3 percent (on about $22 a barrel, in 1982 dollars) that Anderson's equations are unable to explain. This unexplained variation rises sharply in periods of oil market turbulence, suggesting for those periods a marked divergence from a single market-clearing price. This evidence, though not conclusive, seems to support the view of market disruption that underlies the IEA.

As time passes, the economists' standard model of a single market-clearing price is more likely to be accurate, since arbitrage will otherwise occur. Still, it is noteworthy that for two decades after the

273

FIGURE 8-1
ESTIMATED QUARTERLY STANDARD ERROR OF PRICE EQUATION, 1973–1984
(1982 U.S. cents per barrel)

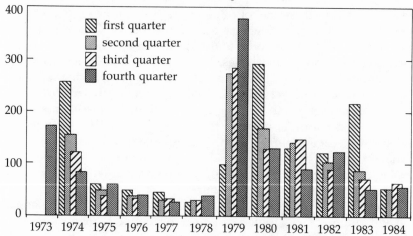

first quarter
second quarter
third quarter
fourth quarter

SOURCE: Standard errors of estimate on Anderson's quarterly regressions on U.S. oil import prices.

opening of the London Metal Exchange in the mid-1950s the London spot price of electrolytic copper typically differed from the U.S. producer price of copper, occasionally being substantially above it, sometimes substantially below, and always more variable. Here is a phenomenon that most economists would argue *cannot* occur for a homogeneous product for any length of time because of arbitrage; but it did occur. Many things that are not possible in the purely competitive model are possible in a world dominated by a few producers, even when they have a competitive fringe. Economists can retort that they are concerned with long-run equilibrium analysis, and it is true that the pressure of the London copper market along with other factors eventually put irresistible pressure on the U.S. producer price structure. But it took over two decades for the "long run" to become manifest. Similarly, OPEC arguably "collapsed," as some economists in 1974 predicted it would, in 1986, although even now it is unclear whether the collapse is merely temporary.

Policy makers do not have either the luxury or the leisure to await such a long run in the presence of major disturbances. If economists are unwilling or unable to deal with the dynamics of disturbed markets, if they feel obliged always to put their analysis into the mold of long-run competitive equilibrium, they will doom their advice to

274

irrelevance in many of the practical problems faced by governments and business firms in a rapidly changing world economy. Particularly in the immediate aftermath of a serious disruption, the economists' model may be a very poor characterization of the market. Yet because of the oligopolistic price-setting possibilities in the oil industry, short-run dynamics may have enduring effects. The IEA emergency sharing scheme is predicated on the assumption that the average price after a disruption will be lower with successful collective management of the period of supply uncertainty than it would be if left to market forces alone. Smith's conventional analysis implicitly rules out that possibility by assumption.

The assumption of a single market-clearing price renders irrelevant for policy in an emergency the otherwise able and fascinating analysis of the section of Smith's paper "The Economic Consequences of Supply Disruptions and Oil Sharing." Without this assumption neither his estimate of gains and losses nor his analysis of the political consequences attendant on those gains and losses is applicable to an actual emergency.

Incidentally, it is worth noting that pricing problems under the IEA oil-sharing scheme, though unresolved and hence difficult, are not likely to be insurmountable in practice. Countries that still receive substantial oil at contract prices below spot prices can sell some of their oil at prices above the contract price but below the prevailing spot price and make both buyer and seller better off. The dispute will be over the magnitude of the "loss" the seller should take relative to his apparent opportunity cost in the spot market. But this dispute should be less acute if it is realized that the spot market price clears only the noncontract market and would be lower once the two markets were integrated.

Oil Import Ceilings

Smith argues that oil import ceilings, such as the IEA adopted for 1980, could lead to OPEC price increases. That suggestion identifies "ceiling" with "quota," as indeed some officials did at the time. But oil import quotas were not in fact imposed. "Ceiling" should rather be interpreted as a serious target to be achieved by a variety of means, including, for example, the imposition of consumption taxes, of subsidies to domestic production, or of subsidies to substitute products such as alcohol. In other words Smith, and implicitly in their analysis also Horwich and Miller, have taken "ceiling" too literally. How does one best convey a serious national objective? Vague generalities that involve politically difficult actions are not likely to be implemented. The ceilings were asymmetrical quantitative targets, allowing—indeed

275

encouraging—diversity of national means to achieve them, involving reasoning similar to that underlying the IEA "yardsticks" set in 1980 to be achieved by 1985, although the latter were not in the context of immediate emergency action.

Import quotas certainly lend themselves to exploitation by a monopolist or a core oligopoly, as Horwich and Miller call it. Targeted ceilings, without specification of instrument, are quite a different thing, just as a quarrelsome oligopoly with extremely divergent interests is very different from a monopoly or a monopoly-like core oligopoly. In terms of Smith's figure 2–4 the import ceiling can be achieved by a quota—in which case it runs the risk Smith and Horwich and Miller see for it, of encouraging OPEC price increases—or by imposing a tariff equal to the difference between P_2 and P_0 or by subsidizing a substitute product (such as alcohol, as Brazil has done), thereby shifting both the demand and the marginal revenue schedules to the left. In the last two cases, even a monopolist cannot exploit the existence of the ceiling. IEA targets left the instruments to member countries with no particular pressure to introduce import quotas.

The discussion of import quotas versus import ceilings as targets and their possible exploitation by a monopoly supplier raises the question of just what kind of entity OPEC is when it comes to setting oil prices. OPEC is clearly not a monopoly; it lacks the cohesion to act as a monopolist, and the interests of its members diverge sharply. But neither is it a collection of perfect competitors. Horwich and Miller identify the problem as one of a core oligopoly with a nearly competitive fringe. But there is also a band of parties between the two that are large enough to have some voice in OPEC decision making but not large enough individually to determine the course of events. In short, OPEC has just the kind of structure that economists have most difficulty in analyzing, because there is no well-defined equilibrium solution in the presence of such a market structure. The problem is confounded further if consumers have an analogous structure, so that one cannot treat oil importers as atomistic competitors.

There are substantial and well-known divergences among OPEC members, both political and economic. The price "hawks" in 1979–1980 were Iran, Libya, and Algeria. Iran and Libya were revolutionary regimes with well-known hostility to the West and especially to the United States as the putative leader of the West. Algeria was a professedly radical leader within the nonaligned movement. All three had political reasons for wishing to harm the West politically and economically, to make the West feel the power of oil. Saudi Arabia, Kuwait, and Indonesia, in sharp contrast, were politically conservative and saw their political future as dependent on a strong West.

On the economic side a number of countries—most notably Algeria—had low reserve-to-production ratios and saw a strong advantage in raising prices to a point that would come close to maximizing current OPEC revenue. Others—most notably Saudi Arabia—had high reserve-to-production ratios and therefore had to concern themselves with long-run price elasticities of demand, which are bound to be considerably greater than short-run elasticities, although no one was sure by how much.

Given these divergences, agreement within OPEC was always tenuous and fragile and so could be influenced by outside events—among them not only what consumers did but what they said they might do and what they might do even without saying so. It is worth recalling that in 1979–1980 the OPEC posted prices followed the spot price up in an irregular pattern but with a considerable lag, as OPEC members jockeyed with one another and were jostled about by outside pressures and events. The emphasis on OPEC power and its reinforcement, conveyed by the bilateral beseechings of European countries and others in 1973–1974, were what Kissinger wanted to deflate by creating a consumer coalition. And in the conditions of 1979–1980 the IEA wanted its members to reduce demand for imported oil in ways that would incur a lower macroeconomic cost than would a sharp price increase in the pattern of 1974.

The actions to accomplish this most effectively would no doubt vary from country to country, but some form of "burden sharing" was necessary to avoid the temptation of many countries to free-ride on the actions of the larger oil-importing countries. Countries therefore had to be given concrete, quantitative assignments, making due allowance for their different circumstances. The first question American congressmen as well as members of the public asked when the Carter administration requested new actions to reduce oil demand was, What are other countries doing? They did not want to incur the costs while some of the benefits accrued to others. They clearly understood that oil conservation had the nature of an international public good for reasons outlined in Badger's chapter, with all the attendant problems of a public good. The import ceilings were designed to address this problem of burden sharing. They should be seen as asymmetrical targets, not to be exceeded, but neither as quotas nor as midpoint estimates. The means used to achieve them should be effective but should not weaken the position of the doves in OPEC, as a disruption tariff, for example, might have done.

If the import ceilings had been taken literally and seriously by OPEC, if it had known the elasticity of demand with confidence, and if it had not been conscious of the macroeconomic damage that a

277

sharp price increase could cause, it could have raised the price at once to ensure a drop in oil import demand by IEA countries to the least binding of the national ceilings. It is worth noting in this connection, however, that it is much easier to draw a marginal revenue schedule such as that in figure 2–4 of Smith's paper than to specify it in practice when a producer is dealing with an exhaustible resource, such as oil. The producer in that case is not interested in the marginal revenue only in the current period but rather in the marginal contribution of additional sales to the present value of the resource. That calculation requires, *inter alia*, concern for the influence of *today's price* on *future* consumption and imports. In particular, the producer must be concerned with the possibility that short-run profit-maximizing behavior will permanently drive consumers to alternative sources of supply and products, even at some short-run cost to themselves, with the motive of breaking the monopoly.

Such a course is what the national energy policy of many countries was concerned with—not only hastening movement along the demand curve for OPEC oil but shifting and flattening the demand curve. This consideration would, of course, be more important to oil suppliers with large reserves and hence with a strong stake in future demand than for producers with low reserves, and therein lies one of the sources of dissension among OPEC members. That the long-run price elasticity of demand for oil is almost certainly much higher than the short-run elasticity should be a matter of serious concern to countries such as Saudi Arabia, for it suggests that the potential for price exploitation is much lower in the long run. And it could well be that how rapidly the "short run" becomes the "long run" in the relevant sense is influenced by the short-run pricing behavior of oil-exporting countries.

As it turned out, the IEA countries underestimated the contractionary effects of the oil price increases, as they had done in 1974, and of their own policy response to the price increases. Levels of economic activity and hence oil demand were therefore considerably lower in 1980 than governments had foreseen—or could admit to— in 1979 when the oil import ceilings were established.

On Stock Management

Smith and Horwich–Jenkins-Smith–Weimer assume that after an oil shortfall private oil users will draw down their stocks in a way that limits the price increase. This is not the way the world works, at least not always. A private stock drawdown should occur when (1) the price is known to have fully adjusted to the shortfall and (2) the shortfall is known to be temporary. Unfortunately, we rarely if ever

278

have a chance to test this proposition. Typically, users and speculators do not know whether the price has fully adjusted to a disturbance, even if the disturbance is widely believed to be temporary (caused, for example, by crop damage due to a storm), and they often do not know whether the shortfall is temporary.

The air is filled with uncertainty after an unfamiliar disturbance. Instead of being able to *assume* that stocks will be drawn down, both market participants and policy makers face the issue of whether users and speculators, seeing a sharp rise in the spot price, particularly in face of what seems to be a considerable shortfall of supply, will attempt to *build up* their stocks. Speculators will build stocks on the assumption that the prices will go higher, at least temporarily, in the reigning confusion; users will build stocks on the assumption that there may be physical shortages, at least temporarily, or that the price may increase in the long run as oligopolistic suppliers take the occasion of even a temporary disturbance to fatten their margins and then cut supply to maintain the new margins. Either of these responses will put further upward pressure on the spot price, as increased stock-building demand adds to apparently reduced supply.

What about the situation in 1979, when substantial stock building went on despite the sharp rise in spot market prices? Presumably buying agents expected a further rise in the price. That is easy to understand in the case of contract prices, which did not yet reflect the full pressure of apparently reduced supply. But why would buying agents continue to buy on the *spot* market even at higher prices? This should not happen on Smith's view of the world, without new information about supply shortfalls. Indeed, when all the initial pressure of a supply shortfall is thrown onto the spot market before contract prices are adjusted, the spot price should rise above the long-run equilibrium price and gradually subside as average contract prices rise to the new equilibrium price. But that is not what happened in the Iranian crisis, at least not for nearly two years. The spot price continued to rise as demand pressed it up. The rise continued even after it became clear that there was no supply shortfall after all: increased production in other OPEC countries more than compensated for the Iranian shortfall of about 2 million barrels a day. Total OPEC oil production in 1979 exceeded that in 1978 by over 1 million barrels a day, despite the sharp reduction in Iranian output. Apparent OECD consumption in 1979, in contrast, was up only moderately over 1978. The difference was a substantial buildup of stocks, which added to price pressures and total demand.

What interpretation can be put on such apparently perverse behavior? Two possible explanations come to mind, not mutually exclusive. The first I call the "medical school syndrome." In the early

279

1970s the number of American college students wanting to become doctors increased, and applications to medical schools rose. Since the capacity of medical schools was limited in the short run, the probability of a student's being admitted to the school of his choice dropped correspondingly. So instead of applying to two or three schools, as students had done in the 1960s, they applied to six or seven schools or even more. *Applications* to medical school grew much more rapidly than the demand for entry into medical school. The apparent increase in demand rose much more than the actual increase.

A similar phenomenon occurred in the world oil market when traditional oil-supplying firms, particularly those dependent on Iranian oil, told their customers in early 1979 that they could not guarantee oil supplies later in the year. The customers frantically sought to ensure new sources of supply. In seeking apparently scarce oil, some oil refiners placed multiple orders. Their behavior had two consequences. First, it fostered the appearance in the broad oil market of much greater demand than in fact there was, an appearance that created a speculative climate conducive to rapid price increases in the spot market. Second, since we now know that oil was not scarce, at least after the first few weeks of 1979, customers ended up with some unplanned increases in oil stocks, as a higher portion of deliveries occurred than was expected.

The second explanation for a sharp rise in oil stocks in 1979 arises from a perception that the OPEC price itself was sensitive to market developments and therefore that a rise in spot price would, with a lag, lead to far greater increases in OPEC posted prices than were justified by the underlying supply-demand situation. This possibility arises precisely because OPEC is *not* either a monopoly or a tightly run oligopoly but is a loose coalition of oil producers with divergent as well as common interests. In particular, it cannot be assumed to be a profit- or revenue-maximizing entity. As is well known, in this kind of market structure the price is not determinate within a possibly wide range and can be influenced by seemingly irrelevant events, such as political pressures, spot prices on a fringe market, or even the illness of a key negotiator at an important pricing meeting.

The continuing rise in spot market prices weakened the position of the price doves in OPEC councils by seeming to give market legitimacy to higher prices (a legitimacy that was only partly valid, because of the operation of Le Chatelier's principle). That in turn implied that speculative stock building on higher prices even in the spot market could become a self-fulfilling prophecy. Two events in particular weakened the negotiating position of the doves. First, the United States, following statutory requirements, auctioned some Elk Hills petroleum reserve oil during late 1979, and the highest sales price, well publicized, was $40 a barrel while OPEC posted prices were still $25. Second, a major oil firm lifting crude oil in the United Arab Emirates at posted prices sold refined products back to the country at spot prices, implying huge markups on oil on which the United Arab Emirates had restrained its prices. So the OPEC posted price rose fitfully from $13 a barrel over the course of nearly two years to $34 a barrel by late 1980 (Saudi Arabia held at $32 well into 1981).

The IEA emergency oil-sharing plan is designed to ensure "fair shares" of the supposedly limited supplies of oil and also to ensure that no IEA country can get more oil by going out on its own. Thus the scheme should encourage conservation instead of a scramble for limited supplies. It is designed, therefore, to limit the overall price increase that occurs under circumstances such as those that prevailed in 1979–1980. The emergency sharing scheme was not tested during that period, because the actual shortfall was not sufficient to trigger it.

In view of the large buildup of oil stocks in 1979, it is surprising that Smith suggests that stock building was not abnormal in that year on the basis of the regressions reported in appendix B of his chapter. In fact, OECD stock building at 34 million metric tons was quite exceptional, although below the 45-million-ton increase of 1974. How can this be reconciled with Smith's regressions? Smith specifies his "normal storage rule" for oil stocks as being dependent among other things on total oil supplies. If supplies go up, desired stocks also go up. But why should this be so, except ex post? It seems more appropriate to specify desired oil stocks in terms of oil consumption. As can be inferred from figure 8–2, oil supplies went up sharply in 1979, but consumption went up only moderately, the difference being the sharp rise in stocks. Moreover, "consumption" here means sales to users. It was widely observed at the time that home and car owners were keeping their tanks topped up much more than usual (and homeowners sometimes also installed second fuel tanks); so stocks very likely rose more, and true consumption less, than shown in the figure.

In addition, Smith inexplicably defines the year of the Iranian disturbance to include the fourth quarter of 1978 and to exclude the fourth quarter of 1979, when the U.S. hostages were taken. Since the labor disturbances in Iran's oil fields occurred near the end of 1978 and the shah left in January, the calendar year 1979 or even a somewhat longer period should be taken as the period of disturbance. This shift in timing is important, because considerably greater stock building took place in the fourth quarter of 1979 than in the fourth quarter of 1978. The conventional view, which I share, is that the stock buildup

FIGURE 8-2
OECD OIL CONSUMPTION AND CHANGE IN STOCKS, 1973–1984
(millions of metric tons)

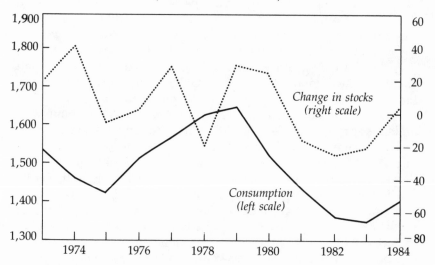

SOURCE: OECD, *Energy Balances in the OECD Countries* (Paris: OECD, 1984, 1986).

in 1979 was exceptional, Smith's equations notwithstanding.[5] To that extent the IEA must be judged to have failed during this emergency. We can only speculate on whether the exceptional stock buildup could have been avoided if the IEA sharing scheme had been triggered.

Concluding Observations

How does all this bear on the application of static economic analysis to an oil emergency? As long as OPEC is a loose oligopoly, for which external events can help determine price, oil-consuming countries have an interest in trying to influence those events in a way that keeps prices lower than they would otherwise be. Detailed management of the crisis takes on a critical importance. This kind of detailed management in a fluid setting is completely ignored by equilibrium analysis.

The results during the crisis of 1979–1980 were terrible, and neither the IEA nor its member states can be given very good marks. But we do not know the alternative against which to compare the actual outcome. Certainly prices did not rise to the short-run revenue-maximizing level. OPEC could have charged much higher prices, and

282

indeed there was widespread expectation that prices would rise to $45 or $50 a barrel, against which expectation countries such as Mexico and Nigeria borrowed heavily. So while the management of that crisis was far from a striking success, it was perhaps not a complete failure either.

Smith concludes decisively that the incremental effect of the IEA was negligible if not actually perverse. He may be right, but it is unclear on what basis his judgment is made. He does not specify an empirically adequate model to indicate how oil import demand would have responded under the counterfactual case of a pure market response. Furthermore, even that would not give us a confident basis for comparison, since there is a further possibility, the independent use of national energy policies, which were vigorous in most countries and were definitely not market policies in many. In assessing the value of the IEA as a forum for information exchange, exhortation, and coordination, one would need another counterfactual scenario, quite different from a pure market model, to determine whether government actions would have been stronger, weaker, or roughly the same in the absence of the IEA. For example, under either scenario, would even greater stock building have taken place during 1979–1980? Would OPEC have increased contract prices faster than it did? Would the United States have removed price controls on domestic oil? Smith does not address any of these important questions, but that does not keep him from passing severe judgment on the IEA, a judgment that is not warranted on the basis of his analysis.

The assumption underlying the creation of the IEA is that it is better to meet a loose coalition of producers with a loose coalition of consumers than to have consumers scramble to make separate deals with OPEC, thereby enhancing the cohesion of OPEC and in particular the price hawks within it. This general proposition is surely valid, but how successful it turns out to be depends on the skills of the practitioners during each crisis. Economic analysis can help them avoid serious mistakes, but in its present state of development it cannot guide them to the best course of action in a fluid and constantly changing situation.

Notes

1. Henry A. Kissinger, *Years of Upheaval* (Boston: Little, Brown, 1982), p. 906.

2. France demurred but not on grounds of support for unimpeded market forces, which French governments have interfered with extensively for three

283

centuries. Rather, France desired to maintain its freedom of national action, and it objected to American leadership in the matter.

3. Robert O. Keohane, "International Agencies and the Art of the Possible: The Case of the IEA," *Journal of Policy Analysis and Management*, vol. 1, no. 4 (1982), pp. 469–81.

4. Le Chatelier's principle is drawn from the physics of fluids. As applied to markets, it says that in response to a given exogenous change, the larger the number of collateral constraints on the equilibrium system, the more a price that is free to move will vary in the new equilibrium. See Paul A. Samuelson, *Foundations of Economic Analysis*, enlarged ed. (Cambridge, Mass.: Harvard University Press, 1983), pp. 36ff.

5. Anderson ran regressions of quarterly changes in crude and product stocks over the period 1970–1984 against explanatory variables that included the change in consumption, stock levels, interest rates, spot oil prices, marginal prices for contract oil, and quarterly dummy variables to capture the seasonal effects. He got a reasonable fit, with $R^2 = .73$, although none of the nonseasonal variables showed strong statistical significance. An examination of the residuals from this equation for the United States suggests that exceptional stock building took place in the second half of 1979 and the first quarter of 1980.

9
International Oil Sharing and Policy Coordination: A Critical Summary

George Horwich and David Leo Weimer

The major case for coordination of the consumer response to oil shocks by the International Energy Agency is made by Daniel Badger and Richard Cooper in chapters 1 and 8. They endorse the IEA's role in all its dimensions, including what they consider the essential emergency sharing agreement. In other chapters John Weyant analyzes strategies for coordinating stock drawdown by IEA members, Douglas Bohi and Michael Toman establish a preference structure for ordering alternative policies among nations, and Joseph Anderson examines the empirical record of the international oil flow. The remaining chapters, which are by Rodney Smith and by ourselves and collaborators, are essentially critical of both the de facto and the possible IEA contribution to stability of the world oil market.

This concluding chapter attempts to reconcile the positions of Badger and Cooper with that of our own. We draw on our understanding of the present institutional structure of the world oil market and the general framework of economic theory, as we interpret it. Our discussion is also based on the common ground presented in the papers by Weyant, Bohi and Toman, and Anderson. Obviously, we speak only for ourselves.

Markets in Disruption

We demonstrated graphically in chapter 3 that if all regional oil markets are at the market-clearing price during a disruption, mandated transfers of oil between regions reduce economic welfare. This followed from the fact that prices rise in donor regions and fall in recipient ones, causing the oil to be valued more highly by those who lose

285

it than by those who receive it.[1] The difference in valuation is a deadweight loss relative to the level of welfare before the transfer. IEA sharing can therefore be justified on efficiency grounds only if markets are not in equilibrium or otherwise adjusting efficiently in that direction. Even then, of course, alternative methods superior to sharing may be available for facilitating the adjustment.

Both Badger and Cooper argue that, after a supply disruption, oil markets are indeed far removed from the market-clearing ideal. Badger sees the disrupted market as driven by highly politicized allocation decisions of both exporting countries and oil companies. Cooper, with a similar perspective, criticizes the economists' traditional reliance on "well-defined supply and demand schedules" based on competitive or pure monopoly situations and yielding a single market-clearing price. He questions the perception of the oil market as determined by "atomistic agents" instead of "uneven coalitions of households and firms in nations and uncertain coalitions of nations in international groups such as OPEC and the IEA."

Although Cooper acknowledges that the negotiating skills and bargaining power of such coalitions have not been mastered analytically by economists or others, he is quite explicit about the nature of much of the market dynamics he believes IEA oil sharing can improve. He, like Badger, sees sharing as dampening price increases and producing a higher level of welfare than is likely to obtain without sharing. While we disagree with his particular analysis, we find that it falls well within the tools and constructs of traditional economics, as the following section indicates.

The Spot Price–Contract Price Connection. Cooper identifies as the basic market imperfection the stickiness of crude oil contract prices and their failure to rise swiftly in response to a shock. As a consequence, unsatisfied demand in the contract market spills into the spot market, where prices rise disproportionately. Cooper cites Le Chatelier's principle from the physics of fluids to make his point precise: "In response to a given exogenous change, the larger the number of collateral constraints on the equilibrium system, the more a price that is free to move will vary in the new equilibrium."

In Cooper's account the increase in the spot price gives rise to two forces that tend to sustain it at its higher level or raise it further. As contract prices rise to the level of the spot price, OPEC will reduce output so as to maintain "the new contract price, whatever it be." The second force is an increased demand for stocks, fed by "a perception that the OPEC price itself was sensitive to market developments and therefore that a rise in spot price would, with a lag, lead

286

to far greater increases in OPEC posted prices than were justified by the underlying supply-demand situation."

Spot prices rise further because of an increased tendency of customers in disruption episodes to place multiple orders at any given level of total demand. Cooper likens this to multiple filing of applications to medical schools, reflecting not a greater number of applicants per se but a perception that the probability of admission has suddenly dropped owing to a de facto increase in demand. The apparent increase in the demand for oil is thus greater than the actual increase, driving spot prices higher still.

We are not persuaded that a component of demand with no actual purchasing power behind it is likely to exercise any perceptible and enduring influence on price—even in the volatile disrupted oil market. The belief that sticky contract prices cause a disproportionate rise in spot prices, however, is widely held, and we shall address it.

Contract flexibility. We believe that Cooper's argument rests on a somewhat unrealistic view of the nature of crude oil contracts. According to a recent Rand Corporation study of contract provisions, almost all domestic and international oil contracts have flexible pricing and quantity provisions.[2] Although contracts are usually multiyear, prices are typically set for three-month periods and are subject to renegotiation for successive periods.[3] It would be misleading, however, to view prices as firmly fixed even for three months. On thirty days' notice sellers may terminate contracts or offer discounts; and because contract provisions binding governments are largely unenforceable, national companies may unilaterally impose premiums and altered credit terms.[4] Both national and private companies also have wide discretion over the quantities lifted, allowing them to divert crude oil directly to the spot market.[5]

The Rand study on contracts and a later one on the IEA emphasize the high degree of price flexibility in oil contracts of the 1980s:

> Only a small and declining share of oil market contracts still specify a fixed price. Much more frequently, prices are specified as premiums or discounts relative to any one of a number of published spot prices or posted prices, which tend to follow spot prices with a slight lag.[6]

> The results of this research strongly indicate that contracts per se are unlikely to constrain those who control crude oil supplies during a crisis or to disrupt the reallocation of supplies in response to the market's price signals.[7]

In particular, after an oil shock,

287

The contracts themselves typically provide for rapid adjustment to such disruptions. Where contractual provisions do not allow for appropriate adjustment, breach of contract does.[8]

The degree of possible price flexibility also varies directly with the size of the disruption and appears to be effectively complete for the sizable disruptions—7 percent or more of the supply of any single IEA member or the group as a whole—to which the sharing agreement applies.[9]

Thus there do not appear to be any inflexible restraints on contract pricing in a disruption. The report notes, nevertheless, that long-term informal relationships between buyers and sellers of crude oil and products could result in more "complicated [behavior] during a crisis than that implied by an auction-market model on a spot-transaction basis."[10] In other words, suppliers have in the past and may in the future favor their long-term contract customers with prices below the spot market and larger quantities than pure spot market responses would generate.

Influence on the spot price. It does not follow, however, that rigidity of the contract price, whether mandated by the contract or not, has any necessary or significant bearing on the spot price. We show this by analyzing a reduction in the supply of crude oil under contract. Our analysis emphasizes the relationship between the crude oil market and the market for refined products, from which the demand for crude oil is derived and by which it is constrained.

Assume that the contract market for crude oil, initially in equilibrium at some price and quantity, is disrupted by a leftward shift of world supply. The schedule after the disruption is a vertical line, indicating that no additional quantities are forthcoming at higher prices. Indeed, in the aftermath of a shock, any incremental supplies will invariably be directed to the spot market.

Suppose, first, that contract prices are rigidly fixed. The loss of available crude oil will force a reduction in the output of refineries. In the market for refined products, the supply schedule thus shifts to the left, raising the product price. The higher price forms the basis for additional purchases of crude oil by refiners who, in the circumstances, must turn to the spot market. In the attempt to secure spot oil, the spot price is driven up.

Now suppose that contract prices, after the same disruption, are perfectly flexible. The shift of crude oil supply raises the contract price to the intersection of the vertical supply line and the demand schedule. The effect on the refined product market is identical with that of

288

the fixed-price case. The product supply schedule shifts to the left in response to the same loss of crude oil supply previously experienced. The product price rises to the same level and funds the same increase in spot market purchases and the spot price as before.

On this analysis, the rigidity of the contract price of crude oil serves only to limit the wealth transfer to OPEC and other exporters. Even if Le Chatelier's principle were an accurate analogy, we would have to balance the losses attributed to higher spot prices against the wealth gain from lower contract prices. But Le Chatelier's principle, based on simple mechanical relationships, is in fact a poor analogy to the interaction between the contract price and the spot price of crude—mediated, as they are, by the product market. There are, however, alternative scenarios that could qualify our explanation.

• Refiners enjoying rigid contract prices after a disruption could choose to share some of the gain from low crude prices with their customers by lowering the prices and increasing the output of products. Although these refiners would forgo short-run profits, the resulting increased market share might yield greater long-run returns. An increase in product output would, of course, entail the purchase of additional crude oil on the spot market, increasing the spot price further.

• The rigidity of the contract price may induce fear of later increases against which traders may protect themselves by adding to stocks. Again, spot market purchases and the spot price would tend to increase.

These may both be real possibilities, although we view the stockpiling response as somewhat ad hoc and less than compelling. The decision to increase market share by passing on low contract prices to product customers is more plausible. We believe, however, that it is overshadowed by the U.S. system of petroleum regulations as a stimulant of spot market purchases in the 1970s.[11] Against the averaging of contract and spot prices à la Le Chatelier, we would cite the averaging of domestic and imported crude prices under the entitlements program. The evidence is incontrovertible that entitlements, under which the average price became the marginal cost of crude, forced firms to increase market share by passing on the savings from low-cost domestic oil.[12]

The ability of refiners and other resellers under the regulations to pass crude oil costs through to product prices, as long as profit margins were not enlarged, also stimulated spot market buying and additions to market share. U.S. product prices could, of course, be

289

altered in response to crude oil costs only if the prices were not determined in international markets. Perhaps half such costs could be passed through to product prices.[13]

We conclude that while stickiness of contract prices may cause spot prices to rise disproportionately, we can find no basis for this relationship in the underlying structure of markets.

Market Failure: An Alternative View. The case for oil sharing seems to run on two tracks. One is the contract-spot price connection that Cooper and others seek to undo by sharing. Another, older view is that sharing is necessary to overcome selective embargoes, such as that against the United States and the Netherlands in 1973–1974, or otherwise to speed the reallocation of supplies following any disruption. In the first instance a disruption will, of course, fall disproportionately on particular countries, raising their oil prices relatively to those of the rest of the world. In the absence of a robust market response after a sufficiently large and narrowly concentrated disruption, prices may be widely dispersed among regions and move only slowly toward equalization. This is the same point made by Cooper when he refers to the existence of multiple market-clearing prices after a disruption.

This scenario is not only different from that of the link between spot and contract prices but different in that sharing may be its only effective antidote. The rise of the spot price may be controlled equally well or better by stock drawdown or disruption tariffs. A relaxation of the ban on exporting crude oil from all IEA nations would both exert downward pressure on spot prices and improve the regional distribution of oil. But a sluggish world oil market may justify the allocations of the sharing program as a mechanism for spreading the burden of disruptions.[14] We investigate the behavior of prices in post-disruption markets using the price data presented by Anderson in chapter 7.

Price dispersion during disruptions. An examination of prices paid by major IEA countries and France in 1973–1985 for imports of crude oil provides little evidence for the existence of persistent multiple clearing prices that are significantly different—at least after the embargo period. Using the unadjusted quarterly prices of chapter 7, table 7–3, we take the dispersion of prices attributable to the disruptions as an indicator of the lack of market adjustment. To do so, we must separate the dispersion of prices into components due specifically to the disruption and those due to the normal variability of prices occurring in both normal and disrupted circumstances.

290

We identify three periods of disruption in table 9–1: (1) the fourth quarter of 1973 (1973:IV) through the second quarter of 1974 (1974:II); (2) 1979:I through 1980:II; and (3) 1981:I. Column 1 shows the mean price paid for imported crude oil by the United States, Japan, West Germany, the United Kingdom, France, Italy, and the Netherlands and the percentage change in each price over the preceding quarter.

Our general rule was to count as a disruption quarter one in which the mean price rose 7 percent or more. The first disruption could thus have included the second and third quarters of 1973, since the price increased 8 percent in each of them. But we excluded those quarters because U.S. prices were unavailable for them. Price increased only 6 percent in 1979:I, but that quarter was included because it marked the beginning of the post-Iranian decline in free world output.

For all nondisruption quarters after 1974:II, we expressed the difference between the highest and lowest of the seven prices as a percentage of the quarter's mean price. The average of these ratios (for thirty-five nondisruption quarters) is 7.4 percent, and we take this as the normal dispersion of prices about the mean. Column 2 gives the observed price ranges of each disruption quarter; in column 3 the ranges are reduced by the product of 0.074 and the mean price

TABLE 9–1

THE MEAN PRICE OF CRUDE OIL AND THE RANGE OF PRICES PAID BY
MAJOR IMPORTERS IN THREE PERIODS OF DISRUPTION, 1973–1981
(dollars per barrel, except where noted)

	Mean Price^a (1)	Price Range (2)	Adjusted Price Range (2) − 0.074(1) (3)	Ratio: (3)/(1) (percent) (4)
1973:IV	4.75 (32)	2.97	2.62	55
1974:I	9.47 (99)	4.08	3.38	36
1974:II	11.52 (22)	1.77	0.92	8
1979:I	14.81 (6)	1.69	0.59	4
1979:II	17.59 (19)	3.23	1.93	11
1979:III	21.74 (24)	3.66	2.05	9
1979:IV	24.55 (13)	4.98	3.16	13
1980:I	30.29 (23)	5.18	2.94	10
1980:II	32.98 (9)	3.87	1.43	4
1981:I	37.06 (7)	4.35	1.61	4

a. Percentage increase over previous quarter in parentheses.
SOURCE: Chapter 7, this volume, table 7–3.

of the quarter, leaving a price range attributable to the disruption only. In 1979:II, for example, the difference between the highest and lowest price is $3.23 per barrel in a quarter in which the mean price is $17.59 per barrel. The variation about the mean due to normal dispersion is $0.074 \times \$17.59 = \$1.30$, and the range due to the disruption is $\$3.23 - \$1.30 = \$1.93$ per barrel. The adjusted range is 1.93/17.59, or 11 percent of the mean price, as indicated in column 4.

Anderson's prices are unadjusted for differences in quality, transportation costs, and the proportions of contract and spot market crude oil.[15] Transportation costs, which were about $1.00 per barrel for the United States in the early 1970s, may explain a good portion of the wide range of prices relative to the mean during the embargo period when the average price was $4-10. U.S. controls, even before entitlements were introduced late in 1974, enabled high spot market oil to be passed through more or less automatically to controlled product prices and may thus also have contributed to the enormous dispersion of prices in 1973-1974. U.S. prices are consistently at the high end of the range throughout the 1970s in both disruptions and normal periods (see chapter 7, table 7-4). This suggests that U.S. controls and transportation costs may have been a decisive influence on international price dispersion until after 1980, when controls were removed and refineries upgraded and a larger fraction of U.S. oil imports of more variable quality originated in the Western Hemisphere.[16]

However one interprets 1973-1974, the experience in 1979-1980 and 1981:I hardly reflects an international oil market that had become stuck. This was the period of the Iranian convulsion and the outbreak of the Iran-Iraq war, during which prices rose in every quarter, galloping from $14.03 in 1978:IV to $37.06 in 1981:I. In spite of these repeated shocks, the adjusted absolute difference (that is, the difference attributable to the disruptions) between the highest and lowest price paid by major importers never exceeded approximately $3 on a price base of $25-30 (see 1979:IV and 1980:I in table 9-1). More often the price range was about $2 or less. This is particularly significant in view of the fact that the original prices are unadjusted for various attributes, including transportation costs.

Overall, during the 1979-1981 disruptions, the mean of the ratio of adjusted price ranges to the corresponding mean prices was a modest 8 percent. This percentage was loosely proportional to the size of the accompanying price increase. It fell to just 4 percent in 1980:II and 1981:I, when the price increases were only 9 percent and 7 percent and were not succeeded by new increases in the following quarter. But even when the price shocks recurred in successive quarters, the price dispersion did not appear to grow, accumulate, or linger beyond the current quarter and the accompanying price increase. In

292

all three quarters immediately following disruptions—1974:III, 1980:III, and 1981:II—the unadjusted ratios of price range to mean price were 10 percent, less than three percentage points above the normal dispersion ratio of 7.4 percent.

In view of these findings, we regard the assumption of Smith (chapter 2) and ourselves (chapter 3) that after an instantaneous disruption markets equilibrate *before* sharing can be implemented as a reasonable working hypothesis. From the evidence it is most unlikely that sharing, unavoidably a time-consuming process, can be imposed more rapidly than the uncontrolled market adjusts.

Anderson's econometric analysis of petroleum *quantities*, which change simultaneously with prices, is also relevant here. He was not able to reject the hypothesis of no structural change between disrupted and nondisrupted periods for most petroleum variables of the seven major importing countries (see chapter 7, table 7–7). The hypothesis was rejected for U.S. and Japanese imports, United Kingdom production, West German crude stocks, and Netherlands product stocks but accepted in twenty-eight other tests of the basic variables.[17] Most important, the hypothesis of no structural change could not be rejected for total petroleum consumption of each of the seven countries. The combined evidence from Anderson's econometric analysis of quantities and our investigation of prices thus suggests to us that, overall, oil markets continued to adjust in disruption as in nondisruption circumstances.

Atomistic supply and demand? Although our brief examination of the data cannot be the final word on this subject, we find the tendency to price equalization compatible with price paths we would expect atomistic economic agents to generate. This is not to assert that the political dealing and coalition bargaining stressed by Badger and Cooper were absent from the adjustment—only that if they were present, they did not operate in a direction opposed by the traditional market forces (they may even have functioned as an expression of those forces) or, alternatively, did not prevent those forces from determining, at the margin, the final distribution of given supplies. There were, after all, no price ceilings on crude oil in international markets and no effective restraints on bidding for imports by anyone among or within the major IEA countries.[18] Any significant conflict between political forces and atomistic forces would ultimately have thwarted or seriously delayed the process of price equalization.[19]

Even a rapidly adjusting (price-equalizing) market is not one, however, that sharing advocates are necessarily happy with. The spot-contract price connection remains a source of exacerbated price increases, including a higher long-run price due to OPEC responses.

Cooper, as we have seen, is also deeply concerned with the increased demand for stockpiles, which he regards as a perverse result and reinforcement of the rise in spot prices. We turn now to the evidence on stockpiling.

Stockpile Accumulation. Cooper sees the rise in demand for stocks as a psychological phenomenon spurred by the spot price in a period of disruption and not necessarily related to whether world oil supplies have actually fallen. Thus he cites the feverish increase in stockpiles of 2 million barrels per day during 1979–1980 and the rise in the spot price "even after it became clear that there was no supply shortfall after all: increased production in other OPEC countries more than compensated for the Iranian shortfall of about 2 million barrels a day." We find Cooper's characterization of the Iranian shock in terms of the ex post change in quantity simply inadequate. The underlying disturbance of the crude oil market was a leftward shift of world supply (an inelastic schedule, but not perfectly so) owing to the Iranian disruption. The increased demand for stocks then shifted world demand (also inelastic) to the right. Each shift of a schedule contributed to the rise in prices; the combined shifts left the market quantity essentially unchanged or marginally higher.

These events do not suggest to us an absence of shortfall. Nothing would have happened without the initial supply shift, whose economic effect is best measured by the rise in price (as Cooper recognizes in other contexts). The demand shift was in fact a response to a leftward shift of supply, whose political and long-run economic implications were momentous. The shock of 1973–1974 had been a calculated assertion of the sovereignty of oil-exporting countries over oil properties left unprotected by the decline of the British empire—manifestly a one-time event.[20] The fall of the shah and the rise of Islamic fundamentalism in 1978–1979 were far more ominous. There were no warnings or recognizable precursor signs in the preceding decade; the shah's successors, whoever they might be, had been universally expected to continue his maximal oil-producing policies, and they did not; and Islam in this manifestation threatened to spread uncontrollably and destabilize the entire region. In this setting a mass movement into stocks could scarcely be called a panicky reaction. It was a coolly rational response to an event that, unlike the earlier shock, was both repeatable and uncontrollable even by its perpetrators. It is, in any case, a gross oversimplification to view the price rises during this period as due solely to increased demand for stocks.

Anderson finds that stockpiling behavior followed the same structural pattern in normal and disrupted periods in most, but not

294

all, countries. Smith similarly found that stockpiling was not "abnormal" in 1979, although it was for several quarters afterward. The absence of a finding of abnormality may simply reflect the fact that high levels of stockpile determinants fully incorporated the special circumstances of the Iranian revolution. These determinants included interest rates for Smith, which entered positively in half his equations, and various oil prices for Anderson, which also had positive coefficients.

Does Sharing Reduce Costs?

Both Badger and Cooper see the sharing program as the buyers' coalition, a mechanism for consumer countries' cooperation in restraining demand, and a forum for the exchange of information. The limitation of demand is aimed, above all, at avoiding the scramble in the spot market and curtailing the rise of the spot price. This goal supersedes the IEA's earlier concern with overcoming selective embargoes or any desire to correct regional imbalances of supply and promote regional price equalization. Containing the spot price and equalizing it among regions are not incompatible goals, but if spot prices are influenced by the rigidity of contract prices, they could be inordinately high though equalized among regions. To sharing advocates that would not be a satisfactory outcome.

In view of the analysis in this chapter and in the rest of the volume, is oil sharing the most efficient way to restrain demand and contain the spot price, whatever its determinants? We submit that sharing is not likely to meet these goals and is seriously inferior to several alternatives. The following summarizes our views.

Administrative Lags. Smith's discussion and our own investigations indicate that full implementation of the sharing system could take up to four months after the onset of a crisis. Not only are the system and its procedures complex, but information, which at best is reported monthly, will not be complete because many companies will be outside the reporting network. If the crisis sets in incrementally, as it did in 1978–1979 with a gradual shutdown of Iranian wells, it may be some time before the 7 percent threshold loss of supply materializes.

Quantity as Trigger instead of Price. Implementing the system in response to a given loss of supply instead of a specified increase in price means that sharing will not be invoked against truly serious disruptions.[21] We have seen that in 1979 world oil output actually rose slightly while prices more than doubled in response to the partial

295

Iranian cutoff and the increase in world demand. In 1974 world output also dipped and rose again, leaving output roughly constant for the year. But world oil production had been on an upward trend throughout the century, and 1973 marked the end of a growth trend of 7 percent per year dating from 1918. In the thirteen years before 1973 the annual growth rate was 8 percent, and just before the embargo, in the twelve months ending September 1973, it was over 10 percent. The de facto loss of oil can be said to equal the loss of the long-term trend of 7 percent of world production or the thirteen-year trend of 8 percent to which the world's economies had fully adapted. Because short-run demand is highly inelastic and neither world oil stocks nor excess production capacity outside the Organization of Arab Petroleum Exporting Countries (OAPEC) was available to offset this abrupt and traumatic trend reversal, crude prices quadrupled.

The real costs of oil shocks are thus easily missed by the IEA's quantity rule. The only meaningful trigger must relate to price. Achieving consensus among IEA members on a price trigger, however, is probably impossible.[22]

The Use of Import Quotas. Countries whose supplies exceed their supply rights under the agreement may impose import quotas to achieve compliance. This is particularly undesirable because, in an oligopolistic market, a reduction of imports mandated by a quota can cause a perverse increase in the world price. Although the agreement does not require the use of quotas to reduce consumption, we believe they are the instrument of choice in the context of sharing during a disruption. Cooper and other advocates of sharing insist that IEA import "ceilings" cannot be taken too literally; they are "targets, allowing—indeed encouraging—diversity of national means to achieve them. . . . The import ceiling can be achieved . . . by imposing a tariff . . . or by subsidizing a substitute product."

We believe that this interpretation constitutes a misreading of the IEA Emergency Management Manual. Supply rights, calculated by formula, are precise point limits, not a suggested range, within which imports are expected to fall without delay. As Horwich and Miller observe in chapter 4, quotas are expressed in the same quantitative units as the supply right, leaving no doubt or delay in compliance. Setting a tariff or any other measure to restrain demand involves a continuing trial-and-error attempt to produce the target level of imports.[23] That is not a realistic procedure, either politically or as a way of promptly meeting the emergency sharing requirements.

Imposing a tariff is politically unpalatable to governments because the resulting increase in the domestic price of oil, already higher

296

because of the disruption, will be readily attributed to them. Quotas, on the other hand, create the same effective rise in the domestic price as tariffs, but the rise takes the form of the newly created value of a license or other right to import oil under the quota. If the rights are simply assigned and are not tradable (as in the U.S. mandatory oil import quotas of the 1960s), the value of the right will not be public knowledge. Even if the rights are tradable, it is a rare citizen who will link the government's imposition of the quota to the price of the right.

We find Cooper's suggestion that governments might subsidize an alternative fuel to reduce oil consumption unrealistic. It is not that private markets adapting to higher prices will not hit on alternative fuels—even or particularly in emergencies—if regulations permit. It is the suggestion that a government can be the agent of such a movement, rapidly selecting the right fuels that come on stream in adequate amounts for the sharing obligation, that we find unconvincing.

Cooper readily acknowledges the perverse effect quotas can have on the world price in an oligopoly market. Chapters 2 and 4 describe in some detail how a restriction of imports mandated by a quota introduces a kink in the demand schedule for imports. Oligopoly producers will respond by raising prices while reducing output by an amount somewhat greater than the mandated import reduction. This is a well-known theorem in international trade theory. What is less well known is the theorem's wide applicability to the world oil market.

The simulations of chapter 4 indicate that even small reductions in the demand for imports enforced by quotas of individual countries can cause significant increases in the world price. The volume of oligopoly output, at the same time, can be very small. For sufficiently low but realistic elasticities of supply and demand, import reductions of as little as 250,000 to 500,000 barrels per day against oligopoly output of 2 to 6 million barrels per day cause nontrivial and often substantial increases in the world price. It is particularly ominous that any individual or small group of countries controlling 2 or 3 million barrels of daily output can reap enormous benefits by restricting output only slightly more than the mandated reduction in imports. Such countries need not be members of OPEC and may behave quite competitively in the absence of quotas. They can be members of the Soviet bloc or even the IEA. They need not act openly or deliberately. A seemingly accidental shutdown or a mere slowdown of production will suffice.

Assuming that the sharing agreement will actually be implemented, we find the instability that quotas can impose on the world oil market a sufficient reason for abrogating the agreement. Given the

297

likelihood that countries will find quotas the most practical means at their disposal to limit consumption, given the incentive to restrict output that quotas provide even competitive producers, and given the considerable price increases that can result from such restrictions under a wide range of conditions in the world oil market, we think it ill advised to retain oil sharing as an IEA emergency program.

At What Price? The IEA has declared that transfers of oil under the sharing program shall be priced at the level of "comparable commercial transactions." The IEA has made no clarification beyond this statement and instead has established an arbitration procedure to mediate disputes about price between buyers (recipients) and sellers (donors). It is virtually certain that transfers of oil under sharing will not take place at the highest spot price of each grade of oil. We argued in chapter 3 that there would be no incentive for transactions at those market prices. Nor do Badger, Cooper, and other advocates of the sharing system endorse the use of such prices. They see a price below the highest spot price as adequate compensation for sellers and one that buyers, of course, will readily accept. In this light sharing is clearly a mandatory allocation program that will incur the costs endemic to any such program. These are the "transactions" costs of sharing described or referred to in chapters 2 and 3.

Countries with a selling obligation will require domestic companies to supply oil at less than its opportunity cost. Although appeals to the national interest will be made, the abandonment of price-directed allocation will subject companies to de facto coercion.[24] Simultaneously, oil will be diverted from its highest-value domestic uses, as expressed in free market prices. In response to anticipated government expropriations of supply, the oil industry will tend to underinvest in stocks in normal periods and overinvest during crises. Whatever size of government-controlled stockpile was optimal in the absence of a commitment to sharing, a larger size will be optimal under such a commitment. Companies participating in the program will seek regulatory protection of their markets as nonparticipating firms attempt to fill any gap. This, indeed, is what "fair sharing," recommended by the IEA, is designed to do. And consumer interests can be expected to lobby for prices at least as favorable as those enjoyed by countries with purchase rights under sharing. All these forces will tend to build a political environment conducive to industry-wide price ceilings and mandatory allocations. Such an environment is present, of course, in most countries even without sharing and does not require much additional stimulus to result in pervasive controls.

298

In countries with a purchase right, government is likely to determine the distribution of oil priced below market. In the United States, which our simulations (chapter 3) indicate will be a recipient under complete-information sharing, the record of mandatory distribution is not encouraging.[25] Our study of the 1970s indicated that the mandated distribution was neither efficient nor, by conventional standards, equitable. The beneficiaries under the small refiner bias program, the buy-sell program for refiners, and exceptions relief were generally but not always small, wealthy (after participating in the program, if not before), and arguably grossly inefficient in comparison with those who bore the costs. The supplier-purchaser freeze imposed widespread patterns of fuel use outside the retail level that were hopelessly outmoded within weeks or months of their imposition. At the same time the freeze insulated established firms from competitive forces. There is no evidence that retail product controls, such as gasoline price ceilings, benefited the poor as much as they did the affluent middle class. The combined effect of the controls created huge macroeconomic costs that fell disproportionately on the poor.

Therefore, another reason why we oppose the sharing system is our belief that its implementation would increase the likelihood of domestic price controls and mandatory allocations.

A Better Alternative

The advocates of sharing defend it for its ability, in the wake of a disruption, to limit demand, contain the spot price, and provide a broadly equitable distribution of supply. We believe there are far more efficient ways to accomplish all these goals. The alternatives may but need not involve coordination of consumers' responses.

A Disruption Tariff. If the structure for cooperation already exists, as in the IEA, the imposition of a disruption tariff by all members could be highly effective. It would function without the panoply of mandatory allocations and import quotas that the sharing program requires or encourages. A tariff creates a simple leftward shift in the demand schedule facing producers at all prices. Monopolists, oligopolists, and competitors alike will find the profit-maximizing response to be a reduction in price. An appropriate tariff will reduce the spot price by as much as any program of sharing imposed under the most favorable circumstances—and without the complex administrative procedures and data gathering involved in sharing.

299

If imposed by all members, the tariff will tend to reduce the world price of oil—so much, in fact, that domestic prices including the tariff will be only slightly higher, if at all, than before the tariff. This will be a result of the highly inelastic world supply along which demand will probably shift after a disruption. The collective action of all the IEA members can thus overcome the political risks faced by countries imposing tariffs individually. Cooper's objection that tariffs will discourage the production efforts of OPEC's doves may be accurate but is applicable to effective sharing as well.

Stock Drawdown. We are not, however, advocating tariffs as the optimal response to a disruption. We see them rather as a better *collective* response, far superior to the attempt of sharing to establish prices, to mandate consumption levels and import ceilings, and generally to control individual members' participation in the world market. Our preferred emergency program is the use of national or nationally controlled stockpiles. Now exceeding 1.1 billion barrels in IEA countries, with 540 million in the United States, they are, we believe, the first and most logical line of defense against interruptions of world supply.

Drawdown of stocks offers the disarmingly simple option of replacing lost oil with new oil. Acting through the self-regulating mechanism of the world oil market, the incremental supply will quickly supplement existing flows to regions directly hit by the disruption. In place of the draconian attempt of the sharing program to limit the access of a score of individual countries and thousands of individual traders to world markets, stock drawdown uses those markets to restrain prices at the source. Whatever forces determine or are determined by the spot price, they will be tempered if not neutralized by the infusion of new supplies. To resolve the difficult problem of when to draw down stocks, we favor some involvement of the private sector in the drawdown decision.[26]

The IEA has, of course, played a useful role in encouraging the development of stockpiles. As Badger and Weyant have detailed, coordinated stock drawdown has been featured by the IEA since July 1984 as a paramount emergency program. The problem of achieving coordination remains unsolved, but the emphasis on the use of stockpiles is unmistakable.

The use of government-controlled stocks to offset supply losses is readily endorsed by all but one of the contributors to this volume. The main difference among the group is whether stock drawdown should supplement the sharing program or replace it. We support the latter because of our objections to sharing's administrative complexities and the numerous economic inefficiencies it gives rise to. To those who believe existing stockpiles are inadequate for the likely disruptions of the future, we suggest that the rate of drawdown already obtainable from world stocks, 4 million barrels per day for nine months, is a sufficient buffer for most of the likely cutoffs of the Persian Gulf.[27] We favor, in any event, continued and aggressive buildup of stocks in all IEA countries. If, nevertheless, a response beyond stocks is still required, we urge the coordinated use of tariffs in place of sharing.

Must Drawdown of Stocks Be Coordinated? Unlike sharing and disruption tariffs, stock drawdown has the further advantage that it need not be a coordinated response to be effective. We endorse the kind of proposal put forward by Weyant, although we are mindful of the pitfalls in achieving any coordination, as described by Smith and by Bohi and Toman. For the United States, however, unilateral action can clearly be justified. Although the benefits of drawdown are and were assumed to be worldwide, the many dynamic programming simulations conducted at the Department of Energy support the unilateral creation and drawdown of a U.S. stockpile of 1 to 2 billion barrels.[28] Simultaneous drawdown of reserves by all IEA members would yield even greater net benefits but does not lessen the desirability of an independent stockpile initiative by the United States. The role of IEA coordination, as Weyant and Bohi and Toman note, is far more important in encouraging stock buildup than in drawdown.

To those who regard IEA coordination as the sine qua non of effective stockpile policy, we offer the following counterarguments:

- With significant levels of government-controlled stocks now present in the major IEA importing countries, drawdown by any country lowers the expected price and raises the cost of failing to draw down to all other countries. As Weyant observes, there are now strong built-in incentives for cooperative action.
- The United States, along with Canada, has the highest rate among IEA members of total energy use per unit of GNP—roughly twice that of Japan and some European countries. The gain from containing the price of oil and of substitute fuels is thus significantly greater for the United States than for other countries. In general, the optimal time and rate of drawdown will vary among nations with the amounts and ways in which they use energy.
- The alternative disruption policies (other than sharing) that members may choose to employ, as described by Bohi and Toman, all have

301

the effect of lowering the price of oil to all users. Whether it be stock drawdown or a variety of demand restraint measures (other than import quotas), the external benefits are equally present in all cases. It is extremely doubtful that unilateral and vigorous stock drawdown by the United States will confer greater benefits on its allies than their demonstrated ability to reduce energy use early in a disruption will confer on the United States.

We conclude that despite the benefits of IEA coordination, the benefits of unilateral action with respect to stockpile use or demand restraint are substantial enough, particularly for the United States, to avoid overemphasis on the IEA's role. It would be a costly mistake for the United States to cite a lack of formal coordination as its excuse (1) to maintain its historical reluctance to draw down any strategic mineral reserve in time of crisis and (2) to resort instead to disastrous control policies into which the failure of prompt drawdown could catapult us. If, however, coordinating drawdown among IEA members increases the probability that the United States will in fact draw down its reserve, the effort to coordinate may be justified.

Will Sharing Be Fully Implemented? In our many discussions with officials of the IEA and members of the international energy community, we are constantly reminded that the sharing agreement will probably never be implemented or, if implemented, never fully implemented. We find this expectation unpersuasive. Under complete information (that is, about the market response before sharing and after a disruption), our simulations in chapter 3 give the United States a buying right under sharing. In the U.S. political climate after a disruption, it may be difficult to avoid invoking the agreement.

Once the agreement is implemented, our simulations indicate the possibility of net benefits to the IEA if members fulfill their selling obligations but do not exercise their buying rights (and do not reduce demand by invoking quotas in oligopolistic markets).[29] This ignores the likelihood that oil under sharing will be priced below the spot price, making it almost certain that countries will exercise their buying rights. But partial implementation seems likely to break down in any case. If, for any reason, recipient countries refuse to accept oil bid or coerced from consumers or drawn from government stockpiles in donor countries, the oil will be sold on the world market. This seems utterly unrealistic. More plausible is that governments in recipient countries will exercise control over incoming oil and add it to their stockpiles or allocate it to "hardship" refiners and distributors and move thereby to full implementation.

In spite of these problems, one person compared the sharing agreement to the sword that often hangs on the wall of a Japanese home; although no one expects it ever to be used, it nonetheless reminds the family of the authority of the father. If the agreement were terminated, members might be less willing to use the IEA as a forum for the informal cooperation that is perhaps the IEA's most important benefit. We believe this is unlikely. The IEA enjoys strong constituencies in the bureaucracies of its members among those who have witnessed its cooperative role at the IEA headquarters in Paris. The IEA can thereby continue to perform a positive role as a forum for cooperation in stockpile accumulation and drawdown, in gathering and disseminating information, and in continuing its salutary historical role of discouraging the use of price ceilings by member countries (including the United States). For these reasons, the "sword on the wall" (sharing) could be removed without diminishing the IEA's role in international energy cooperation. In light of the danger that the sword might actually be used some day, we believe that it should be removed.

On the basis of our work and other contributions to this volume, as we interpret them, our recommendations with regard to the U.S. role in the IEA are as follows:

- The United States should remain in the IEA.
- The United States should withdraw from the IEA sharing agreement.
- The United States should continue to work for coordination of stock drawdown among IEA members in a disruption but should not hesitate to draw down unilaterally.
- The United States should seek an agreement among IEA members to lift all restrictions on the export of crude oil and crude oil products.

Notes

1. Given equal prices in all countries, any given transfer of oil will tend to raise price more in donor countries than it will reduce price in recipient countries, thereby raising the average level of prices worldwide. This is because demand in a donor country tends to be relatively inelastic (causing it to lose relatively less oil in a disruption) and demand in a recipient country tends to be relatively more elastic (causing it to experience relatively greater losses in a disruption). This point is made by Daniel F. Kohler, William B. Trautman, and Mary Anne Doyle in *The International Energy Emergency System: Issues and*

Sources, N-2295-DOE (Santa Monica, Calif.: Rand Corporation, May 1985), pp. 6–8. The effect can be seen visually in our fig. 3–1, chap. 3.

2. Fred Hoffman, David Seidman, and John Haaga, *Legal Constraints on Market Response to Supply Disruptions*, N-1864-DOE (Santa Monica, Calif.: Rand Corporation, June 1982).

3. Ibid., pp. 10–12.

4. Ibid., p. 11.

5. Ibid., p. 12.

6. Kohler, Trautman, and Doyle, *International Energy Emergency System*, p. 6.

7. Hoffman, Seidman, and Haaga, *Legal Constraints on Market Response*, p. v.

8. Ibid., p. 30.

9. Ibid., p. 12.

10. Ibid., p. vi.

11. Estimates by Kalt attribute an average of 407 million barrels per year, or 1.1 million barrels per day, of additional crude oil imports to the entitlements program during 1975–1980. See Joseph P. Kalt, *The Economics and Politics of Oil Price Regulation* (Cambridge, Mass.: MIT Press, 1981), p. 191.

12. A dramatic example of the influence of entitlements on spot prices occurred in May 1979 when entitlements were reinstituted for imports of distillates. Although entitlements were usually granted on purchases of crude oil, products were occasionally covered. In this instance the entitlement for distillates was worth $5.00 per barrel. To the consternation of many European governments, it quickly raised the price of distillates in the Rotterdam spot market by $6.70 per barrel. See the account by William C. Lane, Jr., *The Mandatory Petroleum Price and Allocation Regulations: A History and Analysis* (Washington, D.C.: American Petroleum Institute, 1981), pp. 78–79.

13. Kalt estimates conservatively that 40 percent of the entitlements subsidy was passed through in the form of lower product prices. Increases in crude costs would presumably raise product prices in the same ratio. See Kalt, *Economics and Politics of Oil Price Regulation*, p. 184.

14. For a sufficient lack of adjustment, sharing may be able to nudge the distribution closer to the free market allocation even though the sharing formula ignores differences in demand elasticities among nations and is biased toward countries with domestic production.

15. Anderson does carry out adjustments for the United States with regard to transportation and quality of oil. The adjustments cannot be made, however, for areas other than the United States.

16. While the United States has frequently paid the highest prices, particularly during disruptions, the United Kingdom has often paid the lowest prices. Its experience may reflect its net exporter status beginning in the mid-1970s. See table 7–4.

17. Anderson (this volume, chap. 7, n. 6) observes that the decline of U.S. imports in 1980 (a disruption year) occurred during the phase-out of domestic crude oil controls, which had, of course, heavily subsidized U.S. imports (see n. 11 above). This phenomenon, it appears, could have contributed to

Anderson's finding of structural change in U.S. imports during disrupted periods.

18. See Smith's empirical results in chap. 2 on the failure of demand restraint policies in the sections "Actual Effects of IEA Policies" and "Informal Assessments of the IEA."

19. Badger is less explicit than Cooper about why sharing will dampen the movement of prices. Badger (chap. 1, the section "The Formal Response Plan") argues that sharing relieves the pressure on prices by "(a) limiting the allowable level of imports by the group as a whole to the amount of undisrupted oil available to them on the world market, and (b) specifying each member's allowable share of those imports, thereby removing the incentive for competition among members." But reallocating a fixed supply does not in itself alter aggregate demand or reduce prices. In fact, Kohler, Trautman, and Doyle argue that it increases prices owing to differential price elasticities of demand among donors and recipients of oil (see reference in note 1). Only if sharing is partially implemented, as described in chap. 3, or reduces the incentive to stockpile does it dampen aggregate demand and the price of oil.

20. See the expression of this view in Joseph S. Nye, "Energy and Security," in David A. Deese and Joseph S. Nye, eds., *Energy and Security* (Cambridge, Mass.: Ballinger, 1981), pp. 3–22. See also Walter J. Mead, "An Economic Analysis of Crude Oil Price Behavior in the 1970s," *Journal of Energy and Development*, vol. 4, no. 2 (Spring 1979), pp. 212–28.

21. In this connection see Douglas Bohi and Michael A. Toman, "Oil Supply Disruptions and the Role of the International Energy Agency," *Energy Journal*, vol. 7, no. 2 (April 1986), pp. 40–41. The data in the remainder of this paragraph are taken from George Horwich, "Coping with Energy Emergencies: Governmental and Market Responses," Department of Energy Staff Review, May 1984.

22. Not the least of the complications is that nations face different effective prices of oil, which, customarily denominated in dollars, translate into different amounts by way of each country's individual dollar exchange rate.

23. See Smith's evidence on the ineffectiveness of demand restraint measures in 1980 outside the framework of the sharing agreement in chap. 2, the sections "Actual Effects of IEA Policies" and "Informal Assessments of the IEA."

24. See George Horwich and David Leo Weimer, *Oil Price Shocks, Market Response, and Contingency Planning* (Washington, D.C.: American Enterprise Institute, 1984), p. 185.

25. Ibid., chap. 3.

26. Ibid., pp. 128–33.

27. The flow of oil from the Persian Gulf is 8–10 million barrels per day, of which 2–3 million move through overland pipelines. A worst-case scenario is unlikely to involve the loss of more than 6 million barrels per day, two-thirds of which could be replaced by the existing strategic stocks for up to nine months. This would certainly be adequate for an interruption lasting less than one year. For a permanent loss, the available drawdown would enable the necessary adjustment to be made at a gradual and realistic pace.

28. See the discussion and analysis in David Leo Weimer, *The Strategic Petroleum Reserve* (Westport, Conn.: Greenwood Press, 1982), chap. 5 and pp. 128–30; and Glen Sweetnam, "Stockpile Policies for Coping with Oil-Supply Disruptions," in George Horwich and Edward J. Mitchell, eds., *Policies for Coping with Oil-Supply Disruptions* (Washington, D.C.: American Enterprise Institute, 1982), pp. 82–96.

29. As noted in chap. 3, our simulations calculate net benefits without taking account of adjustment costs incurred in moving from a predisruption to a postdisruption equilibrium. These costs, associated with domestic prices that incorporate any tariffs or quota rights imposed by sharing, tend to rise more than proportionately with the size of the disruption and could easily dominate other costs due to the disruption.

Index

307

310

313

A NOTE ON THE BOOK

*This book was edited by
Trudy Kaplan and Janet Schilling of the
Publications Staff of the American Enterprise Institute.
The figures were drawn by Hördur Karlsson,
and the index was prepared by Grace D. Egan.
The text was set in Palatino, a typeface designed by Hermann Zapf.
Merri Typesetting, of Columbia, Maryland,
set the type, and Edwards Brothers Incorporated,
of Ann Arbor, Michigan, printed and bound the book,
using permanent, acid-free paper.*

HD9565
R47
1988

957589

H: 1

DATE DUE

	JUL 2 6 2007		
MAR 1 3 2009			
APR 0 2 2009			
GAYLORD			PRINTED IN U.S.A.